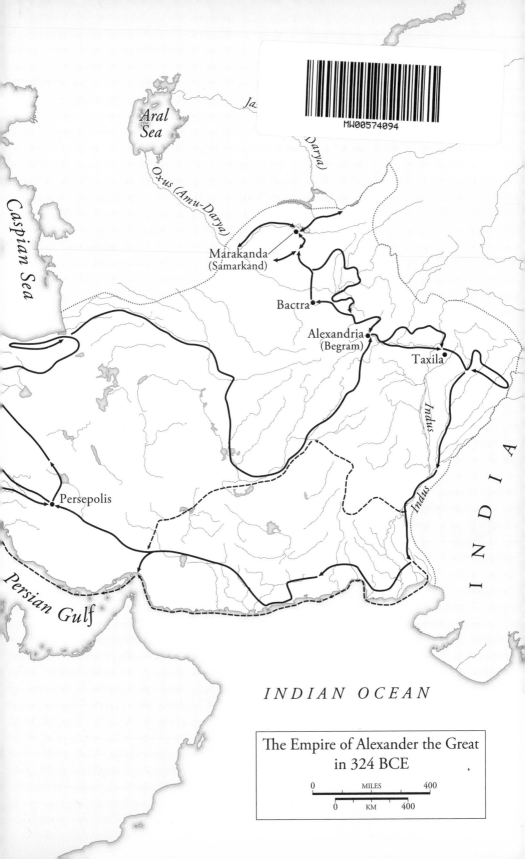

Aral
Sea

Ja...

Oxus (Amu-Darya)

...Darya

Caspian Sea

Marakanda
(Samarkand)

Bactra

Alexandria
(Begram)

Taxila

Indus

Indus

Persepolis

Persian Gulf

I N D I A

INDIAN OCEAN

The Empire of Alexander the Great
in 324 BCE

0   MILES   400

0   KM   400

ALEXANDER AT THE END
OF THE WORLD

ALEXANDER AT THE END OF THE WORLD

The Forgotten Final Years of
Alexander the Great

RACHEL KOUSSER

MARINER BOOKS

New York   Boston

Grateful acknowledgment is made to the following for the use of the photographs that appear in the art insert: Archaeological Museum, Istanbul, TurkeyTarker/Bridgeman Images (page 1; page 10, top); Wikimedia Commons, Ronald Slabke (page 2, top); Metropolitan Museum of Art 05.44.388 (page 2, bottom); © Patrice Cartier. All rights reserved 2023/Bridgeman Images (page 3, top); Persepolis, Iran/Bridgeman Images (page 3, bottom); NPL—DeA Picture Library/Bridgeman Images (page 4); photo courtesy Ephoria Archaiotheton Periphereias Thessalonikes (page 5; page 11, bottom); photo courtesy Wikimedia Commons (page 6, top and bottom; page 7, bottom); Louis Dupree and Nancy Dupree Collection. Photo courtesy Afghanistan Centre at Kabul University (page 7, top); Hermitage Museum, St. Petersburg. Fine Art Images/Bridgeman Images (page 8, top); photo by Wolfgang Kaehler/LightRocket via Getty Images (page 8, bottom); Private Collection. Photo © Leonard de Selva/Bridgeman Images (page 9); Metropolitan Museum 1989.281.30a, b (page 10, bottom); photo courtesy Claude Rapin (page 11, top); photo by uniquely India via Getty Images (pages 12–13); photo courtesy Photo Dharma, Wikimedia Commons (page 13, top right); photo by S. M. Rafiq Photography via Getty Images (page 14, top); Private Collection © Mike Andrews. All rights reserved 2023/Bridgeman Images (page 14, bottom); *American Journal of Archaeology* 104.3, 531-60. Drawing courtesy Stavros Paspalas (page 15, top); photo © Novapix/Bridgeman Images (page 15, bottom); The Palaces of Nimrud Restored. Fergusson, James (fl. 1817–58). Image courtesy The Stapleton Collection/Bridgeman Images (page 16, top); and Alexandria, c. 50 BCE © 2023. Digital reconstruction by John Goodinson (page 16, bottom).

HarperCollins books may be purchased for educational, business, or sales promotional use. For information, please email the Special Markets Department at SPsales@harpercollins.com.

FIRST EDITION

Designed by Renata DiBiase
Endpaper and interior maps by David Lindroth Inc.

Library of Congress Cataloging-in-Publication Data has been applied for.

ISBN 978-0-06-286968-5

24 25 26 27 28 LBC 5 4 3 2 1

This book is dedicated to Ilyon Woo

Contents

ALEXANDER AT THE END
OF THE WORLD

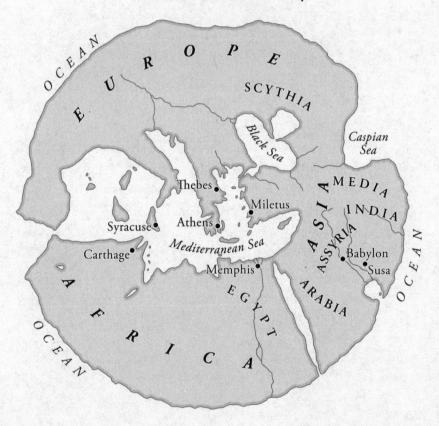

Map of the World, as Imagined by the Greeks of Alexander's Day

OCEAN

EUROPE

SCYTHIA

Black Sea

Caspian Sea

Thebes

Miletus

ASIA

MEDIA

INDIA

Syracuse

Athens

ASSYRIA

Babylon

Carthage

Mediterranean Sea

Susa

AFRICA

Memphis

EGYPT

ARABIA

OCEAN

OCEAN

Prologue

Alexander's Choice

THROUGH THE TOUGH MOUNTAIN PASSES of northeastern Iran, the pursuers tracked their prey in the blistering summer heat of 330 BCE. They moved so fast that they left the landscape littered with the bodies of exhausted men and dying horses. But finally Alexander, the young, wildly ambitious, and improbably successful ruler of the upstart kingdom of Macedonia, caught up with his adversary, Darius III, Great King of Persia.

Alexander had spent the past four years fighting Darius across the vast reaches of his rival's enormous, wealthy empire. Twenty-two years old at the start and with an army a fraction the size of the Persian king's, he had nonetheless dared to challenge Darius, a seasoned war hero and leader of the hegemonic power of his day. By the time Alexander reached the Great King in northeastern Iran, he had defeated Darius in two major battles, received the submission of his most important subordinates, emptied his treasuries, and taken the royal family hostage. Already legendary, Alexander had trekked thousands of miles from his homeland on the Balkan Peninsula across Europe, Asia, and Africa: an exhilarating yet grueling journey, farther and longer than any Macedonian army had gone before.

By the summer of 330 BCE, Alexander could dream of ending it all with one last battle against Darius. But he arrived too late to meet the Great King face-to-face. Instead, in an abandoned cart covered with grimy animal skins, he found his rival bound in golden chains and stabbed to death by assassins. Generous in victory, Alexander covered Darius's mangled body and arranged for its burial. He had just become king of the most powerful empire the ancient world had ever known.

Alexander had won, unexpectedly and definitively. What would he do next? His soldiers, who cheered and cried at the news of Darius's death, hoped it meant their king would lead them home. Ancient biographers, and many modern scholars, have concluded that he should have. But Alexander made a different choice: instead of a triumphant return to Macedonia, he kept going east. He wanted to reach the literal ends of the earth, to see the Ocean that he believed encircled them. He wanted to conquer the known world.

In choosing to pursue his dreams of worldwide conquest, Alexander initiated what would become a dangerous, fascinating, momentous, and at times disastrous seven-year odyssey. On his journey, he would go far beyond the confines of the Classical world, and would irrevocably alter them. In these new places, from the barren Central Asian steppe to the fertile river valleys of Pakistan, he would meet nomadic Scythian warriors and naked Indian ascetics, face enormous battles and small but dangerous conspiracies, lose an army, find a new home. By the time he died in Babylon at the age of thirty-two, Alexander would create the largest lifetime empire in history save that of Genghis Khan. His choice had world-historical repercussions, destructive but also transformative, that echo to this day.

Alexander's choice to go east has perplexed—and vexed—his biographers. So have many other decisions he made in his last years. Time and again, Alexander had the opportunity to turn back, take the easy way out, go home. He never willingly did. For some, this made him an unhinged megalomaniac; for others, a visionary. The truth is more complicated.

As he struggled eastward, Alexander was transformed from the invincible young conqueror of popular legend. He became instead a pragmatic, opportunistic, mature man—frequently unorthodox, and at times unheroic. During his last years, Alexander knew defeat as well as victory. He faced down a seemingly intractable guerrilla war and two major army protests; married (three times; Macedonian kings were polygamous); survived, barely, a direct hit to the neck, several assassination attempts, and a deep chest wound; and buried his closest friend. In the eyes of many observers (and perhaps his own as well), in his last years Alexander had failed, and his failures, like his victories, were immense. Historians pass over these years quickly, or highlight only a few lurid incidents. There is more to tell.

The last years of Alexander were not just the sordid aftermath of a once impressive career; they were in fact what made him "Great." It is true that Alexander failed, hugely and repeatedly. But he also responded to his failures with grit, resilience, and an open-minded flexibility uncommon for his age, or for any other. He learned, slowly but surely, that although he had the best army in the world, the most brilliant generals, and an unsurpassed military budget, he could not solve his problems through force alone. Instead, he had to compromise, to integrate, and to live with imperfect solutions, so that in the empire he had created, the conquered had a stake as well as the conquerors. In essence, Alexander became great only in his neglected final years, after his empire struck back.

So Alexander's story is not, as so often, one about a charismatic leader changing the course of empire and history. Instead, it is about how the empire changed *him*. As he faced external rebellions, internal conspiracies, protests, and a brutal, unforgiving landscape, Alexander learned to think, fight, and love differently. Out of this crucible, he forged his legacy: the integrated and globally interconnected Hellenistic world.

Alexander's was not the ancient world's first global empire, but it was by far the most ambitious and integrated in the years before Roman rule. Its creation was unexpected, perhaps even by the great conqueror himself. It was formed from the union of the Persian Empire with the ambitious, yet constantly quarreling Greek city-states and Alexander's own kingdom of Macedonia. Of the three, few would have predicted that Macedonia would lead.

In the years just preceding Alexander's conquest, Persia was an immense, powerful, and at times vulnerable empire. Under its first kings, Persia had rapidly expanded from its center in present-day Iran east to Pakistan, west to Turkey, and south to Egypt. By Alexander's day, the Persian kings had ruled this huge territory with a light hand and impressive efficiency for the better part of three centuries. They could raise an army of a hundred thousand men with one royal order, and send a letter from the western border to the empire's heartland in twelve days (normal travelers took three months). Despite their extraordinary power, the Persian kings had experienced astonishingly few revolts and fewer challenges to their rule. In the fourth century BCE, however, they suffered from internecine power struggles—due to their practice of maintaining a large harem, there were always too many half brothers contending for the throne—as well as occasional external threats. The greatest of these threats came from Greece.

The city-states of the Greek mainland had, by Alexander's day, a long and complicated relationship with Persia. They had provoked, then repelled, two Persian invasions in the early fifth century. For the Greeks, these were existential struggles that cemented their cultural identity as tough, freedom-loving, independent states, opposed to the luxurious and corrupt inhabitants of a despotic empire. From a Persian perspective, the wars looked quite different: minor squabbles in the remote western borderlands. For both parties, the wars' aftermath brought a century and a half of relative peace, complicated by the Greeks' tendency to enlist as mercenaries in Persian power struggles—frequently, on both sides—and the Persian kings' to use their abundant gold to undermine dominant Greek city-states and empower their enemies. Since the Greek states were not one unified nation but many small, acrimonious cities, the Persians had frequent opportunities to do so. Still, the Greeks were formidable soldiers, and there was always the danger that they would put their quarrels aside long enough to threaten Persia. It is an irony of history that they did so only after they had lost their independence to Macedonia.

While the Greeks had always conceived of themselves in opposition to Persia, in the years before Alexander's birth they had paid scant and scornful attention to Macedonia. Alexander's father, Philip II, was the most effective military commander of his era, who doubled the size of his kingdom during his twenty-three-year reign. Still, he was sneered at by the Athenian orator Demosthenes as "not even a barbarian from any place of which one can speak well, but a pest from Macedonia, where it was never yet possible to buy a good slave"—in Greek eyes, the ultimate insult. But as Philip grew in power, he began to command Greek attention, and the wary notice of the Persians as well. He did so by creating the ancient world's most formidable army (a combination of a large, heavily armed infantry and a smaller, but brilliantly trained, cavalry) and then deploying it selectively, along with diplomacy and deceit, against his Greek opponents. After Philip had conclusively annihilated his last Hellenic adversaries at the Battle of Khaironeia in 338 BCE, he turned his sights to Persia. He sent an advance force of ten thousand soldiers, commanded by his powerful general Parmenion, across the Hellespont—the thin sliver of sea separating Europe from Asia at the western border of the Persian Empire—but was assassinated before he could join them. He left his army and his dreams of conquest to the twenty-year-old Alexander.

Philip's legacy was a formidable one for a boy just out of his teens, but Alexander was ready for it. Short but strong, with large brown eyes and chin-length, artfully tousled hair, he was determined, physically fearless, and accustomed to command. He had been brought up in the tense, combative atmosphere of his father's court, with its constant jockeying for power among high-ranking officers and ambitious royal wives (Philip had, eventually, seven). From this court, Alexander had been schooled in leadership and intrigue from an early age. He also learned philosophy from Aristotle and generalship from his father, the superb military leader. His training showed in the early years of his kingship, as he dealt swiftly and effectively with nearby threats; the Greeks were the first, but by no means the last, to pay a heavy price for underestimating the young monarch. Alexander then invaded Persia in 334 BCE. In a series of extraordinarily rapid, brilliantly fought campaigns across the Middle East, he succeeded in subjugating the western half of the Persian Empire in a little over three years.

By the time Alexander reached Darius in northeastern Iran, he had fulfilled his father's dreams—and then some. He could have stopped, ruling the immense empire he now held from the Great King's throne at Persepolis, or heading back to Macedonia with an inordinate quantity of loot. Instead, he kept going east. If he had known what was coming, even Alexander might have blanched. His early, easy victories were behind him, and during his years in Central Asia and the Indian subcontinent, he faced more complicated challenges from his new enemies, from the tough terrain they fought on, and most insidiously, from his own men.

Alexander also faced the challenges posed by his rapid and unprecedented early success. He had conquered an empire that straddled three continents, and united under one man what are now the nation-states of Greece, Albania, Turkey, Armenia, Syria, Lebanon, Israel, Palestine, Jordan, Iraq, Iran, Turkmenistan, Afghanistan, Uzbekistan, Tajikistan, Pakistan, and Egypt. Alexander had neither the army nor the bureaucracy to police this enormous, heterogeneous territory effectively, and the larger his empire became, the more pathetically understaffed it was. Nor were the chief inhabitants of Alexander's empire easily compatible. Instead, the Persians, Greeks, and Macedonians followed different religions, were governed by radically opposed political systems, and had been battling each other for centuries.

Alexander rose to these challenges, but his success was neither straightforward nor easily achieved. Instead, it was a slow, stuttering process of stalemate, experimentation, failure, and then further experimentation, as Alexander felt his way gradually toward the integrated global empire he eventually created. The story of how he did so is intriguing in its own right, as the saga of a man coming to terms with a world far more complicated than the one in which he was born. It is also resonant. Alexander struggled with such questions as: How to convert military success into an effective, stable government? How to integrate new peoples into the state, without alienating long-standing inhabitants? And how to mitigate—for the conquered, the army, and those on the home front—the horrific costs of war? In his final years, Alexander encountered these challenges repeatedly, and he tried, failed, and tried again to solve them. His story is all the more relevant given its historical setting, the first European empire in the Middle East.

Alexander's story is generally told from the accounts of Classical authors: powerful men, writing about the most famous ruler in antiquity for Greco-Roman aristocrats like themselves. Few Persians recorded their impressions of Alexander's empire, and their accounts have been preserved fragmentarily or not at all. Even the Classical texts are limited. Apart from the fulminations of orators like Demosthenes, and a handful of sedate inscriptions in fourth-century bureaucratese, our extant Greek and Roman literary sources stem from the late first century BCE at the earliest—that is, some three hundred years after the death of Alexander.

These Greco-Roman texts quote, excerpt, and tendentiously revise earlier writers, particularly those from Alexander's era. They had a lot to work with, since like many later politicians, the Macedonian king spawned a veritable cottage industry of historians and memoirists. Some were famous, like Alexander's close friend and later king of Egypt, Ptolemy, and his official historian, Kallisthenes, nephew of Aristotle. Along with these significant historical figures came many others, less celebrated but with useful details on their areas of expertise: Alexander's admiral; his master of ceremonies; one of his architects or engineers; his helmsman; even his seer, with details on dreams and divination. Taken together, these numerous and varied authors make it possible to write about Alexander—where he went, what he did, even what he said—in a manner almost unequaled in Classical antiquity. We know the details of his life far better than those of, say, Cleopatra or Constantine.

Useful as they are, these writers, and the later ancient historians who used them, come with certain inherent biases. They favor the king's military adventures over his personal life and political accomplishments; they sensationalize, like the tabloids of today, and with a similar preference for a good story over the sober truth; and most significantly, they view Alexander's life through a Greco-Roman lens, never a Persian one. Sometimes it is possible to read these sources against the grain and catch glimpses of, for instance, Babylonian priests, South Asian kings, or Iranian aristocratic women. For the most part, however, the Classical authors remain resolutely parochial.

To tell the story of Alexander's life without these texts would be neither possible nor desirable, but recent discoveries allow us to complement them with other sources, radically different in character. We now have access to cuneiform tablets recording the observations of contemporary Babylonian astronomers, for example, and inscriptions in Aramaic—the lingua franca of the later Persian Empire—from what is now Afghanistan. Advances in Persian studies over the past half century mean that we now know far more about the empire Alexander conquered than we did previously; a similar renaissance in Macedonian studies has given us a better sense of where he came from. And while these reevaluations are still primarily based on texts, there is also a tremendous amount of evidence available from archaeology. Alexander's swift, violent passage through Africa, the Middle East, and Asia left *traces*—from the ashes of the city he destroyed at Persepolis to the towns he founded in Central Asia to battlegrounds in Pakistan.

These archaeological traces of Alexander's empire are not always comprehensively published, nor are they easy to interpret. They have consequently been neglected by most previous historians, who are more comfortable with literary texts than with coarse pottery and the fragmentary foundations of undistinguished buildings. For this book, however, archaeological remains are critical, because they offer us a perspective unavailable elsewhere. The archaeological evidence helps to re-create the world of Alexander in all its fullness and complexity, to show what ancient writers obscure, omit, or consider unimportant. It gives voice to those who remain voiceless when history is written only by the victors. The result is a new perspective on Alexander's conquest of the Persian Empire, one that integrates into his history the experience of the conquered.

To study Alexander is to analyze power. What the archaeological evidence does is to allow us to trace the effects of power not only on the Macedonian king himself, but also on those on whom power was exercised. In doing so, this book brings new attention to those who are often considered bit players in "great man" history; for instance, Alexander's women, enemies, subjects, and soldiers. It also conveys their agency: how the power *they* wielded affected Alexander.

In recounting the story of Alexander, historians generally begin with his birth, as the son of an embattled ruler in the provincial kingdom of Macedonia. But the true story of Alexander starts later on. It begins in his last years, as his character was revealed—and transformed—by failure. During these years, Alexander hunted lions in Uzbekistan and was almost killed himself by a South Asian warrior. He celebrated a dazzling wedding with nine thousand guests, and buried his lover with a funeral pyre the size of two football fields. He journeyed as far as Begram and Samarkand, but died still dreaming of fresh conquests. In his last years, as he faced down Afghan warlords, Indian elephants, and his own angry veterans, Alexander became a far more complex and compelling individual than he had been as an effortlessly successful young king. It was also in his final years that he began to have a lasting effect on the empire he had conquered. His story truly commences when Alexander—in defiance of his advisers, his army, and perhaps good sense as well—chose to leave behind everything familiar and set off on a quixotic quest for the end of the world. It begins with a burning city.

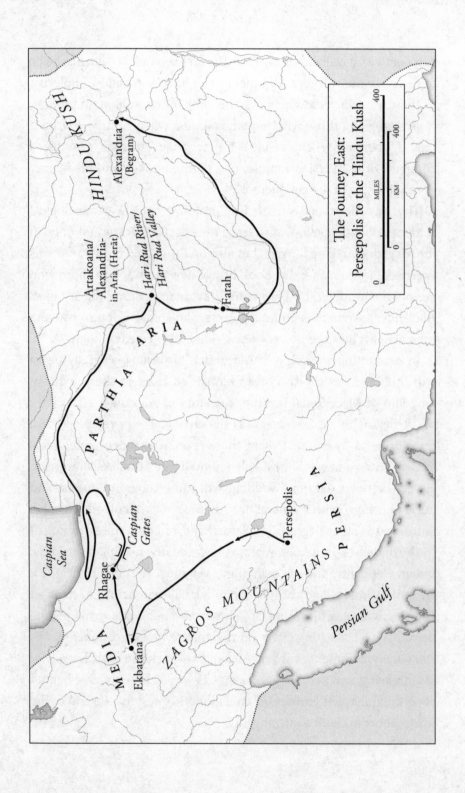

The Journey East:
Persepolis to the Hindu Kush

HINDU KUSH

Alexandria
(Begram)

Arakoana/
Alexandria-
in-Aria (Herāt)

Hari Rud River/
Hari Rud Valley

ARIA

Farah

PARTHIA

Caspian
Sea

Caspian
Gates

Rhagae

Persepolis

PERSIA

MEDIA

Ekbatana

ZAGROS MOUNTAINS

Persian Gulf

MILES 400

KM 400

ONE

A City on Fire

Persepolis, Iran
Winter–Spring 330 BCE

HIGH UP ON THE CENTRAL IRANIAN PLATEAU, in the thin, chill February air, the twenty-five-year-old Alexander of Macedon waited with his army at the gates of the royal city of Persepolis. He'd spent the past month chivying his troops on a forced march over the tough mountains of western Iran, fighting his way through enemy territory, foraging for food, bridging rivers swollen by winter rain.

Alexander had rushed to Persepolis, desperate to secure the treasure stored within its walls. Almost within his grasp was a fortune several orders of magnitude greater than his own inheritance: massive quantities of coins, bullion, and precious objects extracted from their empire by the ancient world's wealthiest kings. If he delayed, he might lose it all to his rival, the Persian ruler Darius III. If he hurried, Alexander could take possession of riches that would fund his journey to the end of the world.

That February day, as he gazed up at Persepolis, Alexander could see that the treasure was well guarded. The city's walls topped out at ninety feet above the plateau he stood on; at its back was the mountain Kuh-i-Rahmat. Set on a high terrace were thirty-three acres of monumental buildings; audience halls and palaces with soaring cedar roofs, columns ornately carved and elaborately painted; lush gardens filled with greenery. Beyond them, tucked away inconspicuously at the back of the complex, was the treasury, a low, mazelike building housing the riches Alexander sought. If he had to fight, they would be exceptionally hard to win. The city's walls were thick, its gates few. Small wonder that Darius I, the revered and long-dead founder of Persepolis, called it his fortress.

Since its founding in the last years of the sixth century BCE, Persepolis had never been attacked; no hostile army had penetrated to this, the symbolic heart of the Persian Empire. A few short months later it would be devastated, with all the magnificent buildings and lush greenery turned into a smoky, blackened ruin.

When Alexander arrived, however, Persepolis remained intact. Its high walls functioned like the exterior of a strongbox, a rough and imposing sheath for the extraordinary riches within. Alexander could not be certain just what was inside: A treasure, but perhaps also an army, an ambush, or a host of outwardly compliant, dangerously resentful inhabitants? At Persepolis, as so often in his short and violent life, Alexander was preparing to rush headlong into the unknown. But for him the risk was far outweighed by the potential reward. Persepolis's treasure was a prize he could not afford to lose in his high-stakes contest with Darius III.

Alexander had been fighting Darius since his arrival in Persia in the spring of 334 BCE. Then he had been a brash young man with big dreams and an army he could scarcely afford, the legacy of his father, Philip II. No one, perhaps not even Alexander himself, had expected him to make much headway against his adversary. He'd begun with the rhetoric of a Panhellenic crusade against Persia, which was de rigueur if one needed the support of the Greeks. But some victories along the western coast of Turkey, followed by a return to Macedonia with a decent quantity of plunder, were all most Greeks had envisioned when Alexander started out, and his advisers were only slightly more sanguine.

Alexander proved them both wrong. Since that spring day when he had invaded Persia, success had followed success in his war against

Darius. He had won two massive set-piece battles at Issos and Gaugamela; taken by siege a host of wealthy, prominent cities; and annexed all the Persian provinces from northern Turkey to Egypt, Syria, and Mesopotamia. Proud and supremely self-confident, the young king had prevailed—against Darius, and against all those doubters from Greece and Macedonia. Demosthenes had once insisted that Alexander would be content to remain sauntering around his hometown and consulting omens. The headstrong young king must have been pleased to demonstrate how drastically the aging orator had miscalculated. Far from staying in Macedonia, Alexander had conquered the western half of the Persian Empire in a little over three years.

The Greeks, reckoning the odds from their dusty marketplaces and verdant philosophical academies back home, revised their estimation of Alexander. Perhaps he could win that Panhellenic crusade he'd talked of, echoing (however cynically) the advice Greek rhetoricians had given to his father. They began to hope that Alexander, despite his unpromising Macedonian origins, could be their instrument of vengeance for the Persian invasion of Greece a century and a half earlier. The Greeks nursed long grudges, even by ancient standards, and for them it seemed entirely reasonable for Alexander to punish Darius III for the sins of his great-great-great-grandfather, or burn down Persepolis in exchange for Xerxes's sack of Athens. They dreamed of an extraordinary conflagration, grand and destructive enough to rival that of Homer's Troy. If Alexander obliged, they might even give him a hero's welcome upon his return.

Alexander's Macedonian advisers did not share the Greeks' preoccupation with vengeance, but they, too, wanted him to return to his homeland. They had been the top generals of Philip II and had known his son since childhood. As they followed Alexander on all his conquests, they were a fount of well-intentioned, frequently ignored advice for the young king. By the time they reached Persepolis, they had been on campaign longer than any Macedonian army officers had before. They were also farther away, with the high limestone walls of Persepolis some 2,300 miles from the decidedly less imposing fortifications of their own capital, Pella. Philip's old generals felt Alexander had gone far enough, perhaps too far—beyond what his father had anticipated, and beyond what was strategic, and sustainable, also. The young king had already faced one serious rebellion in Greece, led by the Spartans. He'd quashed it—or rather, his Macedonian regent, Antipater, had—but the advisers were worried.

Alexander's advisers were especially frustrated because the impetuous young king had already turned down at least one credible overture from Darius. After his first major loss at the Battle of Issos in 333 BCE, the Great King had written to the Macedonian upstart, offering all the lands west of the Euphrates River, the hand of a Persian princess in marriage, and ten thousand talents, an immense fortune, in silver. It was far more than Alexander had yet achieved, and an offer of wealth, land, and status beyond what any Macedonian ruler had had before.

"If I were Alexander, I would take the offer," insisted Parmenion, Philip's best general and now Alexander's second-in-command.

"So would I, by Zeus, if I were Parmenion," the young king shot back, all brevity and contempt.

The offer was tabled; Alexander fought on, and won again. By the time he reached Persepolis, his riches and territorial gains far exceeded what Darius had offered. Alexander's achievements hardly placated his Macedonian advisers. If anything, they made matters worse. Unlike the Greeks, the advisers weren't interested in conflagrations—don't destroy your own property, said Parmenion to Alexander, grumpily but pragmatically, when the young king considered what to do with Persepolis. What they sought was restraint and a clear stopping point. In their view, it was high time for Alexander to settle down and profit from his conquests. He needed to bring his immense wealth back to Macedonia, keep a closer eye on those unreliable Greeks, perhaps even marry and produce an heir.

Alexander was, predictably, less than enthusiastic about this vision for his future. He had no interest in sitting on a throne, particularly one situated in Macedonia, for any length of time. He had seen the wealth, power, and sophistication of the Persian Empire—a place far better suited to his outsize aspirations than his small, provincial homeland. He wanted more, needed more. Some of his needs were practical, others less so. Practically speaking, Darius was still at large and a potential threat that Alexander needed to defuse. So were the governors of the Persian Empire's borderlands in eastern Iran and Afghanistan. Farther east, the Indian subcontinent beckoned, with reports of its fabulous wealth and exotic natural resources: spices, gems, elephants. Beyond them all, but not so very far away, according to the scientific theories of Alexander's former tutor Aristotle, was Ocean, the immense body of water the Greeks believed lay at the end of the world.

Ocean fascinated Alexander, at once a physical entity he sought to reach, a mythological character familiar from his favorite book, the *Iliad*, and a scientific hypothesis he hoped to prove. Ocean was the counter and the antithesis of the Mediterranean Sea, which was in Greek minds the center of the world. Around that wine-dark watery core, philosophers imagined thin strips of land, on which the peoples of the world were distributed "like ants or frogs around a pond," in the words of Aristotle's teacher Plato. Beyond the Mediterranean Sea, and the narrow bands encircling it, lay the vast gray depths of Ocean: cold, uncanny, boundless, filled with monsters. If Alexander could conquer up to Ocean, it would be an achievement that might satisfy even his enormous ambition—and it would be the ultimate secure border.

But before he could reach Ocean, Alexander had to deal with Persepolis. As he stood with his shivering and weary soldiers outside the city, he had done all he could. It was the Persepolitans' choice what came next. In a letter to Alexander, their treasurer had been encouraging. But he had also made clear that the inhabitants of this powerful royal city were not fully under his control. Would they welcome Alexander into Persepolis, with the acquiescence befitting a royal city whose king had fled? Or would they resist? Given the strength of Persepolis's fortifications and the timing of Alexander's arrival, resistance would be at best an inconvenience, at worst a real danger. The young king and his army would have to blockade the city, settling in for a prolonged and chilly siege.

That February day, Alexander's luck held (he was generally lucky, and even more frequently virtuous, according to the Roman biographer Plutarch, who wrote two essays on the topic). The Macedonian king faced no substantive resistance as he entered the city. There was no siege—the one at Tyre, in present-day Lebanon, had taken Alexander nine months—no gates were barred, no arrows fired.

Alexander walked unimpeded up the immense, broad staircase that led to the terrace buildings and passed through the gatehouse that, on its own, compared favorably in scale with the palace he grew up in at Pella. The inhabitants of Persepolis were accommodating, if unenthusiastic. At Babylon, Alexander had been greeted with roads carpeted with flowers and garlands, silver altars burning with frankincense and other rich perfumes, and a great procession of ambulatory gifts, including herds of cattle, horses, lions, and leopards. At Persepolis, the Macedonian king made no ceremonial entry into the city, and received no such exotic gifts. But he could afford to dispense with costly formalities. His chief goal, the treasury, remained intact.

Upon Alexander's arrival, the treasury was intact, but by no means easy to get to. He had to walk through the gatehouse and into a courtyard that was roughly the size of a soccer field, where his Persian predecessors had once held elaborate outdoor ceremonies. He had to pass the enormous audience hall of the Persian kings, with its forest of columns sixty feet high and brightly decorated staircases. He then walked through a triple-gated building whose main function seemed to be to separate, in properly grandiose fashion, the more public area of the terrace from the more intimate private sphere of the palaces. And finally, after four palaces—three of them larger and more richly decorated than the one he grew up in at Pella—a staircase on the left led him to his goal. Before him stood the blandest and most inconspicuous building on the terrace, with plain mudbrick walls and stubby wooden columns: the treasury.

The treasury was visually unimpressive, but what it held was astonishing. The ancient sources disagree on just how much precious metal Alexander found there. (Classical historians were not statistically minded, and their budget figures tend to vary wildly, as do their calculations—frequently and grossly inflated—of the number of enemy soldiers killed.) Still, even the low estimate was forty thousand talents, at a time when the annual tribute of the Athenian empire topped out at twelve hundred. Nor did it begin and end with the more pedestrian forms of wealth, such as coins and bullion. Instead, the treasury was packed, from its flattened dirt floors to its wooden rafters, with the exotic, beautiful objects that the Persian kings had accumulated during their two centuries of imperial power: high-polished stone bowls once owned by Egyptian pharaohs, jewelry made of amethysts from India and lapis lazuli from Afghanistan, a spectacular Greek marble statue of Odysseus's wife, the patient Penelope, waiting for him to come home. Alexander would have to decide what to do with it all—how to take what he needed for his quest for Ocean, where and how to store the rest. But on the day he arrived in Persepolis, all that lay in the future. For the moment, he simply cordoned off the terrace to ensure the treasure's safety, then let his soldiers loose on the lower town, to rape, pillage, and slaughter as they wished.

The sack of Persepolis marked a new low in the relationship between Macedonians and Persians. The two peoples had much in common—both came from militaristic upstart kingdoms with more powerful, better-established neighbors—although the Persians had the advantage of conquering those neighbors far earlier. By the time they had their first substantial encounter with the Macedonians in the early fifth century BCE, the Persians had already extended their realm from Afghanistan to Turkey, and had recently added the once great land of Egypt to their empire. The Macedonians, by contrast, held only the broad, well-watered plains at the apex of the Aegean Sea, and were regularly preyed on both by nomadic peoples to their east and by the covetous city-states of southern Greece. When those Greeks drew the ire of Persia by supporting a rebellion of their fellow Hellenes in western Turkey, the Great King vowed to retaliate—and the Macedonians lay directly in his army's path.

In 492 BCE, the Great King, Darius I, sent ambassadors to all the city-states of southern Greece, as well as to the kingdom of Macedonia. He demanded earth and water: simple everyday materials, but ones that symbolized submission to the rule of the Persian king. In Athens, the king's ambassadors were thrown into a pit used for the execution of criminals; in Sparta, they were dumped into a well (where they had, said the Spartans, earth and water aplenty). In Macedonia, King Amyntas I—the great-great-great-great-grandfather of Alexander the Great—complied with the Persians' demand. He likely felt he had no choice. His small, poorly equipped army was no match for the enormous one fielded by the Persians, and no Greeks, however bellicose, would put themselves at risk for their Macedonian neighbors, who still had a king and lived in villages rather than self-governing cities like the Hellenes. So Amyntas I submitted, and left the way to southern Greece open for the Persians. In fact, he went further, supplying troops to the Persian army, negotiating with the Greeks on their behalf, and marrying his daughter to the son of a high-ranking Persian general.

Amyntas's son, Alexander I, benefited considerably from the collaboration with the Persians. He used Darius's invasion as an excuse to expand his realm at the expense of his less compliant neighbors. More surprisingly, he managed to hold on to his gains even after this first Persian invasion of Greece had been roundly and implausibly defeated in 490 BCE. He even pulled off the same feat with the second invasion, by Darius's son Xerxes, in 480–479. To judge from the ancient literary sources, Alexander I was an impressive operator, who played very cannily his initially quite unpromising hand of cards. He was also lucky and long lived, dying long after his Persian counterpart, in 454. In this, Alexander I was unusual. Between battle, hunting, and palace conspiracies, few Macedonian kings lived long or died in their beds. The same went for the Persians, although in the Greek sources at least, their most frequent cause of death was poisoning by their high-ranking eunuch officials, an outcome the Macedonians didn't have to worry about.

For the next century and a half, the Persians and Macedonians had relatively little to do with one another. The Persians did not attempt a third invasion of Europe, and concentrated their efforts on destabilizing their Greek neighbors through selective alliances and bribery instead. Their kings continued to be plagued by palace conspiracies. Xerxes I, for instance, was assassinated with the collusion of a eunuch official, as were two later rulers. But despite these dynastic hiccups, the Persian Empire itself held together well. The only major loss was the far-off and traditionally autonomous province of Egypt, which broke away in 400 BCE and was successfully reconquered only ten years before the arrival of Alexander the Great. Elsewhere, the Middle East and Central Asia remained in what might be called a Pax Persica, their immense territories united and peaceful for more than two centuries.

The Persians' successful empire in the east contrasted strikingly with the Macedonians' beleaguered western kingdom. Following the death of Alexander I, the Macedonians cycled through a series of weak and ineffective rulers, whose internecine struggles were gleefully exploited by their neighbors. In the period from 399 to 393, for example, the Macedonians had four kings in six years, of whom all but the last died violently. The decade between 370 and 360 was even worse: two short-lived kings; one dangerously powerful but equally short-lived regent; invasions by the nomadic Illyrians from the west, the Thracians from the east, and the city-state of Thebes from the south; and hostages, ransom, and near-constant warfare, with Macedonia always on the losing side.

Ironically, the Macedonians suffered these losses because of their region's abundant natural resources—they had what everybody in the ancient world wanted. Their well-watered plains were ideal for agriculture; even today, the traveler in Macedonia is struck by the abundance of fruit trees and vegetables that cloak the landscape in vivid green. The Macedonians in consequence attracted the attention of their less well endowed neighbors, especially the Illyrians, whose drier, more mountainous territory was far less suited to farming. During the fifth and fourth centuries BCE, the Macedonians were regularly raided, and intermittently invaded, by massive bands of these nomadic peoples, who swooped down from the mountains to steal cattle, terrorize villagers, and demand protection money before disappearing back across the border.

The city-states of southern Greece also coveted the natural resources of Macedonia, although they had different priorities and strategies than did the Illyrians. What they wanted most was timber. Within the northeast Mediterranean, the Macedonians had a near monopoly on the tall, sturdy trees the Greeks needed for shipbuilding. Since ships were required for both sea trade and naval warfare, two key Hellenic activities, the Macedonians were constantly at risk. The Greeks invaded their kingdom, established colonies on its outskirts, and imposed treaties, predominantly favorable to themselves, to regulate control of this valuable asset.

The Macedonians' relationship with Greece was further complicated by their intermittent emulation of all things Hellenic. By the Classical era, the Macedonians spoke and wrote Greek, although they likely used another language among themselves. They also encouraged Athenian painters, philosophers, and shipbuilders to emigrate, offering them royal patronage. And they trained their army in the most up-to-date methods of Greek warfare.

Despite their Hellenizing efforts, the Macedonians were only grudgingly and sporadically accepted as members of what was, to the Greeks at least, a very exclusive club. Some prominent Hellenic intellectuals refused royal invitations to the Macedonian court. Others visited, then mocked the king when safely out of reach.

The Greeks' cultural resistance extended even to athletics. When the early Macedonian king Alexander I attempted to participate in that quintessentially Hellenic activity, the Olympic Games, he was initially disqualified; the Olympics, said the judges, were only for Greeks. He responded by producing an elaborate genealogy tracing his ancestry back to the Greek city of Argos, and likely to its most famous former resident, the Argive hero Herakles. With this suitably illustrious, and impeccably Hellenic, pedigree, Alexander I won over the Olympic judges, and he was allowed to compete. He may even have won, since there is a fragmentary poem by Pindar praising his victory in the pentathlon.

While the Macedonians' emulation of Greece is well attested— the Athenians chattered incessantly, in a self-congratulatory manner, about the Hellenic cultural ambitions of their arriviste neighbors— their connection to Persia is less familiar. Still, it was critical. During the Classical era, the Persians were the most prominent, and most effective, imperial power in the Mediterranean world. They exemplified precisely what the Macedonians aspired to. The Persians also had a king, a court, and royal institutions the Macedonians could emulate, and thus offered a far more appealing precedent than did the democracies and oligarchies of the Greek world.

By the time of Alexander's youth, the Macedonians had taken on key Persian practices. They had an informal council of high-ranking aristocrats, the Companions, who advised the king and executed his orders. These were closely analogous to the Kinsmen (not always blood relations) who surrounded the Persian king. The Macedonians had Royal Pages, aristocratic youths who attended the king and were educated alongside royal family members. As in Persia, these young men were honored, but also instrumental. They served as hostages for their fathers' good behavior, since a powerful aristocrat would think twice about rebelling when his heir would pay the price. Macedonian kings, like their Persian counterparts, were polygamous. In both cases, they had the same motivation, the need for an abundance of heirs, and the same problem, a superfluity thereof. The Macedonians even adopted a fashionable Persian bowl, known as the calyx cup, and used it the same way, for drinking and gift-giving.

By the time Alexander launched his invasion, the world he was attacking had critical connections to the one he had left behind. He was able to navigate the Persian imperial system—its court, its bureaucracy, its rituals—because it was what his own kingdom aspired to. Of course, the Macedonians did not adopt all Persian practices seamlessly. When one high-ranking Macedonian aristocrat first observed Persian courtiers bowing reverentially before Alexander, he burst out laughing (the king in response slammed his head against the wall). But Alexander was familiar enough with the Persian modus operandi to harness it effectively for his own purposes. He used it to plan his travels, feed his troops, and persuade Iranian administrators to switch sides. More ominously for the inhabitants of Persepolis, he also used it undermine Darius and demonstrate the Great King's inability to protect his people.

When Alexander unleashed his men on the lower city of Persepolis, the thin, chill air was filled with the sounds of the sack: men shouting, heavy running footsteps, women screaming in terror, the dull, sickening thud of swords meeting flesh. Soldiers fought each other for precious objects, and killed captives whose ransom paled in comparison with the wealth that surrounded them. Some Persians committed suicide, dressing in their most expensive clothes before throwing themselves off the city's high walls with their wives and children. Others set fire to their houses and burned themselves to death. It was a terrible fate for the symbolic heart of the Persian Empire.

It was not, however, an unprecedented or unexpected fate for a powerful imperial city. Ancient generals regularly permitted, if they did not encourage, attacks on civilian populations. For generals, such attacks were useful, because they allowed the soldiers to acquire plunder, a key component of military pay in the ancient world. They also served as a warning for other cities, making clear the penalties for resistance. Alexander had carried out several attacks on civilian populations already, at the Greek city of Thebes, the Carian Halikarnassos, and the Phoenician Tyre. The Macedonian king treated Persepolis no differently; he was brutal and implacable, but even-handed. Every other military leader of his era, Persians included, had done the same.

After the sack, Alexander and his army remained for four months in Persepolis, waiting. Slowly, his soldiers lost the hungry look they had had when they arrived that winter, though they remained tired. They had been fighting in Persia for the better part of four years, thousands of miles from their homeland and families. They had no idea when, or if, they would ever return. The soldiers must have been uneasy as they stayed, unusually for Alexander's army, so long in one place, without a major battle to fight or a siege to undertake. They were prevented by the harsh winter weather from any substantive campaigning, and in any case, they didn't know exactly where Darius was, or what new stratagems he was formulating to continue the war.

The soldiers could see that the Great King had not come, as Alexander had hoped he would, to give himself up: to submit to his conqueror, acknowledge the Macedonian's sovereignty, and receive, in return, some portion of his kingdom back again. With Darius still free, the soldiers would have to keep fighting, at least once the weather permitted and they figured out where their enemy was. In the meantime, they waited. For four months at Persepolis they rested, however warily, and enjoyed the proceeds of the sack.

Brutalized by the sack, Persepolis's residents had spent those same four months adjusting to the difficult reality of living under occupation. They had seen the lower part of the town sacked, but the looters had not left, and the fate of the palaces was still in doubt. In the meantime, they had to share their elegant columned homes with Alexander's soldiers; to supply them with food, drink, and whatever else they demanded; to watch them performing sacrifices to their unfamiliar gods, and taking part in athletic competitions—nude footraces, discus throws, and the *pankration,* a kind of all-in wrestling match that was the mixed martial arts of its day—that were considered bizarre by Persians. Persepolis's residents saw the soldiers departing on a brief sortie against recalcitrant mountain peoples in the region, and returning, inevitably, victorious. It was disheartening, unpleasant, and, most of all, crowded. Alexander's troops and followers likely rivaled the total population of the Persepolis region before the arrival of the Macedonians, and most were adult males, armed and demanding, a constant threat.

While the army rested for four months, Alexander was far from idle. The Macedonian king presided over his soldiers' athletic games, awarding generous prizes, and personally conducted the army's sacrifices. Throughout his career, Alexander was assiduous in cultivating the gods, and by the time he got to Persepolis, he had a good deal to thank them for.

In addition to his pious duties, the Macedonian king had another, more ominous agenda. He began by summoning twenty thousand mules and five thousand camels from the surrounding region, the snowy midwinter weather notwithstanding. He brought them as close as he could to the Persepolis treasury, which he had carefully preserved

intact when he let his soldiers loose on the lower town. Then methodi-
cally and inexorably, he removed from it the riches he had sought.

Alexander took coins, bullion, perhaps a few precious objects—
whatever he believed would help his cause, and whatever he feared
to let fall into Darius's hands. The treasure he had pursued so desperately was his, and he wanted to keep it safe. He loaded it up onto
the mules and camels and sent them to make their slow, ungainly
journey across the western mountain passes to the royal palace at
Susa, 388 miles away. It was an extraordinarily difficult logistical challenge, even by Alexander's standards. One scholar has estimated that
the procession was so long that the last animals in line were five days
behind the leaders.

Only once the treasury was safely en route did Alexander carry out
his dangerous and devastating plan for Persepolis.

On a soft spring day in 330 BCE, Alexander set the crown jewel of
the Persian Empire on fire. First, he organized a second sack of the
city, concentrating his efforts not on the lower town and its already-
brutalized inhabitants, but instead on the buildings of the upper
terrace. He allowed his soldiers to ransack the palaces and the treasury, seizing whatever valuables they desired. Practiced looters, the
soldiers took every single one of the gold and silver bowls on the
terrace, because these were light, easy to carry, and possible to melt
down, but left the beautifully polished ones in hard, too-heavy stone.
The men also found all the precious metal swords and daggers that
were once stored within the heavily guarded palace buildings, leaving
only a few shabby bronze weapons and a scatter of arrowheads.

The soldiers had to work quickly; Alexander didn't give them much
time. For him, the sack was only a prelude. He let his soldiers loot
whatever he had left behind. But he must also have warned them that
those who worked too slowly might be burned to death.

The traces of the soldiers' looting show their reckless speed. They had no patience for the mazelike windings of the treasury, so they created a faster thoroughfare, running up a ramp, across the building's flat, low roof, and down a closed-off staircase, breaking down the door in the process. At the bottlenecks in their escape route, the soldiers dropped valuables: six gold rosettes and fragments of a gold band on the staircase, gold scraps and coins along the ramp. The men had taken so much, and needed to move so quickly, that they failed to notice what they'd lost. Then the fire intervened, and they never came back.

It was an extraordinary fire. Alexander had his men prepare it, heaping up richly ornamented wooden couches and intricately woven textiles to burn in a storeroom on the south side of the audience hall. The soldiers set alight masses of flammable material in the largest room of the treasury, the portico of the throne hall, and the audience hall's center. Their work ensured that these buildings, the largest and most prominent on the terrace, would be devastated. Elsewhere the arsonists of Alexander were less meticulous. Some rooms of the treasury show only minor scorching, and the triple-gated building that led from the public area to the palaces was left virtually intact. The arsonists aimed at destruction, but also speed; even if a few buildings were still standing, they had done enough.

When Alexander's soldiers had done their work, the fire raged all over the city of Persepolis. Flames scorched the walls of the palaces on the terrace. Their heat shattered limestone column bases; fused together the shafts of arrows; melted iron. The fire devoured cloth-of-gold canopies and tapestries, turned gold-encrusted couches into heaps of ash, and baked the mudbrick walls of the treasury light red. Sparks from the fire reached sixty feet in the air to the ceiling of the audience hall, lit and consumed its great cedar beams, and brought the remnants crashing to the ground. When it was all over, Alexander had turned the palaces on the terrace into ruins, blanketed in one to three feet of heavy gray ash. The accumulated wealth of the great Persian capital, its lush gardens, its ornate sculptures, and its immense, seemingly eternal buildings—all had been irrevocably destroyed.

In wantonly burning down a rich and powerful city like Persepolis, Alexander took a calculated risk, one of the greatest in a career full of audacious moves. It was stunning, dramatic, and—from the perspective of Alexander's Macedonian advisers, at least—a senseless, self-destructive choice. Persepolis had been an imperial center, a nexus of control at the intersection of royal highways that stretched to the four corners of the Persian realm. As the advisers could clearly see, destroying it risked fragmenting that control, and called into question Alexander's claim to be the new Great King.

Perplexed by the Macedonian king's behavior, most ancient writers blame wine and a woman. Their story is that at a drinking party of Alexander and his companions, an Athenian courtesan came up with the idea, and the whole group lurched drunkenly after her, waving torches.

The reality was more deliberate and more sinister. Alexander had, after all, spent four months emptying out the treasury. He did it so thoroughly that of the forty thousand talents the building once held, only thirty-nine coins were left: nine gold, two electrum, twenty-seven silver, one bronze. He also organized the soldiers' sack of the treasury before it burned, and set fires selectively to target the largest, most impressive buildings on the terrace. As the archaeological remains demonstrate, Alexander acted with ruthless, purposeful violence, not drunken impulsivity.

When Alexander burned Persepolis, he was attuned to several audiences. He knew it would please the Greeks, who had been agitating for vengeance against Persia for roughly a century and a half. It may also have appealed to Alexander personally. The Macedonian king slept with the *Iliad* nearby, and this was as close as he would ever come to the fire at Troy.

But Alexander likely aimed the destruction of Persepolis primarily at the Persians. In burning down the crown jewel of their empire, he sent a message: He had conquered, definitively and ruthlessly. Further opposition was futile. For those who might consider protecting Darius, or joining him in resisting the Macedonian king, the destruction of Persepolis was a warning of the retribution they would face. It was a sign that Alexander would not be satisfied with what he'd already won. He would keep going: to Darius, to the eastern empire, to the end of the world, if he could. Alexander torched Persepolis so thoroughly that it was never again substantially inhabited. Then he marched his army out of the smoking ruins. He was headed to the high mountain region of northwest Iran, where rumor had it Darius had fled. Winter was over, Alexander's treasure secure. It was time to resume his pursuit of the Great King.

TWO

The Hunt for the Great King

Iran
Spring–Summer 330 BCE

THE FIRE'S HAZE STILL LINGERED as Alexander left Persepolis. Beyond the city it dissipated, and the countryside was blanketed with the bright green leaves and pale blossoms of spring. There were apple, mulberry, pear, quince, olive, date, and pomegranate trees; the plains around the city were like an immense orchard. Spring rain and melting snow fed them with a crisscrossing network of irrigation canals, dams, and ditches, organized by the Persian kings to keep the heartland of their empire fertile and well watered. On the plains, cattle and horses nibbled tender new grass, while along the rivers, a rich variety of aquatic birds taught their hatchlings to swim and fly. Through it all marched Alexander, and with him some seventeen thousand armed men.

As Alexander led his army through the springtime plains and orchards around Persepolis, he faced the uncomfortable quandary of what to do next. For the moment, he was headed toward Ekbatana, a powerful city in the mountains of northwestern Iran. He had heard from his own scouts or Persian deserters that Darius III was there, gathering a new army with his allies among the nomads who lived along the northern borders of the Persian Empire. At Ekbatana, his informants doubtless told him, Darius had treasure to fund such an army—far less than the better-endowed capitals of Babylon, Susa, and Persepolis, but enough to buy an army if the allies were willing.

Alexander was fiercely determined to find Darius. He wanted to fight it out with his rival, confident that he would defeat the Great King and destroy his army as thoroughly as he had Persepolis. His dream was to capture Darius, as he'd tried and failed to do, to his immense frustration, at their two previous encounters at the battles of Issos and Gaugamela. Like Achilles—Alexander's hero, and a legendary ancestor on his mother's side—the young Macedonian king wanted constantly to be the best, and to be acknowledged as such. By defeating Darius, his greatness and preeminence would be clear. So would his royal legitimacy. If he could put the Great King in chains, Alexander would become, inarguably, the new Great King.

Alexander raced along the Royal Road from Persepolis to Ekbatana, some 514 miles, fearful that Darius was about to slip away from him once more. Ancient armies often missed one another; earlier in his career, in the immediate lead-up to the Battle of Issos, Alexander had in fact marched within thirty miles of Darius without knowing it. Now the Macedonian king was in even more unfamiliar territory, while his rival, a former governor of Armenia, knew the landscape better. If Darius escaped, Alexander's best hope of finding him would be his knowledge that every army has deserters—particularly an army in retreat.

Alexander's own army posed another problem. As he marched along the Royal Road, they spread out before him, an immense, heaving sea of men. Their bronze armor glittered in the sunlight, contrasting with the cold gray of their iron weapons and the quivering sheen of their horses' coats. Dangerous men, well trained and formidable, they had prevailed in every battle they'd fought. And in the uncertain, potentially hostile territory through which they now moved, the soldiers were critical. Alexander had spent long enough in the Persian Empire to know that resisters could be anywhere, even among the pale blossoms and placidly munching cows of the Persepolis plain. The Macedonian king needed his soldiers, especially when another major battle with Darius threatened. But if the Great King chose to flee eastward, Alexander's enormous, complex army became more of a liability than an asset. His soldiers moved too slowly, took too much effort to discipline, rest, and feed. For the hunt, when it came, he would need to let some of them go.

Alexander looked over his army, weighing his options. Most prominent, but most unwieldly, were the Macedonian heavy-armed infantry, with eighteen-foot spears tipped by cruel iron spikes at both ends. Their spears, known as *sarissas*, weighed so much that the soldiers had to use both hands to hold them, and carried their shields on straps slung around their necks and swords in belts. They marched in battle with their spears pointed outward, an outsize, bristling porcupine of a formation. Well trained and properly organized, the sarissa-bearers were unstoppable in warfare; no enemies could get close enough to harm them. But in pursuit they were a disaster in the making, difficult to maneuver and highly vulnerable on uneven ground.

Next to the sarissa-bearers marched the old-fashioned—and far more flexible—infantrymen known as hoplites, Greek and Macedonian. Their name derived from their *hopla* ("panoply"): a heavy bronze-plated shield, metal helmet, breastplate, and shin guards. They needed this panoply because their spears were comparatively short and light, a mere eight feet long and 2.2 pounds, one-fifth the weight of the sarissas. In battle, they moved like a tank, with shields overlapping so as to be almost impenetrable; they fought by shoving shields and jabbing spears against their opponents, until one side broke and ran.

The hoplites' heavier armor and lighter weapons allowed them to perform tasks impossible for the sarissa-bearers, such as scaling walls—a key component of Alexander's numerous city sieges—and scouting unfamiliar territory. But on the march, their heavy equipment made them slow, especially as Alexander generally forced them to carry all their gear. This reduced the need for pack animals, which had to be fed and slowed the whole proceedings down. But it made the march an astonishing athletic workout for everyone involved, especially at the speeds Alexander demanded (probably around thirteen miles per day, depending on the weather and terrain).

Infantrymen made up the bulk of Alexander's army, but the cavalry was the Macedonian king's own unit, and the one closest to his heart. Cavalrymen, too, could wield the eighteen-foot sarissa—a particularly impressive accomplishment given that they rode without stirrups (which were a later invention) and with only light, perfunctory saddles. They wore metal helmets and breastplates but no shin guards, because when charging, they had to keep their seats by gripping their horses' sides with their legs, requiring incredible inner thigh strength.

When he came to power, Alexander inherited a large, well-equipped cavalry, to which he and many of his best friends belonged. He expanded and transformed it in order to fight the Persians, who had access to what were at that time the ancient world's best horses. These horses came from Nesaia, in what is now northern Iran, and they were stronger, larger, and faster than those found in Macedonia (ancient horses were generally much smaller than those of today; even Alexander's famous stallion, Boukephalos, his mount in all his most important battles, was likely the size of a modern pony). To counter the Nesaian horses, and the enormous Persian army generally, Alexander trained his cavalry in new tactics: coordinating with infantry, fighting at close range rather than launching spears from afar, and using the horse itself as a weapon, so that with rearing, checking, and charging it terrified the opponent's horse, or any man unlucky enough to get caught beneath its hooves. For battle, Alexander aimed to hold on to as many of his cavalrymen as possible, and in pursuit they gave him speed, as they moved far faster than could the infantry. But in the dry, desertlike territory of eastern Iran, they would struggle, as they needed not only food but fodder and water for their horses; they could not go far on lean rations.

Along with infantry and cavalry, the mainstays of his army, Alexander had a range of other troops marching along the Royal Road.

There were light-armed javelin men for skirmishing, archers for long-range attacks, scouts for reconnaissance, sailors for rivers and sea journeys, and engineers for siege machines and bridge building. All were organized into territorial units (Phoenician sailors, Cretan archers, etc.), and many hailed from outside the Greek world, including areas Alexander had recently conquered. He would soon give orders for thirty thousand Persian youths to be trained in the Greek language and Macedonian fighting tactics, with the goal of integrating them into his army once their training was complete. Later on, these youths would play a pivotal role, transforming Alexander's forces and protecting the king when he was most in danger. But even before their arrival, Alexander's army was a complex, heterogeneous, and multiethnic entity, disparate in many ways but unified by loyalty to the Macedonian king. In this way it was a microcosm of the society Alexander hoped to create in the Persian Empire at large.

Together with the soldiers traveled an even more motley and disparate group, the noncombatants who followed the army and provided various services to it. Some were official, others less so. Among those with official status were doctors—including Alexander's personal physician, Kritoboulos—along with the attendants of the horses and pack animals and servants for the higher-ranking officers. Alexander limited their number as much as he could, since they had to be fed and looked after. He also armed them when desperate for reinforcements, though they rarely proved distinguished soldiers.

Similarly inept at battle, but important to Alexander, were a group of intellectuals and entertainers. They included historians, philosophers, seers, poets, actors, boxers, and flute players. They were prominent members of Alexander's traveling court, although he often found them wanting. After one particularly sycophantic but unimpressive poet performed, the king remarked that he would rather be Homer's Thersites—a low-class antihero of the *Iliad*—than his own poet's Achilles.

Along with the servants and courtiers came a range of unofficial camp followers, including artisans (metalworkers, carpenters, stone-masons, etc.), merchants, and women. These women, and eventu-ally their children as well, appear infrequently in the ancient literary sources, and scholars have paid them little attention. But judging from the remote and inaccessible places where they are mentioned—for instance, the Makran Desert in what is now Pakistan—they must have been a constant presence, following in the wake of the army and intimately connected to it. These women served the sexual and romantic needs of Alexander's soldiers, who were not allowed to bring their wives on campaign and who had now been absent from their homeland for four long years. While there is no evidence for their forcible coercion on the march (Alexander was not about to waste soldiers guarding them), the women were not there of their own free will.

The women were primarily drawn from the conquered popula-tions of the empire, whose lives had been radically disrupted by Alexander's arrival in Persia. Now, far from their homes and families, they were dependent on their conquerors. As they moved east, the march grew harder, and the separation from their homeland more acute. Eventually, many of them formed new relationships with Alexander's soldiers, despite the strong linguistic and cultural bar-riers separating them, and the element of coercion that must always have been present. Later, when Alexander himself was celebrating his wedding, he offered to formalize the unions of any of his men attached to Persian women. Reportedly, nine or ten thousand of them took him up on the offer—a surmounting of cultural barriers on an enormous scale.

For now, the women came along, doing their best to keep up with the swift marching pace Alexander required. By ancient standards, or even those of more modern eras, Alexander's army traveled extremely quickly. Even in the eighteenth century, armies averaged a mere seven to eight miles per day, and Alexander was constantly surprising his enemies by arriving faster, and by more difficult routes, than they had anticipated. Given the length of the road between Persepolis and Ekbatana, their journey likely took about a month.

Three days before they reached Ekbatana, Alexander and his army encountered an unexpected visitor to their camp. He was a son of the Great King Artaxerxes III, who had ruled Persia during Alexander's youth. When Artaxerxes died, this son was passed over. In retrospect, he was lucky, as the successful candidate, one of his siblings, was dead within two years. The passed-over son survived, becoming part of Darius's entourage, and had followed him throughout his reign. But as Darius fled east, he recognized that the Great King's hold on power was weakening. With the fine sense of political timing that had enabled him to survive so long, he deserted.

The son of Artaxerxes arrived in Alexander's camp trusting to the well-publicized mercy of the conqueror, and with important news to guarantee his welcome. Darius's northern reinforcements had not come, and the Great King had slipped away from Ekbatana. Taking the city's treasury along with three thousand cavalry and six thousand infantry, he was heading east. Artaxerxes's son let Alexander know how close he was to tracking down his rival. The Macedonian king could thrill to the fact that his prolonged and frustrating wait was almost over. With mounting excitement, he could ready himself for the hunt.

Before he began the chase, Alexander rested his army briefly at Ekbatana. He likely stayed in the elaborate Persian palace, constructed of imported cedar and cypress wood, and with rafters, ceiling, and columns plated with silver and gold. He fed his soldiers with the rich produce of the region, famous for its fruits and vegetables and now, in high summer, at its peak. And he must have appreciated the comparatively temperate climate—the reason that the Persian kings had chosen Ekbatana as their summer capital—and the spectacular natural setting, with snowcapped mountains to the north and west, and the fertile plain of the Qareh Sū River to the east.

At this royal capital, Alexander behaved differently than he had at Persepolis. Still eager to add to his treasure, he stripped the palace of its gold and silver plating. But he did not encourage his soldiers in destruction or atrocities as he had before.

Alexander had already begun to regret the burning of Persepolis. It was a difficult decision that had brought him short-term success—satisfying the Greeks and momentarily cowing the Persians—but over time, it created problems. It called into question his claim to legitimacy as Great King and his trustworthiness as a ruler. It also reminded the conquered of the destructive aspects of his conquest. Alexander could not be certain how bad the long-term consequences of his choice would be. But by the time he arrived at Ekbatana, he considered it a mistake, one that he learned from by behaving more mercifully to this northern royal city.

During his stay in Ekbatana, Alexander focused on the pursuit of Darius, and on the discharging of soldiers necessary for it. Demobilization was a tricky business. It involved releasing a flood of well-trained, belligerent men, who would leave his service thousands of miles from their homeland. He needed them to leave happy and to go where they could settle down, or at least find appropriate service elsewhere. For the demobilization to succeed, he had to choose the men and their leader carefully.

Alexander's choice at Ekbatana fell on the Greek hoplites drafted from his allies, and on the non-Macedonian cavalry; all told, about eight thousand men. He gave them rich discharge payments, enough to guarantee a life of wealth and prominence in Greece if they made it back with their lives—and savings—intact. He also appointed a high-ranking officer to lead them west to coastal Turkey. There, in a prosperous region inhabited by Greeks for centuries, they would find safe passage home.

Alexander's choice was wise, and the demobilization proceeded successfully. The veterans left contented—those who wished were allowed to stay and volunteer for mercenary service—and they do not appear in the ancient sources again. They had served long enough to see Alexander repeatedly victorious against the Persian king, and to benefit from the rich proceeds of his western Persian conquests. As Greeks, they likely viewed the burning of Persepolis with satisfaction, and they brought memories of it home to an audience of Hellenes who assuredly would do so. With the destruction of Persepolis, and Darius's flight to the eastern borderlands of the Persian Empire, the Greek veterans may reasonably have seen their war of vengeance against Persia as brought to its successful conclusion. They were superfluous, and their part in the great crusade completed. What Alexander did next was his own affair. He could pursue victory to the ends of the earth, if he so desired. They were going home.

The Greek veterans were not the only members of the army left behind at Ekbatana. So, too, were the aging general Parmenion and Harpalos, a childhood friend of Alexander's and his chief of finances. Parmenion was charged with depositing the king's enormous treasury at Ekbatana and handing over the money to Harpalos. In doing so, he was entrusting the funds to a canny but also luxury-loving and at times unscrupulous administrator who had already fled the king's service once.

To carry out the handover—and to trim the army further for the pursuit of Darius—Parmenion had six thousand Macedonians, cavalry with some light-armed troops. They would remain in Ekbatana for the foreseeable future, safeguarding the treasury. Parmenion also had other troops, meant to stay only temporarily in Ekbatana: Greek mercenaries, Thracians, and all but three thousand of the cavalry. Once the treasury was securely in Harpalos's hands, Parmenion was supposed to lead them east toward the south coast of the Caspian Sea to eliminate resistance there.

This was the first time Alexander had departed on a major campaign without Parmenion, a significant move for the young king. It was a declaration of independence, though Parmenion was still, to all appearances, honored and trusted—Alexander had, after all, left him with a sizable portion of the army, some fifteen thousand men. But it meant that Alexander could now proceed on the hunt for Darius without his highest-ranking general, and without his advice: the cautious, pragmatic counsel Alexander so often ignored. It must have been satisfying, though Alexander was still not entirely free. He had to bring along a reminder of Parmenion in the form of his sons. Alexander particularly disliked one named Philotas, an arrogant man only a few years his senior. Philotas was cordially detested by Alexander's closest friends but nonetheless, due to his father, was commander of the all-important Macedonian cavalry.

Alexander and Philotas bid Parmenion farewell, and led the rest of the army east from Ekbatana. As they marched, the fertile territory close to the city soon turned barren: low-lying plains with salt steppes and little drinkable water. The soldiers moved as fast as they could through the harsh desert landscape, going so quickly that many men were left behind exhausted and horses died.

Alexander wanted to overtake Darius before he reached the Caspian Gates, the narrow defile that offered safe passage through the steep ravines and crumbling rock of the Kuh-i-Namak Mountains. But despite the army's speed and sacrifice, Darius eluded them. Alexander and his troops learned from the other army's deserters that the Great King had made it to the Caspian Gates before them.

Fast as they had traveled, the Macedonians had failed to take their quarry. Now they would have to fight their way through the Caspian Gates, if Darius chose to defend them, or search the desert beyond for the elusive Great King. For an impatient man like Alexander, the delay and suspense must have been exasperating. But in case of a battle, he needed his men in good condition. He rested them at the nearest sizable city, Rhagae, until after five days they had recovered enough to move on. Then he resumed the chase.

When they finally reached the Caspian Gates, Alexander and his soldiers did not immediately see Darius's army. But the landscape they faced was formidable enough. Surrounding them were mountains formed of a rock that easily disintegrated, where one false step could leave the unwary traveler plunging from crumbling cliffs into a deep ravine. The soldiers had to move carefully in this last leg of their exhausting and dangerous hunt.

At the gates, Alexander and his soldiers entered through a pass only twenty yards wide, squeezing between sheer cliffs. Then they picked their way along the defile, avoiding the salt stream winding through it and the snakes that, according to ancient authors, made it almost impassable in summer. For hours, the soldiers marched through the weird, uncanny landscape where rocks overhung them, oozing liquid salt. As they exited the pass and headed for a campsite with potable water, the soldiers could be grateful that they had faced no human adversaries. Despite the advantages for military strategy, Darius had chosen not to defend the Caspian Gates on his desperate journey east.

Darius's focus was now entirely on flight. But trying to elude Alexander left him ill prepared to deal with the dangers posed by his own men. The Great King was surrounded by ruthless, ambitious individuals, often of royal blood, who commanded their own troops and had, in the decentralized Persian Empire, their own power bases and regional loyalties. One of them was Artabazos, former governor of northwest Turkey, who had close ties to Darius's Greek mercenaries. He had been exiled for rebellion by Darius's predecessor, and had in fact sought sanctuary at the Macedonian court; he must have known Alexander as a child. Artabazos had been honored by Darius and owed him allegiance, but it was unclear how far that would extend.

Bessos, governor of northern Afghanistan and Central Asia, was another high-ranking official whose loyalty was in doubt. He had distinguished himself for bravery and fighting prowess at Gaugamela, and was affiliated with the most formidable remaining portion of the army, the Bactrian cavalry. Bessos ruled the largest province unconquered by Alexander, a veritable kingdom in its own right. His colleague Satibarzanes, a governor in what is now southwestern Afghanistan, was also dangerously powerful.

These men had all remained loyal to Darius after his devastating defeat at Gaugamela the preceding autumn, following him to his winter retreat in Ekbatana and now on his desperate, harried rush to the east. They had seen some high-ranking companions, and many of the soldiers they commanded, slip away to Alexander. They were likely aware of how kindly the Macedonian king had received them, and of the clear material benefits offered by desertion.

In the hilly, almost waterless country east of the Caspian Gates, some of these men formed a conspiracy. Led by Bessos, they surrounded the Great King and forced his abdication. Artabazos, unable to prevent the conspiracy but unwilling to countenance it, took the Greek soldiers and headed for the nearby hills, away from both armies.

Alexander learned quickly of Darius's fall. He had the intelligence from two high-ranking deserters at his camp just beyond the Caspian Gates. Anticipating difficulties with the food supply in the wasteland ahead of him, Alexander had sent many of his soldiers out on a foraging expedition. When the news of the conspiracy arrived, he knew he needed to move quickly. Without awaiting their return, he set out again on the trail of Darius, taking only his top cavalry unit, his mounted scouts, and the best, fastest foot soldiers. They carried just their weapons and two days' rations, trusting that they would find Darius (and food), before these were exhausted. To avoid the brutal summer sun, they traveled that night and into the cooler morning hours, until by noon they could go no farther. After an uneasy siesta in the wasteland, they marched all night again.

At dawn Alexander and his remaining troops found the abandoned camp where Darius had been deposed. From a few disheartened deserters still left there, they learned more details of the Great King's fate. Darius was still alive, for now. But he had been arrested and put in chains—golden chains, appropriately for a Persian king—and was being transported in a carriage covered with animal skins, for secrecy. Darius was meant to be used as a bargaining chip with Alexander, one that might help ensure the conspirators' own safe getaway. The deposed king was being dragged along, unhappy and superfluous, while Bessos had been named commander in his place.

By deposing Darius, the conspirators had made Alexander's pursuit an even more dangerous game. The Macedonian king had hoped to capture Darius with his power intact, so that Alexander's claim to the title would be assured. But the conspirators didn't give him the chance. Instead, they did what the Macedonian king had hoped to do—put Darius in chains—and made Bessos a new and very plausible contender for the title of Great King.

After resting in Darius's former camp, Alexander and his soldiers resumed the chase in late afternoon, traveling all night and through to the following midday. As the sun was at its height, they reached the place where Darius had stopped the day before. Alexander knew then how close his enemy was—almost, but not quite, in his grasp. The Macedonian king would have to continue the cat-and-mouse game he had embarked on with his Persian enemy just a little longer.

From nearby villagers, Alexander learned that there were two roads leading in the direction Darius had gone. One was longer but better for travelers, the other a waterless deserted path. Darius's party, with their horses and covered carriages in mind, chose the easier road. Alexander, focused on speed, took the shortcut. He dismounted five

hundred cavalrymen and replaced them with his best infantry officers. Then he took the cavalry, some three thousand soldiers, to race
along the waterless road after Darius. The rest would follow more
slowly along the route the Persians had taken, as backup.

That night, Alexander and his cavalry traveled forty-five miles—an
extraordinary distance for men moving in darkness through a harsh and
unfamiliar landscape, and already near the point of exhaustion after a
relentless five-day chase. By the next morning, they could barely keep
going, much less defend themselves against a sustained attack. But as
Alexander had likely predicted, they didn't need to. The Persians were
just as tired and far more discouraged, due to the desertions, conspiracy,
and flight they had endured in recent days. After a token resistance, they
fled before Alexander's men, or allowed themselves to be captured.

The conspirators kept Darius with them as long as they dared. But
as they saw Alexander drawing near them, they decided to thwart the
Macedonian king one final time. They stabbed Darius and left him
alone in his grimy carriage.

At the very last moment, after Alexander's four years of campaigning, his monthslong pursuit of Darius, and his desperate final push,
the Macedonian king found the glory he had hoped for snatched
from him. Alexander had sought to kill Darius heroically in battle,
like Achilles, or to defeat, then mercifully pardon, his foe. Either alternative would have provided a cleaner, clearer ending to the hunt,
and greater legitimacy for Alexander.

But when he pushed aside the animal skins and entered the
carriage—yearning to see his enemy for the first time face-to-face—
the deposed king was already dead. All Alexander could do was to
cover his former enemy with his cloak, and send him back to the
Persian Queen Mother, Sisygambis, for burial. The chase was over.

Alexander's soldiers, with Darius's death, were certain they were
finally going home. They had burned Persepolis, scattered the pitiful

remains of the Persian army, and seen the mangled body of the Great King sent back to his homeland for burial. At Ekbatana, they had also watched their Greek allies depart, with honor and enviable discharge payments. Now, they were sure, it was their turn.

Alexander, for his part, was in an awkward negotiating position. He had been moving through a landscape that would have been difficult under the best of circumstances, doing so at the worst possible time—high summer, and generally at night, with only the moon and torchlight to see by. He had necessarily relied on people for guidance who were by rights his unconquered enemies, the Persians living in the area and deserters from his rival's army. And Alexander had shed soldiers relentlessly as he rushed toward his final encounter, so that by the time he made his last push, the army of seventeen thousand he had set out with from Persepolis had shrunk to three thousand, a fraction of its former size. He'd left the remainder of his men with various officers along the way, trusting that they would manage to meet up again—and that they would not revolt, though the quantity of soldiers they commanded in several cases outnumbered his own. Given that the king he was pursuing had just been forced to abdicate due to a conspiracy of his top military officers, Alexander cannot have been blind to the risks he was running. A gambling man, he was now risking his wins on an extraordinarily high-stakes wager. It was unclear how much further the Macedonian king could push his luck.

To the astonishment of his soldiers, Alexander decided to keep going east. In defense of his decision, he likely pointed to Bessos and the other conspirators, who had set out with six hundred cavalrymen for Bactria, and would doubtless raise a better army there. Alexander may also have emphasized that the provinces of Central Asia, though marginal from a Hellenic perspective, were a key part of the Persian Empire. To leave them unconquered was to abandon his great task half-finished: an unglamorous decision, and from a strategic viewpoint, a dangerous one. Given the way Darius died, Alexander was not yet securely in possession of his kingdom. The young Macedonian would have to prove himself to be accepted as Great King.

Beyond the strategic considerations Alexander highlighted for his soldiers, the Macedonian king likely had other motives, no less potent for being unvoiced. According to his ancient biographers, Alexander was driven by *pothos,* a Greek word signifying desire, and in particular a desire for what one does not yet possess: a dangerous, but perhaps inevitable, attribute of empire builders. Pothos was not the king's only motivation, and he was often more rational, and less romantic, than Classical writers suggest. But he was ambitious; he wanted to be "Great." His present achievements could hardly assuage his yearning for greatness.

Alexander's precise words at this moment are uncertain, but two key facts are clear. The first is that the Macedonian king prevailed, despite his soldiers' surprise and disappointment. The army went east, heading around the southern tip of the Caspian Sea that summer. At the same time, it is obvious from their response to Darius's death that Alexander's soldiers were not prepared for this decision. Whatever his own plans had been when he invaded Persia, Alexander had not suggested a conquest this thoroughgoing to his followers. And if his ambitions had grown over time, with his unexpected and rapid success, the Macedonian king had not communicated this well either. Now he was faced with a situation in which the difference between his plans and his soldiers' expectations was thrown into relief. For the time being, Alexander won out. The soldiers followed along obediently, perhaps after some cajoling and distribution of bonuses. But their discontent and disappointment would continue to fester.

THREE

Old Friends and New Clothes

Eastern Iran, Turkmenistan, and Afghanistan
Summer–Fall 330 BCE

WITH DARIUS'S DEATH, Alexander was deluged by a flood of Persian aristocrats switching sides. He had to decide whom to trust and how much. His decisions would transform his empire—integrating Persians into the highest echelons of the command structure—as well as the king himself. In doing so, they simultaneously strengthened and endangered both.

Few individuals had more at stake in Alexander's decision-making process than one Persian aristocrat already in his camp: his mistress, Barsine. Barsine was the daughter of Artabazos, the loyal courtier of Darius III. She was also half-Greek. Her mother, Agerros, hailed from the island of Rhodes, an important supplier of mercenaries to the Persians; her uncles were Mentor and Memnon, high-ranking condottieri in the king's service. The family's cultural fluency proved important when they ran afoul of the Great King and headed for the man best able to protect them: Philip II of Macedon.

Barsine arrived at the Macedonian court with her parents, her siblings, and her uncle Memnon when Alexander was about four years old and Barsine herself likely a few years older. They all stayed there for around a decade, so that Alexander grew up with Barsine and her complex Greco-Persian family nearby. It was an educational experience on both sides. Alexander saw firsthand what an intercultural marriage looked like; it must have impressed him, as he went on to emulate it in his own life three times. Barsine and her family learned different lessons. They had front-row seats at the court of the most powerful man in the Mediterranean. There they witnessed Philip's strengths and weaknesses—and those of his son and heir, Alexander. They then applied this knowledge when circumstances changed, and they found themselves no longer the guests, but the enemies of the Macedonians.

By the time Alexander was in his midteens, Barsine's uncle Mentor had distinguished himself so prominently in the Persian king's service that he asked for his relatives' pardon. He was successful, and Barsine and her family returned to Persia. Artabazos became one of the Great King's highest-ranking courtiers and advisers, while Mentor and Memnon went on to ever-more-prominent positions as generals. Barsine, likely in her teens or early twenties, married her uncle Mentor. Marriage to a close relative was at that time common in both Greece and Persia; it cemented family ties, and in Barsine's case, perhaps rewarded Mentor for his role in her father's pardon. After Mentor's death, Barsine married her other uncle, Memnon. When she encountered Alexander as a prisoner of war in 333 BCE, Barsine had thus already married—and lost—two of the most capable Greek generals of her time.

After her capture by Alexander, Barsine entered into a relationship with her late husband's adversary, a man whom her father and brothers were still fighting. She likely did not choose to do so, any more than she chose to marry either of her uncles, men easily twice her age and selected on grounds more political than romantic. Like most women of her time, Barsine had little autonomy when it came to marriage and sexual relationships, and as a prisoner of war, she was particularly vulnerable. She could not refuse to share Alexander's bed.

Alexander saw his relationship with Barsine more positively. She was famously beautiful, and had also received an excellent Greek education; this made her highly unusual in a time when few Greek or Persian women received any educational instruction at all. Alexander was also likely attracted to her because he had known her since childhood. Throughout his life, the Macedonian king loved, trusted, and promoted his childhood companions above all others, even when, as with his treasurer Harpalos, they repeatedly betrayed that trust. When he encountered Barsine in the aftermath of the Battle of Issos, she was no longer the young girl he had known, but a mature, twice-married widow with children of her own. Nonetheless, of all the Persian aristocratic women he captured, he chose her. And he brought her along with him from that time onward, while other captive women, such as Darius's family members, were left behind.

By the summer of 330 BCE Barsine had traveled farther east than she likely ever had before, past the Persian Empire's heartland to the fertile, humid territory surrounding the Caspian Sea. To Barsine, who had spent most of her life by the Mediterranean, this must have been an exotic seascape, with unfamiliar fish and deep, almost sweet water, far less salty than the sea she knew. In this strange region far from home, her father and brothers arrived in Alexander's camp, along with members of Darius's family and nervous envoys from the Greek mercenaries. They had come to surrender to the Macedonian conqueror. Finally, if Alexander was merciful, Barsine and her family would find themselves together again.

Alexander's reception of Artabazos was an impressive sight and a study in contrasts. Alexander had just turned twenty-six, and his youthful appearance was enhanced by his clean-shaven face and fair, loosely curled hair. He was probably dressed lightly in a knee-length short-sleeved tunic, a cloak pinned at one shoulder, and a floppy beret-like Macedonian hat. Artabazos, on the other hand, if he appeared as befitted his status as a high-ranking Persian courtier and grandson of the Great King, wore a heavy floor-length robe with wide sleeves, a long-sleeved belted tunic, a flat-topped hat, and elegant low shoes with leather thongs. If he had in addition the long, luxuriant hair and heavy beard of the typical Persian noble, he must have been, in the warm, humid summer of eastern Iran, extremely hot.

At their meeting, Alexander received Artabazos's formal submission. No doubt to Barsine's relief, he pardoned her father and brothers, giving Artabazos his right hand as a sign of special favor. The men's loyalty to Darius was rewarded and they were even allowed to intercede for the apprehensive Greek mercenaries. One of Barsine's brothers was dispatched to bring them to Alexander's camp, where they were scolded for their support of Persia, then pragmatically incorporated into the Macedonian army. At the same time, Barsine's father and brothers became members of Alexander's traveling court and eventually received top postings in the conqueror's government and army—though Alexander kept them with him for some time first, perhaps to make sure that their contrition was genuine.

Alexander's generous treatment of Artabazos and his sons contrasted sharply with his brutality toward the inhabitants of Persepolis. He may have acted mercifully for Barsine's sake, and because of the long-ago friendship between their families. But likely more important was the changed political situation. Darius was dead, and Alexander hoped to be accepted by the Great King's other prominent followers as readily as by Artabazos. To attract leading Persian aristocrats, he had to be willing to trust them. He knew that his Macedonian officers resented his openness to those they had defeated. Nevertheless, he persisted. His efforts were all the more important given the disturbing news he soon received about the leader of the conspirators and his new archrival, Bessos.

From his provincial capital at Bactra in northeastern Afghanistan, Bessos issued a direct challenge to Alexander. He put on kingly robes and gave himself the royal name of Artaxerxes after the penultimate Persian ruler. He also began wearing the upright tiara, a type of Persian headgear constructed of fur-lined silk or leather and stiffened to stand erect about the head; this was the Persian equivalent of a royal crown, the distinguishing sign of the Great King. In doing all this, he raised the stakes of the game he was playing with Alexander. Bessos was no longer simply the governor of a remote, unsettled province. Now he claimed for himself the whole of the empire and the rank and title of the man he'd killed. Given his status as a governor, war hero, and close blood relative of Darius III, Bessos was dangerous. For inhabitants of the Persian Empire opposed to the Macedonian conquest, he was a plausible alternative to Alexander. And he had close ties to the governors of nearby provinces as well as a personality well suited to guerrilla warfare: brave, calculating, ruthless.

In response to this news, Alexander decided to head for Bessos. He claimed his goal was vengeance for Darius III. In order to present himself as Darius's legitimate successor, Alexander needed to punish the leader of the conspiracy against the Great King. More pragmatically, he wanted to eliminate a rival who threatened his control of the Persian Empire. Alexander had failed to capture Darius alive, to his frustration, and Bessos had seized the opportunity to challenge him as Great King. Alexander knew enough about Persia to recognize the Bactrian governor as a political threat. But Bessos was also a philosophical threat, challenging Alexander's policy of rapprochement with Persian aristocrats, suggesting it made him look not generous, but weak. As a military commander already facing resistance to this policy from his own officers, Alexander could not afford to appear vulnerable.

Alexander could not attack Bessos immediately, however, because his way was blocked by one of Bessos's coconspirators, Satibarzanes. Satibarzanes was among the most powerful governors of Central Asia and "remarkable both for generalship and bravery." He had fought against Alexander at Gaugamela, leading the contingent of soldiers from his province, and in the aftermath of the defeat, he had followed Darius east. But his loyalty had extended only so far. Satibarzanes joined the coup against the Great King and was among the men physically responsible for stabbing Darius. Then he fled east, hoping to raise a new army and fight again.

From his stronghold in the Hari Rud valley of southwestern Afghanistan, Satibarzanes was well placed to oppose Alexander. His region was a crossroads, with routes leading north to Bessos's territory, east to the best road through the Hindu Kush, and south to the main road through Afghanistan. With the Hari Rud in his possession, Satibarzanes controlled the key arteries Alexander needed to move east. He also blocked the Macedonian's westward access, cutting him off from supplies and reinforcements sent by Parmenion at Ekbatana.

By the time Alexander reached his province in the late summer, however, Satibarzanes had not been able to put together enough soldiers for his defense. Instead he made the risky but not unprecedented choice to approach the Macedonian king in person at the border of his territory and offer his submission, hoping for pardon. Satibarzanes was likely making the best of a difficult situation. Though still very much in charge of his rich river valley province, he had not yet assembled an adequate defense against the invaders' large, carefully trained army.

The governor of the Hari Rud likely knew that Alexander had a history of pardoning Persians, even when they had previously opposed him. Satibarzanes was in fact the third regional governor to submit that summer, and one had been not only pardoned but reappointed to his administrative position. Satibarzanes had good reason for optimism, since of the twelve governors Alexander appointed between 331 and 327 BCE, eleven of them were Iranian. Submitting to Alexander must have seemed a chance worth taking to the governor of the Hari Rud valley, particularly since by doing so, he could help to preserve his territory from the ravages of the conquerors—an important responsibility of a regional governor, and one with significant personal repercussions if, as often, he had his own landholdings within the area he ruled.

Satibarzanes was not disappointed. He received the pardon he sought from Alexander and was also reinstated as governor, just as his colleague had been. He was even given a troop of Macedonian

soldiers led by one of Alexander's Companions for the specific pur-
pose of guarding the province and protecting it from the army as the
Macedonians marched through. If his goal had been to safeguard his
territory, then Satibarzanes had succeeded brilliantly.

The deal was also convenient for Alexander. Although it called into
question his claim to be avenging Darius, the Macedonian conqueror
benefited from leaving the regional administration intact. Working
with the Persian governor and his local network, Alexander could
take over and collect tribute more easily. He could also secure the
province with fewer soldiers from his own forces, a significant consideration given the number he had recently left with Parmenion or sent
back to Greece. Now that Darius was dead, Alexander could hope to
conquer the remaining portion of his empire with comparatively little
effort. So he pardoned Persian governors quickly, reinstated them,
and left them with minimal garrisons.

Satibarzanes, like Artabazos, was one of the most powerful individuals Alexander encountered that summer. Despite their different
backgrounds, positions, and roles in Darius's death, he pardoned both
of them. More quickly in Satibarzanes's case, more slowly in Artabazos's, he entrusted them with important roles in his empire and a
share in its administration. With Artabazos and his family, Alexander's trust was abundantly repaid. Satibarzanes, by contrast, waited
for Alexander's departure and then used his position as governor to
aid Bessos, the aspiring Great King.

Alexander bid farewell to Satibarzanes with another enormous conflagration. He needed to put a stop to Bessos's pretentions fast, so
he planned to lead his army on a difficult and uncertain route to the
northeast through mountains and arid steppe. He had to bring all
his forces—including the recently acquired Greek mercenaries led
by Artabazos—and they traveled no faster than before. Indeed, the
soldiers moved more slowly, encumbered by the spoils of Persepolis

and their many previous victories. They were sitting ducks, prime targets for ambush along the circuitous mountain roads they had before them. Alexander could not be sure when Bessos would attack, whether he would move quickly or wait for the Macedonian to draw closer to him. But he knew that a slow march would aid his rival, allowing more time for the would-be Great King to gather reinforcements and rally his longtime subjects against the new Macedonian invaders.

Alexander assembled his troops and ordered all their baggage loaded on wagons, absolute necessities excepted. He had the draft animals unyoked from the wagons and led away, then headed for his own baggage with a flaming torch in hand. He saw one last time his accumulated treasures, the fruit of four years' bloody labor: gold and silver dining vessels, gem-encrusted jewelry, purple clothing, royal tents. Then he set them all alight with his torch, and told his soldiers to do the same.

Everything burned. Precious metals melted and ran together, gems cracked, robes flared, then vanished into ashes. Wooden wagons collapsed like kindling, and their bronze and iron fittings fell away. The soldiers saw the loot they had fought so hard to gain disappear in clouds of billowing smoke. They had created a fire to rival the one at Persepolis. But now it was not the treasures of the Persian king they were burning, but their own. Alexander, that inveterate gambler, was risking all their gains in the hope of winning more. As he set the wagons and their contents afire, he showed his soldiers how much he was willing to sacrifice to win. And he made clear that he was the kind of leader who expected all his men to do the same. The Macedonian king and his army left behind their treasures in a heap of glowing coals.

Alexander and his soldiers moved faster now that their baggage was gone. It marked a new beginning, a foretaste of the very different kind of war they were now fighting—one that rewarded speed and flexibility over wealth and entrenched power. They would have to become a new kind of army, with a different, more open-minded ruler, to win it.

As his new lighter and faster army headed toward Bessos, Alexander was experimenting with other changes, too. Particularly now that his rival claimed the throne, Alexander had to act like a Great King in order to offer an attractive choice for powerful, ambitious men such as Satibarzanes. So he integrated Persian aristocrats into his court and Persian customs into his self-presentation, to make his rule more acceptable to the inhabitants of his growing empire.

Alexander began with the idle, disaffected Persian aristocrats who had flooded his camp. He selected around five hundred to serve as bodyguards, though he trusted them too little—or feared his officers' opinion too much—to give them the same rank and access to his person as the seven Macedonians with the same title. He also added Darius's brother to the circle of his Companions. It must have been awkward for all concerned, but by fostering a relationship with his dead enemy's relative, Alexander legitimized himself in the eyes of Iranians and rewarded the highest-ranking Persian aristocrat to join his cause. Integrating Darius's brother among the Companions was also instrumental in that it allowed the Macedonian king to keep a close eye on a potential rival.

Alexander's transformation of his court primarily concerned elite Iranian men—they were his target audience—but his changes also affected women. He adopted or re-created Darius's retinue of concubines, who reportedly numbered 365, one for every day of the year. And he added to his entourage a group of eunuchs, most prominently one named Bagoas.

Like most ancient Persian eunuchs, Bagoas had probably been castrated before puberty in order to preserve his smooth face, high voice, and youthful good looks. Without his consent, he was marked for a role in Persian court society. Before encountering Alexander, Bagoas had formed part of the Persian royal retinue of eunuchs and concubines, guarding the king's women but, like them, also sexually available to the ruler. He had in fact been the lover of Darius III. An expert navigator of court politics, Bagoas formed a relationship with his new Macedonian overlord after the Great King's death. He was a talented singer and dancer, appealing to a king who loved the arts. The eunuch also clearly knew how to please powerful men, though he was despised by Persian aristocrats, whose high status preserved them from ever suffering his fate.

Among new Persian members of his court like Bagoas, and perhaps a few sympathetic Macedonian friends, Alexander first made his appearance in a modified form of Iranian dress. He put on a floor-length long-sleeved tunic used by Persian courtiers, belted at the waist and white with a sumptuous purple border. Over it he wore his familiar Macedonian cloak, dyed all over an expensive shade of purple. And he adorned his floppy Macedonian hat with a purple-and-white band of a type used by high-ranking Persians, but which also fortuitously resembled a diadem, the ribbon given to victors in Greek athletic games. It was a heavier, more constraining, and more grandiose ensemble than his previous Macedonian outfit, and must have felt very different to Alexander when he first put it on. But it soon became his habitual costume—initially only among his intimates indoors, but gradually for more public outdoor appearances as well.

Alexander's new clothes, together with his retinue of Persian body-guards and concubines, were the concrete, visible signs of more far-reaching changes. As he moved east and incorporated ever more Persians into his empire, Alexander needed to navigate a court culture far more cosmopolitan and sophisticated than his own. Years before, after his first major victory over Darius, he had gotten a taste for this culture when he entered the Persian royal tent. On that occasion, he looked around at the finely worked precious metal drinking vessels, the luxurious couches, the exotic and carefully prepared food, and reportedly said, "So this, it seems, is living like a king."

In his outreach to Persians, Alexander had few supporters and even fewer role models. His own tutor, Aristotle, reportedly told him "to deal with the Greeks like a leader, and the barbarians like a despot; to treat the Greeks like friends and fellow-citizens, but to behave toward the rest as though they were animals or plants." And when he tried to co-opt his Companions by giving them purple-bordered Persian robes to wear and Persian harnesses for their horses, they were disgusted and bewildered by the new clothes, and had to be appeased with gifts.

If Alexander had any models for his pragmatic yet open-minded efforts to navigate between two worlds, they were perhaps Artabazos and Barsine. Artabazos had been interacting closely and effectively with Greeks, Macedonians, and Persians since before Alexander was born. His practice equipped him well for the new king's service, and so despite his advanced age, the Persian commander took on increasingly important roles in Alexander's government. Barsine had no such public status, and she is seldom mentioned in Classical texts. But as the most prominent woman in Alexander's life—and as a bilingual, bicultural Greco Persian—she offered a compelling example of what integration might look like. As such she was a natural inhabitant of the new world Alexander hoped to create.

Alexander's changes upset the Macedonians, but they didn't always succeed in reconciling Iranians to his conquest either. As the humid summer gave way to cooler autumn weather in 330 BCE, Alexander learned that Satibarzanes had revolted. The newly reinstated governor had killed the minimal Macedonian garrison that Alexander had left in his province quickly and without warning. Then Satibarzanes fortified his capital and proclaimed his allegiance to Bessos.

Satibarzanes was the first important regional governor to submit and then renege on his commitment to Alexander. He offered a warning for the Macedonian king about the difference between his previous western conquests and the new war he would be fighting in the east. As Alexander would learn, it was one in which submission, and even military victory, meant little—a war that the king did not yet know how to fight.

Caught between the so-called Great King and the rebellious governor Satibarzanes, Alexander decided to deal with the threat from the governor first. He turned back and raced with his fastest troops to Satibarzanes's capital of Artakoana, near present-day Herāt in northwest Afghanistan, covering around seventy-five miles of twisting mountain road in a mere two days.

When Alexander arrived at Artakoana, he found the provincial capital well protected, standing on a high plateau and surrounded by thick, heavy ramparts. Nonetheless, Satibarzanes abandoned it and fled northeast toward Bessos with two thousand cavalrymen. While Satibarzanes and his horsemen escaped, the rest of his followers were less fortunate. His soldiers disappeared into the hills around Artakoana, where Alexander piled trees around their mountain fortress, then lit fires and smoked them out.

After killing or enslaving Satibarzanes's followers, Alexander laid siege to the city of Artakoana itself. To deal with the city's ramparts, he brought out the large, technically sophisticated siege engines— tall, mobile scaling towers and powerful battering rams—that had been key to his military success throughout his campaigns (and were carefully preserved when he set fire to his loot). At the sight of these unfamiliar machines, the inhabitants nervously capitulated. Alexander pardoned them, preferring to blame their defection on Satibarzanes himself rather than widespread dissatisfaction with the Macedonian conquest. Then, from his base at Artakoana, or perhaps the new city he likely founded nearby, Alexandria-in-Aria, the king spent a month battling the rebels of western Afghanistan. He also gave the inhabitants a new Iranian governor. Alexander could only hope that this one would be more faithful.

Fighting his way through the Hari Rud valley, Alexander had time to reflect on how much Darius's death had complicated his conquest. His soldiers might believe that their task had ended with the assassination of the Great King. But the revolts of Bessos and Satibarzanes had shown how dangerous these powerful Central Asian governors remained—and how much effort it would take to be accepted by them and their subjects as a true Great King. And Alexander was still hampered by his own Macedonian cultural biases and shallow understanding of Persia. Even when he meant to please, he could still offend.

An incident at Susa, just before he left for Persepolis, had demonstrated how much Alexander still had to learn. He had received a present from his family: Macedonian wool, finely woven and dyed purple, along with expert women weavers. Proudly he sent the cloth and the women to the Persian Queen Mother, Sisygambis. With his gift, he instructed a messenger to tell her that if she and her granddaughters liked the textiles, the women could teach them how to make more.

From a Macedonian perspective, weaving was the paradigmatic women's work, expected of every good wife and mother. With Odysseus's wife, Penelope, as a mythological model, even high-ranking women wove. From the point of view of an aristocratic Persian like Sisygambis, however, weaving was degrading, the work of servants. The messenger reported to a disappointed Alexander that when she received his gift, the Queen Mother had tears in her eyes.

Alexander hastened to Sisygambis and apologized. He explained that his clothes were made for him by his own mother and sisters (though one wonders how much time powerful royal women really spent at the loom). "My own customs misled me," Alexander told the Queen Mother, as he dropped his suggestion that the Persian princesses learn to weave. But this high-profile cultural faux pas showed how difficult it would be to bring Macedonians and Iranians together. Despite his efforts to master new customs and reach out to his new foreign subjects, Alexander would fail repeatedly in the next few years: trusting the wrong people; preferring fighting to diplomacy, and vice versa; alienating those he meant to court; ignoring advice he should have heeded. His failures would have dangerous repercussions for the king and those he ruled. As Alexander would learn, integrating an empire was far more complicated than just putting on new clothes.

FOUR

Lovers and Conspirators

Afghanistan
Fall 330 BCE

BY THE TIME ALEXANDER had finished pacifying the Hari Rud valley in late autumn, it was too late in the year to head straight toward Bessos and Satibarzanes through the snowy mountains of northern Afghanistan. Instead the Macedonian king planned a longer, more circuitous path south and east around the mountains, hoping to find an easier way to reach his rival. He had only gotten as far as present-day Farāh in the far west of Afghanistan when the next rebellion struck.

This time the conspiracy was launched not by a Persian, but instead by Macedonians. Among those involved was a man named Dimnos, one of Alexander's Companions. Dimnos's particular grievances are unknown—he never got the chance to state them—but with the rest of the Macedonian officers, he likely resented Alexander's unexpected prolonging of the war as well as the king's recent embrace of Persian dress and court ceremony.

In response, Dimnos joined a conspiracy against Alexander's life. As he did so, he could not help confiding in his same-sex lover. Boasting that the conspiracy reached as high as one of Alexander's seven Macedonian bodyguards, Dimnos urged his lover to join him. He laid out the whole story to the person he believed, due to their relationship, was least likely to betray his trust.

The same-sex relationship of Dimnos and his lover was not unusual for their place and time. In Macedonian society, men fought, hunted, drank, and worked together, while women lived separate and more secluded lives. Macedonian men consequently often fell in love with other men, and these relationships, both sexual and companionate, were encouraged rather than repressed.

In Dimnos's case, the relationship approximated the Classical Greek ideal, in which a mature male lover pursued and educated a beloved adolescent boy. Other powerful Macedonians did the same. Alexander's father, Philip, for instance, had at least two young male lovers, one of whom, Pausanias, proved as dangerous to him as his own lover did to Dimnos. But in the predominantly male society of the campaign against Persia, same-sex relationships were more diverse and varied than the Greek ideal—and also very common. Given the foreign nature and limited number of women available to the soldiers, this proliferation is not surprising. In the army that conquered the Persian Empire, more men likely slept with other men than with women.

By confiding in his lover, Dimnos made a serious error of judgment in what seems to have been, at best, a haphazardly planned assassination attempt. Terrified of the conspiracy's likely consequences, his lover revealed the plan to his brother, Kebalinos. While the young man remained in his tent, so as not to raise Dimnos's suspicions, Kebalinos made straight for the king.

Kebalinos soon arrived at Alexander's tent, which was easy to find, being larger, more centrally located, and more visually impressive than any other. But due to his low rank, Kebalinos was not permitted inside it, particularly now that Alexander had surrounded himself with so many Iranian bodyguards and other appurtenances of Persian court ceremony. All he could do was wait outside, hoping to find someone high-ranking enough to enter the tent and convey his message to Alexander.

Soon Kebalinos saw Philotas, son of Parmenion and commander of the top cavalry unit in Alexander's army. Philotas was famous in the camp for his bravery, his toughness, and his devotion to his friends, all virtues rated highly by the Macedonians. Even his faults were appropriate to his rank and decidedly Macedonian in character: arrogance, boastfulness, ostentation. Kebalinos approached him eagerly and revealed the plot against Alexander. Philotas listened, agreeing to tell the king. Then he swaggered off to the inner recesses of the royal tent.

All day, Kebalinos remained outside the tent, waiting for a summons. He expected to be called in, questioned closely, and, with luck, believed. Then Dimnos would be arrested and the plot foiled, while he and his brother would be vindicated, perhaps rewarded, as loyal subjects ought to be. But that day, Kebalinos received no summons, and when he confronted Philotas at its end, the cavalry commander said breezily that he hadn't had the occasion yet to mention the matter to Alexander. Tomorrow, no doubt, he'd find the time, said Philotas, as he went off to his own luxuriously appointed tent.

Kebalinos waited another day, and still, no summons came. He feared for Alexander, whose life was threatened while his potential assassins remained at large. He also feared for himself and his brother, who would be blamed if the plot was by some chance uncovered, and their knowledge of it revealed. He needed to get to Alexander as quickly as possible. But now that he had involved Philotas, he had the cavalry commander to fear, too. As Kebalinos knew, if he told his story to another friend of the king, he risked angering Philotas—and the wealthy Macedonian aristocrat was not a man to be antagonized lightly.

A second full day passed, and Philotas did nothing. Finally Kebalinos spoke. He confided in a young nobleman who was in charge of the royal armory. The young man reacted with gratifying speed, notifying Alexander and bringing Kebalinos in to see him as quickly as possible. Kebalinos told his tale, explaining what he knew of Dimnos's plot and doing his best to exculpate his brother. Then he noted that he had tried to warn Alexander earlier, but that he had made the mistake of choosing a messenger who clearly did not have the king's best interests at heart: Philotas.

Alexander responded quickly to Kebalinos's story. He sent a group of soldiers to Dimnos, who either committed suicide or was killed while resisting arrest (ancient biographers differ, though they all agree that he died on the spot). With Philotas, however, the king had to proceed more carefully. He called in Parmenion's son along with some of his closest companions, then inquired delicately about his interactions with Kebalinos. To Alexander, Philotas freely admitted that he had been accosted by Kebalinos and informed about the plot. But given that the informant was Dimnos's young, low-status lover, he simply hadn't taken it seriously. Philotas apologized, and he and Alexander shook hands. When the cavalry commander left the king's presence, the matter appeared closed. But he had made himself vulnerable to Alexander, who had long been resentful of him and his powerful family. Philotas would pay dearly for it.

Though Philotas claimed he had not taken the plot seriously, palace conspiracies were a frequent—and often deadly—feature of the Macedonian court. They had taken the lives of Alexander's uncle, his stepgrandfather, and a series of earlier Macedonian kings. Though the young king had not yet been born when these conspiracies occurred, he must have known about them from his surviving relatives or longserving Macedonian councilors like Parmenion. And Alexander had experienced firsthand what such a conspiracy looked like when his father, Philip II, was stabbed to death in front of him six years earlier.

At the time of his assassination, Philip was about to depart for his much-anticipated conquest of the Persian Empire. The king had already sent out an advance guard of ten thousand soldiers led by Parmenion and an important Macedonian aristocrat named Attalos.

Philip had long-standing ties to Parmenion, and he had recently conducted a marriage alliance with Attalos's niece Kleopatra. To conquer
a wealthy and powerful empire like Persia, Philip knew, he needed to
have the Macedonian elite solidly behind him—and if that required a
seventh marriage, to a beautiful young woman half his age, then the
king was certainly willing to do his part.

Unfortunately for Philip, the marriage antagonized other individuals
whose support he required: Olympias, the most prominent of the king's
previous six wives, and her son, the heir apparent, Alexander. Mother
and son both saw Kleopatra, not unnaturally, as a threat. They were not
reassured when Kleopatra's uncle Attalos made a toast at the wedding
banquet expressing his hope that now Philip would finally have some
legitimate children (a slur on Olympias, whether for her ancestry—
she was from Epirus, a nearby kingdom—or something worse). At the
banquet, the young heir responded angrily to Attalos's toast, and Philip
drew his sword; bloodshed was averted only by the fact that the king
was too drunk to walk. Alexander and Olympias left the court, angry
and disgusted. Philip was angry, too, but he was at length persuaded
to patch up the quarrel, primarily due to his Persian ambitions. The
king could not afford to have a furious teenage heir as he began his
conquest.

Some months later at Vergina, ancestral home of the Macedonian
kings, Philip planned a grandiose multiday ceremony that would
commemorate his reconciliation with Alexander and Olympias,
showcase his accomplishments, and provide a fitting send-off for
his departure for Persia. He invited all his Macedonian nobles and
an enormous number of well-born Greeks, who were meant to be
properly impressed by Philip's power and generosity. There Philip
celebrated the marriage of Alexander's sister, also named Kleopatra,
to her uncle, another Alexander (the northern Greek elite, like the
modern-day British monarchy, had a limited repertoire of favorite
names, and so Alexanders and Kleopatras cycle through their history
with astonishing regularity). The marriage honored Olympias—it

was her daughter and her brother who were involved—and reiterated Philip's commitment to her line of the family. In this way, it was meant to placate Alexander, too.

At sunrise, Philip held a religious procession to the theater of Vergina. There, on a cool green hillside overlooking the Macedonian plain, he entered the theater, flanked by the two Alexanders, his son and his new son-in-law. As Philip acknowledged the cheers and acclamations of the crowd, he kept his bodyguards at a distance, demonstrating to those assembled that he relied for his safety on their goodwill, rather than on men with spears.

Philip was unwise. Among his bodyguards was his former Royal Page and lover Pausanias, who was bitterly angry with the king. Earlier, Pausanias had jealously driven a fellow page and rival for Philip's affections to suicide. In doing so he had antagonized his rival's friend Attalos, who had in retaliation gang-raped and publicly humiliated the young man. To Pausanias's frustration, Philip had not punished Attalos. Instead, the king had put him in charge of the Persian expedition, while attempting to placate his former lover with an appointment as bodyguard. If Philip hoped that this powerful and honorable position would appease Pausanias, however, he was wrong.

At Vergina, Pausanias saw his chance, and took it. With a dagger he had concealed under his cloak, he ran up and stabbed the king repeatedly, then fled. As Pausanias tripped on a vine on his way out, he fell and was killed by two friends of Alexander's. By then, it was clear to the huge crowd assembled in the theater that the bodyguard had assassinated the king.

Pausanias was physically responsible for the king's death, but it was uncertain how far the conspiracy reached. The young bodyguard may have acted alone, given his resentment of the king and the ever-increasing prominence of his enemy Attalos. Alternatively, Pausanias may have been encouraged by others, who used his well-known grievance for their own purposes. Alexander—the undoubted heir, quickly acclaimed king by Philip's top generals—blamed and executed a cousin, whose royal blood made him a plausible candidate for a conspiracy, along with two other members of the royal house. Later, he also accused Darius III of complicity in Philip's death, although the involvement of the Persian king was decidedly less convincing.

Despite Alexander's efforts to avenge his father, rumors persisted that the young prince himself was complicit, that he or Olympias had encouraged Pausanias in his plot. It is certainly possible, since Alexander had much to gain from Philip's death, and the most to lose if the king's new wife bore a son. Still, conspiracy was a dangerous game to play, and Alexander had years before any child of Kleopatra's would be old enough to challenge his position as heir. He was likely guilty, at most, of encouraging Pausanias, and profiting very effectively from the angry young man's actions. For the conspiracy surrounding Philip's death, Alexander stayed on the sidelines; Pausanias acted.

Now in 330 BCE at Farāh, Alexander was himself the target of a conspiracy, and he could not afford to stand aside. Initially he seemed to accept Philotas's apology. But later he changed his mind. He was egged on by his childhood companion Krateros, who had long been jealous of Philotas's prominence and suspected him of treason. Alexander himself also disliked the cavalry commander, whose boastful personality and illustrious birth grated on the competitive, glory-seeking king. He decided to hold a formal trial of Philotas, on the charge of aiding and abetting the conspirators. In accordance with Macedonian custom, Alexander called on the entire army to assemble. He needed to follow the legal procedures impeccably for a case like this one, where the penalty for guilt was death.

At the assembly, Alexander spoke first, as was his right as king. He was followed by Kebalinos along with several of his generals. All presented the case against Philotas in the most aggressive and dire terms, and the soldiers' roars of anger portended no good to the accused. But when Philotas himself appeared before them in chains, the soldiers wavered. As they knew, he was a powerful and important commander, whose father, Parmenion, had led them, ably and victoriously, for the better part of thirty years. They seemed potentially sympathetic to Philotas, though they were unimpressed by his speech. Their wavering was recognized by Alexander, who could read the mood of his soldiers better than anyone. So the king delayed their decision to the following day.

That night Philotas was subjected to torture. Such treatment was a familiar punishment for Persian aristocrats suspected of conspiracy against the Great King. It was also seen in Greek legal circles as a method to uncover the truth. The phrase, "I offer my slaves to be tortured," was a regular opening gambit for accused criminals in democratic Athens, and torture could also be carried out on free men in cases where the security of the state was at risk. In Philotas's case, Alexander himself remained aloof. But the torture was executed by the king's closest friends, so it was certainly approved, if not initiated, by him.

The leader of the torturers was Krateros, a huge, imposing man a decade older than Alexander. An upholder of conservative Macedonian values, he liked the king's new Persian customs no better than Dimnos and Philotas—but he hated traitors more. Krateros was Alexander's most faithful and capable general, and he probably recognized that the conspiracy gave him a chance to replace Parmenion. His combination of genuine indignation against Philotas and powerful self-interest made Krateros implacable as he laid out the torture implements.

Next to Krateros was Koinos, a brave and much-injured cavalry commander around the same age as the angry general. Koinos was caught in a very difficult predicament. Just before the invasion of Persia, he had married Philotas's sister. Now, with his wife and young son back home in Macedonia, he was particularly at risk of guilt by association. At the trial, Koinos did not defend his brother-in-law. Instead he became one of Philotas's most vociferous accusers and even tried to convince the army to stone him to death (whether to protect himself or, as some believed, to spare Philotas what he feared was coming). When his effort failed, Koinos participated in the torture—whatever his personal feelings may have been.

Spearheading the torture along with Koinos and Krateros was Hephaistion: Alexander's closest companion, very likely his lover, certainly his most trusted friend. An age-mate of Alexander's, Hephaistion often accompanied the king on his public appearances, similarly dressed, but taller, more handsome, and more regal. He was indeed mistaken for Alexander by the Persian Queen Mother Sisygambis when she first met them both (fortunately for her, the real king approved of her choice, saying that Hephaistion, too, was Alexander). Hephaistion was promoted to bodyguard early in the conquest, and often took the lead in protecting what he perceived as the king's interests. He was one of the first to speak out against Philotas, and as ready to torture him as Koinos and Krateros—all the more so as he had a rivalry with the latter that would one day spill over into violence.

Philotas was well known for his ability to endure hardship, but he could not withstand what the king's friends did to him. He cried out, begged for mercy, and made a very full confession. His words were read to the army the next day, as he was carried to the assembly—the torture had left him unable to walk. Still, the confession convinced the soldiers, and they voted for his immediate execution. The punishment was carried out by the entire army, stoning Philotas to death or killing him in a hail of spears. It was a horrible way to die, particularly for Philotas, whose crime was likely no more than acquiescent silence. But Alexander had seen the opportunity to eliminate Philotas, and he grasped it, quickly and irrevocably. In doing so, he reestablished his soldierly preeminence and royal authority by quelling dissent with brutal, perhaps gratuitous violence.

Alexander used the conspiracy and its outcome to redistribute power and reward his friends. He made Hephaistion coleader of Philotas's cavalry unit, balancing him with Kleitos, a well-respected officer whose sister Lanike had once been Alexander's wet nurse. He gave increasingly prominent commands to Krateros and Koinos, and replaced the bodyguard (executed shortly after Philotas) with his close friend Ptolemy.

The conspiracy gave Alexander the opportunity—and, perhaps, the motive—to promote his loyal inner circle of young friends, while older, more traditional officers were left out. With these promotions, he created a cadre of trusted and highly effective generals to whom he could safely delegate power. He also fostered resentments that would lead to further conspiracy and protests later on.

With Philotas removed, Alexander had to eliminate Parmenion as well. However extensive Philotas's manufactured confession, the old general would never accept the execution of his son. So Alexander sent a close friend of Parmenion's on racing camels to Ekbatana. With local guides, he made the monthlong trip across the Iranian desert in a mere eleven days. Upon his arrival, the messenger delivered a letter from Alexander to the general in charge of the territory. In it, the king described his fortunate escape from assassination and demanded Parmenion's death.

The messenger met his old friend walking in the Great King's gardens at Ekbatana. He distracted Parmenion with another, very different letter from Alexander, an anodyne account of military campaigns accomplished and new ones planned. He then gave the old man a letter purportedly from Philotas. Delighted, Parmenion began to read. Relaxing in a grove full of beautiful trees planted for the Great King's delectation, and accompanied by his close friend and high-ranking Macedonian officers, the old general became absorbed in the news from his long-absent son. He was still reading when the messenger and officers surrounded him and stabbed him to death.

Parmenion's soldiers were angered by the extrajudicial killing of a man they had honored and followed for so many years. They threatened mutiny, and even when the confession was read out to them, they remained angry. The army demanded to be allowed to bury Parmenion with honor, and the assassins were forced, albeit grudgingly, to permit their request. The soldiers received the body of Parmenion and gave him a fine military funeral. For his part, the messenger hurried back across the desert to Alexander, carrying with him a grisly memento of his errand—Parmenion's severed head.

Parmenion and Philotas were dead, but the effects of the events at Farāh lingered. With ruthless improvisational brilliance, Alexander had used the threat of conspiracy to consolidate his hold on power by eliminating the family most capable of challenging him. He had also strengthened himself by advancing his close friends to higher positions, creating an inner circle of officers he trusted because they owed their rise to him. Seen from this perspective, the king had succeeded, unexpectedly and thoroughly.

Still, the fact remains that Alexander faced a conspiracy, however half-baked. It suggested the dangers posed by his Macedonian followers, who resented his outreach to Persians and his increasingly autocratic ways. Even if it did not succeed, the conspiracy showed that Alexander had failed to understand the officers' anger. Nor did he change his modus operandi. Instead, he continued down his chosen path, alienating his Macedonian followers further. He also failed to placate the rebellious Central Asian governors who posed a more immediate threat.

FIVE

Epic Combat

Afghanistan
Fall 330–Spring 329 BCE

WHILE ALEXANDER WAS PREOCCUPIED with the trial of Philotas, Satibarzanes struck. The former governor returned to his old province with troops supplied by his ally, Bessos. There, in his rich and strategically located homeland, Satibarzanes launched a second insurgency. He threatened the villages Alexander had recently believed were pacified, as well as the city, Alexandria-in-Aria (present-day Herāt), that he had just founded. It was a clever move, one that demonstrated Satibarzanes's determination, resilience, and keen grasp of the essentials of guerrilla warfare. The governor had seized the initiative, endangering Alexander's lines of communication and resupply from the center of his empire. By coordinating his actions with Bessos, he also forced the Macedonian king to fight on two fronts.

To deal with the threat posed by Satibarzanes, Alexander tried a new strategy. He did not choose to engage with the rebellious governor himself, but instead sent west a high-ranking Greek officer named Erigyios, plus a sizable portion of the army, about six thousand infantry and six hundred cavalry. More significantly, he made his old Persian friend Artabazos cocommander. And he sent messengers to the neighboring province's governor, a Persian named Phrataphernes, asking for assistance. Phrataphernes had fought against Alexander at the Battle of Gaugamela, but had been among the first Iranian governors to submit and be reinstated after the death of Darius. His loyalty to the Macedonian king was thus far unblemished, though given the recent track record of Persian governors, Alexander must have been aware he was taking a chance.

In dealing with Satibarzanes, Alexander depended heavily on top-level Persian officials, particularly Artabazos and Phrataphernes. His action was intentional and significant. On the one hand, it showed how far Alexander had come in integrating Iranians into the command structure of his empire. With Artabazos and Phrataphernes leading Alexander's military contingents, something extraordinary had happened: Persians were giving orders to Greeks and Macedonians.

On the other hand, Alexander's decision to make Artabazos and Phrataphernes leaders in the fight against Satibarzanes also turned out to be a canny political decision. It isolated the rebellious governor from his compatriots, pitting members of the Persian aristocracy against one another and depriving the revolt of its potential nationalist overtones. And it ensured that Alexander's Iranian allies had to make a very public demonstration of their loyalty to him vis-à-vis other Persians. By fighting with Alexander and against Satibarzanes, Artabazos and Phrataphernes committed themselves indissolubly to the Macedonian king's side.

The Persians and Macedonians hastened to the Hari Rud valley. They sought out Satibarzanes and his followers, who, despite their superior knowledge of the countryside, chose not to use guerrilla tactics. Instead, the two sides faced off against each other in battle.

On the Macedonian side stood a substantial and well-equipped infantry force, probably sarissa-bearers with an admixture of hoplites and javelin throwers. Surrounding them were their cavalry, protecting the flanks. Satibarzanes, by contrast, likely had fewer and more lightly armed foot soldiers and a much larger number of horsemen, the traditional strength of Bessos's Bactrian command. With their superior cavalry, Satibarzanes's forces could strike hard and fast, searching to push through weak points in the Macedonian line. But the sarissa-bearers' eighteen-foot spears were a formidable obstacle, and they had years of experience countering Persian cavalry; they knew how to stand their ground.

Back and forth the two sides fought, both tiring but neither able to overcome the other. Just when it seemed that the clash might end in stalemate, Satibarzanes removed his helmet and rode to the front line.

The Central Asian governor issued a challenge to the opposing army. Bravely, with the pride of a man defending his homeland, he offered to fight any champion they selected in single combat. He would spare both armies bloodshed, if they agreed that the winner would decide the fate of the battle.

The man who stepped forward from the Macedonian side was Erigyios, a close friend and longtime Companion of Alexander. He was Greek in origin, but his father had settled in Macedonia, and Erigyios had grown up alongside Alexander at King Philip's court. Erigyios was older than his friend—at the time of the battle, one ancient author calls him "white-haired"—but the two men were close. Due to their friendship, Erigyios had even suffered banishment when Philip was enraged with Alexander shortly before his death. Following Alexander's accession, Erigyios returned to Macedonia and received increasingly prestigious commands. He led the Greek cavalry at Issos and Gaugamela; organized the baggage train during Alexander's pursuit of Darius; and had recently participated in the council about Philotas. Loyal, brave, and capable, Erigyios had long been a stalwart supporter of Alexander, but he had never stepped into the spotlight so dramatically as he did now.

In volunteering for single combat against Satibarzanes, Erigyios was acting in accordance with Macedonian heroic ideals that found their most profound expression in Homer's *Iliad*. Like Erigyios, Homeric warriors fought one-on-one, with two champions introducing themselves to one another—often with extraordinarily detailed histories of their ancestors—and exchanging courtesies before proceeding to hack each other to death with spears or swords. Macedonian aristocrats sought to emulate this Homeric mode of fighting, with its emphasis on single combat and heroic *arete* (bravery). Traditionally, young Macedonian warriors were not even allowed to wear a belt before they had slain an enemy in battle.

The Macedonians retained these Homeric ideals and practices even in the age of Alexander. But they rarely had the opportunity to flaunt their heroic tendencies in the king's battles, where close coordination and the subordination of the individual to the demands of the whole were central to the army's success. So when Erigyios saw the chance to act like a true Homeric warrior, he seized it, despite the fact that at the conclusion of the battle, he had a 50 percent chance of ending up dead.

Satibarzanes's motivation for offering the challenge is less clear. Perhaps he, too, was inspired by epic literature, in his case stories of the Mesopotamian cultural hero Gilgamesh, far famed for his prowess in combat. But the Persian leader may also have been emulating a closer historical prototype. As Satibarzanes no doubt knew, before his accession Darius III had come to prominence by killing an enemy king in single combat. With Darius dead and his succession disputed, Satibarzanes's action was a regal one.

The champions faced each other on horseback in a space between the two armies. Their weapons were spears and swords. For Erigyios, this mode of fighting was familiar, a key component of Macedonian military training from childhood on. Even as an adult and a high-ranking cavalry commander, Erigyios would have maintained his skill with the same weapons and with close-range combat, central to Alexander's battle strategy. Persians like Satibarzanes, by contrast, had particular expertise with the bow, though they trained with spears as well. And like most Persian aristocrats, Satibarzanes likely went into battle most often in a chariot, preferably one adorned with cruel curved scythes that rotated with the chariot wheels and cut to pieces any unlucky man or beast who came too close.

Satibarzanes threw his spear first, but Erigyios evaded it, then charged forward and rammed his own into his opponent at close range. The Greek knocked Satibarzanes from his horse, but wounded him only slightly. Satibarzanes rose to fight again.

Erigyios managed to extricate his spear from his enemy's body and plunged it in a second time. With this final strike, he killed the tenacious Central Asian warrior. To commemorate his success, he sliced off Satibarzanes's head.

Following their general's death, Satibarzanes's army melted away or submitted as necessary to Alexander's side. The rebellion in western Afghanistan was over.

Their mission successfully concluded, Erigyios, Artabazos, and their soldiers headed east. They finally reunited with Alexander the following spring after both armies had made the trek across the Hindu Kush. They brought him the good news—and, ancient writers claim, Satibarzanes's severed head.

While Erigyios was enjoying his moment of epic combat in western Afghanistan, to his east Alexander was continuing his pursuit of Bessos. He was also contending with a more immediately dangerous and damaging opponent: winter. Raised in the Mediterranean climate of Macedonia, Alexander had not experienced anything as extreme as the harsh continental winters of Asia, apart from his stay in Persepolis the year before. For the winter of 330–329 BCE, however, Alexander had no large, elegant city in which to quarter his troops, and no well-established network of supplies with which to feed them. And due to his pursuit of Bessos, Alexander had moved far beyond the fertile valley of the Hari Rud. Instead, as winter struck, Alexander's route had taken him north and east toward the mountains, to the area of what is now Afghanistan's capital city, Kabul.

Modern travelers often remark on Kabul's spectacular natural setting—nestled within the Hindu Kush and surrounded by dramatic snowcapped peaks—but Alexander and his followers had a far less enthusiastic response to the region. They experienced it as a desolate, treeless landscape, blanketed in snow. They found few birds or other animals and saw no proper cities, only small clusters of low-lying brick houses, covered to their roofs in snow and perceptible only through the smoke issuing from their chimneys. Within these houses they encountered members of an "uncivilized tribe, extremely coarse even for barbarians," as one cosmopolitan Roman writer disdainfully put it. Alexander's followers were the first foreigners they had encountered and they surrendered quickly, but had few provisions to share.

Alexander and his army had traveled extraordinary distances over the course of the year. Leaving Persepolis in May, they had marched nine hundred miles by July, when they ended their pursuit of Darius. Another thousand miles brought them to Satibarzanes's capital of Artakoana in early fall, and it had taken them almost another thousand to complete their great arc south of the Hindu Kush and enter the bleak, barren region in which they found themselves for the winter.

Difficult enough for soldiers, the journey must have been extraordinarily hard for the women and children who accompanied the army. They struggled with frostbite, a perplexing condition for the sandal-wearing inhabitants of the Mediterranean. They were also blinded by the glare of the bright white snowy landscape surrounding them. The followers were exhausted, hungry, close to despair.

Despite their exhaustion, Alexander's followers kept heading north. However desperate they were—and however exasperated with their leaders—they could see that there was no way out but onward. Not far from what is now Kabul, they came upon a city in a broader, more cultivated valley. With rich stores of provisions and a substantial population, the place made a good headquarters for the winter.

Alexander's headquarters were part of the Persian king's administrative landscape, one that had eluded the king and his followers elsewhere along their winter journey. It was a landscape of way stations, granaries, and corvée workers; of flocks of sheep and farms owned by the king; of seals, sealings, and accounts sedulously recorded on cuneiform tablets. Alexander had encountered this carefully constructed and highly organized system almost from the moment he crossed the Hellespont back in 334 BCE. Together with his own sophisticated planning, it guided his movements through unfamiliar territory, fed his troops, and paid them with the monies he found stored up at capitals like Sardis and Susa. Throughout his early campaigns, Alexander used the Persian imperial system very successfully against the Great King. The system helped make his conquest possible, though it has rarely been acknowledged by ancient or modern historians.

At his winter headquarters in the Hindu Kush, Alexander took full advantage of the Persian imperial system. He also renamed the city, declaring it another Alexandria (it is likely the site now known as Begram, and continues to be a strategically important position; it was the location of a major US military base prior to the withdrawal of American forces from Afghanistan). The king settled several thousand veterans and camp followers on the site, so that as he crossed the mountains, he would have fewer and less-debilitated mouths to feed.

As Begram and Herāt demonstrate, throughout his years of conquest, Alexander was an enthusiastic founder of cities. Beginning when he was sixteen with an Alexandropolis in northeastern Macedonia, he founded scores of other cities in Egypt, Afghanistan, Uzbekistan, Tajikistan, Pakistan, and Iran, some seventy all told, according to one author. As often with the Macedonian king, that number is an exaggeration. But it is clear that Alexander used city foundation as a regular part of his strategy of empire building, particularly during the difficult years in Central Asia when his conquest was most challenged.

Alexander placed his cities at strategic locations; for instance, along major routes that he and his army followed. Often he chose a choke point, where the city commanded a river valley, as at Herāt, or guarded a pass through the mountains, as at Begram. Where possible, Alexander selected sites that were easily defensible, with a high natural citadel or a river preventing access from one side. He also regularly garrisoned his cities, or settled them with veterans. Too old or injured for campaign, these men were nonetheless tough, aggressive, and well trained, eminently capable of defending their city in case of attack.

The inhabitants of Alexander's cities needed to be well trained— and their locations defensible—because they were repeatedly at risk. Islands of Macedonian power within an immense Iranian sea, the cities showcased the attractions of Hellenic civilization. Eventually they were equipped with theaters for entertainment, gymnasia for exercise and education, and temples with masterfully carved statues of the Greek gods. But the new city-foundations of Alexander were also focal points for attack during periods of rebellion against Macedonian rule. They were an incarnation of the locals' worst fears: that these aggressive foreign conquerors meant to stay.

For their part, the veterans and camp followers who populated Alexander's city-foundations were often frustrated by being demobilized and settled in remote Central Asian towns. After many years of constant military campaigns, they were not well suited to the sedentary agricultural life on offer in these cities, or to the region's climate or customs. In the view of Alexander's Greek and Macedonian veterans, settling in a city like Begram meant they were living at the end of the world. They even identified a nearby site as the place where the Titan Prometheus had been chained by Zeus: a mythological paradigm for an imprisonment at the earth's outer limits much like their own.

What the veterans failed to see was how, from a broader Middle Eastern perspective, Begram was not the end of the world but its crossroads, a critical way station on the southern Silk Road with close links to the South Asian subcontinent. Alexander recognized the site's strategic potential, but he failed to communicate its importance to his settlers. Or perhaps they just didn't care.

Though the veterans may not have seen themselves as lucky, they were likely envied soon after by the rest of the king's followers. By settling in Begram, they were spared the forthcoming, exceptionally difficult journey across the summit of the Hindu Kush. They also escaped what would turn out to be a brutal three years' struggle for Central Asia, one that would test Alexander and his army as never before.

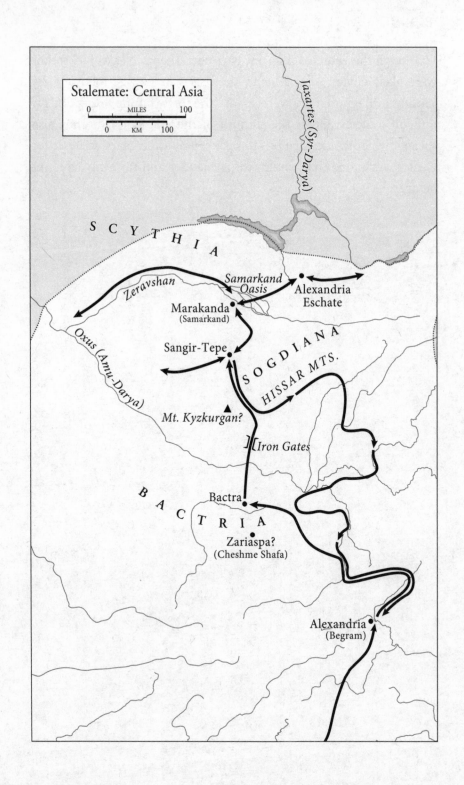

Stalemate: Central Asia

0   MILES   100

0   KM   100

Jaxartes (Syr-Darya)

S C Y T H I A

Zeravshan

Samarkand
Oasis

Alexandria
Eschate

Marakanda
(Samarkand)

Sangir-Tepe

Oxus (Amu-Darya)

S O G D I A N A

HISSAR MTS.

Mt. Kyzkurgan?

Iron Gates

Bactra

B A C T R I A

Zariaspa?
(Cheshme Shafa)

Alexandria
(Begram)

SIX

Across the Hindu Kush

Afghanistan, Tajikistan, and Uzbekistan
Spring–Summer 329 BCE

IN EARLY SPRING, Alexander left Begram to face the last obstacle between him and his rival Bessos—the Hindu Kush. Formed by the clash of the Eurasian and Indian continental plates some fifty million years ago, the Hindu Kush mountains were the coldest, highest, and most barren Alexander had ever encountered. Linked in the east to the Pamirs and Himalayas, in the west to the deserts of Iran, they spread laterally across what is now the center of Afghanistan, a line of tall, jagged peaks, deep gorges, and rushing torrents. Alexander had been skirting their foothills throughout the fall and winter, but these were minor in comparison with the central crests. There the Macedonian king would find two dozen snow-covered crags more than 23,000 feet above sea level. Nothing in his previous life had prepared him for climbs like this. Mount Olympus, so tall the Greeks believed the gods lived at its summit, was less than half as high.

Alexander set out with his army, pack animals, and camp followers one chilly day in March. He may have taken the Khawak Pass—more than 11,000 feet above sea level, but with reasonable gradients, decent water and forage, and open valleys that precluded ambush—or the neighboring Shibar Pass, a lower but longer route, with a deep gorge on the descent that offered little in the way of camping sites, food, or protection from possible attack.

It is uncertain which pass Alexander took, because the armchair historians of the Hellenistic and Roman eras knew too little of Afghanistan to describe the terrain accurately. What is clear is that the crossing was, in early spring, distinctly premature. Later travelers note as a matter of course how all passes through the Hindu Kush were covered by snow from November to March, and caravans made the journey only between July and September. Indeed, when one intrepid Victorian attempted the Khawak Pass in mid-April, he found the road "one glistening sheet of frozen snow."

Alexander and his followers climbed slowly through the snowy landscape. As they moved relentlessly upward, they had to acclimate to the thin air of the peaks. They also suffered from lack of provisions, finding little but terebinth, a shrubby tree related to the cashew. Desperate, they ate some of their pack animals—raw, since the treeless mountain slopes offered no wood—along with a medicinal plant that was likely asafoetida, a familiar ingredient in Indian cooking. With these foods, Alexander's army and camp followers made it across the mountains in seventeen days, a herculean effort given their numbers and the quantity of pack animals and weaponry with which they traveled.

Alexander pushed his followers hard, though he had a comfortable winter camp at Begram and could easily have waited to cross the Hindu Kush. But by wintering on the southern side of the mountains he was cut off from news of what was happening in Bessos's territory. Alexander did not know what kind of army his rival had assembled, what funds he had collected, or what cities he had fortified. He was certain, however, that Bessos's potential resources were enormous.

Bessos commanded an immense, rich, and populous territory: the double province of Bactria-Sogdiana, stretching from northern Afghanistan into the former Soviet Republics of Turkmenistan, Uzbekistan, and Tajikistan. His center of power was the city of Bactra (present-day Balkh), which dominated the fertile lowlands of northern Afghanistan. Here he could draw on the bountiful agricultural produce of the region, where snow-fed rivers from the Hindu Kush and an extensive irrigation system produced large harvests of grapes, tree fruit, melons, and wheat. For this reason, Bactria was known in antiquity as the land of a thousand cities, with agriculture facilitating, on a grand scale, a settled civic life.

Although the rest of Bessos's realm was less immediately appealing than Bactria—desert, mountains, steppe—the governor knew how to profit from it. On the steppe grazed massive numbers of horses, the foundation for the famous Bactrian cavalry. Bessos had led some nine thousand of them at the Battle of Gaugamela, and they provided critical backing for him in the coup against Darius III. Well trained and disciplined, the Bactrian cavalrymen were among the most formidable units in the Persian army, and one of the few to hold their own against Alexander. At Gaugamela, for example, they fought bravely against the best of the Macedonian cavalry, and managed to retreat in order once the battle was lost (most of the soldiers fled, and their formations were cut to pieces by the victorious Alexander).

Along with the Bactrian cavalry, Bessos could draw as well on the nomad riders of Sogdiana and his allies beyond the borders in Scythia (located in present-day Russia). He had led Sogdians, too, at Gaugamela, where they had fought with the Bactrians on the powerful left wing of the army. And he knew that Darius had summoned the Scythians to him when he tried to make a last stand at Ekbatana, although they likely recognized the king's weakness, and did not come. But as the long-established governor of Bactria-Sogdiana, Bessos had close ties to the Scythians; he could plausibly hope for better. Even without these allies, Bessos had an impressive fighting force with which to oppose Alexander, and the resources to hire and feed them. If they stood their ground and fought, they could wreak serious damage on Alexander's troops, particularly as they emerged from the mountains weak and hungry.

Despite his advantages, Bessos decided not to attack Alexander immediately after his crossing of the Hindu Kush. Instead, he tried a strategy that the Persians had hitherto avoided using against Alexander, although it had been proposed by Darius's Greek commander Memnon upon the Macedonian king's arrival in Persia five years before. As Memnon had suggested, Bessos retreated, taking or destroying everything that could be of use to Alexander: wood, livestock, and most of all, food.

Early spring was the lean season, when the fall harvest was almost eaten up and the year's crops barely planted. Bessos likely seized what was left in the large imperial granaries of his well-organized province; burned woodpiles and stretches of forest; and moved north with herds of cattle, sheep, and goats from the royal flocks. His army's great braying retreat was a ruthless, Alexander-like move that left the local inhabitants with nothing. But it was also potentially devastating to the Macedonian king and his army, some twenty-five thousand strong and exhausted from their journey across the Hindu Kush.

To Bessos's frustration, however, Alexander kept up his pursuit. He and his followers lived off freshwater fish—which Bessos could not remove from the numerous rivers of northern Afghanistan—more pack animals, and herbs, which doubtless seemed too unimportant to uproot. Here Alexander benefited paradoxically from the hardscrabble diet available to most inhabitants of Macedonia and Greece. His soldiers were used to eating fish and greens, abundant in the dry, sea-ringed territory from which they came. They may not have been pleased, but they had extensive practice in surviving in a country with limited agricultural resources in a way that Bessos, accustomed to fertile Bactria, may not have imagined.

Alexander and his army advanced into Bactria with deep snow still on the ground. They were headed for Bessos's capital, Bactra. The city stood at the foot of the Hindu Kush mountains, a strongly fortified town with thick ramparts and a river running to one side. Like Satibarzanes's capital of Artakoana, it was a strategic location and a regional administrative center from which Bessos controlled the countryside. As such, it was a prize that Alexander sought and Bessos wanted to keep.

As Alexander marched closer, however, Bessos made the difficult decision to abandon the city. He had fought the Macedonian king at Gaugamela, and perhaps he feared the outcome of another pitched battle. He and his cavalrymen withdrew from Bactra, hoping to preserve their forces and fight another day. They did not destroy the town's heavy brick citadel, but instead left the inhabitants to defend it, giving their governor time to make his getaway. They must have been aware, though, that against a determined besieger like Alexander, no town with Bactra's defenses would be able to hold out long.

The Macedonian king surrounded Bactra with his troops. He also likely threatened its walls with his dangerously effective siege machines. Despite the city's strong walls—and Alexander's weary, hungry soldiers—he captured Bactra on his first attempt.

After the siege, Alexander met up with Erigyios, Artabazos, and their troops, fresh from their victory in western Afghanistan. The king often planned to rendezvous with those he'd left behind at major cities: fixed points they could be expected to encounter in the vast, unfamiliar territories of the Persian Empire. As he met his friends again at Bactra, Alexander could feel pleased that his choice to split his forces and deal with Satibarzanes separately had been a good one. He could also congratulate himself on having eliminated one of Darius's killers, and Bessos's strongest ally.

At Bactra, Alexander settled most of his pack animals, baggage, and equipment and appointed Artabazos as governor to replace Bessos. In this way, Alexander rewarded his old Persian friend for his fidelity to the Macedonian side. He also left the important province of Bactria-Sogdiana in capable and loyal hands.

With a lighter, leaner army, Alexander followed Bessos into the desert. Beyond the fertile river valleys of Bactria lay arid wastelands where few plants or animals lived, and where the roads were frequently effaced by windblown sand. Alexander and his soldiers crossed them at night, since despite the snowy weather elsewhere in Bactria, the desert remained implacably hot. Even with this precaution, the soldiers suffered terribly from thirst, and in the absence of dependable roads, they had to navigate by the stars.

When Alexander and his army arrived at the Amu-Darya River, Bessos had slipped away. Around them was a desert landscape, with only a few smoldering trees due to Bessos's scorched-earth tactics. Across the wide, deep, and swift-flowing current, all they could see were the blackened hulls of the boats he had burned in his retreat.

Bessos had again shown his determination and ruthlessness by destroying his own resources in order to deny them to his enemy. For the Macedonians, who had borne so much on their journey through Bactria, Bessos's actions compounded their frustration. Stymied by the formidable guerrilla warrior they were chasing, they were too late.

On the banks of the Amu-Darya, Alexander faced a discouraging if not impossible situation, one that Bessos doubtless hoped would lead to a retreat. But Bessos had miscalculated. One of the Macedonian king's strengths as a military leader was his ability to think differently, generating unorthodox solutions to the seemingly impossible challenges his conquest posed.

Alexander ordered his soldiers to take out the animal hides they used for tents. Then he told them to fill the skins with straw and sew them closed, turning them into makeshift life preservers. With these to hold on to, the entire army floated across the river in only five days.

Once past the river, Alexander headed north, taking charge of the province of Sogdiana as he went. On his march, he came across a town in what is now Uzbekistan whose inhabitants claimed to be Greek. They gave the king an enthusiastic welcome and told him that they were the descendants of the Brankhidai, caretakers of the important oracle of Apollo at Didyma in southwestern Turkey. The Brankhidai had collaborated with the Great King during the Persian Wars and were subsequently relocated by him to defend them from their angry neighbors.

It's not clear if the story of the Brankhidai was accurate—no archaeological traces of Greeks have been found in Sogdiana prior to Alexander—but similar migrations across vast territories were a familiar practice of Mesopotamian and Persian kings. They could come as punishment (for instance, the Babylonian Captivity after the Jewish-Babylonian wars of the early sixth century); as a pragmatic redistribution of laborers; or, as perhaps with the Brankhidai, as protection. Such migrations help put Alexander's city-foundations in a wider historical context. Innovative to the king's Greek and Macedonian soldiers, for his Persian followers they were simply business as usual.

The Brankhidai offered a foretaste of what Alexander's city-foundations might become, and the Greek soldiers in the army did not like what they saw. They observed that although the townspeople claimed to be Hellenes, they were now bilingual. The Greeks also resented their status as alleged collaborators—even though the war in which they had collaborated was a century and a half old. Alexander called together those soldiers who came from the same region as the original Brankhidai and asked them to vote on the fate of the town's inhabitants. When they could not agree, he nonetheless went ahead and massacred the townspeople. As in Persepolis, the king killed innocent civilians who had surrendered to him, justifying it as vengeance for the Greeks.

Throughout his conquests, Alexander faced competing pressures: the need to be merciful and pragmatic toward subject peoples in order to incorporate them into his empire, countered by the push to assert his dominance violently so as to intimidate others. With the massacre in Sogdiana, violence won out. If Alexander thought he would appease his Greek soldiers, he was wrong, which he would later find out. If he thought he would intimidate the Sogdians, he was also wrong, as he would find out more quickly.

In Bessos's camp, Alexander's seemingly unstoppable journey north was causing difficulties for his rival. First the members of the Bactrian cavalry deserted, returning to their own homes. Although they did not join Alexander's army, their departure was an enormous blow to his rival. They were the foundation of Bessos's fighting force, and had followed him faithfully in the past, despite the defeat at Gaugamela and the killing of Darius. Now they melted into the countryside, leaving their former leader vulnerable to the shifting loyalties of the Sogdians.

Among the most formidable Sogdians in Bessos's camp was a man named Spitamenes. Possibly of Iranian descent, he had his power base in northern Sogdiana, with close ties to the Scythians who populated the borderlands of the Persian Empire there. A generation older than Alexander, Spitamenes had children, including a teenage daughter named Apama, and a long-married wife. He was also a brilliant military strategist with a particular expertise in guerrilla warfare, as Alexander would soon learn.

Spitamenes was closely associated with Bessos, to whom, as a local leader in Sogdiana, he was theoretically subordinate. He did not fight at Gaugamela, but instead likely joined the aspiring Great King upon his arrival in Bactria in the fall of 330 BCE. There he observed firsthand Bessos's scorched-earth tactics, his decision to leave the richest, most fertile portion of his double province devastated and open to Alexander. As the Macedonian king approached, Spitamenes retreated with Bessos across the Amu-Darya River, burning the boats. By the time the Macedonian king had managed to cross, Spitamenes had had enough. He sent messengers to Alexander asking for men and promising to betray his former colleague. The Macedonian king in response sent a small force led by one of his most trusted friends, Ptolemy.

In choosing Ptolemy for the mission to Spitamenes, Alexander was singling out a close companion who had never previously received so important an assignment. Ptolemy was the son of a high-ranking Macedonian nobleman and had, like Erigyios, been close to Alexander at the court of Philip II. With Erigyios, Ptolemy had suffered banishment due to his friendship with Alexander, returning to Macedonia only after Philip's death. In the years since, he had been loyal but not particularly distinguished, playing no major roles in Alexander's great battles, but serving as his bodyguard after the trial of Philotas the previous autumn. Following the deaths of Philotas and Parmenion, Alexander's own friends began to take on more prominent responsibilities in the Persian conquest, while men of his father's generation moved to the background. Ptolemy was one of these friends, who showed his aptitude for new, more high-profile missions during the conquest of Central Asia. He began with Bessos and Spitamenes.

According to his later, rather self-aggrandizing memoir, Ptolemy raced with his small force toward Spitamenes. With Alexander-like speed, he covered what should have been a ten-day march in only four. Arriving in the Kashka-Darya River valley in Uzbekistan, he learned that Bessos was in a nearby town. Ptolemy hurried to the town, perhaps the site known as Sangir-Tepe, which boasted strong walls, a citadel, and an elaborate sanctuary outside the walls at this time. He surrounded it with his cavalry and demanded Bessos, promising the town's inhabitants they would not be hurt if they surrendered the would-be Great King. After they nervously complied, he seized Bessos and departed. Then he wrote to Alexander, asking how he should bring the former provincial governor to him. Ptolemy followed his friend's commands to the letter, presenting Bessos naked—the ultimate humiliation for a normally well-dressed Persian nobleman—and bound in a wooden dog collar, waiting along the road where Alexander and his army would march.

Other ancient writers give Ptolemy a lesser role. They focus on Spitamenes, describing how he and his coconspirators surrounded Bessos, deposed him, and put him in chains. In these accounts, Ptolemy was responsible only for receiving Bessos from them and bringing him to Alexander; even the dog collar was Spitamenes's idea. Given Spitamenes's leadership abilities and Ptolemy's tendency toward self-glorification, they may well be right.

A year after the conspiracy against Darius III, Alexander finally met the chief conspirator face-to-face. He saw Bessos after he had been stripped of his upright tiara and royal robes, and with the degrading dog collar that Alexander himself had perhaps mandated. Halting his army on the road, the Macedonian king interrogated his former rival in full view of his soldiers, staging an elaborate public demonstration of his victory over Darius's assassins. Alexander towered high above Bessos in a chariot as he asked the usurper why he had betrayed his liege lord and close relation, Darius III. He did not accept Bessos's attempted excuse, that he had only done so to negotiate for his own safety with the Macedonian king. Instead, Alexander ordered the chief conspirator to be whipped in public, with a herald all the while reciting his crimes.

After Bessos's capture and punishment, Alexander could begin to relax. His travels in the early summer of 329 BCE must have felt like a victory lap, as he moved through the mountains, deserts, and oases of what was finally, indisputably, *his* empire.

On his journey, Alexander could reflect on the successful conclusion to his first few months in Bactria. He had taken possession of the province and named as its governor Artabazos, a trustworthy individual with connections to both Macedonians and Persians. He had seen, perhaps, the severed head of his former enemy Satibarzanes, and knew that western Afghanistan had been pacified. And he had punished Bessos, though he had left him alive for now. The landscape Alexander was journeying through was harsh and his followers suffered from it, but he had dealt with mountains and deserts before. As he headed for the northern borderlands of the Persian Empire, he likely anticipated adding those regions to his conquest as easily as he had others in the past. But he had misread—and wildly underestimated—their inhabitants.

Spitamenes meanwhile was far away. After betraying Bessos, he headed to his own fiefdom on the northern border of the Persian Empire. There he would await Alexander's next move, pondering how long his collaboration with the Macedonian king would last, and when and for what reasons it might end.

SEVEN

Fighting the Hydra

Kazakhstan, Tajikistan, Uzbekistan, and Afghanistan
Summer–Winter 329 BCE

AS ALEXANDER MOVED NORTH in the summer of 329 BCE, he was aware of occasional rumblings of dissent—a Macedonian foraging party attacked, a few insubordinate villages. They must have seemed like rounding errors within the immense empire he now controlled. In fact, they were warning signs of the worst rebellion he had yet faced.

Disregarding these tremors, Alexander marched his troops all the way to the empire's northern frontier. To safeguard his realm, he wanted to establish a secure border, and that meant dealing with the people living just beyond it, the Scythians. He sent an ambassador named Derdas, one of his Companions, ostensibly to conclude an alliance, following initial peaceful overtures from the Scythians. In reality, Derdas was a spy, intended to observe the Scythians' land, their customs, and their weapons, in advance of a possible invasion by the Macedonian king.

Derdas found the Scythians in their summer quarters, among the vast plains of waist-high grass on the Eurasian steppe in what is now Kazakhstan. As he approached, he had to make his way through flocks of horses, cattle, sheep, and goats to the large domed tents where these roaming pastoralists lived. He was greeted by men who were heavily tattooed, with extravagant gold jewelry, fur-lined coats, and loose, baggy pants tucked into their boots. The women were, from

Derdas's perspective, even stranger. Expert horseback riders, they possessed weapons and knew how to use them; they may have been the real-life models of the Greeks' mythological Amazons.

Derdas did not come unprepared to the Scythians. He likely brought an interpreter with him, or even several, as the Scythians spoke an Iranian dialect that was similar to, but not identical with, the court Persian of Darius's nobles. He also presumably brought gifts. Wine was likely, since the Scythians loved to drink, but as nomads, had no vines; he may also have brought gold jewelry and ornate gilded weapons. A splendidly crafted Greek-style golden quiver, now in the Hermitage Museum in Saint Petersburg, may have come from Derdas; it was so prized by the Scythian chief who received it that it was buried with him when he died. In return for the gifts, the Scythians would have invited Derdas into their yurts, brightly decorated with felt-covered pillows and wool carpets, and fed him their delicacies: a drink made of fermented mare's milk, enormous portions of meat.

As an ambassador and covert spy, Derdas had to make the best of what must have been an uncomfortable situation. He was accustomed to chairs and couches, but was now reclining awkwardly in the Scythians' tents, which were barren of furniture apart from low tables and stools on the floor. His conversation with his hosts would been similarly awkward: slow and stilted, given the likely number of interpreters required.

Derdas also had to contend with a radical difference in worldview. As one of Alexander's Companions, he came from a settled agrarian society, where the majority of the population made their living as farmers. He was used to people who spent their lives in a small, confined area, clearly demarcated and fiercely protected from outsiders. Of course, Derdas himself had traveled, moving over the vast reaches of the Persian Empire together with his king. But his perspective was shaped by a place where citizenship was a closely guarded privilege and where immigration, save for the very rich, was strongly discouraged.

The Scythians saw things differently. As nomads, they ranged widely over the course of the year, moving their flocks to the best pastures, irrespective of political boundaries. They had capacious, unfettered horizons, traveling up to six hundred miles per year, and trading indiscriminately with everyone. Their political affiliations, too, were fluid, as they formed part of a loose confederation of associated but not identical tribes. Even their jewelry reflected their wide-ranging cosmopolitanism, incorporating Greek palmettes, Persian winged lions, and Chinese dragons.

The Scythians were aware that the Persians had established a loose demarcation along the Syr-Darya River, one that theoretically separated those inside the empire from those beyond. But the Scythians crossed and recrossed this boundary regularly, whether to feed their flocks, trade with their more settled agricultural neighbors, or conduct raids on them. Even with the raids, it was a mutually beneficial relationship, one that the Persians had wisely left it in place during their two centuries of rule.

As Derdas knew, Alexander intended to disrupt this relationship. At that very moment, the Macedonian king was camped along the banks of the Syr-Darya River, sketching the foundations of a city he called Alexandria Eschate ("Alexandria the Farthest"). His goal was to police the border, using the new, well-fortified site to observe or prevent movement across the reinforced boundary line. As Derdas was perhaps also aware, Alexandria Eschate had another potential function. It could be used as a staging ground if Alexander decided at some later point to invade the region beyond the Syr-Darya, and to bring the northern pastures of the Scythians fully under his control.

It is uncertain just how much Derdas told the Scythians about Alexander's intentions, or how much they guessed from their own spies or observers along the Syr-Darya. What is clear is that his feint at an alliance that summer failed. As Alexander moved his army up toward the Scythians' territory, the tremors he had been ignoring grew stronger, until the entire region erupted into a revolt.

Both the Sogdians within the borders and the Scythians beyond them joined the rebellion. Farmers and nomads alike resented Alexander's heavy-handed military presence in an area where the Persians had been careful to tread lightly. The Sogdians had long been part of the Great King's empire, but due to the difficult geography of their region and its distance from the imperial center, their local leaders exercised greater autonomy than elsewhere; they would not give up their freedoms without a fight. The Scythians had even more at stake, since Alexander's border policy threatened their way of life.

Earlier in Alexander's career, he had calibrated his approach to different regions with considerable cultural sensitivity: acting as a pharaoh in Egypt, for example, and proclaiming "freedom and autonomy" for the Greek cities of western Turkey. In Central Asia, he failed to do so. The revolt highlighted the limits of the king's open-mindedness and outreach to his subjects, his inability to understand what mattered to the Scythians and Sogdians. It signaled a philosophical failure, one Alexander would pay dearly for.

The Scythians and Sogdians resented Alexander, but they needed a leader to catalyze their rebellion. They found that leader in Bessos's betrayer and Alexander's former ally, Spitamenes. From his stronghold in northern Sogdiana, the powerful Central Asian warlord ruminated on his peoples' accumulated grievances—and his own. Spitamenes could see the garrisons that Alexander had imposed on every major town in the region and the checkpoints he set up. He heard a pressing invitation from the Macedonian king to an assembly: a military review where Alexander claimed he would select troops for his planned invasion of India. To Spitamenes, this demand for compulsory military service was grating, perhaps ominous. He was losing faith in Alexander, who had failed to recognize or reward him for his aid in capturing the Macedonian's greatest rival.

Spitamenes decided to take vengeance on the unwelcome foreigner he had made the mistake of trusting. He spread the rumor that at the military review, Alexander intended to assemble the best fighters of Bactria-Sogdiana together—and then kill them all. His rumor was all the more plausible given the resentment and suspicion the inhabitants of Central Asia felt toward the Macedonian king, as well as the massacre of the Brankhidai just a few months earlier.

Before the military review could even occur, Spitamenes and his followers broke out in open revolt. The Central Asian warrior had received an optimistic messenger from Alexander when the first signs of rebellion appeared, asking for his assistance. Spitamenes was, after all, just the sort of local leader the Macedonian king had made use of previously: one who, like Phrataphernes and Artabazos, came over to the Macedonian side, but still retained credibility with Iranians. Spitamenes, however, responded to Alexander's plea by mustering a fighting force, one primarily composed of Scythian cavalry. Then he headed to the Sogdian capital, Marakanda (present-day Samarkand in Uzbekistan), to oust Alexander's garrison.

When Spitamenes arrived at the walls of Marakanda in the dusty late summer of 329 BCE, he saw before him a spectacular city located in one of the most fertile oases of Sogdiana. Set on a natural citadel, Marakanda had been fortified with enormous Persian ramparts, extending in a circuit nearly four miles long. With only his cavalry force and no siege machines, Spitamenes knew that he would have difficulty taking the city and forcing out its garrison. But for his rebellion to succeed, Marakanda was key: a royal capital with rich stores of grain and treasure, it occupied a critical choke hold on the road to the border.

Spitamenes laid siege to Marakanda. Given its grain supply, as well as the canal that brought fresh water to the city's inhabitants, he could not expect swift results. He settled in for a long siege, ready to harass the Marakandans and, slowly, starve them into submission.

Spitamenes kept a close watch on Marakanda, but he could not prevent messengers bringing word of his siege to Alexander. He knew they would make their way north and arrive at the camp of the Macedonian king. Spitamenes could not be sure how Alexander would react. But he must have anticipated that the news would surprise and anger the man with whom he had so recently collaborated. Spitamenes must also have been mentally prepared for the prospect that Alexander would send soldiers to attack his men and raise the siege. They would be better trained, better equipped, and, in all likelihood, far more numerous than his ragtag cavalry force of Scythians. He would have to rely on his superior knowledge of the countryside and his guerrilla tactics to survive.

Far from Marakanda on the northeastern frontier, Alexander was stymied by a place that was difficult to conquer, and even harder to hold. Across the Syr-Darya River from him, the Scythians had begun gathering their horsemen for an attack. To the south, the cities that he had garrisoned in Sogdiana killed or expelled the Macedonian king's soldiers, then strengthened their defenses. And even in Bactria the rebellion reverberated. There it was led by the cavalrymen who had followed Bessos, suspicious of their new ruler and of the military review he had ordered. Dealing with the revolt was like fighting the Hydra, the monster attacked by Alexander's mythological ancestor Herakles: when he cut off one head, two more grew in its place.

All the lands north of the Hindu Kush were in an uproar, with Alexander pinned down at the Persian Empire's border—cut off from his baggage train in Bactra and his supply lines and communications via Iran. It was an extremely dangerous position, and one that Alexander, typically so adept at anticipating his opponent's every move, in no way foresaw. As he gazed at his city, he must have wondered how he had so entirely miscalculated.

For the moment, however, Alexander could not afford to reflect on his miscalculations. He needed to react swiftly, before the revolt got completely out of hand. Alexander cannot have been pleased to have been forced into responding to the actions of another, particularly since that other was Spitamenes, his former trusted ally. Alexander trusted easily—too easily, according to some of his advisers, when those he trusted were Persian. Now he had gone against their advice, and been betrayed.

The revolt in Central Asia was dangerous on several counts. Not only did Alexander have to deal with the rebellion itself, but also with the concerns it raised among his officers about his leadership and judgment. The Macedonian king had by this point had his policy of rapprochement challenged by three different Central Asian leaders—Bessos, Satibarzanes, and Spitamenes—and his officers were growing increasingly skeptical. Though Alexander exerted a powerful control over his followers, even he recognized he could not rule if they lost faith in him.

Alexander did not choose to deal with Spitamenes himself. He likely feared to leave the border region, with its towns in an uproar and the Scythians nearby. He also hoped, despite everything that had happened, to patch things up with Spitamenes. He sent a limited force, some two to three thousand mercenary infantry and cavalrymen, and put in charge a diplomat rather than a military leader. His choice fell on a man who was neither Macedonian nor Greek but a likely Iranian named Pharnoukhes, who could speak to the Sogdians in their native language and was considered to be particularly skillful in dealing with them. Alexander must have believed that Pharnoukes's dealmaking, combined with a limited show of force, would succeed with Spitamenes.

Pharnoukhes and his men traveled south toward the oasis of Marakanda. As they neared the city, they likely hoped to catch Spitamenes, hemming him in between their forces and those of Marakanda's Macedonian garrison, then working out a deal. But they were thousands of heavily armed men moving through the unfamiliar Sogdian landscape—noisy, conspicuous, taking the most obvious road—and Spitamenes must in any case have been expecting them. When the Macedonian soldiers neared Marakanda, they saw the Sogdian leader and his followers riding away from the city on their swift steppe horses. Their orders were to deal with Spitamenes, so as he and his men headed north and west toward the Zeravshan River, the Macedonians unwisely followed.

Pharnoukhes and his men allowed themselves to be lured far from the safety of Marakanda and its Macedonian garrison. As they moved along Spitamenes's trail into a heavily wooded royal Persian hunting preserve, Pharnoukhes grew increasingly uncomfortable. He confronted the infantry and cavalry commanders and tendered his resignation. He was a diplomat and a foreigner, he told them, while they were military leaders, Macedonians, and Companions of the king. In a situation like this one, Pharnoukhes thought, he should not be in charge.

Alexander's Companions, however, were just as unwilling as Pharnoukhes to take responsibility for the situation. As their king had become increasingly autocratic in his ways, concentrating power in his own hands and those of a few select friends, they feared to contravene his orders. They also recognized the dangers inherent in their current circumstances, as well as the errors of judgment that had already been made, and they did not want to be blamed if their encounter with Spitamenes went badly. In a tense conversation at the edge of the lush Persian wilderness, the military commanders refused to accept Pharnoukhes's resignation. It was at that moment that Spitamenes struck.

The mercenary soldiers, unbeatable fighters on open, level ground, had far more difficulty in the irregular wooded glen in which they found themselves ambushed by Spitamenes. With trees in every direction, they could not always see their attackers, nor could they form themselves into the tight defensive formations—shields overlapping, spears bristling—that protected them in conventional battles. Their enemies followed none of the usual rules of engagement, and would not come near enough for the close-quarter combat at which the soldiers excelled. Instead, the mercenaries found that their enemies remained frustratingly out of reach: two to a horse, they would fire a barrage of arrows at their unlucky targets, then wheel around and retreat, repeating this sequence again and again.

It is possible that a brilliant, creative general like Alexander himself would have been able to improvise a solution on the spot for the Scythians' unconventional guerrilla warfare tactics. Pharnoukhes, however, could not, and his military commanders were no help to him. When the cavalry leader headed toward the Zeravshan River in an attempt to save the horses, he failed to inform his infantry comrades. Instead of covering his retreat, they began to flee as well. They ran in a chaotic, disorderly fashion that left them vulnerable to the Scythians' attack. Horses and men made it only as far as an island in the middle of the river, where they were easy targets for the Scythians' arrows. Almost all of them were slaughtered.

The few survivors of this stunning and unexpected defeat made their way slowly to Alexander. They limped back to the Macedonian king's camp, a pitiful remnant of the proud fighting force that had so recently departed. They horrified Alexander, who had never experienced a loss this grave. If he had feared his officers' questioning of his leadership before, he knew the revelation of Spitamenes's victory would be far more damning. By one account, he was so upset by what had happened that he swore all the survivors to silence.

As bad as the defeat near Marakanda was Alexander's disastrous attack on the nearest large town in the border region, a place called Cyropolis. This was a well-established older city, one that had been founded two centuries earlier by the Persian king Cyrus the Great. Its fortifications were too strong for Alexander and his men to swarm the walls and take the city immediately, so he called for siege machines and put his close friend Krateros in charge of preparing for a full-scale onslaught. Such an effort was precisely the kind of critical but unshowy work at which Krateros excelled.

While the siege machines were moved into place at Cyropolis, Alexander attacked other small towns nearby. These towns had lower, less impressive walls, so he could use his archers and javelin men to pick off their defenders one by one, then scale them with ladders, jump down, and proceed with the sack.

Frustrated by betrayal and failure, Alexander took out his resentments on the towns' inhabitants. In each, he killed all the adult males and made the women and children slaves. It was cruel, unfair, and counterproductive, but the Macedonian king did not care. He responded to this rebellion in the eastern borderlands with ruthless, overwhelming force.

Returning to Cyropolis, Alexander hammered the walls with battering rams and catapults. As at Artakoana, so, too, at Cyropolis, his use of such sophisticated military technology gave him an advantage; the mudbrick walls of Central Asian towns were built to withstand assault by archers and cavalry, not siege machines. While the inhabitants of the city were distracted by his catapults, Alexander noticed another flaw in Cyropolis's defenses. The river that normally flowed beneath the walls and provided water to the city was now, in the hot late summer of Central Asia, completely dry. Taking his bodyguards, archers, javelin men, and elite foot soldiers, he crept beneath the walls along the riverbed, then burst into the city and broke down its gates.

As the Macedonian soldiers flooded into Cyropolis, they faced fierce resistance from the city's inhabitants. Alexander and his men were forced to fight through each street, against people who knew the place far better than they did. For the Macedonians, every building was a potential hive of enemies, every road a death trap. Unlike in battle, they had to fear not only face-to-face combat, but also unpredictable assaults: arrows, stones, even roof tiles thrown down by inhabitants from their houses. Sieges and city sacks were dangerous, and many soldiers' worst wounds came from these military operations. Philip II, for example, lost an eye at the siege of Methone in 355; Pyrrhus of Epirus, a relative of Alexander's mother, Olympias, was hit on the head by a tile thrown down by a woman from the rooftop in the sack of a city, stunned, and killed by a nearby soldier. At Cyropolis, or possibly a second, unnamed city nearby, Alexander was struck on the neck by a stone thrown so hard that when it hit him, he collapsed unconscious. As the fighting raged around him, everything went dark.

Rescued by his men, Alexander was carried back to his new foundation, Alexandria Eschate. There the wounded king busied himself with laying out his city. Given its position on the border, he focused on Alexandria's fortifications, using all his soldiers in order to build its six-mile circuit wall in under three weeks. He settled the new town with demobilized veterans as well as nearby locals, described by ancient authors as volunteers, but more likely moved there by force. Then he commemorated its foundation with religious ceremonies and athletic games, giving his cornered and demoralized soldiers an opportunity to celebrate. Such a respite was important as they would soon have to encounter the Scythians, under circumstances that were, by Alexander's standards, highly unfavorable.

The Scythians appeared menacing to the Macedonian soldiers, but even more worrisome was Alexander himself, recovering from his wound and in no fit condition to lead. His recovery was complicated by the sparse diet available in the border region, where a narrow strip of fertile land tracked the river between harsh, looming mountains. Due to his wound, Alexander had difficulty speaking—perhaps from some damage to his windpipe—and he was too weak to stand in the army's ranks, ride a horse, or project his voice strongly enough to give instructions or encouragement to his troops.

For a commander who had always led from the front, and who depended on his charismatic example to inspire others, Alexander's injury was a major setback. It revealed the fragility of the Macedonian conquest, so dependent on one man. It also suggested the potential danger of Alexander's battle strategy, particularly his tendency to put his own body on the line in every fight.

As he waited in Alexandria Eschate to recover, the Macedonian king consulted his soothsayer Aristander. Men like Aristander had been a regular part of Hellenic armies for centuries—as Alexander knew, they appeared already in Homer's *Iliad*—and it is not surprising that the soothsayer had joined the Macedonian war effort. Despite his up-to-date scientific education from Aristotle, Alexander was a deeply religious man. He appreciated having a prophet to consult, particularly at moments of frustration or crisis. With his wound, as well as the nationalist rebellion he had unwittingly ignited, the present moment certainly qualified.

At the army's camp in his makeshift new city, Alexander ordered his seer to conduct a sacrifice and observe the omens carefully. He also summoned to his tent his bodyguards and closest friends. He asked them to sit close, so that he did not have to strain his voice to speak to them. Then he presented his case for immediately attacking the Scythians.

Alexander's friends discouraged him, and so did the gods, according to Aristander. Even after Alexander demanded a second sacrifice and consultation of the entrails, the omens were unfavorable. Alexander lost his temper, but the seer remained inflexible. He told the king that "the signs from the gods would not appear otherwise just because Alexander wanted to hear something different."

Despite the discouragement of both his soothsayer and his friends, Alexander did not give up his intention of fighting the Scythians. Instead he spent a long, sleepless night planning his battle strategy. He often thought through his military maneuvers at night, when it was dark and quiet and there was no one to disturb him. Before his final showdown against Darius III at Gaugamela, for instance, Alexander stayed up well into the night, finalizing his battle plan. Then he fell into so deep a sleep that he had to be awakened by an impatient Parmenion in midmorning, well after the battle should have begun.

At Alexandria Eschate, Alexander sat in his tent, pulling aside its flaps from time to time to look out on the Scythians' myriad campfires across the Syr-Darya. He needed to figure out how to get across a river that was broad, deep, and swift flowing, as difficult as the Zeravshan, where Pharnoukhes and his men had been caught. He also had to cross it under fire, as his enemies occupied the opposite bank. And he had to counter the Scythians' unconventional battle tactics, particularly their tendency to attack, wheel around in retreat, then attack again. Alexander stayed up all night, contemplating and revising his battle plan. At dawn, he got up, put on his military uniform, and carefully, painfully, went out to speak to his men.

Alexander had not appeared in public in military dress since he was wounded at Cyropolis, and the soldiers greeted him with tears of joy. The king, however, gave them little time for emotional displays; there was a battle to fight. Alexander ordered his men to prepare rafts for the cavalry and heavy infantry, and tent skins for the light-armed forces. Unlike at the Amu-Darya River, he had plenty of trees at his disposal here, and needed his troops to cross fully armed and with their best military equipment. He oversaw the construction of several thousand rafts in two days: a massive endeavor that suggests just how much effort he mustered for the fight against the Scythians. Then he and his army began their perilous river crossing.

In his carefully planned battle strategy, Alexander put men with large, heavy shields at the front of the rafts, kneeling behind their shields for cover against the Scythians' arrows. Behind these soldiers he placed the catapults, with armored men protecting those who worked the equipment, so they could fire volleys at the enemy as they crossed. In the lee of the catapults and hidden by them, Alexander set the heavy-armed infantry, with their shields extended in front, above, to the sides, and behind them like a turtle's shell; they also covered the oarsmen, so they could row without interference. The king made similar provisions for the cavalry, but did not try to put the vulnerable and skittish horses on rafts. Instead he had them swim, with the water obscuring their bodies and affording them some protection. At the back he had the light-armed forces on their tent-skins, floating across as best they could.

Alexander's crossing was difficult. While the Scythians waited menacingly on the other side of the river, the king had to contend with a heavy current pushing his men downriver and threatening to upset his soldiers, who were precariously balanced on their flimsy rafts. Only when they had almost reached the farther shore could he have his javelin-throwers rise and cast their spears. His goal, with them and with the catapults, was to scatter the Scythians guarding the riverbank so his men could disembark safely. Alexander's plan worked, and he got his men onto the shore without serious loss of life. Now he was ready to attack the slippery guerrilla fighters who had been taunting him across the river for several weeks.

The Macedonian king began the battle as he normally did, with a cavalry charge. But this tactic, which had proved so effective against the Persians, did not work against the Scythians. They simply responded, as they had with Pharnoukhes, by wheeling around and retreating before the Macedonians could attack them.

Alexander then put his hopes in a new tactic. He mixed light-armed troops, archers and javelin men, in among the horses, and had the front lines all charge together, fast and hard. With this combined-arms strategy, Alexander's late-night planning paid off. His archers and javelin men had a longer range than the cavalry, so they could wreak havoc among the Scythians even before the horsemen had come to grips with them. They also prevented their foes from wheeling around and retreating, for fear of being shot in the back. Alexander had the enemy trapped at close quarters, for the hand-to-hand combat that showed the Macedonians to advantage. And he had neutralized the Scythians' best tactics, forcing them to fight in a way that played to Macedonian strengths rather than their own.

Alexander's unorthodox battle plan succeeded, and the result was a rout. He captured the Scythian commander and a number of his horsemen, while the remainder of the army fled. Alexander managed to kill relatively few of them—even the ancient literary sources, with their typically inflated casualty figures, claim only a thousand enemy deaths—while the rest retreated in disorder. Despite his fragility, the Macedonian king pursued them through difficult countryside and re-morseless early-autumn heat. Desperately thirsty en route, he stopped for a drink. It was his worst decision of the day, as the water turned out to be dirty, giving him diarrhea and dehydrating him even more thor-oughly than the climate. Nine miles from the battleground he collapsed and lost consciousness, and had to be carried back to camp.

In the aftermath of the battle, Alexander received a profuse apology from the king of the Scythians. He decided to accept the king's claim that rogue elements of the Scythian confederacy were responsible, and that the attack on the Macedonians had not been the considered intention of the high command. As Alexander must have known, this claim was unlikely, if not completely false. But he chose to accept it, and to consent to the offers of alliance from various Scythian groups that now came pouring in.

Alexander is often described, by both ancient and modern schol-ars, as driven insatiably to conquest. The episode with the Scythians, however, testifies to his capacity for restraint, his recognition of the value of a self-appointed stopping point. Alexander could have re-fused to accept the Scythian king's apologies, and pressed forward in his invasion of that territory. He had the men, the weapons, and the insight into a successful battle strategy. Yet he did not. Instead, he crossed back into the Persian Empire at the Syr-Darya and headed south to face the Sogdian rebels before winter came.

Still nursing his wound, Alexander marched with his army toward Marakanda, once more under siege by Spitamenes. He pursued the Sogdian leader, who retreated again in the direction he had led Phar-noukhes and his men earlier, though this time without an ambush.

When they arrived at the site of the massacre, Alexander broke off the chase, and gave the troops who had perished a full military funeral.

For Macedonians like Alexander, giving Pharnoukhes and his men a proper burial was a long and difficult process. First, they would likely have had to collect all the bodies—which had been rotting in the Central Asian heat—and cremate them, probably on a vast funerary pyre like those in Homer's *Iliad*. Then, when the ashes had cooled, the Macedonians would have to comb through the remains picking out the bones, and bury them in an urn or chest underground. Finally, the mourners would intone ritual laments and pour drink offerings for the dead, and perhaps bring flowers. Alexander had to carry out all these rituals—and in the meantime, let Spitamenes go—because for Greeks and Macedonians, the proper burial of the dead was a profound obligation. Without it, the ancients believed, the dead were condemned to wait in eternal restlessness by the River Styx.

When the funeral had been completed, Alexander tracked Spitamenes as far as the desert, where the Zeravshan River disappeared into the sand. He could not safely bring his army any farther, and had to accept that the Sogdian leader had once again eluded his grasp. By this time, the Central Asian summer heat had given way to cool fall weather. Alexander turned back, moving south toward Bactria. He needed to be in a large, well-stocked, and well-fortified city, so that his troops would have food and shelter for the long, cold winter that was coming.

Up in the foothills of the Hindu Kush, situated along the Balkh River and controlling a key pass from the mountains to the Bactrian plains, stands a recently discovered city. It has huge, thick Persian-era walls and masses of Iranian pottery scattered throughout the site. Though a relatively short distance from the royal capital of Bactra, the newfound city has a very different strategic and topographical character: higher and more defensible, with cool, dry mountain air instead of Bactra's malarial swamp. Now called Cheshme Shafa, this was perhaps the city ancient writers called Zariaspa, a safe, healthy place where the king could rest and recover from his wound.

Along with his recovery, Alexander had much to do in the winter of 329–28 BCE. He reconnected at Zariaspa with his loyal Persian governor Phrataphernes, who had just defeated another supporter of Bessos and brought him to Alexander for punishment. The Macedonian king also met up at Zariaspa with soldiers and generals who had come all the way from the Mediterranean to join his army. There were men from Syria, Turkey, and as far away as Greece itself, some twenty-three thousand in total. After the king's losses in Central Asia and the numerous veteran's colonies he had founded, they made an opportune addition to his depleted force. Alexander welcomed as well an old friend: Nearkhos, a Cretan naval officer who was one of Alexander's close companions from his youth in Macedonia, and who would later play an important role as admiral of his fleet.

Alexander had called up the officers and soldiers long ago, before Darius had been assassinated and Bessos usurped the throne. Their arrival at Zariaspa was an uncomfortable reminder of an earlier phase in the king's military plan, when he had blithely assumed that his conquest of Bactria-Sogdiana would be completed by this time, and his invasion of India would begin. The king cannot have been pleased to acknowledge how different the situation was at present, with his wound still troubling him and the entire double province in revolt. Instead of an easy, and highly lucrative, conquest of India, he was stuck losing soldiers to ambushes and city sieges in Central Asia. These were not the battles he had brought them out to fight.

Alexander was likely even less enthusiastic about admitting his disappointments to the other significant arrivals at Zariaspa: the local leaders of Bactria who had not been deterred by Spitamenes's rumor. The Macedonian king had envisioned a triumphant military review, in accordance with a long-established Persian tradition, during which he would examine the troops they had brought and select some for his new campaign. Having fought the Bactrian cavalry at Gaugamela, he was well aware of how talented and well trained these men were and how excellent their horses, a fine complement to his infantry-heavy force. And it made sense to integrate them into his army, binding the local elites more closely to their Macedonian overlords in a shared campaign against India. Asking the Bactrian leaders to assist in guerrilla warfare against their compatriots, however, was likely more than even Alexander dared to do. He seems to have let them go without enlisting any at this time; for another year, they go unmentioned.

If he could not make use of the Bactrian cavalry for his army, however, Alexander could at least give them a spectacle to remember. He summoned everyone—Greeks, Macedonians, Persians, Bactrians—to an assembly, then brought Bessos forward. Alexander's last significant encounter with Bessos had been in early spring, when he met the usurper, naked and wearing a dog collar, along the road. How Bessos appeared on this occasion is unknown, nor are his words recorded. We know only what Alexander did. First, he ordered Bessos's nose and ears cut off in front of everyone. Then the Macedonian king decreed that his rival be sent to Ekbatana to be executed before an assembly of the Medes and Persians.

Alexander's treatment of Bessos was deliberate, and deliberately shocking. He shocked the Greeks and Macedonians, who were not averse to torture—witness Philotas—but tended to use it as an intelligence-gathering strategy, not for punishment. Alexander's behavior toward Bessos was interpreted by them as yet another example of his decline into Persian-style barbarism, and ancient writers moralistically disapprove of it. But Alexander was not putting on the show for their benefit. He aimed his actions primarily at the local members of his audience, who expected to see usurpers punished in just this way. The Macedonian king needed them to understand how he treated rebels, so he "spoke" to them, Persian style, through his actions. His need was all the more pressing in that Spitamenes was still at large, far to the north, gathering troops for next spring's campaign.

EIGHT

Murder at the Feast

Afghanistan, Tajikistan, and Uzbekistan
Spring–Fall 328 BCE

AS SOON AS HE COULD plausibly declare winter over, Alexander began moving north for a counteroffensive against the rebels. He had to thread his way through the Hissar Mountains, an area of wild high peaks, deep gorges, and rushing rivers in what is now eastern Uzbekistan. It was a slow and torturous journey for the king and his army, as they faced resistance from local leaders at a series of hilltop fortresses. The most critical—and difficult—came in the region known as the Iron Gates.

Like the Caspian Gates Alexander had encountered in his pursuit of Darius, the Iron Gates were a choke point, guarding the best pass through the Hissars along the main road north to Marakanda. They were guarded by a defiant local ruler named Sisimithres, who controlled a mountain, likely the present-day Mount Kyzkurgan, that protected the defiles of the Iron Gates. Sisimithres was well provisioned, and many powerful individuals from the region had taken refuge with him. Due to the imposing geography of his fortress, he was initially unresponsive to Alexander's demand for surrender.

Alexander and his soldiers prepared for a long, painful siege. Living in tents as their provisions from Zariaspa ran low, they suffered from cold and hunger. Since they could hardly expect to starve out Sisimithres quickly, they needed to intimidate him with a plausible threat. Alexander had his soldiers cut down junipers, tall as pine trees in that region and very strong, and make them into ladders. With these, they descended into the gorge below and began to fill it. They put stakes in the ground at intervals and then a kind of wickerwork netting between them, strong and flexible, to be filled with earth. They worked constantly, with Alexander supervising one shift of soldiers during the day, and his Companions another at night.

Alexander could tell that Sisimithres thought little of the Macedonians' efforts when they began. Given the size of the gorge and the limited resources available, it was hard to believe that the attempt to fill it in could ever succeed. But as the work continued and the ground rose, the king judged that Sisimithres was becoming increasingly uneasy.

To intimidate the keeper of the Iron Gates, Alexander made use of one of his most significant advantages as a conqueror: his engineers, who built bridges, pioneered siege machines, and formulated technological solutions to whatever military problems the Macedonian king faced. After all, the gorge in the Hissars was by no means the most difficult site Alexander's engineers had been asked to bridge. At Tyre in what is now Lebanon, they had used rocks, nets, and cedars to construct something similar—only underwater.

Finally, the keeper of the Iron Gates capitulated to Alexander. Sisimithres used as his intermediary a man named Oxyarthes, a mature, high-ranking aristocrat from Bactria who had allied with Bessos and continued his rebellion even after the aspiring Great King's imprisonment. Oxyarthes had recently come over to Alexander's side, probably following the king's capture of his wife and daughters. His role as intermediary was the first time Oxyarthes demonstrated his ability to work well with both Alexander and local leaders. The Bactrian and his family would soon take on added responsibilities, far more prominent.

With Oxyarthes as mediator, Alexander offered the guardian of the Iron Gates favorable conditions for his surrender. Neither Sisimithres nor his followers were killed, nor did they lose their land. Indeed, the local ruler even managed to retain his position in charge of his hill-top fortress. In return, the Sogdian leader shared his provisions with Alexander, sending dried meat, wheat, and wine to the hungry Macedonian soldiers. His gesture was well timed and only increased Alexander's respect for him. With his stores still so abundant, it showed that he had not been starved into submission, but surrendered of his own free will.

Alexander's attack on the hilltop fortress of Sisimithres showcased his brilliant generalship. In it, he demonstrated his unique combination of innovative, out-of-the-box thinking; coordinated and determined execution of his ideas; and an uncanny grasp of his enemies' psychology, so that he understood precisely what would make them submit. But the attack also illustrated the limitations of a purely military approach to the war in Sogdiana. Alexander spent weeks securing the surrender of one relatively minor fort, starving and freezing his men in order to do so. Sogdiana was full of fortresses like this. If he had to besiege each one, he would never leave.

As Alexander left the Hissars and moved into the broad, spreading plains and river valleys of eastern Sogdiana, the Macedonian king experimented with a different solution. He divided his forces into fifths, with a trusted commander for each. Working in coordination, they combed through the countryside, destroying those who resisted and accepting those who surrendered. Together, Alexander and his five commanders covered ground more quickly than he could manage on his own. The king ordered them to reconvene at the end of summer at Marakanda for a great hunt and feast. It was a clever plan, well adapted to the challenges of Sogdiana, and a good use of the large army and talented, ambitious officers Alexander had brought with him.

For his commanders, Alexander chose carefully. He did not rely on the men of his father's generation, though they were high ranking and battle hardened, with more years of experience in warfare than he had alive. Instead, he pushed them aside—creating anger and resentment as he did so—to rely on his own friends. He awarded commands to

Ptolemy, the capturer of Bessos; Koinos, the brother-in-law and ac-
cuser of Philotas; Perdikkas, a young bodyguard and rival of Ptolemy;
and his old Persian friend Artabazos (it is telling that the one man of
an older generation whom Alexander trusted here was a Persian). His
final choice fell on Hephaistion, his likely lover and closest friend.

Alexander could scarcely remember a time when he had not known
Hephaistion. They had grown up side by side, and Hephaistion accompanied the young prince to Mieza, where they were tutored for
three years by Aristotle. Beneath snowcapped mountains, in a green
and shady site the Macedonians called the Shrine of the Nymphs,
they learned together. They listened to their tutor's stern, dry lectures
on geography (mostly, as Alexander now knew, wrong) and poetry,
which left them with a lifelong love of Homer. Hephaistion probably
heard Aristotle advise the young future conqueror about the despotic
way he should treat his Persian subjects. Like Alexander, Hephaistion
ignored this advice, and indeed became the king's preferred intermediary to the Persians.

Alexander and Hephaistion developed an intense relationship
when they were very young, perhaps even before the start of Alexander's conquest. It was most plausibly sexual as well as companionate, though the king's ancient biographies never explicitly say so.
Their physical and emotional intimacy is, however, suggested by a
story told in Plutarch. Once, when the king was examining a letter
from his mother, Hephaistion stood close to him and read it over his
shoulder. Because the letter detailed Olympias's complaints against
the Macedonian regent Antipater—expressed with all the clarity and
frankness of a powerful royal woman—Alexander wished to keep its
contents secret. To signal this, without speaking he placed his seal
ring on Hephaistion's lips.

Alexander's relationship with Hephaistion did not correspond to
the Greek pederastic ideal, since the two young men were age-mates.

It is a useful reminder of the lack of fit between the picture of Classical same-sex relationships presented by most ancient writers and Macedonian realities. Nor was it exclusive, at least on Alexander's part. In ancient Macedonia, men were expected to have sexual relationships with women, particularly wives, who could alone bear them legitimate heirs. Alexander had no wife yet, unusually given his age and regal status, but not entirely surprisingly for a man who had spent the past six years continuously on campaign. He would have seen nothing odd about having both a mistress, the half-Persian, half-Greek Barsine, and a Macedonian male partner, Hephaistion—not to mention the entourage of Iranian eunuchs and concubines who now followed him everywhere. In Macedonian society of the fourth century BCE, monogamy was not expected, least of all for a king. Alexander was, however, unusual in the intensity of his relationship with Hephaistion, which seems to have taken precedence over all others.

By the summer of 328 BCE, Alexander was confident enough in his own power and Hephaistion's abilities to give his companion a more prominent military role. His work in Sogdiana was his first major independent command, and it was not exclusively military. Uniquely among his fellow officers, Hephaistion was also given a commission to found cities and establish garrisons, a task that showcased his willingness to engage constructively with Persians.

Along with the king and the other commanders, Hephaistion spent the campaign season fighting his way through the river valleys of Sogdiana. Finally, in the searing heat of the end of summer, he returned to the royal palace of Marakanda. There, in the heavy-walled fortress at the heart of the Zeravshan River valley, he rendezvoused with the king and the other leaders to take stock of their experiences in the region and receive news from elsewhere—little of it good.

The worst news that messengers brought to Alexander and Hephaistion at Marakanda concerned Spitamenes. After wintering with the

Scythians and convincing more of their cavalrymen to join his revolt, Spitamenes returned to the fight. But since Alexander and his commanders were concentrating their efforts on Sogdiana, Spitamenes skirted their forces and took his soldiers south to Bactria. There, with the Macedonians outnumbered and more vulnerable, he could do greater damage.

As Alexander learned at Marakanda, Spitamenes had begun cautiously. He first attacked a fort in the Bactrian region, massacring its garrison and taking its commander prisoner. Then he moved on to Zariaspa, where Alexander had left supplies behind, along with a handful of officers recovering from wounds, some Royal Pages, and a musician. Ravaging the nearby countryside, Spitamenes managed to lure these men out, then feigned retreat. No doubt to Alexander's frustration, the Macedonians fell for this maneuver, though it was strikingly similar to what Spitamenes had done at Marakanda the year before. Also upsetting to the Macedonian king was the outcome: victory for Spitamenes, death or imprisonment for the entire expeditionary force, even the musician. The Sogdian leader was eventually pursued by Alexander's top general in the area, the dependable second-in-command, Krateros. They fought, but he escaped by fleeing to the desert, where the Macedonians could not follow.

The next item of bad news was delivered in person by Artabazos. As he and Alexander both knew, the king's longtime Persian friend had served loyally since the death of Darius. His sons had high-ranking military and diplomatic positions; his daughter was Alexander's mistress. But now he was resigning from his post as governor of Bactria-Sogdiana—due to old age, Artabazos said. It was an enormous blow.

Artabazos was one of the last high-ranking Persian aristocrats to join the Macedonian king's war effort. And given the current scarcity of Persians on Alexander's side, he could not be easily replaced. His resignation was an early sign of the toll that the war in Central

Asia exacted on Alexander's supporters, Macedonian and Persian. It would soon be followed by others, even more ominous.

One messenger with good news did make his way to Alexander in Marakanda. It was Derdas, the ambassador to the far-off Scythians, who returned from his travels with the promise of an alliance. He brought gifts from the Scythians and an offer of marriage between the king's daughter and Alexander. Derdas was also accompanied by a second king, who offered to act as a guide if Alexander wished to extend his empire to the northwest. Given the problems he was having in Central Asia, Alexander politely rejected the opportunity for new nomadic wars. He also turned down the offer of marriage. The Macedonian king was not eager to marry, and he did not need the Scythians enough to make such an alliance worthwhile. He did, however, hold on to the idea of using marriage as a diplomatic mechanism. Whatever his personal feelings may have been, Alexander was coming to recognize the strategic usefulness of marriage alliances— particularly since his brutal tactics the previous year had failed.

When all Alexander's commanders had reassembled at Marakanda, they prepared to celebrate their efforts and relax with an enormous hunt. For the hunt, they traveled away from the city to a place called Bazaira, a royal hunting preserve like the one where Pharnoukhes and his men had been ambushed. There they found a lush, wooded, garden-like site, stocked with the exotic big game the Persian kings loved to hunt: lions, boars, wild bulls. Walled off from poachers, it had lain undisturbed for four generations. Alexander and his men wandered through place that was teeming with animals and extraordinarily lovely—the Persian word for it, *paradeisos*, is the origin of the English *paradise.*

Alexander adored hunting. Along with the pages at his father's court, he had grown up accompanying Philip and his followers to hunts in Macedonia. The young prince had cultivated the skill, bravery, and daring that were essential to big game hunting, and the competitive, but nonetheless strongly hierarchical, behavior that went with it. Like other members of the Macedonian elite, Alexander was not allowed to recline at dinner until he had killed a boar without a net.

Now Alexander was king, and in the hunt as elsewhere, he gave place to no man. As he moved through the woods at Bazaira, he searched for lions—the largest, most dangerous, and most impressive game. Assyrian and then Persian kings had hunted lions for centuries, stocking their *paradeisoi* with the exotic animals even in places like Central Asia, where they were far from native species. One of Alexander's bodyguards had killed a lion single-handedly at a paradeisos in Syria. He had been badly injured in the process, but was nonetheless famous for his deed. At Bazaira, Alexander could hope to equal or outdo his friend.

Suddenly Alexander caught sight of an unusually large lion heading straight toward him. His bodyguard, nearby and trying to protect the king, started to aim his spear at the dangerous animal. But Alexander angrily pushed him aside, shouting that he was just as capable as his bodyguard of killing a lion single-handed. To everyone's terror, he insisted on facing the beast alone.

Alexander raised his hunting spear. With practiced aim, he threw his weapon, killing the animal in one stroke. The Macedonians were relieved, but still furious. They did not understand Alexander's compulsion to excel, or his constant effort to assert his dominance over his Companions. From their perspective, the king's behavior was simply reckless and unnecessary. And in putting their leader's life on the line, it endangered everyone. The Macedonians resolved at Bazaira that the king must be more careful in the future. They decreed that Alexander was no longer allowed to hunt on foot and that he must be accompanied at all times by a select group of officers and friends. They were trying to rein him in, to make the king act with the maturity and consideration appropriate to his role. They were trying to bottle lightning. It didn't entirely work.

The hunt at Bazaira made clear the gulf between Alexander and his followers. With his domineering, unstoppable will, he fought their efforts to control him—even when they were just trying to keep him safe. After the hunt, he agreed in theory to accept new limits. But they applied only to hunting, while Alexander's reckless impulsivity permeated all his actions. Only slowly and imperfectly would he learn self-control.

In the tense aftermath of the hunt, Alexander and his men returned to Marakanda. There, in the Persian royal citadel with its enormous stores of food, the king gave a feast. A messenger had recently come to Alexander, bringing Hellenic fruit from the sea to Central Asia. Thrilled by the taste of home, Alexander invited all his friends to share the messenger's bounty with him. He gave a special invitation to Kleitos, cocommander of the Macedonian cavalry with Hephaistion. Alexander intended to be generous to the older man, who had once saved his life in battle by chopping off the arm of a Persian about to attack the impetuous young king. Instead, the invitation would prove Kleitos's undoing.

As was typical for Alexander, the feast at Marakanda was an extravagant affair. Along with the Greek fruit, it featured meat: remnants of the hunt, perhaps, or the bounty of the nomadic pastoralists nearby, with their flocks of cattle, sheep, and goats. There was bread made from the stores of the huge granaries of Marakanda and likely millet, a popular, long-lasting grain in that region. Above all, there was wine.

At Marakanda, the Macedonians prepared their wine with a careful and ornate ritual. First they likely mixed it with water in deep, wide-mouthed bowls, since Hellenic custom decreed that only centaurs and barbarians drank their wine neat. Then they ladled the mixture into pitchers or wide, shallow cups, pouring it through strainers to catch the lees. Sometimes they passed a cup from drinker to drinker, with the shared vessel a symbol of their communal bonding experience. On other occasions, they drank individually from small two-handled cups that were refilled constantly as the night wore on. Despite the presence of food, drinking was the centerpiece of all Macedonian feasts. The un-looted Royal Tomb II at Vergina, likely contemporary with Alexander, contained nineteen silver drinking vessels—and no plates.

The wine-fueled feasts given by Alexander brought the king and his officers together in an atmosphere that was convivial, but also, frequently, combative. Poets recited, philosophers debated, musicians sang and played. Men boasted, flattered, and fought with one another. Precisely because feasts were so important to the Macedonians, they engendered high-profile, high-stakes fights. And since Alexander had both free-flowing alcohol and weapons at his feasts, these fights could be dangerous for both the king and his guests.

The problems at Alexander's feast at Marakanda began with Kleitos. The cavalry commander was a blunt, outspoken, hard-drinking man of Alexander's father's generation. Now in his late forties or early fifties, Kleitos was battle hardened but still vigorous, and he had just been named the successor of Artabazos as governor of Bactria-Sogdiana. Given that Alexander had recently bypassed Kleitos and his contemporaries in handing out commands in Central Asia, the king perhaps intended this promotion as a concession to the older generation. Kleitos, however, was not grateful.

At the banquet, it is uncertain just what provocation set Kleitos off. One story has him offended by a poet, who was reciting satirical verses about the Macedonians' recent battle losses (Alexander only laughed). In another, Kleitos was angered by the king himself, who was boasting about his accomplishments and denigrating those of his father. Whatever the initial trigger, Kleitos was clearly nursing a host of grudges. In the intense atmosphere of the feast, and under the influence of alcohol, they all came pouring out.

Kleitos began quietly. In response to Alexander's joking or boasting, he recited a passage from the Greek playwright Euripides, whose combination of clear, almost colloquial language and subversive antiauthoritarian content made him the perfect poet for the occasion. "Alas, how terribly Greece is governed," quoted Kleitos, softly enough that only his nearby companions could hear. They all likely recognized the passage, since memorizing poetry was a central part of elite education in the fourth century, and Euripides the most popular of the three great tragedians. But Kleitos went on to finish the quotation nonetheless. Adopting the words of Peleus, father of Achilles, he lamented that the Greeks inscribed their trophies with the names of kings alone, giving their rulers the glory won by others' blood.

Euripides's relevance to the current situation was obvious, as the expressions of Kleitos and his nearby companions made clear. Alexander, seated at a distance, did not hear Kleitos's words, but he could tell from his companions' reaction that something was up. When he asked what his new governor had said, he was met only by prudent silence.

Kleitos grew bolder. He raised his voice and began praising Philip, describing his conquests and ranking his military successes above the war they were engaged in now—a sure way to infuriate Alexander. Then Kleitos noted bitterly that the younger generation had gotten all the plum commands and spoils. But he, who had saved Alexander's life, was left with a thankless province.

Kleitos kept going, excoriating Alexander for adopting Persian customs and favoring barbarians. How wrong it was, said Kleitos, that high-born native Macedonians were forced to beg Persians—*Persians!*—for an audience with the king. He taunted Alexander by saying that the king should invite to his feasts only barbarians and slaves who would prostrate themselves before him, not free-born men accustomed to speak their minds. Like Dimnos and Philotas, Kleitos was furious about Alexander's embrace of Persian practices and his integration of Iranian aristocrats into his entourage. His outspoken protest at the banquet shows how the Macedonians, far from acclimating to the king's new ways, had only intensified their opposition.

It was all painful, but Kleitos's next comment particularly stung. He ridiculed the oracle of Zeus-Amun, claiming to be more truthful than Alexander's "father" had ever been.

Four years earlier during his invasion of Egypt, the king had trekked out to the sanctuary of Zeus-Amun in the Siwa Oasis. He sought out the oracle there, one of the three most important in the Greek world. Far to the west in the Libyan desert, in a sanctuary fringed by date palms, Alexander entered the temple alone. He never revealed exactly what he heard there, but he was likely greeted as son of Amun, as was typical for an Egyptian pharaoh. The king took the greeting as a prophecy: a legitimation of his extraordinary status, a promise of future greatness. By the time of the Marakanda banquet, the tale was clearly familiar enough for Kleitos to cite it—and resent it. Claims to quasidivine status, like the king's part-Persian dress and his new Iranian bodyguards, were exactly the kind of behaviors guaranteed to exasperate a man like Kleitos, because they made clear how much Alexander had changed.

Finally Alexander, drunk and angry, could not contain himself. He leaped up from his couch, looking for a weapon. His dagger was gone—one of his bodyguards had wisely hidden it when Kleitos's rant began. The king seized a spear from a nearby guard and lunged toward his old friend. Before he could strike, two bodyguards grabbed him by the waist, while two others took the spear from the king. In the heat of the moment, as the enormous pressures and frustrations of the campaign reached their boiling point, Alexander panicked. He cried out that he was like Darius, betrayed by those closest to him. He shouted for the trumpeter to sound the alarm, calling his elite troops from their quarters. No one obeyed.

Kleitos was hustled out of the symposium, but managed to return, still shouting. Alexander broke free of his friends, grabbed a sarissa from one of his guards, and struck Kleitos. Like the lion at Bazaira, one thrust was all it took. The man who had once saved his life was dead.

Alexander looked at Kleitos's bloody, lifeless body. He had killed many men in battle, but this murder at a feast was different, and far worse. The king had lost control and brutally murdered a man to whom he was forever indebted. He desired greatness, supremacy, perhaps even divinity. But his desires had led him not to new heights, but to the abyss. For the first and seemingly only time in his short life, Alexander contemplated suicide.

Quick-thinking guards prevented Alexander's suicide. They carried him to his tent, wailing and sobbing. They did their best to comfort him as he tore at his cheeks with his fingernails, a characteristic Hellenic gesture of mourning. Refusing food and drink for three days, Alexander lamented Kleitos's death and cried for his officer's sister, the king's wet nurse Lanike, who had received so cruel a return for her loving care. Panicking at Alexander's suicidal behavior, the Macedonians held a formal assembly and voted that Kleitos's death was justified. At the time, their legal procedures did little to assuage the king's feeling of guilt.

Very slowly, Alexander's grief dissipated. He was persuaded by his friends to eat. He was visited in his tent by Aristotle's nephew, Kallisthenes, the official historian of Alexander's conquests. An odd, ambivalent man, Kallisthenes alternated between bouts of poorly written sycophancy in his job as historian and an unbending anti-authoritarianism in his role as Hellenic aristocrat, philosopher, and tutor to the Royal Pages. In the days after Kleitos's death, though, when Alexander was most vulnerable, Kallisthenes was kind and gentle to him. He comforted the king by speaking softly of ordinary things, skirting carefully around the topic of the murder and Alexander's role in it.

Kallisthenes's rival, the philosopher Anaxarkhos, took a different tack. He forthrightly argued that Alexander was king, kings came from Zeus, and that "whatever is ratified by Zeus is done justly." In essence, Anaxarkhos presented Alexander with the doctrine of the divine right of kings, a millennium before its official debut.

The Macedonian king likely appreciated Anaxarkhos's argument, which resonated with his own claims to authority. Still, in the matter of Kleitos's death at least, his actions suggest that he did not entirely believe it. Alexander ordered a formal funeral ceremony for Kleitos, though the Macedonians had sought to refuse him burial. He also made sacrifices in expiation of his crime to Dionysos, god of wine. Deeply religious, Alexander made sense of his life through his belief in the gods. He took responsibility for his unforgivable act at Marakanda, but at the same time felt it occurred because he had offended Dionysos, bringing down on his head the horrifying drunken vengeance he had dealt out and experienced. Making sacrifices—burning incense, slaughtering and roasting cattle, pouring out that selfsame dangerous wine harmlessly on the altar—offered Alexander a way to acknowledge and accept his guilt, but also to make amends. And by carrying out the ceremony in public, with his friends and soldiers participating, he helped to restore the sense of community that his actions had so painfully fractured.

Alexander spent ten days at Marakanda, making restitution as best he could for the death of Kleitos. Then, as the fierce late-summer heat gave way to cooler fall weather, Alexander left the ill-fated royal capital behind and headed east. He was on his way back to the Hissar Mountains, where rebellion still threatened the all-important main road through Central Asia. Marching out of Marakanda with his army, Alexander sought to leave the panic and despair he had felt there behind him.

For the past year, as his campaign in Sogdiana turned into a quagmire, Alexander had responded brutally: toward his rival, Bessos; toward the Scythians and Sogdians who opposed him; and now, most horribly, to his old friend. In each case, Alexander's anger and impulsivity had proved disastrous. Far from terrifying those he threatened into submission, he had intensified their opposition—both his Central Asian subjects' and his own officers'. After the murder of Kleitos and his own near suicide, Alexander was finally ready to consider less violent alternatives. It was time for something new.

NINE

Three Banquets and a Conspiracy

Uzbekistan and Afghanistan
Spring–Summer 327 BCE

IN THE EARLY SPRING OF 327 BCE, Alexander attended another fateful banquet. This one, however, ended more happily than the feast at Marakanda. At it, he fell in love.

The banquet was hosted by Sisimithres, the keeper of the Iron Gates. It was intended to solidify good relations between the Macedonians and their Central Asian allies. In this, it succeeded beyond everyone's expectations.

By this time, Alexander was familiar with Persian-style banquets like that of Sisimithres. As the guest at such a feast, he would need to bathe beforehand, then put on his most beautiful clothes—in the Macedonian king's case, his best version of a distinctive mixed dress, with a long-sleeved Persian tunic underneath, an expensively dyed purple Macedonian cloak over it, and a purple-and-white diadem in his hair. Then Alexander presented himself, with a select number of his followers in their own purple-bordered Persian robes, at Sisimithres's abode. As the most important guest, the king was placed at the center of the feast with his host, while their assorted followers settled into circles around them, with the top aristocrats close by and the periphery filled with lower-ranking military officers and minor civil servants.

As with all Persian feasts, this one likely centered on meat. Alexander had mutton, goat, beef, and poultry to choose from, and perhaps more exotic options: game, for example, or an Iranian favorite, ostrich. He ate the meat stewed in deep, footed bowls, with bread off large, flat trays. The king was also offered cheese, nuts, seeds, and fruit, as well as large quantities of wine. Alexander drank it unmixed from small handleless bowls or thin, curving vessels shaped like a bull's horn and very difficult to put down; they must have encouraged draining the cup in one long, inebriating draught.

For entertainment, Alexander and his followers enjoyed a departure from both Iranian and Macedonian custom. Instead of a predominantly male affair, with perhaps some concubines to sing or flute-playing courtesans, the banquet featured the daughters of Central Asian aristocrats. Sisimithres had been given charge of many of them at his mountain fortress, and they had fallen into the hands of Alexander when Sisimithres had surrendered earlier. Now they danced for the Macedonian king. To his eyes, they were exotic, with their long, wide-sleeved Persian robes, their hair pulled into a braid at the back, their fine leather hoods and squirrel-skin capes, their elegantly decorated boots. Their dances, too, were likely different from the circling ones popular in Hellenic lands. And their mere presence was unprecedented and thrilling for the Macedonians, who had spent the past seven years in a mostly male, military society and were unaccustomed to seeing women who were their social equals anywhere, least of all at a banquet.

One young woman in particular caught Alexander's eye, and he inquired as to her identity. Her name was Roxane, a Persian word whose root means "shining," "radiant," or "brilliant." She seemed to him more beautiful than any woman in the Persian Empire, the wife of Darius III perhaps excepted. Roxane's lineage, too, was attractive. She was the daughter of the Bactrian noble Oxyarthes, the associate of Bessos and Spitamenes who had gone over to Alexander. Roxane's father was the man to whom the Macedonian king owed the surrender of the Iron Gates, the choke point on the road to Marakanda. Roxane belonged to just the kind of family the Macedonian king needed to ally himself with if he wanted to establish a lasting peace in Central Asia. She was young and beautiful. Alexander himself was nearing thirty, and more aware, after the disastrous banquet at Marakanda, of his own mortality and fallibility than he had been before. Impulsively, he proposed marriage.

Alexander may have been attracted by Roxane's youthful beauty, but he proposed marriage for reasons that had little to do with love. Long before he met Roxane, Alexander had all the eunuchs, concubines, and mistresses he needed, as well as Hephaistion for intellectual and likely erotic companionship. Now he wanted something different: a more solid, official relationship through which he would for the first time create his own family. Roxane's father, Oxyarthes, had already proved his utility to Alexander, and she was of childbearing age. She was a pragmatic choice. Her beauty made her an alluring one as well.

Roxane was likely less impressed. Alexander's clean-shaven face, wavy, light-brown hair, slight build, and small stature were nothing like the ideal in her culture. So, too, he treated his close friends like equals rather than remaining in splendid isolation, as a Great King ought. Roxane was a Central Asian aristocrat, and as such, she had not been brought up to expect that she would marry for love. But a man like Alexander was not the sort of husband she had anticipated. He was probably twice her age, and they had no common language. He had conquered her people. Now he was proclaiming, with the munificence of a conqueror, that he sought her hand in marriage. As Roxane was well aware, he could simply have added her to his entourage of mistresses and concubines. Marriage was better, offering a more powerful, institutionalized position for her as queen. But a union with Alexander was in no way her choice.

Alexander and Oxyarthes, however, left nothing for Roxane to do. They agreed to the marriage, with some romantic fervor on the Macedonian king's part, and a clear sense of its practical value for both. Impatient of delay, Alexander pushed for a wedding on the spot, though doing so likely violated both Macedonian and Iranian norms.

The king called for a loaf of bread from the kitchen. Then, in accordance with Macedonian custom, he cut it in half with his sword. Both parties nibbled the bread ceremoniously. They were participating in a homely tradition, one that recalled the austere, impoverished origins of early Macedonia—as well as the country's militarism—in the midst of a lavish Persian feast. With that, Alexander and Roxane were officially married. Oxyarthes was ecstatic. Of the bride's feelings, we have no record.

Roxane was not the only individual whose feelings were not consulted at this spur-of-the-moment marriage. Hephaistion, too, had every right to feel surprised. He must have expected, of course, that Alexander would someday marry. Given the pressure to produce an heir, no Macedonian king could afford to do otherwise. But Alexander had been successfully avoiding that pressure since he came to the throne at twenty—the age when most royal Macedonian males conducted a matrimonial alliance, at least for the first time. Hephaistion had watched his friend reject the eligible daughters of the top Macedonian aristocrats. He had also seen Alexander turn down Darius's offer of marriage with *his* daughter, though Hephaistion must have suspected, as the Persian princesses were settled at Susa with Greek tutors, that his friend might eventually have an alliance with one of them in mind.

But marriage with one of Darius's daughters was a far-off prospect. In the meantime, Alexander and Hephaistion remained close. They hunted, drank, and fought together, and Hephaistion had no wife, or even a recorded mistress, to distract him from the king. Over the past year, Alexander had given him a series of increasingly high-profile assignments: army commands, city-foundations, the organization of the all-important supply chain over the past winter. With roles like these, Hephaistion could feel confident in the king's favor. But marriage would change things between them, inevitably.

Far more threatened by the marriage than Hephaistion was the king's mistress, Barsine. She was still part of Alexander's entourage, and likely pregnant at just this time. In 327 BCE, she would give birth to a son, Herakles. Named for the mythological founder of the Macedonian royal house, he was the only child of his own blood that Alexander would ever know.

At the time of the marriage to Roxane, Barsine remained with Alexander. So did her siblings, receiving honors and appointments from the openhanded king. But her father, Artabazos, had recently left Alexander's service, depriving Barsine of her most powerful advocate. Now, with Roxane as queen, Barsine's own status was diminished. She lost her role as the king's closest woman companion, and the marriage called into question just how significant that role had ever been. Barsine had been passed over for a young woman from the minor Iranian nobility, while she herself was the descendent of Great Kings. The marriage must have added considerably to the difficulties of a Central Asian pregnancy, along with unfamiliar food, complex terrain, and an army almost constantly on the move. Given the circumstances, Barsine had enough to do to ensure that the child she was carrying survived.

Along with Hephaistion and Barsine, all the high-ranking Macedonian officers opposed the marriage. Ancient writers describe Alexander's high-flown speeches to them, in which he defended his choice of wife by invoking his mythological ancestor Achilles (while failing to note that the son of Peleus did not in fact marry his captive, Briseis, but simply made her his mistress). Despite the Homeric precedent, the Macedonians remained resentful. They could not approve of so impulsive a marriage, particularly with an Iranian rather than a proper Macedonian girl. They said nothing, however, because after the murder of Kleitos, they all feared to provoke the king.

Alexander was perceptive, with an ability to predict others' responses that verged on the uncanny. In proposing to Roxane, he must have known how those closest to him would react, how resentful and upset they would be. And yet he went ahead with the marriage.

The years of campaigning in Central Asia had taken a toll on Alexander, both physical and psychological. His body had suffered particularly from his wound at Cyropolis, and he had not recovered as quickly as he had from earlier injuries, but remained frail and nearly inaudible for months. Less visible, but just as pernicious, was the damage to his spirit. Alexander's army had endured a number of humiliating defeats at the hands of the rebel leader Spitamenes. His soldiers had been forced to fight a guerrilla war—village by village, river valley by river valley—for which they were ill trained and ill equipped. They had won most of the battles, technically, but their enemies had often managed to escape to the desert, returning with reinforcements to fight again.

As dangerous as the enemy had been the geography and climate of Central Asia, always catching Alexander off guard. His soldiers had suffered from thirst in deserts, from frostbite in the mountains. Recently, they had been caught in a terrifying lightning-cum-hailstorm, where in the absence of shelter large numbers of troops, camp followers, and servants died. For a man who prided himself on invincibility in battle, these were horrendous defeats. And as Kleitos's tirade proved, Alexander's soldiers blamed him.

With marriage to Roxane, Alexander was trying something different. For him, the timing was opportune. He had recently received at his camp an unexpected gift: the severed head of Spitamenes. It was the third such head the Macedonian king had received in the past three years, following that of Parmenion and the rebellious governor Satibarzanes. It came from the hands of Spitamenes's exasperated Scythian followers—or, according to some writers, from his even more exasperated Iranian wife, tired of being dragged from one desert to another in the course of the protracted guerrilla war. Whatever the head's source, Alexander was relieved to get it. With Spitamenes gone, Alexander could hope that the most effective opposition to his rule in Central Asia had been terminated.

To keep the Sogdians in check, the king also took Spitamenes's daughter, Apama, as a hostage. Together with Barsine and, now, Roxane, Apama was among the highest-ranking Iranian women traveling with Alexander's army. An unwilling guarantor of her countrymen's good behavior, Apama did not receive a high-profile position at this time. But her role as a hostage was yet one more demonstration of Alexander's power over his subjects' lives.

With Apama and Roxane, Alexander was trying out two different tactics simultaneously. His deployment of Apama as a hostage was familiar; he had treated other powerful Iranian women—for instance, the Persian princesses—the same way. His marriage to Roxane, however, was something new. Through a marriage alliance, he could win over the local leaders whose support was key to success in Central Asia. More than his mixed dress, his Iranian bodyguards, or the young men from throughout the empire whom he was training for his army, a wedding would most thoroughly convince the Persians of his good faith in pursuing a policy of reconciliation. Alexander knew from experience how effective a mixed marriage like this one could be in uniting disparate peoples. After all, his own parents had done the same.

Three decades earlier, Alexander's parents, Philip and Olympias, had met on the remote Greek island of Samothrace. Philip was likely a teenager, the brother of the current Macedonian ruler. Olympias was even younger and the niece of the ruler of Epirus, a kingdom nearby. Like many powerful aristocrats from the fringes of the Greek world, they sought initiation in the mysteries of Samothrace: a secretive cult whose initiation ceremonies—with nighttime ritual processions, chanting, and torchlit dances—promised security to sailors and life after death.

Young and impressionable, Philip and Olympias became engaged during this intense religious experience. Given the utility of the relationship for both parties, they married soon after, likely once Philip became king. From that time onward, their two kingdoms worked in concert. Macedonia and Epirus collaborated against the militarily powerful Illyrians, with whom they both shared a border. The two kingdoms also reaffirmed their ties through further marriages. Though Philip and Olympias had their personal differences, their marriage was a political success—and just the kind of alliance Alexander needed.

However impromptu, Alexander's marriage banquet was a momentous affair. Far from the centers of power of either Macedonia or Persia, the king gave his clearest indication yet of how he meant to turn his ephemeral victories into a lasting empire. In his mind, it would not be a kingdom of, by, and for the Macedonians, with the Persians as a permanent underclass. Instead, Alexander sought to create a new ruling elite of individuals from both civilizations, and eventually, following intermarriage, their bicultural children. In marrying Roxane, the Macedonian king entered a new phase in his conquest of Persia, one that signaled a decisive turn toward fusion and power sharing. It was a key move that allowed him to make peace in Central Asia. It was also wildly unpopular with the Macedonians, to an extent that even Alexander had not anticipated.

The Macedonians' frustrations with Alexander came to a head at the second major banquet of 327 BCE. By this time, the king and his court had moved south. Eager to leave Sogdiana behind—now that Spitamenes's death and Alexander's marriage offered at least a hope of stability for the region—the army headed for Bactria. Once there, Alexander had a change to make, one that was key to his increasingly elaborate court ceremonial. It concerned the Persian greeting ritual that the Greeks called *proskynesis.*

In the status-conscious society of ancient Persia, even a simple greeting was heavily freighted. It signaled one's place in the social hierarchy for all to see. Two people of equal status greeted each other by kissing on the lips, which for the Persians was not a romantic gesture but one that suggested a peer-to-peer relationship. By contrast, one saluted a person of slightly higher rank by kissing on the cheek: a less intimate but still amicable and associative greeting. And if one encountered an individual of *much* higher status—an aristocratic woman, say, or someone of royal blood—one performed proskynesis. Exactly what this entailed is debated, but the most likely guess is that one made a bow, put one's right hand to the lips, and blew a kiss: an appropriate gesture given that the Greek word *proskynesis* means, literally, "sending a kiss forward."

As with other cultures with a tradition of bowing, Persians could vary the gesture to reflect the status of the two individuals involved. Those self-confident in their own rank might make just a slight bow, while those with less authority might kneel or even prostrate themselves on the floor. Proskynesis was thus a social gesture capable of near-infinite calibration, well suited to Persia and especially to the court of the Great King. As Alexander adopted Persian dress, Persian customs, and, now, an Iranian wife, it is small wonder that he also found proskynesis appealing. Through it, he could show himself the true successor of the Persian king.

Proskynesis was not reserved for the Great King, but unlike other Persians, he could not be greeted otherwise. If he were not saluted with a proper degree of humility by his subjects, he was hardly, in Persian minds, a king at all. Alexander had consequently been greeted with proskynesis almost as soon as he arrived in Persian territory. As battle followed battle and he received the submission of more Persian aristocrats, Alexander found himself increasingly surrounded by people who performed proskynesis to him—and who must have viewed the free and easy manners of the Macedonians toward their king with distaste, if not outright alarm.

Alexander had sought to integrate high-ranking Persians into his court, adding Darius's brother to his Companions and making Barsine's family military and diplomatic leaders. But it was difficult to bridge the cultural barriers between Macedonian and Persian aristocrats when something as basic as a greeting divided them. Alexander decided to put everyone on equal footing with regard to proskynesis. Since there was no way he could convince the Persians to abandon the gesture—it was tantamount to calling his legitimacy as a king into question—he needed to persuade the Macedonians to adopt it. To do so, a convivial setting and a certain degree of peer pressure would be necessary. Alexander determined to make his attempt at a banquet.

To this banquet, Alexander invited both his Persian and his Macedonian companions. As host, he offered food first, and then, when hunger had been satisfied, he and his men settled down to the serious matter of drinking. They did so according to Greek custom, with a shared cup of wine passed from hand to hand around the room. Appropriately for Alexander, they used a golden vessel, perhaps one encrusted with jewels, as was popular in the court of the king. As it circulated around the banquet, it created a sense of inebriation, community, and good fellowship, functioning as a kind of "loving-cup."

Alexander's closest companions led the way. Beginning most likely with Hephaistion, each one performed proskynesis, drank from the cup, then came up to receive a kiss from Alexander in return. The kiss from the king was a departure from Persian custom, perhaps intended to signal the close relationship of Alexander with his companions despite the subordination that proskynesis implied. For some at the banquet, however, a kiss from the king was not enough. The older men in particular were resentful. They saw the new ritual as yet one more instance of Alexander's hateful Persianizing. They also disliked his attempt to replace the more equitable relationship he had had with his followers with one that exalted him at their expense. And proskynesis in particular brought up powerful negative feelings, deeply embedded in Hellenic cultural memory.

For two hundred years, Greek and Macedonian ambassadors to Persia had been expected to perform proskynesis to the Great King. A few had managed to evade the ritual—dropping a ring on the floor, for example, to give themselves a pragmatic reason to bow down, or asking for a religious exemption on the grounds that in Hellenic lands, one made proskynesis only to the gods. In making a religious excuse, the ambassadors were not being entirely truthful. As they were well aware, Persian proskynesis in no way implied the divinity of the Great King.

In refusing to perform proskynesis, the ambassadors used religion to express a deep-seated cultural abhorrence. As people who prided themselves on their freedom and autonomy, they hated the appearance of subordination to the Great King. Perhaps appropriately given the tendentious nature of their refusal, however, the ambassadors were nonetheless often forced to comply. They wanted Persian allies, and Persian gold, too much to refuse.

Alexander's introduction of proskynesis brought back these angry memories of subordination to Persia. His older companions were all the more frustrated in that they, who had finally succeeded in conquering the Persians, were now being pressured to adopt the customs of those they had conquered. They felt entrapped: invited to a banquet, then forced to humiliate themselves before their host. They cared little for the Persians and still less for their feelings, however much Alexander himself might wish to accommodate them. The king's older companions did nothing, however, until the Greek historian Kallisthenes received the golden cup.

Kallisthenes, nephew of Aristotle and official historian of Alexander's campaigns, was a complex and contradictory man. Thoughtful and sensitive when he comforted the king after the murder of Kleitos, Kallisthenes could also be stiff necked, abrasive, and decidedly pompous—particularly in contrast with the more pliant philosopher Anaxarkhos. He also had a complicated relationship with monarchical authority. Kallisthenes had reported, and likely embellished, the story of Alexander's visit to the oracle of Siwa, where the king had been greeted as son of Amun. He had also described a convenient ebbing of the tide along the Cilician coast as a miraculous event, where the very waves performed proskynesis to the king as he led his troops beside them.

But it was one thing for the Mediterranean Sea to perform proskynesis, in a sycophantic literary conceit, and quite another for a respectable Greek intellectual like Kallisthenes himself to do so. And so when the golden cup came to him, Kallisthenes omitted the gesture, drank, and went up to receive his kiss from Alexander.

In some versions of the story, there was a debate in which Kallisthenes made a speech, exhorting Alexander to be honored as a man, not worshipped like a god. It was an excellent rhetorical production, much quoted by later philosophers who made Kallisthenes a model for their own opposition to authoritarian monarchy and ruler cult. It was also likely apocryphal, as was the similarly grandiloquent speech attributed to Anaxarkhos, and arguing the other way.

More plausible is another story told about the episode, which left out the speeches, described the omission of proskynesis, and suggested that Kallisthenes expected his behavior to go unobserved by Alexander. According to this account, the historian almost pulled it off. The king was occupied talking to Hephaistion and did not notice, but a busybody pointed out Kallisthenes's lack of cooperation. When Alexander withheld his own greeting in return, Kallisthenes's response was the verbal equivalent of a sullen shrug: "I will depart the poorer by a kiss."

Kallisthenes's remark was meant to sting, and it was indeed resented by Alexander, as later events would show. But on its own, it was not likely to have scotched the king's attempt to introduce proskynesis, despite the claims of subsequent generations of antiauthoritarian philosophers eager to make Kallisthenes a hero. More damning, though less intentional, was the behavior of Alexander's bodyguard Leonnatos.

A boyhood friend of the king's and distant member of the royal house, Leonnatos was one of Alexander's most trusted and capable military officers. He had played a key role in the trial of Philotas, and had recently done his best to intervene during the fight with Kleitos, taking away the king's spear as other bodyguards grabbed Alexander by the waist. Tall and good-looking, with a taste for shiny weapons and Persian luxury, Leonnatos was a paradigmatic Macedonian aristocrat. At the banquet, Leonnatos had likely been one of the first to perform proskynesis. But he is also recorded as bursting out in laughter at the obsequious manner in which one of the Persians executed the gesture. Alexander was furious, and for a time Leonnatos was out of his favor. The king realized from his bodyguard's instinctive reaction, though, how fundamentally alien proskynesis was to the Macedonians. Alexander read the room, abandoned his effort, and eventually forgave Leonnatos. His resentment of Kallisthenes, by contrast, lingered.

Alexander's differing responses to his two friends reveal as much about his own character and aspirations as their actions. Leonnatos's spontaneous laughter was something the Macedonian king could understand; he himself often acted impulsively, and, equally frequently, regretted it later on. Kallisthenes's premeditated action, and the bitter remark that followed it, were harder for Alexander to take. Even more galling was the historian's subsequent behavior, as he gloried in his defiance and attracted young men "as though he were the sole free man among so many thousands." For the increasingly authoritarian Alexander, Kallisthenes's rebelliousness on the matter of proskynesis was a turning point. It transformed the historian from an occasional pompous annoyance into a direct threat.

Alexander soon had an opportunity to act on the threat posed by Kallisthenes. As was typical for the supremely resourceful king, he made the most of what chance had thrown his way, with severe long-term repercussions for Kallisthenes himself, as well as for Alexander's reputation among philosophers. The king's opportunity arrived in the autumn of 327 BCE, with the episode known as the conspiracy of the Royal Pages.

The Royal Pages were the teenage sons of powerful Macedonian aristocrats. Summoned to court to complete their education, they received military training and gave personal service to the king. Theirs was an honorable but not entirely voluntary post. Trained to constitute the king's elite officer corps, they also ensured their fathers' obedience to the ruling power.

In their day-to-day duties, the Royal Pages combined extraordinary intimacy with the king and profound subordination to him. Like servants, they held his horse as he mounted—in the absence of stirrups, a challenging endeavor—accompanied him in the hunt, brought the lovers he summoned to his tent, and guarded him as he slept. If they offended the king, they could be whipped by him: a painful and servile punishment, unusual for freeborn men and especially aristocrats like themselves.

Given their closeness to the king, as well as their age—fifteen to eighteen, what Greeks considered the acme of attractiveness—it is not surprising that the pages sometimes served the king's erotic needs as well. At least two Royal Pages were recorded as lovers of Philip II, though given the power dynamic involved, to call them "lovers" is problematic: it implies that the relationships were consensual. One of the two, Pausanias, was also Philip's assassin. Alexander had no known lovers among the pages, but like his father, he made enemies. The foremost among them was a youth named Hermolaos.

Hermolaos was the son of a well-born Macedonian, though not an especially prominent one. He had likely journeyed to Alexander's mobile court in 331 BCE, when a group of fifty new pages met the king at Babylon. Hermolaos had spent the impressionable years of his late teens accompanying the king on his chaotic, unnerving, and physically demanding campaign through Central Asia, fighting a very different war than either he or Alexander had envisioned. Between battles and ambushes, Hermolaos was tutored by Kallisthenes, whose antiauthoritarian streak and critiques of the king resonated with, if they did not inspire, the page's own.

Four years after his arrival at Alexander's court, Hermolaos was nearing what should have been the end of his term of service. But no new pages had arrived to replace Hermolaos and his companions. Instead of graduating to become junior officers, as was normally the case, they were kept on in their subordinate roles as pages. In a militaristic and hierarchical society like that of Macedonia, their period of prolonged adolescence was not a pleasure. Instead, it probably felt like punishment.

Hermolaos and Alexander ran afoul of one another when they were hunting together in the woods near the royal capital of Bactra. After Alexander's encounter with the lion at Bazaira the year before, the king was closely accompanied by bodyguards and companions during such hunts. All were on high alert: they could not allow the king to be killed or severely injured, however recklessly he himself might wish to behave. As Alexander strode through the woods, with Hermolaos attentively nearby, a boar appeared. As the beast charged right at the king, Hermolaos threw a spear and killed it. In accordance with the army's wishes, he had safeguarded Alexander. He had also achieved something for himself. As required by Macedonian custom, he had killed a boar without a net, and could now recline like a man at dinner. For a youth forced to prolong his service as a page beyond the normal time, this achievement was no small matter. Unfortunately, Hermolaos had also infuriated the king.

As with his bodyguard at Bazaira, Alexander could not bear to be preempted in the hunt. But whereas the year before the king had shouted at his friend and succeeded in killing the lion for himself, Hermolaos left nothing for Alexander to do. The king, enraged, took his horse away and subjected Hermolaos to a public whipping. Keenly sensitive to dishonor, the page began plotting to assassinate the king.

Hermolaos began his plot by confiding in his lover, an age-mate and fellow page. He also carefully and secretively recruited other pages, at least four and perhaps as many as seven.

Like Hermolaos, the other conspirators were all the sons of moderately prominent men: commanders of infantry or cavalry squadrons, conveyors of recruits from Macedonia, a former governor of Syria. Their fathers, who had probably begun their careers under Philip II, were of an age to appreciate the divergence between the former king's reign— with its economic success, military victories, and down-to-earth, accessible monarch—and that of his son. The fathers were also precisely the generation that had begun to be passed over. As the best military commands went not to them but to men like Hephaistion and Ptolemy, Alexander's trusted friends among his own generation, the fathers had strong grievances. They passed their grievances on, like an inheritance, to their sons.

While the fathers continued in the service of the king, the sons entered eagerly into a conspiracy against him. They were adolescents, coming of age in the competitive hothouse atmosphere of Alexander's campaign, where risk taking and the courting of danger were encouraged if not mandatory. Now their daring had a new focus. As they were all well aware, the assassination of the king was a serious undertaking, and they faced certain death if the plot was discovered. Nonetheless, they volunteered readily. Then they waited for an opportunity to act.

The conspirators agreed that they would carry out their plans against Alexander in a month's time, when they were all assigned to guard him at night. In this way, they could make use of their privileged access to the king's person. They would attack when Alexander was asleep and could not easily fend them off or call others to his aid. They hoped to be able to kill him quickly, without complications. What they expected would happen afterward is less clear.

On the chosen night, Alexander attended what would prove to be his third significant banquet of 327 BCE. As with many Macedonian feasts that the king attended, this one devolved into a late-night drinking party. When Alexander reeled back toward his tent in the early hours of the morning, he met with a Syrian prophetess on his way home. She was one of the camp followers, considered by some members of the army to be mad, but tolerated by the king. Alexander was, after all, a superstitious man, who preferred to give those claiming divine inspiration the benefit of the doubt: perhaps the prophecies would prove correct.

That night the Syrian prophetess told Alexander to return to drinking. Between his superstition and his intoxication, the king was happy to obey. He went back to the party. Meanwhile, the pages assembled in his tent had time to reflect on their plan, and become afraid. They must have wondered why the king did not return, and whether their carefully maintained secret had been betrayed. Even if Alexander knew nothing, his absence was an immense blow to the conspiracy. Should he fail to return, their best chance at assassination was over, and it might be weeks if not months before they were all assigned to guard duty together again. They were resolved to act, but how long could they hold out?

By the time Alexander returned to his tent after the drinking party, it was dawn. The conspirators were all still there, but they had been joined by the next shift of pages, ready for morning duty. Alexander, with the affability conferred by a long night's inebriation, commended them for their conscientious efforts, gave them a considerable tip, and sent them home to bed. He then retired to his own chamber to sleep off what must have been a monumental hangover.

The long night watch, with its culmination in Alexander's unexpected kindness, profoundly affected one of the conspirators, Epimenes. Wracked by guilt, he confessed the plot to his own lover, who passed on the information to Epimenes's brother. The brother was old enough to recognize the extraordinary danger in which he and his family had been placed. He had likely witnessed the trial and execution of Philotas, and knew that his father, Parmenion, had been assassinated as well. Epimenes's brother was also aware that in the three years since Philotas had been killed, Alexander had only become more autocratic, less tolerant of dissent. And even if Alexander had been different, no king could afford to ignore a conspiracy against his life—even if the conspirators were a group of frustrated teenagers. The brother knew what he had to do, to retain the hope of preserving himself and his family. As quickly as possible, he needed to convey the plot to one of Alexander's Companions. Fortunately for him, he lighted on an officer who took his concerns as seriously as the brother did himself: Alexander's bodyguard and close friend Ptolemy.

Upon learning of the plot, Ptolemy sprang into action. He immediately woke up and informed the king, rounded up the conspirators, and had them tortured, Epimenes alone excepted. As with Philotas, so here too with the pages, the Macedonian high command relied on torture to reveal the full facts of the conspiracy. If the pages' stories were consistent and they named no further names, even under duress, Alexander could rest assured that he was safe.

According to most ancient writers, the pages remained steadfast under torture. They gave their interrogators no names beyond those already offered by Epimenes and insisted the plot involved no one beyond their circle. Ptolemy's own memoirs, however, tell a different story. By his account, the pages named another man as instigator of the plot: the historian Kallisthenes.

Kallisthenes was a natural object of suspicion for the Macedonian high command. He had close contact with the pages, and as their teacher, he had regular opportunities to exert influence, shaping their values in accordance with his own. The historian was also known to give an ear to the pages' criticisms of the king. And Kallisthenes had recently thwarted Alexander at the proskynesis banquet. In doing so, he made his opinion of the king clear, in a public forum sure to inspire a group of impressionable youths.

It is likely that Kallisthenes had no more planned the pages' conspiracy than Philotas had the plot of Dimnos before him. But like Philotas, he had alienated Alexander, and there was just enough plausibility to the accusation to make him vulnerable to attack. Kallisthenes was rounded up and tortured along with the pages. Even if they never mentioned him, the convenient fiction that they had was easy enough to promulgate—particularly for Ptolemy, who was closely involved enough to know the truth.

After their torture, the pages were put on trial by the Macedonian army assembly. Hermolaos reportedly defended himself with an eloquent speech that included a long list of Alexander's offenses: his arrogance; his unjustified killing of Philotas, Parmenion, and Kleitos; his Persianizing costume; his drinking and sleeping habits; his attempted introduction of proskynesis. As with Kallisthenes's speech at the second banquet, Hermolaos's eloquence here may be apocryphal. His grievances, however, were real. But despite his youth and the failure of his conspiracy, he and the other pages, apart from Epimenes, were granted no mercy. With the entire army participating, they were stoned to death.

Kallisthenes's fate is less clear. Ptolemy claims he was hanged on the spot. Another story holds that the king delayed a decision until Kallisthenes could be put on trial by the League of Corinth, the governing body of the Greek city-states. Given that the league was dominated by pro-Macedonians, it was a safe bet for Alexander: a token acknowledgment of Greek autonomy and self-determination that would cost him little.

The latter story seems plausible, although in the event, the league never had a chance to rule on Kallisthenes's fate. Perhaps fearing an escape, Alexander brought the accused along with him on campaign. Eventually Kallisthenes died—according to this account, of ill health, obesity, and lice.

Kallisthenes's fate and the stoning to death of the Royal Pages had a profound effect on Alexander's followers. Despite their accumulating grievances, they planned no more conspiracies for the rest of the king's life. From Alexander's perspective, they had learned the right lessons from the third fateful banquet of 327 BCE. They saw the harshness with which even unsuccessful conspiracies would be punished. They understood as well how easily men like the outspoken traditionalist Kallisthenes could be eliminated by a king eager to enforce new customs, even when guilty of no greater crime. Dissent would continue, but after the conspiracy of the Royal Pages, it would take new forms.

What Alexander learned from the conspiracy is less certain. If he took any lessons from the teenagers' violent outburst, it was perhaps the extent to which his Greek and Macedonian followers saw his efforts to conciliate the Persians as a zero-sum game. When the king married an Iranian wife, or attempted to impose proskynesis, he was in their view not simply conciliating the Persians. He was rejecting, or attempting to humiliate, the Macedonians as well. From Hermolaos's litany of complaints, Alexander could see, if he wished, how difficult it would be to build the bicultural society he dreamed of. He would not stop trying, but he would hold off for the time being. And when he made his next attempt, it would be more emphatic and thorough-going. Still an impatient and impulsive man, as he turned thirty, Alexander was beginning to learn to wait.

When the king left Bactria behind and headed south to the Hindu Kush, however, he could look forward to having at least one of his long-awaited desires satisfied. He was finally going to India.

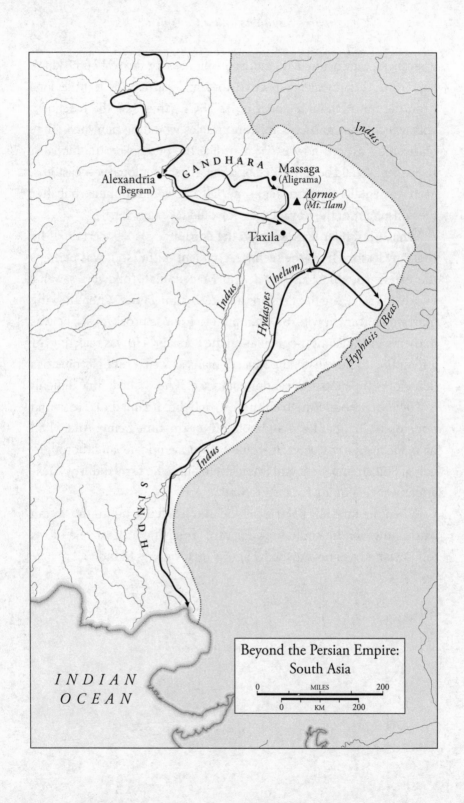

Alexandria
(Begram)

GANDHARA

Massaga
(Aligrama)

Aornos
(Mt. Ilam)

Taxila

Indus

Indus

Hydaspes (Jhelum)

Hyphasis (Beas)

Indus

SINDH

INDIAN
OCEAN

Beyond the Persian Empire:
South Asia

| 0 | MILES | 200 |
| 0 | KM | 200 |

TEN

Following in the Footsteps of the Gods

Afghanistan and Pakistan
Fall 327–Spring 326 BCE

FROM THE CRESTS OF THE HINDU KUSH, Alexander looked with anticipation toward India. Far off in the distance, he hoped to see a glint of water. Many years before, Aristotle had written that from where he now stood, he would be able to see all the way to Ocean and the end of the world. As with many Greek fantasies about India, Aristotle's was laughably inaccurate. But as Alexander would learn, the reality was just as remarkable—though it would also prove more dangerous than he imagined.

With Alexander on his journey to India came an unusual group of soldiers. The king had received reinforcements from his Central Asian allies, and now boasted an army larger—and far more diverse—than the one with which he had entered Afghanistan. Ancient estimates run as high as 120,000 men, an enormous, implausible number, four times that of the army he brought to invade Persia (45,000, including followers, is more likely, and still huge).

Alexander somehow managed to get his immense army over the Hindu Kush. The king is even recorded as generously giving his crack infantry troops silver to plate their shields, in preparation for the invasion of wealthy, ostentatious India. From this time on, they were known as the Argyraspides (Silver Shields). A famous and much-fêted battalion, they long outlasted the man who had created them, growing more powerful—and more avaricious—every year.

As such, they were appropriate for the land they were entering: a place of extraordinary riches, and one more foreign to the Macedonians than anywhere they had yet been.

For the Silver Shields, as for all Greek speakers, "India" was not limited to the boundaries of the modern nation-state. Instead it comprised the whole of the South Asian subcontinent, from the alpine valleys of Kashmir to the Baluchistan desert and the jungles of the Southwestern Ghats. Of these territories, only the wide, spreading plains of the Punjab, the Arabian Sea coast, and the narrow strip of fertile land that tracked the southern Indus River valley had belonged to the Persian Empire. They were likely all conquered by Darius I in the late sixth century BCE, and contingents from them had served loyally under the Great King in the Greco-Persian Wars at the dawn of the Classical age. A few still fought for Darius III at Gaugamela, but it is clear from the accounts of Alexander's time in South Asia as well as the archaeological remains that Persian control was neither as strong nor as pervasive as before. On the subcontinent, Alexander had to deal with a land that was politically fragmented and only theoretically subordinate to the Great King. It housed no pretenders to the throne, or any immediate rivals. From a strategic point of view (or that of Alexander's weary soldiers), the Macedonian king had no need to conquer India. In modern terms, his was a paradigmatic "war of choice."

Despite his lack of a strategic rationale, Alexander was drawn to India. His officers' memoirs suggest why. According to their descriptions, India was exotic, bountiful, and wondrous. It had two harvests a year, they reported enviously, with the inhabitants sowing flax, millet, sesame, and rice in the summer, followed in the winter by wheat, barley, beans, and vegetables; its fruit was more abundant and delicious than that of Greece. The officers claimed that Indians were less given to thieving and had fewer court cases—in contrast to the litigious Hellenes—and were also healthier, perhaps because many of them were vegetarians. They wore long tunics, shawls, and turbans made of "wool that grows on trees" (i.e., cotton), all vibrantly colored and ornamented with ivory, pearls, and gold. No opportunity for adornment was lost. Even the men's beards were vivid, being dyed white, dark blue, crimson, purple, and grass green.

Above all, it was the wealth and natural resources of India that attracted Alexander. In the Greeks' stories, its rivers ran with gold, its seas cast precious stones and pearls onto the shore. From its land grew spices, rare as Arabia's: cinnamon, nard, and other aromatics. Everything was larger and better on the subcontinent. Its oxen so impressed Alexander that he would eventually send the finest of them home, to improve the stock of Macedonia. Its elephants, ancient writers maintained inaccurately, were as tall as African ones—not to mention stronger and far more formidable in war.

Beyond India's fertility, its wealth, and its opportunities for combat— all attractions for Alexander—the subcontinent also fascinated him because of Ocean. He failed to glimpse the end of the world from the Hindu Kush, but he still hoped and believed it was nearby. If he made it to the great body of water he dreamed of, then he would have a satisfactory culmination to his conquest. Without it, he would never willingly stop.

Alexander began his campaign in India by splitting his forces, so as not to risk his entire hungry army on one potentially desolate stretch of road. He sent his close friends Hephaistion and Perdikkas along the main route to the Punjab, in charge of the bulk of the army. The king himself took another route, farther to the north and through radically different territory. Instead of the flat, well-watered plains of the main road, he was headed to what are now the borderlands of Afghanistan and Pakistan, a region of deep, precipitous gorges, high mountains, and spectacularly beautiful river valleys.

Among the most beautifully sited towns Alexander encountered was a place the Macedonians called Nysa. This was a large town perched high in the cool, thick-wooded mountains of what is now northeastern Afghanistan. The king and his army arrived at Nysa shortly before nightfall. Barred from entry, they pitched camp before the walls. They were cold in the high mountain air and lit fires, but these unluckily spread to the cedar tombs of the Nysaeans' cemetery. The besieged, seeing the monuments of their ancestors aflame, poured out to fight. Then they hesitated. Alexander, perceiving their uncertainty, held his own soldiers back. Ordering a blockade but no bloodshed, he waited.

By their heavy walls, the Nysaeans looked out through the flickering firelight at their attackers. They could not know for sure how many there were, hidden among the shadows. But they could hear the whinnying of the Macedonians' horses and the clang of their armor and weapons: iron helmets and breastplates, bronze swords, shields, and spears, while the Nysaeans likely had only metal-tipped arrows, shields of rawhide, perhaps swords, and wooden bows. The Nysaeans could guess that they were outnumbered by powerful, determined soldiers. Still, they noted that the Macedonians had, nonetheless, held off attacking them; perhaps they might be persuaded to be merciful. The Nysaeans opted for negotiation. They sent thirty envoys led by a man named Akouphis to sue for peace.

Akouphis was a wily, clever civic elder. When he met the young king, he brought these advantages to his negotiations, but also faced serious challenges. Akouphis needed to gloss over the Nysaeans' initial attack on Alexander, present their subsequent capitulation as trustworthy, and obtain the best terms he could. He particularly feared what might happen if Alexander asked for hostages. Nysa was not a monarchy and Akouphis was not its king. Rather, he was an eminent man in a collectively run, likely oligarchic town. Nysa could ill afford to lose many members of its high-ranking governing class, and Akouphis would be blamed if he allowed it. So he formulated the most impressive story he could, and hoped for the best.

Akouphis claimed that Nysa had been founded by the Greek god Dionysos, the great mythological conqueror of the east. The envoy and his fellow citizens were descended from the god's veterans, settled when they could go no farther, and were thus, in essence, Hellenes themselves. There was a nearby mountain, Mount Meron ("thigh" in Greek), that had given rise to the story that Dionysos was born from the thigh of Zeus. On it grew ivy, sacred to the god, which Akouphis adduced as proof that the story he told was true.

It's not clear how Akouphis, a devotee of an ancient South Asian pantheon, came up with his story about Dionysos. He likely found the germ of it in his own mythology—Shiva, Krishna, and Indra have been proposed as precedents—and in a belief in sacred mountains. He may also have owed some part of the story to his translators, who were accustomed to articulating Hellenic mythological equivalents for foreign gods. But the precision of the story, with its emphasis on ivy and eastern conquest, suggests that Akouphis must have had some prior knowledge of Greek mythology and Alexander himself. Perhaps he had contact with the king's settlers in southern Afghanistan, relatively nearby, or with Indian ambassadors who had visited Alexander in Central Asia. In any case, and whatever the source, his story worked.

Akouphis's account worked because it was brilliantly calculated to appeal to Alexander. The Macedonian king's family had long-standing ties to Dionysos, and his mother, Olympias, was a particular devotee. At the royal family's most important religious center, the city of Dion, stood the theater where Euripides's *Bacchai* may first have been performed. The play, with its story of a Dionysiac revel gone horribly wrong, was hardly an unequivocal celebration of the god. But it highlighted his extraordinary power and, important for Alexander, his conquest of eastern lands. In lines that the king, that inveterate memorizer of Euripides, surely knew, the god sang, "I have left the golden land of the Lydians and Phrygians, the sun-scorched flatlands of the Persians, and the walls of Bactria."

India went unmentioned in Dionysos's catalog of conquests. Still, it must have seemed plausible to Alexander that the god had gone there, too, and that Nysa marked the eastern limit of his adventures. Now the Macedonian king had an opportunity to surpass the god and head farther east. He readily granted Akouphis's request for freedom and autonomy (at least as Alexander understood the terms: internal sovereignty, as opposed to a Macedonian overlord and garrison). In return, the king asked for three hundred cavalry recruits for his army and a hundred of the city's best men as hostages. Akouphis demurred, cleverly insisting that if the best men were sent away, the city would not be well governed. The king and the envoy compromised, with Alexander gaining the cavalry he sought along with just two hostages. Painfully for Akouphis, they were his son and grandson.

After the negotiations, Alexander led his troops to Mount Meron to celebrate. There they found a beautiful pastoral landscape of shade and dappled sunlight, laurel, and berry bushes. For the first time in years, they saw ivy—a common, everyday plant in Greece, but rare in Persia and Central Asia. Homesick and thrilled by the familiar, they crowned themselves with it in true Dionysiac fashion and sang hymns to the god.

Inspired by Akouphis's story, Alexander sacrificed to the deity he now considered his best mythological predecessor. He seized the opportunity for an unequivocal celebration—rare since the wine-fueled death of Kleitos—of the dangerous but pleasurable god. If his rites in India resembled those back home, he first poured libations of wine while praying to Dionysos. Then he conducted animal sacrifice, ritually killing bulls or goats (the god's preferred offering) with one well-aimed blow to the throat, letting the blood drip onto the ground, separating the god's portion, fat and thigh bones, from the rest. Finally, cooking the meat from the sacrifice, Alexander held an immense outdoor feast. Reclining among the ivy and laurel trees, he and his troops ate and drank to their heart's content. It was a rare moment of relaxation after the arduous crossing of the Hindu Kush, followed by weeks of border skirmishes. And it was all the more astonishing in that it took place within what was still in essence enemy territory.

Luckily for Alexander, his Dionysiac revel ended better than that of Euripides's *Bacchai*. No one attacked, although the king and his troops had certainly dropped their defenses. They enjoyed their celebration in safety. Then they came down from the mountain and prepared to fight again.

As summer turned to autumn, Alexander and his troops moved into the Swat Valley in what is now the North-West Frontier Province of Pakistan. Town by town, the king marched north through the dazzling alpine landscape, with fertile lowlands ringed by dramatic snowcapped peaks. As the king discovered, this picturesque region was populated by autonomous cities that resisted him fiercely. His "war of choice" turned out to be a slow, intermittently violent one. He wanted explicit acquiescence to his conquest, and preferably some soldiers for his army also. When the local inhabitants complied, he conducted an alliance quickly and moved on. When they opposed him, he responded brutally: killing the men, taking the women and children prisoner, at times even razing the buildings to the ground.

Among the most intensely resistant places Alexander encountered there was Massaga. Likely identifiable with the present-day site of Aligrama, a city nestled in a broad alluvial plain in southern Swat, it was a strong, thick-walled town, with stone foundations topped by mudbrick. The largest and most powerful city in the region, it was also, unusually, a monarchy ruled by a queen.

Queen Kleophis had been married to Massaga's king, but he had died with no adult male heirs. She had managed to avoid *sati*, the South Asian ritual burning of widows on their husbands' pyres. Queen Kleophis was young and beautiful, and before her husband's death had borne the king a son. Now, with her son still a child, she held power in her own right. When she heard of Alexander's arrival in the region, she engaged a force of mercenaries. As the Macedonian king and his army approached, Kleophis drew her people within the walls and prepared for a hard-fought, drawn-out siege.

Kleophis and her followers trusted to their walls, but they had never encountered a besieger as determined or technically adept as Alexander. As the queen watched from within the walls, the Macedonian king had his engineers construct wheeled siege towers. Nine days later, he had contraptions tall and strong enough to carry catapults and archers, the first to launch projectiles that would break down the fortifications, the second to pick off their defenders. Terrifyingly for Kleophis and her people, they seemed to move on their own, so that the Massagans believed they were propelled by the gods (in fact, they were pushed from within by Alexander's men). Equally terrifying was the fact that they worked, breaching the walls—but still, Kleophis and her soldiers managed to hold out. Then they observed Alexander try a bridge, lowering it down from a siege tower to the breach in the wall, and sending his best infantry over it. But as the soldiers hurtled across the bridge, it collapsed, killing several of Alexander's men. The violence and destructiveness of the siege at Massaga scarred the site, leaving traces still visible even today: broken walls and unburied skeletons.

Finally, after many days of fighting, Kleophis and her subjects decided they could no longer hold out. She had the mercenaries conduct a separate truce with Alexander, and they departed from the city under arms. Then the queen emerged with a retinue of noble ladies pouring libations from golden bowls. Kleophis correctly judged that her beauty and willingness to surrender before being defeated would be looked on favorably by the Macedonian king. Placing her young son on Alexander's knees, she sued for peace.

Kleophis's actions made her even more successful than Akouphis had been at Nysa. She received not only pardon but also restitution

Alexander's portraits vary wildly. Most did not do him justice, but Plutarch claimed that those by the famous sculptor Lysippos (here, an early copy) best captured the king's dynamic upward glance, melting gaze, and long, leonine hair.

Heroic images: Alexander promoted his connection to his mythological ancestor Herakles, putting an image of the hero with his own portrait features on coins (*left*). He was also shown with Herakles's signature lion-skin helmet in later art (*above*).

Kings in conflict: Alexander riding his favorite warhorse, Boukephalos, to battle (*above*); a Persian Great King and ancestor of Darius III sitting on his throne, receiving the homage of his subjects (*below*).

Persepolis, shown here in a modern reconstruction, was a powerful, well-fortified city with lush gardens and grand palaces, until it was sacked and burned by Alexander's army.

The backbone of the Macedonian army was its heavy-armed infantry, superbly trained and carrying eighteen-foot-long spears that kept enemies at a distance.

The first rebel: Men from eastern Iran and western Afghanistan, like Satibarzanes, often rode on camels and wore long sleeves, trousers, and turbans to protect them from their harsh desert environment (*above*). The conditions and clothing remain similar today (*below*).

The would-be Great King and his punishment: Bessos was governor of the rich, fertile region of Bactria, north of the Hindu Kush mountains (*above, in a photo from the 1970s*). Alexander punished him brutally, just as other rebels had been punished by earlier Persian kings (*left*).

Guerrilla fighters: Spitamenes drew his best fighters from the
Scythians of the Central Asian steppes. Nomads, they fought on
horseback and wore elaborate gold jewelry.

Hellenic enemies: The aging Demosthenes was Greece's best orator and most prominent anti-Macedonian politician, until he was forced into exile following Alexander's return from South Asia.

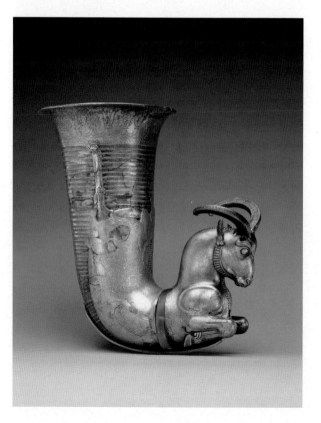

Alexander (*above*) adored hunting, particularly exotic, dangerous animals like lions. He celebrated successful hunts with feasts. Huge amounts of wine in precious metal cups like this rhyton (*left*) and boastful, competitive men with weapons made them almost as risky as hunting.

The remote, well-fortified Mount Kyzkurgan (*above*) in Uzbekistan was likely where Alexander met his first wife, Roxane, when the captured noblewoman danced for him at a banquet. Macedonians of Alexander's day loved feasting so much that they commemorated it even on their tombs (*below*).

The Jhelum River, fed by the snow-capped
Himalayas, posed a formidable barrier for
Alexander when he had to cross it to fight Poros.

South Asian allies and enemies: Kings like Alexander's ally Omphis and his enemy Poros held elaborate public processions like the one shown here, from a relief decorating an early Buddhist stupa in India.

Traversing the Makran Desert in Pakistan (*above*), with its windswept, otherworldly rock formations, Alexander lost more followers to heat and thirst than in any of his other battles. His admiral Nearkhos went by sea, squeezing two hundred men into ships roughly the size of single-family homes (*below, in a modern reconstruction*).

Rebuilding: Alexander restored the tomb of Cyrus (*below*), the first Great King. He also sought to strengthen his ties to Persians by arranging a mass wedding between his top officers and Iranian noblewomen (*right*).

New homes: Babylon (*above, in a nineteenth-century print*) was where Alexander buried Hephaistion and established his capital shortly before his death; Alexandria (*below, in a modern reconstruction*) was the cosmopolitan city where his corpse found its final, appropriate resting place.

of her former status, and no demand for hostages. The more sensationalistic Classical writers, however, insist that nine months later, Kleophis bore a son and named him Alexander—suggesting that she paid in other ways.

Kleophis's mercenaries faced a higher price for their actions. Alexander promised them safe conduct, allowing them to depart under arms and set up camp a short distance away. Then the Macedonian king attacked. When the mercenaries cried out, citing the truce they'd concluded, he replied that he'd agreed to let them leave the city, nothing more. Following this sophistic piece of reasoning, he captured or killed them all.

Ancient writers differ in their judgments of Alexander's massacre at Massaga. For the moralizing biographer Plutarch, it was a terrible blot on the king's reputation as a military commander, because he failed to abide by the well-established laws of war. Arrian, the ceaseless apologist of Alexander, tried to exculpate the king, claiming that he'd learned that the mercenaries were about to abrogate their agreement. Facing betrayal, he simply betrayed them first. Modern authors have also disagreed, blaming everything from faulty translation to the machinations of the queen to a deliberate campaign of terror.

The military writer Polyaenus saw things otherwise. He simply reported the incident, without apology or pathos, as part of his list of useful martial stratagems. From Polyaenus's perspective, Alexander's betrayal of the truce was just one option at the experienced military commander's disposal, comparable to several he included from the crafty trickster Philip II of Macedon.

Alexander's campaign on the Indian subcontinent has been described by modern scholars as gratuitously violent: one cruel, cunning massacre after another. Certainly it was brutal, as the mercenaries at Massaga could attest. It was also very much in line with what the Macedonian king had done earlier. What changed was not the strategy itself but the degree of opposition and autonomy Alexander encountered. In the Persian Empire's west and heartland, he had dealt with powerful governors; if they capitulated, their territories went along. He had experienced more trouble in Central Asia, where he had to contend with a host of local leaders, and the power of the imperial center was less strongly felt. Now Alexander was moving through a land that had barely been touched by the Great Kings. He had to deal with every resistant town separately, and the conquest of one in no way implied success with the next. So he fought his way through the region, town by resistant town.

With the taking of Massaga, Alexander had in his hands the largest and most powerful city in the Swat Valley, but he still wasn't done. Many of the valley's inhabitants had fled to what the Macedonians called the Rock of Aornos. If archaeologists are correct in identifying it with the present-day Mount Ilam, it was a high granite peak that dominated the Karakar Pass, the gateway to the Punjab plains. Snow-capped much of the year and densely forested, this was a tall, pyramidal mountain surrounded by deep gorges on all sides. Alexander was told—perhaps by local informants, or alternatively by some discouraging Macedonians—that Herakles had thrice sought to capture the Rock of Aornos. Each time, the story went, he had failed.

If his informants hoped to dissuade Alexander from attacking the Rock of Aornos, they had radically misjudged the king. For Alexander, Dionysos was an appealing mythological precedent, but even better was Herakles—a mortal who had earned immortality through his labors, and the king's far-off paternal ancestor. Alexander determined to follow in his ancestor's footsteps, and in this case go one better. He would capture Aornos, however difficult it might prove.

Alexander began by securing the countryside around the Rock of Aornos: fortifying Massaga, garrisoning the other towns he had taken, and turning the nearest into his base of operations. He even appointed a governor for the region, a high-ranking Macedonian who had previously been in charge of Alexandria-Begram. He did all this so he could concentrate his efforts on Aornos, without being distracted by rearguard attack or mundane administrative affairs. Alexander emulated the gods—but also planned ahead.

When the king reached the Rock of Aornos, however, it seemed initially as though no amount of planning could help him. He faced sheer cliffs, extremely difficult to scale and protected at the base by deep ravines. He had with him his most agile light-armed troops, as well as experienced generals like Ptolemy. But even after his time attacking mountain fortresses in Sogdiana, Alexander was uncertain how to proceed. Fortunately for the king, a deserter from the surrounding countryside came forward. He promised to show the Macedonians a way to assault the rock. Alexander sent Ptolemy and some of his best men with him, after taking the deserter's son hostage. Then the king and the rest of his forces prepared to wait.

Cautiously and secretively, Ptolemy and his men headed up the slopes of Aornos until they found a place flat enough to camp. They secured the site with a stockade and trench, then sent up a fire signal for Alexander. Dangerously for Ptolemy, the signal triggered both an attempt by the Macedonian king to join them and an attack by the defenders of the mountain. Alexander was beaten back, and Ptolemy only barely managed to maintain his position. Still, it was enough. With the Macedonians established on the slopes of the mountain, the defenders were hemmed in, unable to flee. They could only hope that Ptolemy and his men would become discouraged and abandon the siege before their supplies gave out.

Ptolemy, however, had no intention of abandoning the siege; nor would Alexander have let him. Instead, the Macedonian king made a second attempt to scale the cliffs and join forces with his general. As Alexander's soldiers climbed, they struggled against the arrows, boulders, and other missiles that their opponents rained down. They finally managed to join Ptolemy, though they were still far below the defenders' position and vulnerable to their volleys. To counter these attacks, the king determined to build his own artificial hill.

Alexander ordered his soldiers to cut down trees—abundant on the slopes of Aornos—and construct an elaborate man-made mountain. As with the king's assault on the Iron Gates in Central Asia, so here too, he chose a slow, labor-intensive strategy for his siege, rather than heedlessly risking his men. By the time Alexander managed to mount catapults and siege machines atop his mound, he correctly judged that the defenders of the rock were getting nervous. After some form of negotiated surrender, he removed the Macedonians guarding the paths down the mountain at night, encouraging his opponents to flee. When they did, the king attacked, killing some as they fled. He let the rest go and occupied the top of the mountain. There he sacrificed to the gods and built an altar to Athena. With his advanced technology (and low cunning) he had bested Herakles.

In the months culminating with his attack on Mount Aornos, Alexander was repeatedly told by both South Asians and his own followers that he was following in the footsteps of the gods. For a Macedonian well versed in Hellenic mythology, the idea was a natural one. Alexander had grown up listening to stories about Herakles, the son of Zeus whose labors took him to the ends of the earth, and the great traveler Theseus, who went to the bottom of the sea to meet his father, Poseidon. Alexander expected to encounter the gods more easily in far-off places. He also anticipated meeting there the strange peoples and monsters whose defeat might earn an ambitious man glory, or even immortality. In India, his expectations were abundantly fulfilled.

Alexander's belief that he was emulating the gods did not encourage him to conform to any philosophical ideals of divine morality. Instead, it made him even more ambitious, as well as more willing to resort to violence and deception in order to achieve his ends. As his campaigns in India would demonstrate, it increasingly endangered his relationship with his followers. And his conviction in his godlike invulnerability would threaten his own life. The Greeks had a word for Alexander's conviction: *hubris,* a combination of overweening pride and self-confidence. Their myths also repeatedly illustrated its dire consequences, which they called *nemesis*.

In the winter of 326 BCE Alexander arrived at the Indus, a river so broad and deep it reminded the Macedonian king of the Nile. As in Egypt, so here too, at the Indus he found crocodiles swimming in the river, while lotuses grew along the banks of its tributary, the Chenab. Alexander was fascinated, and wondered if the two rivers were the same. His hypothesis suggests his powers of observation and scientific curiosity—as well as his deep geographical confusion, given that the Nile was more than three thousand miles away and on another continent.

Along with crocodiles, Alexander could see in the Indus a large fleet of boats, which had already been constructed for him by Hephaistion and Perdikkas from the dense forests of this upland region. He planned to use them to bring his army across the Indus as well as the other rivers that spread, like the fingers of a hand, throughout the Punjab plain. But the king had ordered a fleet larger and better built than mere river crossings would require. It suggests that although Alexander was focused on going east toward Ocean, he was also eventually planning to turn back and head south down the river on his way home.

When the Macedonian king was ready to cross the Indus, he linked the boats together into an immense pontoon bridge. Slowly and carefully over many days, he sent his soldiers across. Once they had all made it over safely, he carried out sacrifices, thanking the gods for their help in accomplishing this difficult technical feat and asking for future assistance. Perhaps he prayed for a few good allies. And after the guerrilla warfare of Central Asia, he may have asked for a clearcut opponent as well. But the king was aware that he would have to search for both—and also be able to tell them apart.

Alexander was not sure he could trust the new king of the lands between the Indus and Jhelum Rivers, whom the Greeks called

Omphis (likely Ambhi in Sanskrit). Omphis had encouraged his late father to make contact with the Macedonians while they were still in Central Asia. He had been responsible for the embassy to Alexander then, and had come to the Macedonian king in person as soon as he crossed the Hindu Kush. In all these encounters, Omphis had been careful and submissive, pledging loyalty to Alexander and bringing gifts. He recognized that no army he could field would ever be a match for that of the extraordinary Macedonian conqueror. He also saw that Alexander could, if properly manipulated, be useful to him.

Omphis had a rival: Poros, the wealthy, proud, and powerful ruler in the lands beyond the Jhelum. Likely claiming descent from a king celebrated in the Mahabharata as Paurava, Poros embodied the war-like, aggressive qualities of his heroic namesake. As Omphis could predict, Poros had no intention of surrendering to the Macedonian king. If Omphis could bring the two of them into conflict, he might get Alexander to eliminate his rival for him. So when the Macedonian king arrived at his border, Omphis set out to meet him with the most gorgeous and militarily impressive procession he could muster, eager to present himself as a desirable ally.

For a self-respecting ancient king on the Indian subcontinent, a procession was an opportunity for the display of wealth and power on a scale undreamed of by contemporary Macedonians. For his, Omphis mustered his entire army—about five thousand soldiers—all in battle array, along with more than fifty elephants. With mahouts on their backs and elaborately caparisoned, they looked to the Macedonians like castles from a distance. With them came other animals: large numbers of sheep and at least three thousand bulls, prized by the South Asians of Omphis's day as well as by Alexander. Among the beasts, Omphis himself rode surrounded by his high-level officials and courtiers. If he proceeded in the fashion expected of an ancient Indian king, he was attended by bodyguards and followed by a long retinue of concubines in golden sedan chairs, as well as his queen. A good South Asian king also brought servants carrying silver incense burners to perfume the road along the way, golden vessels and furniture, and golden chariots with trees containing beautiful birds which had been taught to sing.

With this extravagant procession, Omphis succeeded in convincing Alexander of his military preparedness only too well. When the Macedonian king caught sight of the large army approaching from a distance, he feared that Omphis had betrayed him. Anxiously readying for a battle he had not intended to fight, Alexander armed his foot soldiers, moved his cavalry to the army's flanks, and had the trumpeters sound their calls.

Omphis—more relaxed than Alexander and thus better able to read the foreign king's moves—recognized that he had inadvertently alarmed the Macedonians. He called his army, courtiers, elephants, and other animals to a halt and galloped forward with only a few companions. Since this was hardly the behavior of a belligerent attacker, Alexander rode forward, too. Through interpreters, Omphis indicated that he surrendered, and Alexander ceremoniously restored his kingdom to him. Then they reconfirmed their alliance through the exchange of gifts. The sheep and bulls went to feed Alexander's army, the elephants to augment it. Omphis also conferred golden crowns on the king and his companions, and handed over more than two tons of coined silver. Not to be outdone, Alexander returned these gifts and offered far more: gold and silver dinnerware, Persian clothing, thirty horses from his own stables, and a cool twenty-eight tons of silver. In the exchange, Omphis was the clear financial winner, and Alexander's men were furious with him for giving away so much. According to the conventions of gift-giving in both Greek and Persian society, however, the Macedonian king had demonstrated his superior status and put Omphis under an extraordinary obligation to him.

Alexander and his new ally proceeded to Taxila, the capital and largest city in Omphis's kingdom. Nestled in an upland valley near the Muree Hills, it sat at the confluence of three major trade routes:

northeast to Kashmir and, beyond that, to Central Asia; northwest to Afghanistan and Iran; southeast to the Ganges and the eastern sub-continent. Taxila owed its prominence to these intersecting roads and the wheeled traffic that traveled along them, but it also had an enviable physical situation. As the Buddhist monk Hsüan-tsang remarked in the seventh century CE, it boasted rich harvests, flowing streams, sweet-scented flowers and fruit, and a pleasant climate. Particularly in midwinter, when Alexander arrived, it was temperate and mild, a relief after the harsh, freezing temperatures of Central Asia. The Macedonians must have appreciated the soft air and frost-free plains of the northern Indus River valley that winter—though they would have a very different reaction to the following summer's monsoon rains.

For the moment, though, Alexander enjoyed resting his troops in the pleasurable environs of Taxila. It was a large, capacious city, with a broad main road running north to south, and scores of meandering, jostling side streets. Several hundred years old by the time Alexander arrived, it contrasted strongly with his hometown, Pella. The Macedonian king had grown up in a young, grid-planned city, well organized and rather sterile. At Taxila, he saw layers of history.

Alexander passed by large houses, with footprints around 3,600 square feet, and generously sized courtyards as well as upper stories. He also viewed the city's official center, with two large open courtyards and an immense pillared hall. This may have been the Taxilans' most important temple, or the palace where Omphis welcomed Alexander with feasts and drinking parties. Doubtless to the perplexity of the Greeks and Macedonians, however, there were few public buildings: no theater for plays or religious ceremonies, no gymnasium for exercise and education, no *agora*, the large, open square that was the economic and political heart of every Greek city.

Although there was no purpose-built gymnasium, Alexander learned that the city was nonetheless a center for education. Well before his arrival, it had hosted the famous grammarian Panini, whose rules were deployed in the great early religious texts of India, the Vedic Upanishads and Buddhist Sutras. By Alexander's era, the city attracted students from all over the subcontinent. Among them was a young man named Chandragupta, who would later become the founder of the Mauryan dynasty. At its height, Chandragupta's empire would stretch from the Indus to the Ganges, and he would succeed in expelling the last remnants of Macedonian rule from South Asia. When Alexander arrived in Taxila, however, Chandragupta was still an impressionable young man, studying a curriculum that likely included law, hunting, military strategy, singing, music, and Ayurvedic medicine. He was curious about the Macedonian king and may have joined his army. Later he remarked that had Alexander stayed in India, he might have conquered it all.

Along with Chandragupta, Alexander also encountered the teachers who had attracted the ambitious young man to Taxila. The Greeks called them Gymnosophistai—"naked wise men." The Macedonian king was intrigued by them and sent an emissary: Onesikritos, a Greek naval officer and the helmsman of Alexander's own ship. More pertinent for the task at hand, Onesikritos was an intellectual, a student of the Cynic philosopher Diogenes. Curious and broad minded, he was the perfect person to investigate the wise men of Taxila. His impressions of them are preserved for us in his memoir, which—unusually for one of Alexander's officers—primarily concerns philosophy and natural history, not war.

On his mission from Alexander, Onesikritos found the naked wise men congregating in a field outside the city. Despite the heat, he observed that they remained motionless in various postures, in what sounds like an early form of yoga. Through three interpreters, he asked to learn their philosophical teachings. This perfectly rational request—at least from Onesikritos's point of view—did not get the initial response he was looking for. Instead, he was told by Kalanos, one of the leaders, that in order to study, he would have to take his clothes off and lie naked, just like them, on the hot stones.

Fortunately for Onesikritos, a second teacher named Mandanis intervened. As well as the Greek could understand through the interpreters, he chastised Kalanos for arrogance, setting off the kind of backbiting philosophical debate familiar wherever intellectuals are found. Mandanis then offered to expound his own teachings. According to Onesikritos, the Taxilan wise man focused on the removal from men's minds of both pleasure and pain. At the same time, he differentiated between pain—always bad, according to Mandanis—and toil, a useful spur to exertion and teacher of wisdom (as Onesikritos, after the interminable toils of Alexander's campaign, doubtless hoped). The ascetic asked if similar teachings were found among the Greeks. Yes, said Onesikritos eagerly, citing Pythagoras, Socrates, and his own teacher, Diogenes. Mandanis absorbed this array of unfamiliar names and observed politely that the Greeks seemed like good philosophers, too.

Onesikritos was a Hellene. As such, he was heir to a proud philosophical tradition as well as a habit of cultural chauvinism that saw everyone, Macedonians included, as decidedly less than Greeks. Given his heritage, Onesikritos could easily have taken Mandanis's comments poorly, as evidence of intolerable hubris and condescension. Interestingly, he did not. Instead he recorded them in his memoir with remarkable enthusiasm and humility, in a rare moment of cultural rapprochement.

Onesikritos went further, inviting Mandanis to join Alexander's expedition. If the ascetic came, he would form part of the Macedonian king's long roster of intellectual hangers-on, now somewhat lacking in philosophers after the death of Kallisthenes. Perhaps wisely given Kallisthenes's fate, Mandanis declined. He had no need of gifts or fear of punishment, he said, and was thus happily indifferent to Alexander. Onesikritos accepted this and offered a more general invitation. Unexpectedly, the ascetic who chose to come with Alexander was Kalanos. He abandoned his haughty insistence on teaching only those who stripped naked and lay down in the heat, following Onesikritos back to the Macedonian king's court. Throughout his time on the Indian subcontinent and beyond, Kalanos would remain with Alexander, right up until the moment of the wise man's dramatic death.

Who were the ascetics encountered by Onesikritos? In his memoir, the Greek sometimes terms them *Brachmanes*, similar enough to *Brahmins* to suggest to scholars that these were members of Hinduism's highest caste. They resemble later, better-documented Brahmins in their vegetarianism, their high social status, and their devotion to learning. And some South Asians of Alexander's day certainly did have a caste system, which was described by Hellenic writers with considerable fascination—as well as clear misunderstanding, since the Greeks portrayed seven elaborately delineated castes instead of four. In other ways, however, the Gymnosophistai sound more like Buddhist monks, shaving their heads and demanding handouts in the marketplace. Some of their beliefs—for instance, Kalanos's asceticism and insistence on the mortification of the body—even resemble those of Jains. The question is probably insoluble, given the fragmentary nature of Onesikritos's preserved works, as well as his own cultural biases (which make the Taxilan wise men also resemble Cynic philosophers). And indeed, it may be the wrong question to ask, since the fourth century BCE was still a period of flux in South Asian religion, and sectarian differences were far less plainly demarcated than later on.

What does come through clearly from Onesikritos's description is the power of ascetics in South Asian society. Here were a group of influential, high-status individuals who operated outside the conventional political system and were, as Mandanis's example suggests, well able to resist being co-opted by it. In these initial encounters, the Gymnosophistai fascinated and engaged their Hellenic visitor, and he treated them as equals; it all seems rather charming. Later, they would serve as upholders of native tradition against the foreign invaders, and relations would sour. Although Alexander did not realize it yet, they would prove in time some of his most dangerous opponents on the subcontinent.

In Taxila, however, Alexander was busily engaged in finding another, more obvious, enemy. He dispatched a high-ranking ambassador to Poros, Omphis's rival, demanding that the king of the lands beyond the Jhelum meet him at the river, pay tribute, and turn over hostages. How Poros might have responded to a less aggressive message is unclear, but his reaction to this one was everything Omphis might have hoped for. The powerful, proud Punjab king had the ambassador whipped, a deliberate insult, and sent him back to Alexander with an angry missive. Poros told Alexander to turn back, or at least to go no farther. If he ignored this advice, Poros threatened, "Put one hostile foot in my land and you will learn that I am king of the Indians." Only one of Alexander's commands would he follow, said Poros. He would meet the Macedonian at the Jhelum—in arms. Alexander was insulted, as he was meant to be, but given his predilections, he was also likely relieved. After months of following in the gods' footsteps, he had finally found what every aspiring hero needs: a truly worthy rival.

ELEVEN

How to Fight an Elephant

Pakistan
Spring–Summer 326 BCE

ALEXANDER HASTENED EAST FROM TAXILA. When he arrived at the Jhelum River in late April, the mild Indian spring was beginning to turn into a hot, steamy, frequently sodden summer. Through the heavy air, he could see Poros, as promised, camped on the river's eastern banks. Alexander gazed at his rival's large army spread out along the river, a bustling hive of armored men, glittering chariots, archers, horses, and—most dangerously—elephants.

These were Asian elephants, smaller than those of the African savanna, but nonetheless impressively sized. They stood about nine feet tall at the shoulder and weighed between two and almost six tons. With their high, domed heads, soft triangular ears, and convex, gently sloping backs, they were a distinctive presence in the forests of India: the largest animals Alexander encountered there or anywhere else on land.

For the battle-loving Macedonian king, the elephants offered an unprecedented challenge, unlike any in his career. They tantalized. With them and Poros's imposing army, Alexander had the prospect of his first large-scale battle after four interminable guerrilla-ridden years.

Although the Jhelum would be Alexander's first substantive military engagement with elephants, he had encountered them long before. He likely learned about them first from his tutor Aristotle, who was insatiably curious about the natural world. In his *History of Animals,* composed before Alexander's journeys, Aristotle had much to say about the elephant. He was particularly fascinated by the trunk, remarking, "it has a nose of such a kind and so large that it uses it instead of hands. For it drinks and eats by bringing the organ up to its mouth, and with it hands up things to its rider. And with it, [the elephant] pulls up trees, and walking through water, by means of it spouts water up." Aristotle also commented on the elephant's penis (very small), its pregnancy (very long), its tusks (very sharp), and its use among Indians in war.

Of all the ancient peoples Alexander sought to conquer, the Indians had the best access to elephants and trained them most extensively for battle. But since they retained ties to the Persian Empire, they also provided war elephants for the Great King. So at the Battle of Gaugamela in 331 BCE, Alexander had encountered a few elephants on the Persian side. The animals appeared large and intimidating when the king and his soldiers first caught sight of them. However, the elephants were too few in number to be effectively deployed within the huge forces amassed by Persia and Macedonia. Alexander had little to fear from them during the battle. When it was over, he presumably could have added them to his tally of high-ranking prisoners and rich war booty. But he was in a hurry—the powerful cities of Babylon, Susa, and Persepolis awaited—and elephants were hardly the most maneuverable or remunerative of treasures. The Macedonian king captured them but did not take them with him, and the fate of the Gaugamela elephants is unknown. He would not meet such animals again for the better part of four years.

As soon as he entered the Indian subcontinent in the summer of 327 BCE, Alexander began reacquainting himself with elephants. His ally Omphis had brought some to his initial encounter with the Macedonian king, and more when he met Alexander the following winter at his great procession to the Indus River. The Macedonian also acquired some elephants on his own, when his opponents fled after the capture of the Rock of Aornos and left their animals behind. By then, Alexander had added Indian elephant-catchers to his retinue, and they systematically rounded up and brought along the great beasts. In doing so, the Macedonian king was acting defensively—he didn't want trained war elephants falling into the hands of his enemies. But his action must have created enormous logistical challenges, given that each elephant ate about three hundred pounds of food a day and drank up to fifty gallons of water.

By the time he arrived at the Jhelum to face Poros, Alexander had spent some six months with elephants close at hand. Given his wide-ranging interest in animals—he was so fascinated by peacocks that he forbade his men to kill them—he doubtless observed the elephants carefully. After all, as he well knew, his success in the battle against Poros would depend on what he learned.

The elephants Alexander observed combined strength with delicacy. They walked with surprising nimbleness on heavy five-toed feet, their trunks and tails waving fore and aft. Weak sighted, with eyes only about the size of an average human's, they compensated with extraordinarily keen smell and hearing. And for the males, their huge, curving tusks—as tall as a man and weighing around fifty pounds—could be used to batter, spear, and lift whatever got in their way.

In addition to their strength, the elephants Alexander encountered were also remarkably intelligent, sensitive animals. Adept tool users, they had a carefully articulated social hierarchy and extraordinary capacity to remember both kind treatment and slights. They formed strong family bonds between mothers and children, using their trunks to guide, discipline, and lovingly caress one another. And these bonds endured beyond the grave, with bereaved elephants rocking back and forth by the body of the deceased, covering the dead with earth, and being comforted by other members of their herd, who stroked them gently with their trunks.

It was their intelligence and emotion, as much as their strength, that made the elephants so tempting to capture and train. Unsurprisingly

given their own subtle and wide-ranging forms of communication—
including trumpeting, bellows, and rumbles, as well as elaborate
body language—elephants could master a large number of spoken
commands, thirty or more depending on the individual. They could
become strongly attached to their mahouts, treating them with astonishing gentleness while defending them fiercely from everyone
else. They could figure out how to navigate swirling rivers, batter
down walls, and remove otherwise insuperable barriers such as boulders and tree trunks. And while far from natural predators (elephants
are herbivores, with a diet consisting primarily of grasses, leaves, and
seeds), they were accustomed to deploying their size, strength, and
powerful tusks aggressively, whether to establish dominance among
themselves or to frighten off smaller but still dangerous animals. All
these talents and natural tendencies made them extremely desirable
animals for war. And Poros, a proud Punjab king with the largest
number of war elephants in the region, would be sure to have trained
them well.

In addition to his elephants, Poros had a second advantage over
Alexander: the river that lay between the two armies. Known to the
Macedonians as the Hydaspes, it had its origins in the mountains
of Kashmir, carrying the snowmelt of the Himalayas south into the
Punjab plains before finally uniting with the Indus. When the Macedonian king encountered it in late spring, the Jhelum was almost in
full spate. It filled its wide banks and ran far too fast and deep for his
soldiers to wade across. Alexander recognized that he would have to
use the fleet he had assembled for the Indus, transporting the ships
overland slowly and painstakingly by oxcart some 160 miles.

Even when the fleet had reached him at the Jhelum, Alexander
knew that he could not simply launch his forces across the river in
full view of the enemy. To do so would mean leaving his soldiers vulnerable to attack as they navigated the difficult river crossing. And
even if the men were willing to expose themselves to such danger,
the horses would refuse. Even Alexander's bravest warhorses were

terrified by the elephants they could see and smell across the Jhelum. With the elephants in sight, Alexander's cavalry could never cross the river. Poros had chosen his location well.

In putting a river between himself and his enemy, Poros was following a well-established military strategy. Lacking modern fortification materials or defensive weapons, ancient generals frequently relied instead on the landscape's natural features: remote islands, steep hilltops, narrow mountain passes. In Alexander's day, they showed a particular fondness for rivers. Often, the defenders of a region would assemble an army, then select a battle site with a river separating them from their attackers. To force a battle, the aggressors would need to descend into the water—making them easy targets for arrows and javelins from above—navigate the unfamiliar element, with a current that seemed expressly designed to break up military formations, and then clamber awkwardly back up the opposite bank. They then commenced the battle wet, tired, and disorganized: a distinct disadvantage for even the most well trained and effective soldiers.

Despite the dangers of a river crossing, Alexander could feel confident that he had faced, and overcome, this challenge before. Of his four most famous battles—Granikos, Issos, Gaugamela, and now the Jhelum—three began with him forcing his way across a river before facing the enemy's onslaught. But at the Jhelum, Alexander could not simply follow the example of his younger, more impetuous self. He had years of experience and a far clearer sense, following several near-fatal encounters, of his own mortality. He would have to try something different.

Meanwhile, as his men became increasingly wet in their rain-drenched camp, Alexander sent scouts up and down the river, searching for a place to cross. He also roused his soldiers every night and led them out in battle array. At first, Poros countered, arming his own men and moving them into position directly across the river from the

Macedonians. Over time, as the attack he was preparing for failed to come to fruition, Poros stopped. The Punjab king decided that his antagonist was merely playing at war, and that his nighttime expeditions were fundamentally unserious. Poros was all the more convinced when he learned that Alexander was commandeering a massive store of grain from the countryside, enough to feed his camp by the river for months. By winter, the Jhelum would be low within its banks, its current lighter and its flow shallow enough for soldiers to wade across. A sensible man, well provided with food and a convenient (albeit sodden) camp, would wait for winter. Poros began to believe that Alexander—despite his reckless reputation—was just such a man.

Poros was almost right. His antagonist prepared to wait, bringing in supplies and making sure to broadcast far and wide how much he had. But Alexander also continued to get ready for battle, deliberately accustoming Poros to his nighttime activities until his rival failed to react. And the Macedonian king persisted in sending out scouts to search the river. If he kept at it, surely they would find him just the right place for an unexpected midnight crossing. Or so he hoped. Alexander was lucky. One day, his scouts returned from an expedition with welcome news.

Seventeen miles from camp, the scouts told Alexander, they had found a bend in the river. They had made their way through the thickly forested headland to the water's edge, where they saw an island in midriver. When they reached it, they discovered that the island was uninhabited, pathless, and covered in trees. As the scouts likely made clear to Alexander, the island would be difficult to navigate, particularly for a large army traveling over unfamiliar territory in the dark. Still, the king could hide his boats within the forest at the headland, and his soldiers and horses would be well concealed on the island, far from Poros's camp. Under the circumstances, it offered the Macedonian king the best crossing he could hope for. Alexander transported his boats, made his plans, and gave the order to cross as the rain streamed down and thunder boomed on a stormy late-spring night.

The army Alexander brought with him that night looked very different from the one with which he had crossed the Hellespont. Its backbone was still the Macedonian heavy-armed infantry, now handling their eighteen-foot spears as carefully and quietly as possible in the slashing rain. Half stayed with Alexander's best general, Krateros, at the base camp, under orders to cross as soon as the elephants moved away. The other half, along with the Silver Shields, crossed to the island with Alexander. So did many of the king's closest friends: Perdikkas, Ptolemy, and a young man named Seleukos, commander of the Silver Shields and a powerful figure after Alexander's death. Other familiar soldiers came as well, three-quarters of the Macedonian cavalry, with spears approximately three times as long as their small, tough horses. Behind them crept the light-armed javelin throwers as well as archers, both traveling on foot and wearing minimal armor; they fought from afar. All these had been with Alexander from the beginning, as had the Greek mercenaries, hoplites, and cavalry, who were left halfway to the island with orders to cross as soon as possible and aid the fight.

These familiar soldiers were, however, by no means all of Alexander's army. They were not even the majority. The Macedonian king also brought in his train Scythians—baggy pants, jewelry, tattoos, and all—along with Bactrian and Sogdian horsemen, faster and more agile than their Macedonian counterparts. Back at the base camp were more exotic soldiers: cavalrymen from the mountains and deserts of southern Afghanistan, as well as Indian infantry supplied by Omphis and other allies. In all, Alexander's army at the Jhelum was a veritable United Nations, with strong representation both from Greece and Macedonia and from the eastern Persian Empire. It was like no army a Macedonian king had ever led before, astonishing in its range of armor, weapons, tactics, and languages. Somehow, Alexander would have to coordinate their attack, if his battle plan was to have a chance of succeeding.

As the rain and thunder boomed, Alexander's army reached the headland. There they found the boats waiting and assembled for the foot soldiers, along with rafts filled with chaff for the cavalry (the horses, fearful of boats, swam across). The soldiers made it only as far as the island in midriver before Poros's scouts spotted them, then hurried off to warn the Pauravan king. The clock had begun to tick.

When Alexander's soldiers set off from the island for the eastern shore of the Jhelum, they knew that battle was coming. Poros's scouts traveled far faster than they could manage, given their heavy armor and weapons. Nor did the Indians have any need for silence or secrecy. Soon Poros would learn that Alexander had gone ahead after all, despite all his stores of grain and well-advertised plan to wait. The soldiers could not be sure how he would respond. If he sent the bulk of his army to meet them, they would be outnumbered. Only around 5,300 cavalry and 10,000 foot soldiers accompanied Alexander, while Poros had, reports claimed, at least 20,000 men. He also had his elephants—eighty-five or more, according to the ancient sources. Alexander's soldiers did not know when they would face the elephants, or how many they would encounter, but they could be sure it would happen.

In the meantime, the Macedonians arrived at what they thought was the east side of the Jhelum, only to discover, upon embarking from their ships, that it was just another island. After a few panicked moments, they found places to ford, but they were deep and the current strong. The men waded through, up to their breastplates in water, and only the horses' heads were visible (a detail that suggests, incidentally, how small horses were in the ancient world, far shorter than those of today). Finally, drenched and exhausted, the Macedonians reached the Jhelum's eastern bank.

Back at the base camp, Poros was in a quandary. He had learned from his scouts that the Macedonians were on the move, crossing the river far away. But he was unsure just how many of them had crossed—in the dawn light, the numbers in the chaotic flotilla must have been hard for his scouts to estimate—and he could still see a sizable force in camp. Nor was the Punjab king certain where Alexander himself had gone. A small, heavily armored man, he could be anywhere:

at the base, at the headlands, somewhere in between. Caught by surprise, Poros temporized. He sent his son with an advance force of fast-moving cavalry and chariots, enough to stop a small force or delay a larger one. He left a garrison at his base camp, some soldiers and, more important, a sufficient number of elephants to discourage the enemies he could see from crossing. Then he put on his well-made, beautiful armor, mounted his elephant, and gave the order to prepare for battle.

Poros's advance force reached Alexander quickly. The charioteers charged, shooting arrows and trying, with their horses and heavy six-man chariots, to run the Macedonian soldiers down. In a preview of his strategy against the elephants, Alexander countered with light-armed forces, particularly the mounted Scythian archers. As their battles against Alexander himself had demonstrated, the Scythians were nimble: able to fire, wheel around, then attack again. They used their tactics very effectively against the chariots, which were heftier and far less maneuverable. They were aided by the battleground itself, still muddy after the pouring rain the night before. They could pick off the charioteers handily as their chariots got stuck in the mud, while abrupt mud-induced stops also threw the drivers from their vehicles. With the Scythians' help, Poros's advance guard was defeated easily, his chariots captured, and his son killed. Alexander's soldiers headed onward, the full army in their sights.

For his own battleground, Poros chose carefully. He picked a sandy site along the river, broad enough to give his elephants space and not too muddy. He placed the elephants at intervals in the front of his battle line, with infantry directly behind them and cavalry on the wings. By spacing out the elephants, Poros created a longer, more visually impressive line and gave the animals more room to maneuver. At the same time, his choice meant that he had to forgo one of the most terrifying ancient battle strategies: the massed elephant charge. Still, for the Macedonians, his elephants were intimidating enough. They looked like towers from a distance, with the infantry and cavalry filling in like a vast fortress wall.

In the face of Poros's elephant towers and human wall, Alexander paused. He held his cavalry back until his slower-moving infantrymen had caught up. Even when they arrived, he did not move into battle position immediately. Instead he delayed, sending his horsemen to circle defensively around the foot soldiers until they were rested and prepared for battle. Given that his men had already marched almost twice what they covered in an average day—in full battle gear, and under extremely difficult weather conditions—Alexander was wise to rest them. The contrast with his earlier battles, though, is striking. In the eight years since he had charged across the Granikos River in northwestern Turkey, the Macedonian king had learned to wait.

When Alexander determined that his men were fully rested, he began to move into position: heavy infantry in the center, cavalry on the wings, light-armed troops (archers and javelin throwers) sprinkled throughout. Even when his men were in battle formation, he did not attack everywhere at once. He decided to hold off on assaulting the elephants, the most dangerous and unfamiliar element of Poros's army. Instead he began where he and his men had a clear advantage, with his numerically superior, extraordinarily well trained cavalry.

Alexander started the battle by focusing on Poros's left wing. He peppered the horsemen with arrows first, softening them up as he prepared to charge. Before he could do so, however, Poros realized that Alexander was about to attack his left, and countered by re-inforcing it. The Pauravan king pulled his cavalry from the opposite (right) wing, moving them around the back of the army as quickly as he could. It was a risky move, since it concentrated the Punjab horse on one side of the army and left Poros's right vulnerable. But Poros needed all his horsemen—he had only three to four thousand, well below Alexander's count—to have a hope of prevailing in a cavalry battle against the Macedonian king.

Unfortunately for Poros, Alexander had anticipated this stratagem. He had told his close friend Koinos, in charge of the Bactrian and Sogdian horsemen across from Poros's right, to follow the Pauravan cavalry if they began to move. Koinos and his men tracked Poros's right-wing cavalry all the way around the back of the Punjab army, conveniently avoiding the elephants placed at the front. When Koinos arrived at the back of Poros's left wing, the Pauravans were thrown into confusion. With Alexander in front and Koinos behind, they tried to rearrange themselves to fight in both directions. At this moment, with the same flawless timing that had served him so well in earlier battles, the Macedonian king struck. Charging into the Punjab horse while they were in disarray, he terrified them and put them to flight. Back they raced toward the shelter of the elephants, in the words of one ancient writer, "as if to a friendly citadel."

As the Pauravan army struggled to accommodate and protect their fleeing cavalrymen, Alexander pressed forward with his attack. Now was the time, he judged, to take on the elephants. The Macedonian king ordered the main body of his army, the heavy infantry and the light-armed troops, toward Poros's forces. What happened next was terrifying for both sides. As the infantry moved forward, the elephants charged: trampling infantrymen underfoot, spearing them with their tusks, picking them up with their trunks, then passing them helpless to their mahouts or dashing them to the ground. The Macedonian army fought back. They shot arrows and threw javelins at the elephants, hacked at their feet with axes and their trunks with *kopides*, cruel sickle-shaped Persian swords. Blood, weapons, and human and animal body parts flew everywhere. As the Macedonian infantry reeled under the elephants' attack, the emboldened Punjab cavalry charged again.

Attacking with cavalry was an understandable move on Poros's part—in ancient battles, horsemen were almost always the main strike force—but they did not serve the Pauravan king well. These were opponents Alexander was used to fighting, and his stronger, better-trained force quickly devastated the Punjab one. The Macedonian king's cavalry went further, using their larger numbers to encircle the Pauravan army. With the infantry directly opposite the front line of elephants and the cavalry to the back and sides, Alexander's soldiers began to draw a noose around their opponents. They surrounded their enemies, denying them freedom of movement and, even more dangerously, the possibility of flight. Then they tightened the noose, moving in from all sides. The elephants, frightened and in pain, began to retreat. With their huge size and awkward, lumbering movements, they looked to the Macedonians like great ships backing water. As Alexander's men picked off their mahouts with arrows and harried them further, they suddenly stampeded—heading not toward the Macedonians, but toward their own side.

An elephant stampede is extraordinarily dangerous, particularly within a confined space. Although elephants do not run quickly, at least relative to men or horses, they are far larger, heavier, and more destructive. When stampeding, they tend to move together in the same direction, trunks and tails swinging widely, feet thundering. Normally cautious, they become bold and careless of their surroundings, breaking down or trampling any animal that gets in their way. Elephant stampedes in the ancient world were so feared that the great Carthaginian general Hasdrubel equipped his mahouts with weapons expressly to kill their mounts if they began to lose control. Poros, however, did not, and in any case many of the elephants' drivers were already dead. Maddened by pain and deprived of their riders, the elephants charged into Poros's soldiers, killing many. They did Alexander's work for him, as the Macedonian king no doubt intended. Alexander had his own elephants, courtesy of Omphis and his allies, but had absolutely declined to use them in the battle. A situation like this was likely why.

With the elephant stampede, the Battle of the Jhelum was essentially over. Those Pauravan cavalry, infantry, and elephants who could fled the Macedonian noose. They were pursued by Krateros, whose troops had finally made it across the river. Tired and disheartened, the Pauravans were confronted at the very end of the battle by fresh, well-rested men. Poros's troops did their best to escape or, failing that, to surrender. By one account, nine thousand men were taken alive, along with eighty elephants. The death toll on the Punjab side is unclear, but likely heavy, as many as the prisoners or even more. Dead as well were all Poros's chief commanders along with two of his sons.

Alexander, by contrast, lost fewer men. None of his close friends and generals perished, and few of his cavalry. His infantry had suffered most, since they were on the front line against the elephants. As time would show, even those who survived retained strong traumatic memories of the battle, and of the terrible havoc that the elephants wrought.

Boukephalos, the horse Alexander had tamed as an adolescent and ridden in all his major battles, was also a casualty. Enormous for an ancient horse, and, like his master, proudly aggressive, he was now likely fifteen to twenty years old—very old for a horse—and worn out from the extreme conditions prevailing on Alexander's campaign. Some sources say he died from wounds, others from old age and heat exhaustion. Whatever the cause, he perished after the Battle of the Jhelum. Alexander grieved, gave him an ostentatious funeral, and founded a city in his honor.

Poros himself escaped death, though he was severely wounded in the right shoulder. Exceptionally tall and riding the largest elephant, he was a magnet for Macedonian arrows during the battle. Due to his well-made armor, only one got through, but it was enough. Weakened through loss of blood, Poros began to retreat, and his elephant sensed his vulnerability. Elephant and rider slowed down, and Omphis was able to catch up with them. Alexander's main South Asian ally attempted to persuade his longtime opponent to surrender—and got a spear thrown down at him for his pains. Other local leaders received similar treatment, until one the Greeks called Meroes (perhaps the young Chandragupta, future leader of the Mauryan Empire) finally convinced Poros to cease his flight. He rested, drank, and came to Alexander. When the two met face-to-face, the Macedonian asked his Pauravan rival how he wished to be treated. Poros's answer was clear, proud, unrepentant: "Like a king."

Alexander appreciated the chance to demonstrate his magnanimity before a worthy opponent. He restored Poros's kingdom to him—subordinate to himself, to be sure—and even added further territory. As with his gifts to Omphis, Alexander's restoration of Poros put the Punjab king under tremendous obligation to him. It gave him a powerful local ally at the periphery of his empire, in a land where it would always be difficult for Macedonians to exercise control. The Persians had acted similarly, surrounding the core of their empire with client kings; later, the Romans would do the same. It was an intelligent and logical administrative strategy. Unfortunately, it also infuriated everyone on Alexander's side.

The Macedonian king's South Asian allies were upset to see intransigent opposition better rewarded than their loyalty, but Alexander's soldiers were even more furious. They had spent the past month camped by a rainy, swollen river. Their tents had been infested by small, poisonous snakes. By day, they had watched the elephants in the camp opposite. By night, they had sallied out under arms, in feints that came to nothing. Finally, they had crossed the river in pouring rain and fought for hours against unfamiliar, terrifying opponents. And now that they had prevailed, Alexander had chosen to keep the enemy king in power and give him more of the land *they* had won. The soldiers could hardly help concluding that they had suffered tremendously simply in order to reinstate the status quo.

Alexander barely deigned to notice his soldiers' discontent. He rested them, held athletic and equestrian games, founded two cities—the one for Boukephalos and another, Nikaia, in honor of his victory—and sacrificed to the gods. Perhaps in tacit acknowledgment of the army's resentment, he indulged in a round of extravagant gift-giving: a crown plus one thousand gold pieces for every general, and for the common soldiers, lesser but still significant monetary rewards. Alexander could well afford to, since the Indian subcontinent had given him access to extraordinary riches. But even these gifts could not placate his soldiers. As they resumed their march eastward, their resentment only increased.

Then the monsoon struck.

TWELVE

Monsoon and Mutiny

Pakistan
Summer–Fall 326 BCE

AS ALEXANDER'S SOLDIERS RECUPERATED from their battle wounds and their traumatic memories of Poros's war elephants, they faced another enemy: the South Asian monsoon. Gone was the extreme heat of late spring, through which the unlucky troops had fought, sweating in their heavy armor, at the Jhelum. It was replaced by constant rain, thunder, and lightning for seventy days.

The South Asian monsoon rains were like nothing the Macedonians (or, for that matter, the Persians, Bactrians, and Scythians accompanying them) had ever experienced. Distinctive to the tropical belt of eastern Africa and south and southeast Asia, the rains arrived every summer with predictable, implacable ferocity. They poured down in great slashing sheets of water, fast and hard. They turned slow-moving, placid rivers into raging torrents, flooding their banks and engulfing the nearby countryside. Hills became islands; flatlands, lakes. In towns, streets changed to rivers, through which men waded calf-, thigh-, and even chest-high. The rains drummed on houses, then swamped them, leaving standing water at their bases for weeks or even months. The monsoons could be beneficial, spreading nutrient-rich soil throughout the fertile agricultural lands of the upper Indus River valley. But for Alexander and his soldiers—living in tents, exposed to the monsoon's fury—they were brutal.

The monsoons afflicting Alexander and his men in the summer of 326 BCE were the result of the Indian subcontinent's distinctive geographical contours. With the Himalayas to the north and the Indian Ocean surrounding the rest of the peninsula, South Asia is perfectly designed to intensify the monsoon's torrential rain. In early summer, the sun baked the land, with temperatures in June averaging 100 degrees Fahrenheit where Alexander battled Poros along the Jhelum. Since heat rises, like steam from a teakettle, the hot air moved up. Then into the gap rolled cooler, humid air from the ocean, which, when it reached the land, turned to rain. Prevented by the heights of the Himalayas from moving northward, the moist air stayed over the subcontinent, drenching it continuously for weeks. Only with the cooler fall weather would the cycle reverse itself, with dry air from the land blowing out to sea. In autumn, the monsoon would end, the floods recede, and the crops, fed and fertilized, would make a rich harvest. In the meantime, the inhabitants of the Indian subcontinent endured the rains as best they could.

Since ancient geographical theories of India were complex, contradictory, and largely erroneous, Alexander's soldiers understood none of this. And they were likely unprepared for the monsoon's onslaught, since the year before they had been so far north in the mountains as to avoid it nearly or completely. Now, however, they were fully experiencing the monsoon's intensity. Through it, they crossed rivers, watching boats shatter as the swift-moving current thrust them against the rocks. Through it, they besieged towns and ravaged the flooding countryside. They were drenched, frustrated, and completely out of their element. Rain in Macedonia came mostly during the winter, outside of campaigning season, and deposited under twenty inches of water per year. In the Punjab, rain in the summer meant the soldiers still had to fight.

Rain was the most frequent of the soldiers' burdens but by no means the only one. As they moved farther from the highlands and into the foothills, lush forest, and plains of the Punjab, they encountered increasing numbers of unnerving, often dangerous animals. They saw monkeys, likely rhesus macaques, whose expressive faces and clever, highly social behavior initially frightened the Macedonians into thinking they were men. They had to be reassured by Omphis that the small, noisy, furry individuals in the distance were only monkeys. Fascinated, the soldiers exploited the macaques' curiosity and imitative behavior to trap some, adding to the exotic character of what must by then have been an extremely diverse army.

Less visible and more insidious were the snakes. The soldiers encountered vipers, with short, fat bodies and long, erectile fangs, and cobras, with shorter fixed fangs, longer, slenderer bodies, and great shaggy hoods that flared when they were about to strike. The Greeks and Macedonians were familiar with venomous snakes—as witness the myth of Eurydice, wife of the great musician Orpheus, who died of snakebite. But the snakes they encountered in Pakistan were more numerous and more deadly. Men bit by vipers saw their bites swell up in one to two hours, followed by bloodstained spit, systemic poisoning, and often, in two to three days, death. With cobras, death was equally painful but came faster, in about five hours. The soldiers were terrified, sleeping in hammocks to avoid snakes slithering on the ground at night, sometimes fearing to sleep at all. Only later did they learn from locals of natural, plant-based antidotes, so effective they seemed like magic to the Macedonians.

As they contended with the monsoon, monkeys, and snakes, the soldiers kept following Alexander east. They did so with outward obedience, but inwardly, their frustrations mounted. They were still traumatized by their battle with Poros's elephants. They also remained resentful of their king's generous treatment of the enemy who had inflicted so much pain on them.

The soldiers formed an immense human caravan, with an army at least some thirty thousand strong, and with women, children, and other camp followers likely pushing the total number over forty-five thousand. Initially, they were all moving through Poros's kingdom: unified, stable, and, thankfully, well-inclined toward the Macedonians, since Alexander and Poros had become great friends, campaigning together in the months following their battle on the Jhelum. But for all his war elephants, Poros was king only of a limited territory, stretching from the Jhelum to the next river over, the Chenab, an area of perhaps 3.7 million acres. Once the soldiers had traversed his realm, they were back to moving through enemy territory—all the more so, as the militarily aggressive Poros had plenty of foes.

Among the enemies facing the soldiers, the most numerous and potentially dangerous were the Kathaians (likely the Sanskrit *Katha*). Self-governing, they were among the most daring and warlike groups in South Asia, along with the Malli and Sudrakai. Poros had already antagonized the Malli and Sudrakai, having attempted an invasion of their territory before the Macedonians' arrival (he lost). His previous dealings with the Kathaians are unrecorded, but Alexander now faced their antagonism, along with that of a cousin of Poros who had his own realm nearby. Alexander dispatched Hephaistion to the kingdom of the rebellious cousin, and left Krateros and Koinos behind at the Chenab to collect supplies from those already conquered. He ordered Poros to bring troops and elephants, and set out in haste for the Kathaians.

Three days later, Alexander and his men stood before the walls of the Kathaians' capital, Sangala. Inside were thousands of warlike individuals, from a group whose superlative beauty and unusual marriage customs—the bride and groom chose one another themselves and married for love—attracted much comment from Greek writers. Good-looking and (presumably) happily married, the Kathaians had paid little attention to military preparedness before the Macedonians' arrival. As elsewhere in South Asia, they built their city walls of brick, not stone. To reinforce their defenses as the army drew close, they

surrounded Sangala with three rings of wagons, tightly yoked together and filled with soldiers. Alexander led a cavalry charge against
them, but could not thread his horses through the outermost ring.
The Kathaians, meanwhile, sensibly refused to come out and fight.

Stymied, Alexander left his cavalry behind and continued the
battle on foot. He managed with his infantry to penetrate the first
ring of wagons, where a fierce battle ensued. Space was tight, so the
Macedonians were unable to use many of their best maneuvers. Instead, they had a vicious, hand-to-hand melee to contend with, and
casualties on both sides. At length the Kathaians abandoned the
fight, and fled back to their brick walls.

For some time, the Macedonian soldiers surrounded the city, preparing for a siege. They built a stockade and guarded it constantly—a
wise decision, as the Kathaians tried to escape twice. Finally, when Poros
returned with siege engines, the soldiers were able to undermine the
walls and take the city. It was a large one, the center of the region, and
many people from the countryside had fled there for safety. In doing
so, the Kathaians made what proved to be a disastrous choice.

On Alexander's orders, the soldiers were unusually brutal to Sangala's
inhabitants as they took the city. They killed as many as one-quarter of
the city's population in the immediate aftermath of the siege. The rest
they captured, to sell into slavery or to use as hostages. They even razed
Sangala to the ground.

No archaeological evidence for Sangala exists; even its exact location
is unknown. Nor do we have any South Asian inscriptions or literary
sources about the Kathaians to nuance the idealized description of
them provided by Alexander's helmsman Onesikritos. It is unclear how
accurate his picture of the beautiful, romantically married Sangalans
is: True reflection of actual practice, or exoticized, utopian dream? We
will never know, since Alexander and his soldiers destroyed whatever
evidence there was when they devastated the city.

Alexander's harshness at Sangala had immediate repercussions.
Contrary to his hopes, it antagonized the Kathaians' neighbors. Instead

of frightening them into submission, the razing of Sangala intensified their resistance. For the inhabitants of the Punjab, it suggested that Alexander was waging war in a "bloody, barbarian manner," as one Greek writer put it ("barbarian" being the worst insult possible according to the Greeks). The Indians were right. Even by the Macedonian king's standards, the treatment of Sangala was unusually cruel, both in the level of civilian casualties during the city's sack and in the complete destruction of the place afterward. He even pursued and killed about five hundred invalid Kathaians who had fled to nearby towns, but not fast enough to escape his army.

The resistance Alexander faced in the aftermath of the siege of Sangala forced him to change tactics. At the next town he captured, he conducted a treaty and took hostages, as he had with the Dionysos-worshipping Nysaeans the year before. Proceeding onward, he marched with the hostages at the head of his army. Upon arrival at yet another resistant South Asian town, he used the hostages as negotiators. Convinced by their neighbors of the Macedonians' capacity for clemency, the inhabitants capitulated, and other nearby cities followed suit.

The change of course suggests Alexander's flexibility: his willingness, here as in Central Asia, to adopt more malleable and conciliatory tactics when sheer force failed. At the same time, his transformation must have been confusing to his men, who had to adapt very quickly from killing South Asians to safeguarding them. Also to their frustration, Alexander's flexibility had its limits. Despite the resistance, he kept heading east, "for it seemed to him that there was no end to the war while an enemy remained," according to one of the king's ancient biographers.

Alexander's continued march eastward, so exasperating to his soldiers, has also frustrated modern historians. As many have noted, by this point in the campaign the Macedonian king had far outstripped the bounds of the former Persian Empire (it had stretched at most to the Indus River). Alexander's soldiers were tired; the local inhabitants unwelcoming at best. Although the land was rich and fertile, the greater his conquests became, the harder they would be to hold. It is hard not to wonder why he kept going.

The king's ancient biographers blame pothos, Alexander's unquenchable desire for what he did not possess. Modern historians have embraced their own theories, including, variously, love of warfare, megalomania, or a civilizing mission. The truth is likely somewhere in between. Alexander was driven by the logic of empire and by his own forceful ambition. There was always another city to conquer, another powerful king or wealthy autonomous region. And Alexander sought more than just conquest. Despite all his soldiers' suffering and frustration, he still wanted to reach the end of the world. So he kept heading east, dreaming of Ocean.

As Alexander learned from the next powerful king he encountered, however, Ocean was still a long way off. The ruler was Phegeus, king of the territory just to the west of the Beas River. Alexander, Poros, and their soldiers—including Hephaistion, Krateros, and Koinos, who had returned from their own missions—stayed with Phegeus two days. They rested, feasted, and indulged in a round of competitive gift-giving, a game at which the openhanded Macedonian king excelled. Alexander confirmed Phegeus in his kingship, then pressed him for military intelligence. What lay beyond the Beas, the Macedonian demanded. What new challenges would it pose?

Phegeus described a twelve-day march through barren wasteland. Then the army would arrive at the Ganges, India's greatest river. If they managed to get across (no small matter in monsoon season), they faced a mighty realm, larger and more militarily powerful than any Indian kingdom Alexander had yet encountered. The Ganges king, Phegeus claimed, had 200,000 foot soldiers, 20,000 cavalrymen, and 2,000 chariots. Most fearsome of all were his war elephants, some 3,000 to 4,000 of them.

Alexander, who had found Poros's eighty-five or so elephants difficult enough to contend with, was skeptical. He could scarcely believe
in a king with so many war elephants—several orders of magnitude
more than he had faced before. He was certainly intrigued, perhaps
concerned.

As later events would reveal, Alexander was dangerously out of
touch with the frustrations of his soldiers. But even he must have
recognized how much they would fear the Ganges king's war elephants, given the trauma and damage that Poros's much smaller
number of animals had inflicted. Alexander turned to Poros, demanding to know the truth about the Ganges kingdom. Was it really
so powerful and well endowed with elephants? Or was this just an
Indian tall tale?

To Alexander's surprise, Poros agreed with King Phegeus's assess-
ment. He told the Macedonian that the Ganges king was indeed a
strong and militarily impressive ruler, with just as many elephants as
Phegeus said. On the other hand, Poros said encouragingly, the king
was unpopular with his own people. He had killed the previous king
and married his victim's wife, violating any number of Indian taboos.

The story of the militarily impressive Ganges king may well have
been accurate; Chandragupta Maurya, the later conqueror of the
region, claimed the same. Phegeus's description of a powerful kingdom on the upper Ganges is likewise borne out by the archaeological
evidence, which shows an area with large fortified urban centers,
rice-based agriculture, coinage, and sophisticated weaponry. Few
literary records of the kingdom exist, but traces remain from the later
account of a Greek ambassador who went to the Ganges to treat with
Chandragupta. As he negotiated with the Mauryan emperor, trading
territory and a Macedonian king's daughter for war elephants, the
ambassador would observe the Ganges kingdom with fascination. In
his memoir, one of the first Greeks to set eyes on the Ganges would
describe the luxurious wooden-walled capital of Pataliputra, with a
reported 570 towers and 64 gates.

Phegeus's and Poros's comments served only to entice Alexander. But he still had to convince his soldiers. As they camped together by the Beas River, Alexander could see the toll that his conquest of the Persian Empire had taken on them. Their armor and weapons were worn, their horses' hooves thin from the long, shoeless march. With Macedonian woolen clothes long gone, they had been forced to make their garments of recut South Asian fabrics—better suited to the climate, but doubtless strange and uncomfortable to those unaccustomed to wearing them. They had been contending with the monsoon for more than two months.

Alexander recognized that his soldiers' spirits were flagging. To improve morale, he sent them out to ravage enemy territory—callously allowing the nearby inhabitants to suffer for his troops' frustration. While they killed and looted to their hearts' content, he called an assembly of their women and children.

Rarely mentioned by ancient writers, these women and children were nonetheless critical to Alexander's soldiers. Diverse and heterogeneous in background, they likely spoke a cacophony of languages and ranged in appearance from pale, light-eyed Scythians from the Central Asian frontier to dark-haired, olive-skinned Egyptians from the empire's southern borders. What unified them was their subject status: all the women had been forced or persuaded to follow the army as it conquered the regions they called home. By this point in the campaign, they were clearly very numerous, and still very much in evidence despite its difficulties. They were not under constant guard, as their presence at the camp during the soldiers' looting expedition shows. But they had never wanted or imagined joining Alexander's campaign.

To these women, the king made a promise. He tacitly acknowledged the unstable, hazardous, and vulnerable situation they were in: dependent on men who had conquered their lands, exposed to the rigors of the strenuous campaign, raising children amid forced marches, ambushes, battles, and city sieges. Alexander sought to make amends, offering the women a monthly stipend, and the children a payout based on their fathers' military records, with the highest bonuses for the most distinguished soldiers' sons. It was little enough, from the perspective of a fabulously wealthy king who could easily afford it. Still, it was unusually generous by ancient standards, particularly since it was targeted at the unofficial partners of active-duty men; most Hellenic states offered support only to war widows and war orphans.

Alexander's stipends for the women and children of the Macedonian army were intended to aid his soldiers, offering stability and support for their partners, while looting and pay made the men themselves rich. As with many of Alexander's actions, it was pragmatic, not altruistic. If he had really cared for the women, he would have left them in their homes. Still, it was an innovative and thoughtful response to the difficult personal situation his conquests had created, targeted at those who suffered most from his campaigns and benefited least.

Alexander's stipends were also forward-thinking. The children of the camp—the boys, at least—were natural soldiers: schooled from birth in the military ethos, inured to hardship, well versed in weapons, commands, and tactics. They were also bicultural and, in essence, stateless, owing allegiance to the Macedonian army alone. They were thus the perfect recruits for Alexander. Bonuses for them were down payments on the future army of which he dreamed.

As his future soldiers were at most only eight years old, however, Alexander needed to do more for the army he had now. When his men returned from their pillaging expedition, he called an assembly, perhaps of the entire army—or, more likely, given its size, of the officer class. They came to hear their commander in full military dress:

helmets, breastplates, tunics, greaves. They probably brought their weapons as well, since they rarely appeared without them (hence the danger of altercations at banquets and drinking parties). Fresh from their looting expedition, the officers were eager to hear what their leader had to say. They were used to learning of Alexander's major decisions through military assemblies. Perhaps at this one he would finally say the words they were longing to hear, and tell them he had decided to turn back.

Alexander's speech was not what the officers had hoped for. The Macedonian king probably told his officers of Phegeus's stories, and of the vast, rich, militarily powerful kingdom with thousands of elephants that awaited them by the Ganges. Perhaps Alexander mentioned as well his belief that the Ganges ran to Ocean, the great outer sea he had long dreamed of reaching. By now, it seemed tantalizingly close. From Ocean, they could sail to the Persian Gulf. Then they could take their ships around Africa to the Pillars of Herakles, the Greek term for the Straits of Gibraltar, at the mouth of the Mediterranean. Alexander had no idea of the enormity of what he hoped for, the sheer scale and vastness of the continents and oceans involved. But he had conquered the Persian Empire and by this time ventured well beyond it. Having succeeded, however implausibly, why should he not dream of worldwide connectivity and conquest?

As Alexander turned toward his officers, with his huge eyes; long, tousled hair; and aspiring gaze, a long silence followed. He waited, trying to coax them into speech. No one responded. Perhaps no one dared to respond. The officers had their armor, their weapons. As a group, they vastly outnumbered their commander. They could have killed him on the spot, imprisoned him, or forced him to do their bidding. But he was their king, and they had sworn to follow him. He had their allegiance, their respect, even their love. Despite all the exhausting and unreasonable demands he had made on them, and their own angrily whispered frustrations, Alexander's officers hesitated at the thought of open defiance. Instead, some of the men—tough, battle hardened, frequently brutal soldiers—dissolved into tears.

Alexander's relationship with his men was unusually intense, even for a charismatic military leader. He had grown up with many of his officers in the competitive but relatively egalitarian atmosphere of the Macedonian court. He served with them as a teenager, fighting in the front lines at Khaironeia. At Philip's death, as a vulnerable, beardless twenty-year-old, he had depended heavily on their support during his early days as king.

Ten years later, Alexander had in many ways surpassed his men's expectations. Despite his youth, he had demonstrated mastery of all aspects of warfare. Physically daring, he still fought at the forefront of every battle. At the same time, he maintained his grasp of the battle as a whole: exploiting enemy weaknesses, sending reinforcements where they were needed, using innovative tactics to succeed even at heavy odds. When it was over, he honored the dead and visited the wounded, rewarded those who had distinguished themselves, and saw to it that all soldiers had time to recover from their injuries.

Alexander was not only a brilliant general. He also mastered the less glamorous but equally critical military science of logistics, ensuring that his soldiers knew where they were going, avoided unnecessary hardships, and had enough to eat. Given the scale of his army and the fact that they lived off the land in enemy territory, this was an astonishing accomplishment. Alexander chose his subordinates well, giving them the support and direction they needed, but also the autonomy and opportunity for distinction they craved. His officers repaid him with fierce loyalty and exceptional achievement—only rarely, as with Spitamenes's attack at the paradise near Marakanda, do we hear of their defeat.

Even Alexander's flaws bound his men more closely to him. When he pushed his bodyguard away and insisted on facing a lion alone, he killed it—and his frightened soldiers insisted he never hunt alone again. However grudgingly, he acknowledged his foolhardiness and acceded to their wishes. So, too, when he was agonized and disconsolate after the death of Kleitos, horrified by what he had done and refusing food and drink, it was his men who saved him. While his friends spoke to him gently and persuaded him to eat a little, the panicked army voted to declare Kleitos's killing a justifiable homicide. At these moments and many others, there was a reciprocity between the king and his soldiers. They were strong when he was wrongheaded or weak. Alexander recognized and often encouraged this reciprocity, accepting influence despite his claim to absolute rule.

Alexander was the kind of commander soldiers dreamed of: brave, generous, enormously talented. He shared in his men's hardships, knew their names, understood them better than they did themselves. For ten years, they had trusted him enough to follow him everywhere. That was what made his speech at the Beas so upsetting. It showcased the enormous gulf between Alexander and his soldiers. He dreamed of the Ganges, Ocean, and worldwide conquest. They just wanted to go home.

At the assembly, the uneasy silence finally broke. The man who spoke was Koinos, one of Alexander's most capable and trusted generals. Koinos had served with distinction from the very start of Alexander's reign. He had played a prominent role in all the major battles during the Persian conquest and had the scars to show for it, having been seriously wounded at Gaugamela. Given independent commands in Central Asia and Pakistan, he had performed admirably, and had indeed just returned from the last of them, bringing supplies (however unwillingly) for the army's journey east. Koinos was impeccably loyal, and Alexander knew it. After all, he had sided with the Macedonian king at the conspiracy trial of Philotas, despite the fact that he was married to the sister of the accused. Never before had he so much as questioned Alexander's decisions, even with the hardship and heart-break they caused. Now he was tired, perhaps already sickened by the illness that would cause his death a few weeks later. He took off his helmet to signal for the assembly's attention, and haltingly began to speak.

Koinos's speech is imperfectly preserved, but the gist of his argument is clear: Alexander himself might have boundless energy and enthusiasm for an eastern campaign. His men were exhausted. With illness, disabilities, and battle losses, few of his original soldiers survived. Those who did were older and feebler, longing for home. As men wept around him and shouted their agreement, Koinos begged his king to accept their limitations and lead the army back to Macedonia. Then, if he so wished, he could raise another and continue his endless wars of conquest. His soldiers asked only to be left in peace.

Alexander was furious—and also, clearly, astonished. As his treatment of their women and children shows, he had some inkling of the soldiers' discouragement. Still, he was taken aback by the extent and breadth of it. He had been operating on the assumption that the journey eastward was inevitable: securing supplies, forging alliances, gathering military intelligence about the enemies he was likely to face. Now there was opposition. And it came not simply from the rank-and-file soldiers, who might more easily be bribed or cowed, but from his closest friends and top generals. For though only Koinos had spoken, the tears and acclamations of the other officers showed Alexander that he spoke for all.

Alexander dismissed the assembly abruptly and headed for the royal quarters. He refused to admit even his good friends as he remained there angrily for three days. Like his hero Achilles sulking in his tent, Alexander clearly meant to make his men suffer for their opposition. He withdrew what he believed they cared for most—himself—only to discover that he had radically misjudged them. Unlike the aftermath of the death of Kleitos, the soldiers did not hurriedly assemble to ratify his behavior. Instead, they waited. For three days, Alexander and his men remained at loggerheads, watching to see who would blink first.

Concerted opposition to a military commander was rare in the Greek and Macedonian world, and Alexander had not previously faced it. His father had seen complaints—particularly arguments over back pay—and Classical Athenian generals had had their behavior questioned and faced courts-martial in the aftermath of their campaigns. Later, during the tumultuous years of the Late Republic, full-scale mutinies would break out in the Roman army, with soldiers demanding money, food, or less often a change of venue for their campaigns. These events could be violent, involving threats or physical danger to the commanding officers. But they were relatively frequent, and usually resolved peacefully; thirty of them occurred in the last hundred years of the Republic, with even the famous Julius Caesar facing three.

The stalemate between Alexander and his army had little in common with these later Roman mutinies. The soldiers wanted for neither cash nor food—both generously distributed by Alexander—and they never resorted to violence or threats. They also had the support of their commanding officers, Alexander alone excepted, as the response to Koinos's speech makes clear. The soldiers' actions had more in common with a peaceful political protest, as they sought through nonviolent means to change their leader's course of action. They acted as much in sorrow as in anger, weeping even as they opposed their king.

Alexander did not seek to quell the soldiers' peaceful protest with violence. A master tactician, perhaps he calculated the odds and realized it would not work. He was isolated, vulnerable, and on the edge of his empire. He had the whole army—common soldiers and officers, Macedonians, Greeks, Persians, Scythians, Bactrians, and South Asians—united against him. If he ordered Koinos or other leaders imprisoned, who would obey?

Instead, on the third day, Alexander capitulated. He had his sooth-sayers conduct sacrifices at the river, where the omens proved decidedly (and conveniently) unfavorable. Then he called the eldest of the Companions and his closest friends together. He told them that with the gods against him, he could go no farther east. Instead, he would turn back at the Beas and bring the army home.

Some historians have seen Alexander's capitulation at the Beas as an enormous setback: for the ever-victorious commander, an unquestionable, stinging defeat. Certainly it rankled. As later events would show, Alexander remembered the incident, and took care that it would not happen again. But while he was alienated from his soldiers and made an initial insensitive speech to them, the Macedonian king also managed to formulate a flexible, nonviolent response to Koinos. In an unusual, uncelebrated fashion, he showed greatness here.

His men greeted Alexander's new speech with tears of joy. They were astonished and relieved in equal measure. The soldiers had no constitutional right to assembly or free speech, no authority for what they did beyond their own numbers and their absolute united front. They could not have been sure how Alexander would respond, how far he might try to push back against them. They doubtless saw his consultation of the soothsayers for what it was: a face-saving strategy that allowed the king to claim he was obeying the gods, not giving in to his exhausted men.

Before they headed west, Alexander and his soldiers worked together to celebrate and consecrate the site on the Beas. They built enormous altars by the river, twins of the altars they had erected at the Hellespont when they entered the Persian Empire eight years before. Together these altars marked the limits of Alexander's empire, sanctifying its borders with religious power. To hallow them further, Alexander and his soldiers performed sacrifices on the altars, supposedly seventy-five feet high, and commemorated their construction with athletic and equestrian games.

Along with the altars, some ancient writers claim that Alexander ordered his soldiers to erect an immense camp on the Beas. These authors describe high walls, deep ditches, and a circuit three times the size of Alexander's actual camp, intended not for garrison duty but as a permanent abandoned monument, meant to convince subsequent generations of the gigantic stature and ambition of the great conqueror's army.

The story of the enormous camp, with its imputation of the king's archaeological self-consciousness, invites skepticism, all the more so as no traces of the site have ever been found. Most likely it is an ancient elaboration on the (more plausible) tale of the altars, intended to present Alexander as increasingly megalomaniacal due to the malign influence of the East. It fits with a narrative, popular among modern as well as ancient historians, of Alexander's decline and fall: his trajectory from upstanding Macedonian monarch to corrupt, violent Oriental despot.

As with many biographical trajectories, this one should be treated with caution. After all, Alexander was possibly responsible for the assassination of his father at the age of twenty, and certainly for the pitiless destruction of Thebes a year later. He massacred Greek mercenaries at the Granikos River at twenty-two, the entire civilian population of Tyre at twenty-four. Likewise at twenty-four, he visited the shrine of Zeus-Amun in the western Egyptian desert and subsequently proclaimed himself the son of the god. Rather than a trajectory toward corruption, violence, or megalomania, Alexander's career shows a continuous oscillation: between brutality and clemency, egalitarian and authoritarian modes, impulsivity and calculation. The East did not corrupt the Macedonian king. Instead, from the outset he contained within himself the seeds of everything he would one day become.

The events at the Beas River showcase both strands of Alexander's personality. On the one hand, they demonstrate his overweening ambition, his obliviousness toward his troops' feelings, and his absolute fury at their opposition to him—despotic qualities all. On the other hand, the Macedonian king's response to his soldiers' opposition was in no way authoritarian. Rather, it was supple and pragmatic, with a clear recognition of the limits of his royal mandate. And as the aftermath of the events would demonstrate, it was even creative, giving Alexander some room to maneuver despite the promise he had made. At the Beas, the king vowed to bring his soldiers home. But he never vowed how or when.

THIRTEEN

The End of the World

Pakistan
Fall 326–Summer 325 BCE

AS ALEXANDER AND HIS ARMY began heading westward, the king considered his options for the journey back. The site of the protest—a lush, green river valley in present-day Pakistan—was around 1,800 miles from Persepolis, if the heart of the Persian Empire qualified as home, and, if not, a farther 2,300 or so from the Macedonian capital, Pella. And Alexander wasn't traveling light. He had a large army, thousands of camp followers, and a truly extraordinary quantity of loot. Moving was a constant logistical challenge. Even if he had wanted to, Alexander couldn't return quickly.

Unsurprisingly given his predilections, Alexander did not want to go home fast. The simplest thing to do—going back the way he had come, through the now comparatively safe and peaceful territory of Afghanistan—held little attraction for him. Alexander still craved adventure, despite his troops' protests. So, too, his youthful studies with Aristotle had given him an interest in exploration, scientific as well as thrill-seeking in origin. To come so close, in his view, to the end of the world, and then not to see it, was a wasted opportunity. As he headed back west to the site of his battle on the Jhelum, Alexander ordered additions to his fleet. The army would be going home, but on his terms.

Alexander's plan, based on what he knew of Indian geography, was reasonable though not without danger. As he had perhaps envisioned when he first built a fleet, the king and his soldiers would begin by sailing along the Jhelum, following the river as it joined first with the Chenab, then the Ravi, and eventually the Indus, the great north–south artery of present-day Pakistan. Then they would sail to the mouth of the Indus and see Ocean after all. In fact, it would be the Indian Ocean, into which the South Asian peninsula projected. For Alexander, that would be as close as he came to the end of the world.

Alexander's deployment of a fleet, and his interest in waterways, were not arbitrary. Along with his thirst for adventure and his scientific curiosity, Alexander had practical reasons for his action. The Macedonian king had just conquered a sizable portion of the Indian subcontinent, and wanted to keep this wealthy, resource-rich region within his empire. To do so, he needed connectivity, so that the area would be accessible to government administrators, traders, and, if necessary, the army. He could build roads, as had the Persians, natives of the Iranian Plateau. But as a Macedonian, Alexander thought differently. His country supplied the timber that had outfitted generations of Hellenic fleets, and he was oriented toward the sea. As he well knew, in the ancient world travel by water was always cheaper and easier than by land. In sailing down the Indus to Ocean, Alexander sought a way to connect South Asia to the Middle East and Europe by ship, speeding transit and facilitating trade. His goal was understandable, although it would not be fully realized until the Age of Exploration, some 1,800 years in the future. Columbus, after all, had the same idea.

Unsurprisingly given his ambitious plans, Alexander did not manage to bring back everyone. Among those who failed to return was Koinos, the man most responsible for their journey home. Perhaps already sickening when he made his speech at the Beas, he died en route to the Jhelum and was buried by Alexander with full military honors.

Some scholars have seen the timing of Koinos's death as suspicious, suggesting that the Macedonian king revenged himself on his opponent

by killing him. But no ancient writer suggests that Alexander was responsible for Koinos's death, even the most scurrilous. It also seems
plausible that Koinos's illness emboldened him to speak, and that—
with the prospect of his own death imminent—he more freely defied
his king. Already severely wounded five years earlier at Gaugamela,
Koinos was likely more susceptible to the unfamiliar diseases of South
Asia. After all, though the Greeks saw the Indian climate as salubrious
and its inhabitants as unusually healthy, it was not always so for foreigners. The British, for example, sickened and died of tropical diseases
by the thousands under the Raj.

Another death perhaps occurred on the way back to the Jhelum—a
newborn, unnamed son of Alexander and Roxane. Like the soldiers'
women, to whom Alexander had recently given stipends, Roxane
had likely accompanied her husband throughout the rigorous South
Asian campaign. Given her almost two years of marriage, it is appropriate that she produced an heir.

Roxane's pregnancy must have been difficult, particularly in its
later stages. Even as queen, she could hardly be protected from the
monsoon rains, the snakes, the massacre at Sangala, the tension and
stress of the mutiny on the Beas and Alexander's unwilling capitulation. It is unsurprising that as a first-time mother in a dangerous,
unfamiliar environment, she lost the baby. Nor is it unexpected that
her loss went unmentioned in most texts, given the predilections of
Alexander's biographers. Only one source describes the death: the
exaggerated, abbreviated, and gossipy anonymous Roman history
known as the Metz Epitome. The rest, focused on war and politics,
omit all mention of this firstborn, soon-dead son. Here as elsewhere,
they show little interest in women and children, pregnancy and
birth, and ordinary (non-battle) death. Their preferences should not,
however, lead us to disregard the story of the dead child or the sorrow
felt by Roxane and Alexander.

After the events on the Beas, the death of his son was yet another
failure for Alexander. As the king built his child a tomb and made

sacrifices, he buried with him, at least for now, his hopes for the heir and the family he had been seeking for the past two years. It was a political loss, particularly as Alexander was nearing thirty and desperately needed to solidify his dynasty. But it was also intimate and personal.

After two burials with all possible ceremony, Alexander held athletic games and made sacrifices in hope of an auspicious journey. Feasting the entire army, he prayed to his ancestral gods and also those of water: the Jhelum, Chenab, and Indus Rivers. Then the soldiers prepared to embark.

The crack troops—the archers and light-armed infantry, the Silver Shields, the Macedonian cavalry—went by ship with Alexander, even the horses coming along in specially devised vessels. The commander of the fleet was the king's childhood friend Nearkhos, an experienced and capable admiral (at least according to his own self-glorifying memoir). Prominent as well was Alexander's philosophically inclined Companion Onesikritos, helmsman of the king's ship and Nearkhos's nautical and literary rival.

Along with the fleet, the king's best general, Krateros, led additional infantry and cavalry on the left bank, while his close friend Hephaistion took the bulk of the army including two hundred elephants on the right. Like the admiral and helmsman, Krateros and Hephaistion had an increasingly intense rivalry, competing for the most prominent jobs and the king's trust. Their devotion—and their difference from one another—were recognized by Alexander, who called Krateros *philobasileus* ("king loving"), while Hephaistion was *philalexandros* ("Alexander loving"). They also had very different attitudes toward foreigners, with Krateros the foremost representative of the conservative Macedonian position and Hephaistion among the strongest supporters of Alexander's integrative approach. Hephaistion was rewarded with leadership positions that kept him close to Alexander; Krateros, despite his military talents, was ever more frequently sent away.

The high-stakes competition between Krateros and Hephaistion worsened during the South Asian campaign, and at some point they even drew their swords on each other. Alexander broke up the fight and told them that he'd kill them both if he caught them at it again. For the voyage to Ocean the king sought to make them separate but equal, with both men leading important troops on opposite sides of the river. With whom the women and children traveled is unmentioned, but they, too, came along.

They started at dawn to the sound of a bugle. The rowers dipped their oars into the water, the boatswains shouted orders. They made an immense noise, with every sound reverberating in the compressed space, as the river ran between banks so high that they often towered over the ships. The local inhabitants, who had never seen anything like it, lined up along the shores to watch. Sometimes they followed, singing, what must have seemed like an astonishing and colorful parade. It was a glorious send-off, and Alexander could feel satisfied in having made the best of a very difficult situation. Despite everything he had just gone through, the king would manage to see Ocean after all.

Shortly after Alexander's grandiose cruise downriver began, however, it came to an abrupt halt. Rumors of insurrection had reached the king. Despite his promise to head home, Alexander could not resist responding to this new challenge. As the king knew, he was leading his soldiers just where they dreaded going: back to war, when what they wanted was a peaceful journey home. They were sufficiently upset that he was forced to call an assembly—a potentially dangerous proposition, given the protest that the last one had sparked. At this one, Alexander barely managed to cajole his followers onward with the promise of easy victory and rich plunder.

Complicating his promise was the fact that Alexander's enemies, two allied peoples called the Malli and Sudrakai, were formidable warriors. Likely identifiable as the Malavas and Sudrakas mentioned in early Sanskrit texts, they were celebrated as fighters "trained in arms" who fought in the battle that forms the centerpiece of the Mahabharata. They were far-famed soldiers in both Greek and Indian sources—a rare alignment of two very different historical traditions.

The Malli and Sudrakai were excellent archers. They had heavy bamboo, cane, and wood bows strung with cowhide, and huge iron-tipped arrows they pulled back to their ears to shoot. While the Greeks and Macedonians looked down on archery, valorizing instead hand-to-hand combat with spears and swords, Indian warriors saw it as a venerable and heroic mode of fighting. Their great epic heroes, Rama from the Ramayana and Arjuna from the Mahabharata, were preeminently archers.

Besides their military valor, we know only a little about the Malli and Sudrakai. They were both farmers and hunters, catching and taming tigers, accumulating lizard skin and turtle shell. From their own land or through trade, the Malli and Sudrakai had access to precious natural resources: gold and purple thread for their clothes, and a metal the Greeks called "white iron," most likely nickel, pale in color and rare in the Mediterranean. To keep their wealth safe, they built well-fortified cities. Unlike the Greeks, who generally relied for defense on a wall at most, ancient South Asians built complex rings of fortifications. They often used a nearby river to feed a moat, then deployed the dirt from the moat to construct huge earthen ramparts, augmented at regular intervals by gates and towers. Inside their walls, the Malli and Sudrakai had citadels with high mudbrick walls and heavy inner gates. As warlike peoples, they clearly recognized the importance of defense.

Alexander started his campaign against the Malli and Sudrakai with an attack he hoped his soldiers would appreciate: swift and brutal. He trekked twenty-four hours across the desert to reach the Malli's nearest town. When he got there, he caught his victims unawares when they were peacefully out working in their fields. Without giving them time to muster (or even perhaps surrender), the king fell on the agricultural workers and killed many unarmed. The rest fled to the safety of their citadel. Their defenses were strong enough to hold Alexander off, forcing him into a siege.

Outside the Malli's walls, Alexander had a decision to make. Earlier in his career, he would likely have sought a negotiated surrender, preferring a secure alliance, tribute, and army recruits to the dangers of a drawn-out siege. But his Macedonian soldiers had chafed at this merciful attitude toward foreigners, pragmatic though it was, and resented their incorporation into the army. At the citadel of the Malli, Alexander determined to act differently. He led an attack and took the town by assault. Then he massacred the Malli, no prisoners taken. All their wealth fell into the hands of the Macedonian soldiers, just as Alexander had promised.

The Malli and Sudrakai may have been fierce warriors, but they recognized a determined general when they saw one. They did not attempt to oppose Alexander en masse. Rather, they moved eastward, crossing the Ravi River in search of safety. Alexander caught up with them at the ford, then pursued them across the river as they fled to the next fortified town. From their walls, the Malli and Sudrakai fought back strongly in defense of their homes. But again their fortifications proved no match for the Macedonians, who captured and enslaved them all.

By the time Alexander attacked a third city, the Malli and Sudrakai had learned to expect no mercy. When the Macedonians got to the citadel—with the king himself among the first to mount the siege ladders—the inhabitants fought to the death in the streets or set fire to their houses, dying of self-immolation. Their horrible fiery deaths were shocking from a Hellenic perspective, but for the Malli and Sudrakai, they were an appropriately heroic response to extreme circumstances; widows practicing sati, and ascetics facing mortal illness, did the same.

The rest of the Malli and Sudrakai sought to avoid the same fate. They used their superior knowledge of the landscape to their advantage, with some fleeing to the desert, where they knew Alexander would not follow. Others abandoned their city, the region's largest, and moved back west across the Ravi River. They harassed Alexander's cavalry when the Macedonians pursued them to the ford, hoping to prevent their crossing. When the cavalry made it through and the infantry began to follow, the Indians hurried to yet another well-defended town.

The city the Malli and Sudrakai had chosen was large and solid, with a strong outer wall guarded by a heavy gate. Leading his soldiers from the front, the Macedonian king battered down the gate and was the first into the city. He raced toward the citadel as the inhabitants retreated there. When the citadel's gate shut before he could get inside, he called for siege ladders to scale the walls.

To Alexander's impatient eyes, the Macedonians were moving slowly. Perhaps, despite his efforts to wage war their way, they had no stomach for the fight. Or perhaps Alexander was overly sensitive—fearful, after the protest on the Beas, that his soldiers were still unwilling to follow him. He decided to lead by example yet again. Putting his own body on the line, along with fighting mercilessly against foreigners, was something his men would respect.

Alexander seized the first siege ladder and headed up, together with Leonnatos, his bodyguard and relative, and Peukestas, a high-ranking infantryman. As they reached the top, shamefaced Macedonian soldiers raced up the ladders behind them. In their haste to follow and protect their king, too many piled on at once, and the siege ladders broke. Alexander was at the top of the wall, alone save for his two companions. With the ladders gone, no other soldiers could follow, and he made a perfect target for the archers within the citadel. His friends down below called out to him to retreat and made ready to catch him. Instead, in a split-second decision both courageous and ridiculously foolhardy, he jumped down within the walls.

Alexander was now inside the citadel, on his own and massively outnumbered. He landed safely and had for protection his iron helmet, breastplate, sword, and large hoplite-style shield. With them and a nearby tree for shelter, he managed to fend off attacks from the Malli and Sudrakai who came near him. He even killed several before they pulled back. But his armor and weapons were no match for the skilled archers, with their heavy bows and sharp iron-tipped arrows firing at him at close rage. He was shot in the chest, the arrow ramming straight through the metal of his breastplate. Blood poured out of him. Fighting to stay conscious despite the pain and loss of blood, he killed the man who ran up to strip him of his armor. It was clear, however, that he would not be able to hold out long.

On the outside of the citadel, the Macedonians were panicking. They tried frantically to climb the walls, piercing the mudbrick with pegs or standing on one another's shoulders: difficult work, particularly with armor and weapons. From the top of the wall, Leonnatos and Peukestas jumped down to protect Alexander. They reached him too late to prevent the arrow shot and took serious blows themselves. Peukestas was pierced three times by javelins, and Leonnatos wounded in the neck. They did however manage to keep the king safe from further injury, buying time for the soldiers to make it over the walls and open the gate from the inside.

Leonnatos and Peukestas protected Alexander with their own bodies, and also with the sacred shield of Troy. Long ago, at the very start of his invasion of the Persian Empire, Alexander had taken this shield from the temple of Athena. From that time on, he had the sacred object carried before him in battle by a specially designated shield bearer. It was a tangible, very prominent reminder of his time at Troy and his own epic aspirations. Now, near death and half a world away, he sheltered beneath it, awaiting his fate.

When the Macedonians burst inside the citadel, they made straight for Alexander. They bore their unconscious king out of the city, carrying him on his shield. Then, as the best field doctor was summoned to his tent, the grief-maddened soldiers returned to the citadel. They slaughtered everyone they could find—man, woman, or child—in retaliation for what they feared might be the death of their king.

In Alexander's tent, the king was examined by Kritoboulos. An experienced army doctor, he had been trained on Kos, the famed healing center where Asklepios was worshipped and Hippocrates once taught. Kritoboulos was a surgeon, a well-developed field of specialization by his time, with particular expertise in wounds of war. He had treated Alexander's father, Philip, when he was shot in the eye during the siege of Methone, though not perfectly effectively (Philip survived, disfigured and blind in that eye).

Ancient surgeons had delicate and precise instruments: surgical knives with long, narrow blades; scalpels, hooks, and forceps; probes, spoons for removing arrows, scissors, saws. But they had no anesthesia, and they were cautious about cutting deeply into the internal organs of the body. Due to powerful and long-held Greek prejudices against dissection, ancient doctors had only a very rudimentary understanding of the body's anatomical structure. Surgeons could easily do more harm than good.

On Kritoboulos's orders, Alexander was stripped, and the arrow cut off at the shaft. He had the arrowhead so deeply lodged in his chest that the wound would need to be enlarged to get it out. As he regained consciousness, the king learned from Kritoboulos that this would be a potentially very dangerous operation. But if the arrow remained in place, he would die. Alexander encouraged his doctor to operate. He was held down, since any flinching on his part could be fatal. Perhaps he also had leather pillows for support and comfort, as Hippocratic treatises recommended. Carefully, with Alexander holding as still as he could, the doctor opened up the wound. He drew out the iron arrowhead, three finger lengths long and four wide. As he extracted it, the king hemorrhaged massive amounts of blood and fainted yet again. Around him, Alexander's attendants wailed, fearing he had died.

Rumors of the king's purported death spread quickly. They reached Alexander's remorseful soldiers, both those at the citadel and others left behind at a base camp farther west. They made it to the Malli and Sudrakai. Reports even spread across the Hindu Kush into far-off Afghanistan, where they came to the discontented Greek colonists of the king's new cities. Mercenaries deemed too old, sick, or undependable to fight, they had been left behind to garrison the restive province. In Afghanistan, these talented career soldiers had had to become farmers, wrestling with the harsh climate and unfamiliar agricultural system of their new home. The mercenaries were homesick, and only the fear of Alexander restrained them. When they heard rumors of his death, they occupied the capital, Bactra, and chose a leader. Three thousand of the colonists set off with him on the long journey back to Greece.

The colonists' departure was the clearest but by no means the only sign of the dangers of Alexander's charismatic leadership. The king had concentrated extraordinary power in his own hands, making his soldiers, governors, and subjects responsible to him alone. He had for now no clearly preeminent general, no second-in-command authoritative enough to take the place once filled by Parmenion. He had left his only legitimate heir, if he had briefly had one, buried to the north on the Jhelum. And his army was not safely back in home territory. Instead, Alexander and his men were stranded at his empire's extreme eastern border as the king lay near death.

Fortunately for his army, the rumors of Alexander's death proved unfounded. His doctor, Kritoboulos, managed to stanch the bleeding and revive the unconscious king. He convinced his patient to rest, and the penitent soldiers around the tent were finally willing to leave when they heard that Alexander slept. Back at the base camp, though, the rumors persisted. Even when the king wrote a letter announcing his imminent arrival, the soldiers were not satisfied. They suspected a forgery by his friends and bodyguards.

To convince his suspicious army—and perhaps the Malli and Sudrakai—Alexander began to travel as soon as he was fit to move. Even before his wound had closed, he had himself conveyed to a boat on the nearby river. From there he sailed slowly and carefully downstream, lashing two ships together with an open tent on top so that those on the banks could see him. It was a waterborne procession for an audience as much South Asian as Macedonian, celebrating the resilience of the fragile king.

The procession culminated in a carefully choreographed display at the base camp. As Alexander approached on his boat, he held up his hand in greeting to the soldiers assembled to receive him there. He watched them as they in turn raised their own hands in gratitude, shouted, and wept. When the king prepared to disembark, he refused the litter his solicitous infantrymen had brought for him. He demanded his horse instead, so that he could be seen riding by his men. He even dismounted some ways from his tent, to prove that he could walk as well. Then the king allowed his soldiers to approach him, letting them touch his hands, his knees, and his clothing. As they came close, he was showered with wreaths and flowers, like the statue of a god.

Alexander's return to camp was a moment of reconciliation for the king and his soldiers. It offered a public, ritualized occasion for them to reaffirm their connection after their protest on the Beas and his violent, abortive military campaign. The emotional encounter gave the king and the army a way to express their dependance on one another and their remorse for what their differences had cost them—all without overt acknowledgment of wrongdoing on either side. Alexander was wise to arrange and go through with it, though it must have been exhausting for a man recovering from a near-fatal wound.

While the king was reconciled with the rank-and-file soldiers, his top officers were not so easily satisfied. In a gathering at the base camp, they reproached him for his behavior at the South Asian citadel. Ptolemy and Krateros, experienced generals who were likely ten years senior to Alexander, were especially critical. They told him he had acted like a soldier, not like the commander he was. The king was upset because he knew they were right.

Despite his anger, Alexander embraced his officers. Theirs was a highly physical and demonstrative relationship, with the king's hugs and kisses meant to signal his emotional closeness to his men. He also listened to them. He announced that he was still committed to a life of glory. But in fact he was more cautious after the incident at the citadel of the Malli and Sudrakai. He never seems to have led from the front again.

The Malli and Sudrakai had also learned their lesson. One hundred of them arrived at Alexander's base camp, gorgeously dressed in linen embroidered with gold and purple. They came as ambassadors to negotiate terms. Despite the Macedonians' initial successes, the Malli and Sudrakai were still a wealthy and militarily formidable power, and neither side wished to prolong the conflict. They settled on tribute, with the amount formerly paid to the Persians now going to Alexander, and 2,500 cavalrymen to join his army while he remained on the Indian subcontinent. It was little enough, but it allowed the Macedonians to declare victory and the Malli and Sudrakai to free themselves from the threat of further attack. To celebrate their reconciliation, the king invited all the ambassadors to a banquet.

The banquet was a lavish affair, with one hundred golden couches for the guests and tapestries glittering with purple and gold. There was also, as was typical for a Macedonian feast, an inordinate amount of wine—and concomitant quarreling. At this banquet, the chief quarrel was between a boastful and illustrious Greek athlete and an extremely drunk Macedonian soldier. The soldier resented the athlete because he was Greek, a useful reminder of the tensions even among Greek speakers in Alexander's army. He chafed even more at the man's role as a professional athlete, one meant to entertain the troops rather than to fight. The Macedonian scoffed at the Greek's brawny appearance and claimed it was all show. The Greek responded in kind, and although Alexander tried to intercede and make peace, they insisted on a duel.

The following day, the two men assembled in front of a huge crowd including not only Alexander's army, but also the curious ambassadors from the Malli and Sudrakai. The Macedonian soldier arrived heavily armored, carrying his shield, javelin, lance, and sword. The Greek, by contrast, appeared in his role as athlete: stark naked save for a purple cloak, glistening with oil, carrying only a club. It seemed a radically unequal contest. The soldier struck first, throwing his javelin, but the athlete easily ducked to avoid it. Charging with his lance, the Macedonian was again thrown off when the Greek broke the wooden shaft with his club. Before he could grasp his sword, the athlete seized his hand and knocked him off balance. Despite his panoply, the Macedonian soldier found himself quickly overpowered, with the athlete's foot on his neck.

Alexander signaled for the contest to end, and the athlete released the soldier. But the damage had been done. Everyone, including the Malli and Sudrakai, had seen a naked near-defenseless man defeat a heavily armed, well-trained Macedonian soldier: a stand-in for the army as a whole.

The bitterness lingered. Shortly thereafter, the king's Macedonian friends framed the Greek for the theft of a golden cup. Humiliated, the athlete wrote the king a reproachful note and then committed suicide. It was an ugly and unheroic coda to Alexander's failed epic war.

The rest of the journey downriver passed more quietly. Alexander sailed along pardoning those who submitted, attacking those who resisted, and coaxing back to their towns those who ran away. At the intersection of the Indus with the Chenab, the last of the eastern Punjab rivers with which it joined, the king established a city. He appointed a governor for the area and gave him hundreds of soldiers for garrison duty. He also built dockyards, as he would do repeatedly in his cruise down the Indus. Together with the governor and garrison soldiers, the dockyards were meant as a signal to the nearby inhabitants. Although Alexander himself was moving through their territory swiftly, he was establishing a military and governmental structure to hold it for the foreseeable future. The Macedonians, said the dockyards, were here to stay.

The inhabitants whom Alexander encountered disagreed. Foremost among them were the Brachmanes, most plausibly high-status ascetic wise men like those the king had met in Taxila. While the Gymnosophist Kalanos had joined Alexander's entourage, the Brachmanes along the Indus made a different choice. They coexisted peacefully with their own warrior kings—claiming spiritual preeminence while relinquishing overt secular power—but could hardly trust this foreign ruler to respect their status. So the Brachmanes instigated a revolt against Alexander as he cruised down the Indus. He managed to quash it with a number of brutal city sieges, but the revolt cost the king time and effort that he could ill afford. When he finally managed to catch some of the ascetics, he condemned them to death.

The Brachmanes took their revenge at a small town called Harmatelia. When the Macedonians attacked what seemed an easy target, the inhabitants retaliated with dangerous arrows, their tips smeared with the venom of poisonous snakes. Those they wounded, even with a scratch, first became numb. Then their bodies shook with sharp pain and convulsions. Their skin grew cold and livid, bile appeared in their vomit, black froth at the wound site. Death followed quickly, in a few days at most.

The Macedonians were unnerved and horrified by what happened at Harmatelia. The excruciating pain spared no one, not even high-ranking officers; among those wounded was Ptolemy, Alexander's close friend. The king, fearing for his general's life, sought a cure. He likely asked nearby inhabitants for herbal remedies, though he claimed, more mystically, to have seen a healing plant in a dream. Alexander ground the plant up and smeared it all over Ptolemy's body. For good measure, he also made it into an infusion for his friend to drink.

Ptolemy recovered, as did the other Macedonians to whom the plant was given in time. They benefited not from the placebo effect but real herbal medicine. Even today, native plants are used to cure snakebite in Pakistan. And new medical research has shown how they help promote blood coagulation, serve as anti-inflammatories, and guard against excessive bleeding, one of the chief dangers of snake venom. Whether he got the idea from dreams or local informants, Alexander's remedy worked.

Soon after Ptolemy's recovery and the Brachmanes' final submission, Alexander and his men reached a place where they could smell the fresh salt air of the sea. Uncertain, they asked for confirmation from the local inhabitants. Yes, said the locals, the king was only about two days' journey from what they called "the bitter water that spoils the sweet."

Alexander was at the apex of the Indus River delta, a steamy, sediment-rich area of mudflats and mangrove forests. Marsh-filled and swampy, it was crisscrossed by innumerable channels leading to the ocean, only two of which in Alexander's time were navigable. The king built dockyards at the delta's apex and explored its tributaries—with considerable difficulty, as receding tidal waters grounded his deep-keeled Greek-style boats, then smashed them to pieces as high tide flooded in. Alexander finally managed to bring his fleet to an island named Cilluta, where they found safe anchor close to the shore.

Alexander had arrived at the seacoast in early summer: the beginnings of monsoon season, when the air is heavy with humidity and the sea rough and gray. He sailed out from the yellow-brown coast, where enormous monsoon-fueled waves dragged the sand out to sea and left a barren, rocky shore in their wake. Behind him he could see small volcanic hills, strips of desert, and a few scrappy trees. As the king sailed out, he passed a motley collection of offshore islands, small and craggy, with occasional mangroves. Ahead was the gray sky, the diffuse wet air, and the dark, churning sea.

Alexander sailed and sailed. As he went, the ocean floor dropped off quickly and the waves, so rough near shore, calmed. He was surrounded by water, with no land visible on the horizon. Over him, seabirds circled, and in the ocean swam fish as well as twelve species of dolphins, porpoises, and whales. He was likely farther out to sea than he had ever been before. Ships in the fourth century BCE were made to hug the shore, tracking the Mediterranean coast and avoiding the potential dangers of its center. They were not meant to be out, as he was now, in the deep ocean.

Alexander had long dreamed of Ocean. As a child, he had heard recitations of Homer, where Ocean was both a place—a mighty river that encircled all lands—and a character (grandfather of Achilles, husband of Tethys, with whom he had acrimonious marital relations). Growing up, the king encountered more pragmatic and skeptical treatments of geography, but even his own tutor Aristotle made space in his philosophy for "the outer sea, whose end is not visible to those dwelling within." Now, at long last, Alexander had reached that point. Despite war elephants, monsoons, mutiny, and his own near-fatal wounding, he had managed to see Ocean. He was finally at what he believed was the end of the world.

Alexander had not meant to reach Ocean along this route. His goal had been to journey farther east, covering the whole of the subcontinent. Then he would have felt sure that there were no more worlds to conquer; then his quest, so unprecedented and seemingly quixotic when he began it, would have come to its absolute and certain end. His soldiers' protest had frustrated that goal, the wildly ambitious dream of a young man. Alexander had been forced to compromise. Traveling south, and letting go of his vision of world-without-end empire, was one of many compromises he made in maturity.

Was the glimpse of Ocean worth it to Alexander? Did it compensate for the smashed boats, the poison-tipped arrows, the ugly suicide, the high price he had paid in his own and others' blood? Was it worth the suffering that he and his men were shortly to endure? He had aged fast since he first dreamed of Ocean; grown fragile, too, recovering from his wound. Had he learned, with age and suffering, to tame his pothos, his desire for the unknown that had always driven him on?

Alexander's thoughts are unrecorded as he sailed onward, feeling the salt breeze on his cheeks and listening to the seabirds scream overhead. We can't be sure what he imagined or felt. But what he did is telling. The Macedonian king kept going until finally he consented to stop. For a man like Alexander, constantly pushing the limits of the possible, his willingness to close the circle and make an end to the journey is striking. It suggests that even if Ocean was not as he had dreamed it—hardly perfect—it was enough.

Alexander prepared a sacrifice to Poseidon, god of the sea. He slaughtered bulls, slitting their throats, letting the blood pour down, butchering them as best he could in the confines of his boat. He prayed to the sea god and made libations. The king tossed the golden cup and bowls he used into the sea as an offering to Poseidon, asking in exchange for a safe journey back for his fleet. Then he prayed that no one after him would go beyond what he had done, and headed back from Ocean to a far more dangerous realm.

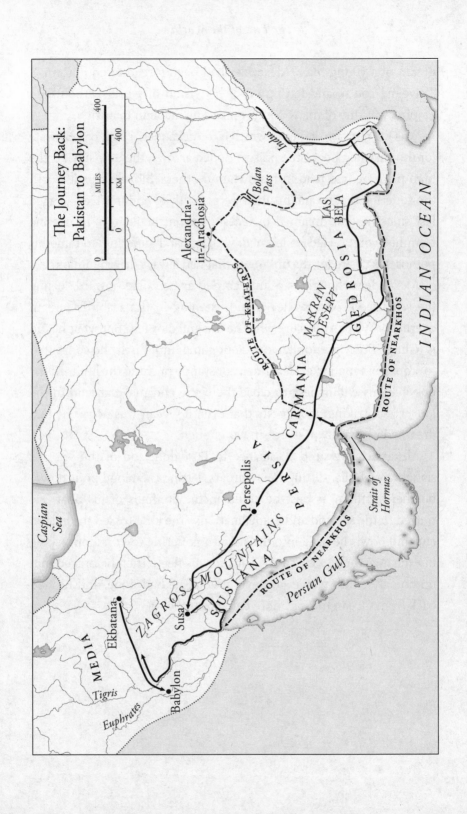

The Journey Back:
Pakistan to Babylon

MILES
0   400

KM
0   400

Caspian
Sea

MEDIA

Ekbatana

Tigris

Babylon

Euphrates

ZAGROS MOUNTAINS

Susa

SUSIANA

Persepolis

PERSIS

ROUTE OF NEARKHOS

Persian Gulf

Strait of
Hormuz

ROUTE OF NEARKHOS

CARMANIA

ROUTE OF KRATEROS

MAKRAN
DESERT

GEDROSIA

LAS
BELA

Alexandria-
in-Arachosia

Bolan
Pass

Indus

ROUTE OF NEARKHOS

INDIAN OCEAN

FOURTEEN

The Land of the Fish Eaters

Pakistan and Iran
Spring 325–Winter 324 BCE

IN THE MAKRAN DESERT, as Alexander and his followers journeyed west to the empire's heartland, sand was all around them: under their feet, so hot it scalded; whipping in the winds, obscuring vision; in their eyes, their clothes, their hair. Walking, the soldiers sunk their feet deep into sand, and the pack animals struggled to get out. They left sunken wagons behind, and carried what they could on foot. They lost their way when sand hid the road markers, and wandered helplessly in what seemed an everlasting landscape of dunes and sky.

Parched, the soldiers could find no water, no oasis, among the dunes, and the wells they dug offered a meager, brackish trickle. Hungry, they scraped by eating dates and the pith of the stubby palm trees dotting the landscape, along with the occasional scrawny sheep. In desperation, the men slaughtered pack animals for food, then told Alexander the beasts had collapsed from exhaustion. Wisely, he turned a blind eye.

There was much the king was forced to see during the march through the Makran. His powerful, proud soldiers, the greatest army in the world at that time, starving and desiccated. The riches of India that they'd fought so ferociously to secure, left behind in the sands. Men, too, left behind: half-dead already, unable to keep up, calling piteously to their friends.

Alexander and his army had been through deserts before: in Palestine, across the Sinai Peninsula, through the western Egyptian desert to the oracle of Amun at Siwa. Never had they suffered so severely. In the Makran, Alexander—master logician, impeccable planner, the king who never left behind a dead soldier unburied—was responsible for thousands, perhaps tens of thousands, of his followers' deaths.

Alexander began the trek westward by sending his general Krateros the safer, easier way home. Halfway down the Indus, the king bid his old friend farewell. He said his goodbyes also to about one-third of his army, including a host of demobilized veterans heading back to Macedonia. With them came the elephants: two hundred massive, hungry, and potentially dangerous animals. Born and raised in the tropical warmth of the subcontinent, they now set out to cross the chilly, barren Toba Kakar Range, just south of the Hindu Kush. The elephants were tricky to manage and highly demanding. But they were also exceptionally valuable in war, as Alexander had seen in his encounter with Poros. In sending them along with Krateros, the king was anticipating future campaigns, despite his demobilization. As Alexander recognized, the elephants had the potential to revolutionize Macedonian warfare. If they did, he wanted a monopoly on their force.

Krateros led the elephants and soldiers northwest to the Bolan Pass, a key artery between Central Asia and the subcontinent. It had an elevation around six thousand feet above sea level, half that of the northern routes through the Hindu Kush. But it was long and narrow, tracking the Bolan River through some forty-four miles of shingly gravel and precipitous gorges, so constricted in places that three horsemen could barely ride abreast. With more than twenty thousand people, at least four hundred pack animals, and two hundred elephants, Krateros's column must have been enormous, perhaps stretching out as long as the pass itself.

Despite the pass's challenges, Krateros made it through. Even the elephants emerged largely intact, at least to judge from their appearance several years later in the wars following Alexander's death. It was an astonishing accomplishment, suggesting that Krateros was a master logistician to vie with the best in military history. The Carthaginian general Hannibal brought a mere thirty-seven elephants on his famous journey across the Alps.

With the Bolan Pass behind him, Krateros's logistical struggles were largely over. His political challenges, however, had just begun. He discovered that he had a revolt on his hands, led by two Persian noblemen named Ozines and Zariaspes. Nothing is known about them prior to their rebellion: not their ancestry, their position, or even where, precisely, they lived. But somewhere along Krateros's route in southwest Afghanistan and southeastern Iran, they catalyzed the anger of those living under Macedonian rule.

Ozines and Zariaspes had good reason to rebel. Their region had suffered from the depredations of its new overlords—Greeks and Macedonians with few scruples about profiting in Alexander's absence from their powerful roles. And disfranchised Iranian noblemen were fitting leaders for a revolt, because they had not been co-opted by the ruling power. Alexander's Persian appointees, by contrast, were among his most loyal governors, and some retained power long after his death.

Krateros managed to suppress the revolt and capture its ringleaders. But the rebellion was an early sign that all was not well in the empire the king had left behind while he fought in South Asia. Return would be more complicated than anyone imagined.

While Krateros was using his troops to quash rebellion in the summer heat of southwestern Afghanistan and southeastern Iran, Alexander set off on his own journey west. When he gave the command, a great moving city—his portion of the army plus everyone from animal handlers to traders and craftsmen—headed out. With them went thousands of women and children. Some were high ranking, like Alexander's wife, Roxane. Other women were less prominent, companions of Alexander's rank-and-file soldiers and mothers of their children. With the stipends the king had recently given them, these camp followers were better cared for than they had ever been. As they moved west, they were also moving toward the center of the empire. By doing so they had a hope of someday stopping their endless marches and, with their partners, settling down.

The people under the king's command walked slowly, probably managing only about ten miles per day given the difficult territory they were crossing and the blistering summer heat. They carried relatively little food, lessening their load and reducing the need for pack animals. For water, they planned to make use of the monsoon rains, which briefly filled the region's otherwise empty riverbeds.

As they left the Indus behind, Alexander's army moved from mudflats and mangrove forests to a desolate landscape of sand and rock. He was headed toward the Baluchistan region in what is now the far west of Pakistan, where serried mountain ranges track the coast of the Arabian Sea. The king had heard enough from scouts and local informants to know that the route he had chosen was dangerous. But the road through the Makran Desert was key to Alexander's goal of connectivity between India and the Persian Gulf. The king believed he could make it through.

Alexander likely pinned his hopes on his fleet. He gave its command to his admiral and close friend Nearkhos, and sent as well his own helmsman, Onesikritos. The king ordered them to head downriver to the Arabian Sea, then follow the coast west to the Persian Gulf. He told them to observe and record the route carefully so that future travelers would know what to expect.

Because ships could carry more provisions, more easily than a land army, Nearkhos and Onesikritos probably took charge of the bulk of the food supply for both themselves and Alexander. They would have to rely on the king, though, to dig wells in case the riverbeds were dry by the time they came through. Since travel by sea was far faster than by land, Alexander presumably expected the ships would catch up with him before his followers needed food.

Nearkhos in his memoir offers a different account, one in which Alexander's land army was expected to supply both food and water to the fleet. But this seems implausible. Alexander knew enough about the desert ahead of him to recognize how little food was available there. He had also collected four months' worth of provisions at his base camp on the Indus, where food was more plentiful. Given the size of the desert and the speed at which the land army marched, four months of food would be just about enough to feed the soldiers. It seems most likely that Alexander gave the bulk of these provisions to Nearkhos, but that the admiral's self-justifying, self-glorifying memoir later elided his responsibility for what was to come.

Alexander's likely plan, with its synergistic relationship of army and fleet, recalled tactics he had used before. He had crossed the desert landscape of the Sinai Peninsula en route to Egypt in the same way and had succeeded brilliantly. Perhaps for this reason, he did not seek to make use of the strategies for crossing the Makran deployed by the Persians. He didn't bring camels, though they were the pack animals of choice for Persian caravans. Nor did he plan his route according to established Persian way stations. And he did not have Nearkhos bring along a local pilot. Perhaps Alexander and Nearkhos could find no one with the necessary expertise, or perhaps these arrogant, fiercely competitive men thought they needed no assistance. In either case, the lack of a guide for the fleet was a departure from Alexander's usual practice. The missing pilot would prove a serious liability in the months ahead.

Alexander ran into difficulties as soon as he started moving west. He marched his army first toward Las Bela, a river delta that constituted the last fertile area before the Makran. Often, when Alexander arrived in a new region, the political leaders of the area met him in advance and preemptively surrendered: an understandable response to the presence of a large army at one's borders. The Macedonian king likely hoped that the inhabitants of this remote region of the Persian Empire would submit quickly. They did not.

The inhabitants of Las Bela were rich and relatively numerous. They were also well integrated into the Persian Empire, since caravan routes from the Indus Valley to central Persia ran straight through their lands. But they were not accustomed to large armies like Alexander's, or to Macedonian, rather than Iranian, overlords. Proud fighters, they chose not to submit to the king.

Alexander could have responded by seeking to negotiate. He had done so in the past—for instance, at Babylon and Nysa—and this strategy had often served him well. Still, even after his attack on the Malli and its disastrous outcome, he had not fully learned to prefer negotiations to battles, leadership to individual heroism. Instead, with the inhabitants of Las Bela, he escalated the situation.

Alexander went on the attack with the light-armed troops, leaving Hephaistion behind with the slower, less mobile portion of the army. Hephaistion's was an unglamorous but critical assignment that showed the king's trust in his closest friend. Alexander was preparing his companion to become, if he was not already, the empire's second-in-command. Given his lack of an heir and his recent near-death experience, the king needed someone he trusted to secure his legacy. He planned for Hephaistion to take on that role.

Like many later foreign interlopers, both Alexander and Hephaistion faced fierce resistance from the inhabitants of Baluchistan. They spent valuable time during monsoon season fighting their way through the river delta. Only when they had killed or captured many of the men of Las Bela did the inhabitants falter, heading north to the hills for safety.

The inhabitants of Las Bela, together with their neighbors from the Makran, rallied at the Kumbh Pass. Like the Caspian Gates in eastern Iran, or Thermopylai in Greece, the Kumbh Pass was a choke point: a narrow, easily defensible route through otherwise impenetrable terrain. It separated the spreading delta of Las Bela from the Jhau Tract, a relatively flat and occasionally fertile part of the Makran. The pass was a good strategic choice to make a stand against Alexander and his army, and perhaps the inhabitants of Las Bela hoped that simply holding it would be enough.

Alexander and his soldiers marched toward the Kumbh Pass, determined to force a passage. Since they were heading for the desert, with all the unpredictability and danger that entailed, they did not want to leave resistance in their wake. They made their way carefully through the treacherous landscape, along the narrow path winding among windswept and utterly barren mountains. At every hairpin turn, they might encounter their attackers: fierce, hard-fighting men who knew the hills far better than they did. But the attack never came.

In the face of Alexander's army, the inhabitants of Las Bela melted away into the mountains. They had suffered many casualties during the king's occupation of their region, and finally—faced with the prospect of imminent battle against a much larger, better-equipped force—they lost their appetite for more. Like many later practitioners of guerrilla warfare, they knew when to stop. Letting Alexander through, and even accepting, as they did, a Macedonian-appointed governor, they would live to fight another day. They put up with a city founded by Hephaistion, and a group of soldiers left in the command of Leonnatos, the increasingly prominent hero of the battle with the Malli and Sudrakai. The inhabitants of Las Bela concluded that if the king wished to try his luck in the Makran, they had no need to stop him. They left him to the desert.

As Alexander headed into the desert, Nearkhos and his sailors were facing a different danger: the monsoon. After parting from the king in mid-July, they held athletic games, made sacrifices to Zeus, then shipped out, too. But sailing down the Indus to Ocean, they were greeted by rough seas and strong winds, blowing firmly and continuously from the south. The sailors pushed westward as best they could until they came to a good harbor, sheltered by an island across its mouth. There Nearkhos determined they would stay until the monsoon winds abated. Nervously, as outnumbered strangers in potentially hostile territory, they fortified their camp with a stone wall. Without Alexander's protection—and with a suspicious, aggressive attitude toward foreigners that was likely widespread among the king's followers—the sailors and their admiral wanted as little interaction with the local inhabitants as possible. So they built a wall, and waited.

Greek sailors like Nearkhos were used to contrary winds. The Mediterranean was full of them, then as now, and they were a familiar-enough phenomenon to figure powerfully in Hellenic mythology. Most famously, the entire Greek fleet at Aulis was held captive by a contrary wind until their leader, Agamemnon, sacrificed his own daughter to appease the gods. Nearkhos is not known to have attempted human sacrifice, but as the days ticked on and the winds continued, he must have understood the Homeric hero's desperation. The admiral let his soldiers hunt for mussels and oysters as he watched the winds. They blew without abating, on and on.

Nearkhos had experienced the monsoon a year earlier, as the army trekked eastward toward the Beas. He had seen the pounding, remorseless rain, the dangerously sudden flooding, the endless mud. He had not, however, anticipated the challenges that the monsoon posed for sailing. And without a local pilot, no one had warned him. As he waited, he realized that the coordinated movement of fleet and army—the key to Alexander's plan—was impossible. Nearkhos was stuck at his harbor while the land army proceeded onward inexorably toward the desert. Pent up behind stone walls and with no idea where the king was, Nearkhos could not even send a messenger.

By the time Alexander concluded an alliance with the inhabitants of Las Bela, he must have recognized that there was a problem with the fleet. He could imagine different scenarios: attacked by locals; shipwrecked; delayed; blown off course. All he could know for certain was that they weren't where his careful planning had anticipated. He was on his own.

Alexander had options, none of them good. He could go back and try to find Nearkhos, making his way through the territory of Las Bela once more. But his army had likely eaten most of the surplus food there already, and a journey east would certainly exhaust it: a poor beginning to the just-concluded alliance. Or he could stay where he was and wait for the fleet, trusting that they had survived and would come before he ran out of supplies, which was implausible. Alexander chose his third, least-bad option. Instead of staying right by the seacoast as he had planned, he headed inland toward what passed for agricultural territory in the context of the Makran. He moved west through the flattest, best-watered tracts of land between the coastal range and the higher central mountains. He must have known that this route would not provide enough food or water for everyone he was leading. But it was the best he could do.

The beginning of Alexander's journey through the Makran was strange and even beautiful. He moved through an austere landscape punctuated by the small, thorny trees that gave the ancient world one of its most valuable organic substances: myrrh. Made from the tree's sap, tapped and allowed to harden into glossy, tear-like beads, myrrh has a sweet, spicy, and slightly astringent scent, as well as antimicrobial and insecticidal properties. It was used in Alexander's time as perfume, incense, and medicine, imported at great cost from the Arabian Peninsula. No wonder the three kings of the New Testament brought myrrh, along with gold and frankincense, to Bethlehem.

The myrrh trees Alexander passed were untouched; no one had ever tried to harvest their resin. The Phoenician traders traveling with Alexander's army quickly set to tapping them, piling pack mules high with the precious substance. The traders also gathered the ginger grass that spread all over their paths, offering a delightful fragrance when trodden by the army. They had no way to monetize the mangrove trees in bloom, but wondered at them nonetheless: trees "washed by the sea" at their roots, with a flower that resembled a white violet.

As Alexander and his army moved westward and the monsoon rains abated, however, the sensory delights of the landscape dried up. They reached what the Macedonian king had feared, but could not avoid: the horrific desert with little water, barely any food, and end- less, scalding sand. The only way out was through.

Alexander's journey through the Makran was slow and torturous. The king and his followers eluded, as best they could, the cavernous gorges and eroded sandstone cliffs that gave the region a spectacular, otherworldly character. They could not escape the deep, hot sand, into which they sank as though walking through untrodden snow or liquid mud. As they traveled by night, with only the far-off stars to light their way, they could barely make out the contours of this strange, barren landscape. Even before the windblown sands covered the roads and their guides grew muddled and uncertain, they felt lost.

On and on they marched through the desert as days turned into weeks, then months. They were always thirsty, hungry as well, and increasingly ill from whatever they had to eat: dates, hearts of palm, pack animals. They pressed on relentlessly, desperate to get out. Those who could not keep up—too exhausted, sick, or demoralized to go on—"perished in the sand, like those falling overboard at sea," in the words of one ancient historian. Those who survived walked on with the cries of their fallen comrades echoing in their ears.

Worst was the night they slept by a riverbed, threaded through with a thin, precious trickle of water. Suddenly in their sleep, rains in the far-off hills swelled it to a monstrous rushing torrent. The fast- flowing deep water carried off baggage, pack animals, and, most horribly, many of the women and children marching with the army. With them gone, the soldiers lost one of their rare present comforts on the journey. The river also swept away hopes for the future, for the next generation and the integrated, bicultural world Alexander had begun to create. According to one of Alexander's ancient biographers, this was the most distressing loss, outstanding even among all the sufferings in the Makran.

Ancient and modern writers have described the march through the desert as Alexander's greatest failure: an error of judgment of colossal proportions, and one with disastrous repercussions for the king, his army, and his empire. Most blame it on hubris and ignorance, though one historian has suggested that Alexander chose the harsh route intentionally in order to punish his army for their protest on the Beas. Historians like this see the king as a megalomaniac, rather than the ambitious, callous, yet overall pragmatic individual his actions generally suggest. Given that Alexander was preparing further military campaigns—as shown, for instance, by his care in bringing the elephants—it seems unlikely that he set out intentionally to waste his soldiers' lives. Instead the king operated as though aware of the difficulties by splitting his army into thirds to distribute the risk, collecting massive amounts of food in advance, timing his journey to take advantage of the monsoon, and planning to coordinate the land army and fleet. He deserves blame, though, for wasting so much of the valuable monsoon season fighting in Las Bela, and for relying on Nearkhos instead of the Persian modus operandi (camels and caravanseray). Throughout his campaign, Alexander oscillated between operating in a Greco-Macedonian way and a Persian one. Here his opting for the familiar Hellenic choice was disastrous.

Somehow Alexander kept going. He saw his plans foiled, his followers tormented, his dreams for the future swept away in a torrent. Still, he managed to keep his army together, incrementally moving forward. His stamina and fortitude, his willingness to place his own body on the line—so dangerous in the siege at the town of the Malli and Sudrakai—served him well. The king watched, planned, and sought to make the best he could of the very bad hand he had dealt himself. In essence, he *led*—not in the glamorous, heroic way he loved to do in battle, but with equal parts willpower and endurance. The Makran would prove the most difficult and unheralded test of Alexander's leadership. He barely passed.

Finally Alexander and his followers reached a place where food was more plentiful, likely the Turbat Oasis near the western end of the Makran. There they found an important way station on the Persian route from Iran to the Indus. It had immense stores of grain, enough to feed whatever was left of Alexander's army, and also individuals tasked with converting raw materials to food (for instance, grinding the grain in order to make flour). The soldiers devoured dates from the cultivated palm trees dotting the oasis, and mutton from its flocks of sheep. Surrounded by plenty, they rested and attempted to recover from the deprivations of the desert.

At the oasis, Alexander was finally able to access the Persian imperial system that he had believed he could do without during his journey through the Makran. Having learned his lesson, the king commandeered grain for the next stage of the journey, which the local inhabitants arranged and sealed in the best Persian manner. (Alexander's soldiers impatiently broke the seals and helped themselves.) The king also sent messengers to his nearby governors, asking them to send supplies to meet the army at the borders of the Makran. And he planned the final stage of his route to take advantage of the Persian imperial system of way stations and food depots.

Alexander passed the coast, two harbors, a river, and a string of oases in a blur of forced marches and stops for resupply. When he arrived at the regional capital, Pura, it was sixty days after he had entered the Makran. He was greeted there by his loyal governor Phrataphernes, who came with a caravan of camels and brought cooked food that lasted well. Alexander and his followers put to good use the bounty of Phrataphernes, clearly an expert in desert travel. If the king regretted failing to profit by his governor's expertise earlier, he did not let on.

By the time he reached Pura, Alexander had lost, if the ancient sources are accurate, thousands or tens of thousands of his followers: a larger population by far than most cities of his time. Still, he had survived, and the army he had left remained a disciplined unit, not a chaotic mass of stragglers. Now the worst was over. It was time for recovery, in Alexander's own inimitable style: a wild, days-long wine-fueled march to the music of flutes and lyres. Then the king was forced to confront the complications of his reentry into the empire's heartland. No one, he would learn, had expected him to come back.

About the time that the king arrived at Pura in late October, Nearkhos was at last able to set sail. Aware as he was of his failure to coordinate with the land army, the admiral must have been fearful of what Alexander would think. But even if he wished for haste, he had no local pilot. Instead he was forced to move slowly and cautiously in his surveying journey along the coast.

Doing his best to fulfill Alexander's exploratory mission, Nearkhos meticulously—albeit often inaccurately—recorded the length of his journey each day, as well as what the coastline and harbors were like. He appreciated the harbor at present-day Karachi, circular, deep, and calm, with a narrow mouth. He also made detailed descriptions of plants and animals as well as the customs of the local inhabitants, though he tended to view the latter with disdain and distrust. Still, he was a vivid and observant memoirist, with a far more wide-ranging curiosity than Ptolemy; in the number of self-aggrandizing stories they tell, the admiral and the general rank about even.

Nearkhos was too late for Alexander, but he did manage to rendezvous with Leonnatos and his soldiers in the territory of Las Bela. He listened to the general's tales of a great battle—with its implausible claim of six thousand enemy casualties—and exchanged his laziest rowers for some of Leonnatos's men.

Despite the battle, Nearkhos, too, had skirmishes with the inhabitants of Las Bela. They may have resented the Macedonians still lingering in their territory: Leonnatos and his soldiers, the colonists Hephaistion left behind, the Macedonian governor, and now the admiral, too, with his enormous fleet. Given the limited agricultural resources of their region, the inhabitants of Las Bela may have been resistant to sharing what they had. Or they may have been provoked.

Nearkhos was certainly willing to resort to force. His suspicion of the local inhabitants made him aggressive even in initially friendly encounters. (Alexander by contrast tended to use force when those he confronted failed to submit, but not before.) When Nearkhos arrived in one town along his route, for instance, the inhabitants greeted him kindly and offered him baked fish in earthenware pans, cakes, and dates. The admiral nonetheless surrounded the place with armed men and demanded more. He got what there was, at the price of alienating the townspeople. Despite his remit, he was hardly smoothing the way for future travelers.

As Nearkhos moved from Las Bela toward the Makran coast, he realized ever more clearly how much he needed a local pilot. But given his belligerent behavior, he unsurprisingly had trouble finding one. At last, about halfway through his journey, he encountered an Iranian named Hydrakes who agreed to take them as far as the Straits of Hormuz at the entrance to the Persian Gulf.

Hydrakes clearly knew the Makran coast intimately. He guided the fleet to safe harbors, good water sources, and villages, astonishing in the region, with date palms, myrtle, and flower gardens. He showed them how to sail faster, and their rate of travel altered dramatically, from a reported twenty-five or fewer miles per day to as many as a hundred. He also told them stories; for instance, one about a dangerous, forbidden island where only a Nereid lived: she would have sex with anyone who came, but then would turn him into a fish. Nearkhos skeptically insisted on exploring the island, and found no one.

More terrifying than the forbidden island were the strange sea monsters Nearkhos and his men found. The sailors were used to the Mediterranean, where the largest marine mammals they regularly encountered were dolphins, relatively small, friendly creatures considered by the Greeks a sign of good luck. But along the coast of Pakistan they encountered sea monsters far more menacing.

First the sailors saw water blown up from the sea as from a waterspout. Startled, they dropped their oars. What they saw was most likely a pod of blue whales, surfacing to expel water through their blowholes. The whales were not aggressive, but they were dangerous, given their size—Nearkhos exaggeratedly claimed they were 140 feet long—and the fleet's lightweight, relatively flimsy ships. A flick of the whales' tails could capsize one of the warships, packed with men, or the supply-laden cargo vessels. To frighten off the whales, Nearkhos had his men blare their trumpets and raise their battle cry. The great sea beasts, to everyone's relief, dove down and did not return.

Almost as strange as whales were the inhabitants of the Makran coast, whom the sailors called *Ichthyophagoi* (Fish Eaters). With nets made from the bark of date palms, they caught fish in the tide pools that dotted the coastline. The tenderest they ate raw, like sashimi; the rest they dried, pounding them into meal, bread, and fish cakes. Their sheep, too, ate fish, since pasture land was scant and valuable; this diet made for fishy-tasting lamb, disgusting to Greeks like Nearkhos. Even their houses were tied to the sea, having beams of enormous whale bones. So extreme are the descriptions of the Ichthyophagoi in the ancient sources that one may be tempted to dismiss them as another of Nearkhos's tall tales. But later travelers record similar practices among the inhabitants of the Makran coast, persisting through at least the 1970s.

With Hydrakes's help and to everyone's relief, the fleet finally made it past the region of the Fish Eaters. As they reached the more wooded, grassy, and well-watered coastline by the Straits of Hormuz, they could see across the water a cape jutting out in the distance:

Arabia. For the sailors, this was a rich and fabled land, full of incense and spices. Onesikritos said they should sail to it but Nearkhos disagreed, in one of their best-recorded feuds. Pulling rank, the admiral told the helmsman they had been commissioned by Alexander to explore the coastline of Asia, not Arabia. They may have failed in their mission to coordinate with the land army, but Nearkhos was not about to violate the king's explicit orders. They stuck to the Iranian coast as they made it through the straits, anchoring at a place they called Harmozia. There they found every food they could wish for (except olives, Nearkhos noted, in a very Greek aside). As they rested ashore, they came across a man wearing a Macedonian cloak and speaking Greek. It had been so long since they had encountered anyone like him that they burst into tears.

The Greek speaker told Nearkhos that Alexander was nearby, some five days' journey inland. The admiral prepared immediately to report to his king. He could not be sure of his reception. Would Alexander be resentful of the fleet's failure to supply the land army? Would he fault his admiral, even if the monsoon delay was out of his control? As Nearkhos was well aware, the king was quick to blame, and after his sufferings in the Makran, his hair-trigger temper was likely to be at its worst. But the admiral knew he would gain nothing by waiting. Instead he made a great show of hastening to his often-impatient ruler. He didn't even bathe.

Mistrustful as always of the local inhabitants, Nearkhos built a double stockade around his ships, an earth wall and a deep trench. Taking with him only one companion—not, notably, Onesikritos—Nearkhos set out on his first substantial land journey in five months. When he reached Alexander, he was virtually unrecognizable: long haired, unwashed, covered in brine, wizened from the sun, and pale from sleeplessness and other hardships. Alexander extended his right hand in a gesture of kindness to Nearkhos and asked how the fleet had been destroyed. The admiral must have been apprehensive. He knew by now just how greatly the king and his followers had suffered, due to his failure to supply the land army. Would Alexander make him suffer, too? Putting the best face on his awkward predicament, Nearkhos told Alexander that all the ships were safe.

The king and his admiral stood together, reunited after their long journeys by land and sea. Alexander had the opportunity to scapegoat Nearkhos, who had waited comfortably in his fortified camp while the land army starved. But if Alexander was resentful, he was also pragmatic, and perhaps, after his own sufferings in the desert, more aware than before of the challenges nature could pose to even the most powerful of men. Nearkhos may have failed to save the land army, but he had kept the fleet intact, and his sailors and marines now represented a substantial proportion of the king's military force.

At least in public, Alexander decided on gratitude. He swore by Zeus and Amun that he rejoiced more at the salvation of the fleet than at his conquest of Asia. Sacrificing to the gods, the king held athletic and musical games, along with a great procession in which the troops showered Nearkhos with ribbons and flowers. The king had more dangerous men to deal with than his childhood friend, a Greek who could never seriously threaten his rule. Alexander was returning to the center of his empire: the powerful heartland where his governors, Persians and Macedonians alike, had armies and treasuries large enough to vie with the king himself. Nearkhos survived. Others would not be so fortunate.

FIFTEEN

A Ransacked Tomb and a Fiery Death

Iran
Winter–Spring 324 BCE

PASARGADAI, THE FIRST CAPITAL of the Persian Empire, stood only some twenty-five miles from the ruins of Persepolis. The Macedonian king had been there once before, during the tumultuous winter of the burning six years earlier. Now he was older, chastened. At Persepolis, he had seen the broken, shattered columns of the audience hall, the treasury covered in ashes three feet deep. He told his friends that he regretted the destruction, that great Homeric fire. He was coming to Pasargadai to make amends.

As Alexander revisited Pasargadai in the winter of 324 BCE, it seemed a world apart from the ruins of Persepolis. Nestled in the lush valley of the Polvar River, Pasargadai was green and bountiful. Alexander looked out on row upon row of carefully planted trees, symmetrically arranged waterways, a man-made pool. He was headed for the tomb of Cyrus, the founder of the Persian Empire and an important role model for the Macedonian king.

By 324 BCE, Alexander was desperately in need of role models like Cyrus. The first Great King offered a long-gone but very attractive precedent for an empire builder like Alexander: a unifier perceived as just by all his subjects, powerful yet beloved. After the protest on the Beas and the disastrous trek through the Makran Desert, Alexander could only hope he would someday enjoy a reputation like Cyrus's. By the time he arrived at the tomb, Alexander was keenly alive to perceived slights to his authority. As he would discover, he wasn't entirely imagining them.

When Alexander neared the tomb, its stepped platform and high, gabled roof stood out against the picturesque natural landscape. Exquisitely constructed by the best Greek craftsmen of Cyrus's day, its exterior had a restrained elegance. But as Alexander knew, the interior was more lavish. On his previous visit, the Macedonian king had marveled at the tomb's rich accoutrements: a golden sarcophagus, a couch with feet of gold and a coverlet of Babylonian tapestry, overlaid with blue robes and trousers, swords, and earrings of gold set with precious stones. He was coming to see them again, bringing offerings in public homage to his most transculturally acceptable model. But when he opened the tomb's door, he was greeted by a very different sight.

Since Alexander's first visit, the tomb had been ransacked. Gone were the clothes, the tapestries, the earrings and swords. The coffin and couch had been broken in a failed effort to get them out the narrow door. Even the body of Cyrus had been removed from its sarcophagus and dumped unceremoniously onto the floor.

The desecration was a threat to Alexander's authority. It was also an insult to the Persians, whose support he was courting. The robbing of the tomb of Cyrus was exactly the kind of incident that could scuttle his efforts to be accepted as a legitimate Persian king.

Alexander started his investigation by seizing the Magi, the powerful Persian ritual experts who dominated the religious life of their society (the three magi who came to the stable in Bethlehem inherited this long-lived tradition). The Magi at Pasargadai were supposed to guard the tomb of Cyrus night and day, receiving housing, food, and wine for their efforts. Despite their power and close attendance, the Magi had allowed the tomb to be looted. Alexander subjected them to torture to find out why, but his cruel treatment of them was in vain. The Magi implicated no one and the king finally let them go.

A second suspect was the governor of the area, Orxines. Orxines was a Persian nobleman, self-appointed to his role when Alexander's representative died. Perhaps in hopes of preempting questions about his behavior, Orxines had met the king with gifts: herds of horses, chariots trimmed with gold and silver; expensive furniture, fine jewels. But his Persian subjects also came to Alexander, alleging that Orxines had desecrated temples and royal tombs and put men to death unjustly. Wary and apprehensive, the king credited the rumors against the governor. Alexander may also have been swayed by his eunuch lover, Bagoas, whom the more sensationalistic literary sources claim Orxines had offended (when asked for presents by Bagoas, Orxines said he gave gifts to the king's friends, "not his whores"). With or without Bagoas's interference, Orxines paid the penalty. Alexander had him hanged and appointed his trusted friend Peukestas as governor in his place.

Alexander executed Orxines, but according to Plutarch, he finally discovered that the actual robber of Cyrus's tomb was a Macedonian officer. Left behind when Alexander went east, the officer perhaps saw the tomb not as a holy place or a hallowed historical marker but as an opportunity, like so many others in Persia, for loot. He likely used his status as part of the occupying force to gain entrance to the site, then robbed it. He had little time to enjoy his ill-gotten gains, however. Macedonian though he was, Alexander had him put to death.

While Alexander took vengeance on the Macedonian officer, Orxines, and the Magi, it was the king himself who was most responsible for the desecration of the tomb of Cyrus. Through his conquest of the Persian Empire, he had created conditions favorable to lawlessness and the abuse of power. And with his lengthy campaigns on the empire's borders, he had left a leadership vacuum in the heartland that was filled by insubordinate and opportunistic men.

The lawlessness seen at the tomb of Cyrus replicated in microcosm the chaos and abuse of power occurring throughout the empire. When Alexander returned from the Makran Desert, he was deluged by complaints from his subjects. They demanded justice for virgins his governors had raped, temples they had plundered, and tombs they had robbed.

The subjects' claims cannot be archaeologically verified, but the devastating impact of Alexander's conquest is clear. From the Mediterranean coast to Central Asia, the king and his army brought fire, death, and destruction to the inhabitants of the Persian Empire. In the caves of Wadi el-Daliyeh on the West Bank, around two hundred refugees from an attack by Alexander were suffocated, likely by the king's soldiers; their skeletons and personal possessions testify to the speed and excruciating manner of their deaths. Far away, at Kyzyltepa in Uzbekistan, Alexander—or others in the turmoil that followed in his wake—shot round after round of arrows at the inhabitants of a powerful fortified site, then knocked down its walls.

While some fortunate individuals saw their towns preserved, their fields untouched, rebels against Alexander suffered terribly. In the Levant, for example, the king's forces were likely responsible for a whole series of important Persian-era buildings destroyed by conflagration, then deserted. And within one well-studied region of southern Uzbekistan, fully 90 percent of the Persian-era sites were abandoned between the coming of Alexander and the consolidation of settled rule in the area by his successors. There and elsewhere, the king's arrival unleashed chaos that lasted a generation, with shattering effects on his subjects' lives.

As archaeological remains like these suggest, Alexander struggled with the transition from military conquest to stable rule. From the perspective of the Macedonians, the king had made war on the Persian Empire to benefit them, and they were entitled to the spoils. But as Alexander was well aware, he could not simply loot and burn—not if he wanted to hold on to an empire in which Persian subjects vastly outnumbered their Macedonian overlords. Nor could he let Iranian governors like Orxines act with impunity, tarnishing the reputation of his new regime. With his return to the center of his empire, the

Macedonian king had to take charge and assert his power over his governors. Along with the complaints of their subjects, Alexander had an additional cause for resentment against these officials: they had committed the unforgivable offense of acting as though he would never come back.

Alexander's response to this offense was swift and violent. He executed six of his twenty provincial governors, along with four other senior commanders. Remarkably, he killed not only Persians like Orxines, but also high-ranking Macedonians.

Alexander's punishment was harsh, but within a Persian context, not unprecedented. If he wished to be seen as a powerful Great King like Cyrus, Alexander could not permit his officials to become insubordinate. A good Persian ruler kept close watch over his governors, summoning them to his court when they were accused of disobedience. If he decided they were guilty, he executed them, often with their entire family. In the high-stakes world of the Persian court, the Great King was expected to exert authoritarian control over all his subjects. Death could be the penalty for far lesser infractions.

Macedonian kingship was different, with a greater commitment to egalitarianism and free speech—at least among powerful men. But strong rulers like Alexander's father, Philip, still concentrated power in their own hands, banishing even high-ranking members of the court for minor misdeeds and eliminating rivals who posed a threat to their authority. Alexander had grown up in Philip's court, a likely heir who was nonetheless constantly uncertain of his status, and he witnessed the exiling of four of his closest friends. The experience made him keenly sensitive to fluctuations in power, and determined to secure his own by whatever means necessary.

Back in Pasargadai, with the torture and executions over, Alexander sought to do better. He decided to restore the tomb of Cyrus: a clear sign of how much the first Great King—and the approval of his Persian subjects—now meant to him. He chose for the task Aristoboulos, the architect or engineer who wrote one of the earliest memoirs of Alexander's campaigns.

Aristoboulos's moment in the limelight was his restoration of the tomb of Cyrus. His memoir describes how he put the Great King's body back into its sarcophagus, repaired the tomb's furnishings, and ordered new garments, tapestries, weapons, and jewels. When he was finished, he walled up the tomb and placed on its door the royal seal. In doing so, he hoped to fend off future tomb robbers, or at least make their depredations visible. A builder rather than a destroyer, Aristoboulos was trying in his small way to make Alexander's empire whole again.

While the tomb of Cyrus could be restored to something resembling its former glory, Alexander could not fix so easily the effects of his conquest on real people. He struggled even with those he meant to favor; for instance, the South Asian sage Kalanos. Kalanos was the ascetic who had joined Alexander's entourage in far-off Taxila. Accustomed to a healthy outdoor lifestyle with simple food and plenty of exercise, Kalanos had grown old without experiencing serious illness. But by the time he reached Persia, the rigors of the Macedonians' campaigns and the king's more luxurious food and drink had taken a toll on Kalanos. At seventy-three, he could no longer perform his naked athletic workouts all day in the sun; he could not even walk. He asked Alexander's permission to commit suicide.

The Greeks and Macedonians had an ambivalent attitude toward suicide. They had no religious prohibitions against it, and honored some important mythological figures—for instance, the Trojan war hero Ajax—who chose to end their own lives. But they also saw it as a response to the kind of desperate or humiliating circumstances a good hero would hope to avoid (fittingly, in Greek tragedy, suicide is often the province of women). For Kalanos to choose suicide due simply to ill health was perplexing to the Greeks and Macedonians, and Alexander tried to talk him out of it. But Kalanos stayed firm.

Kalanos retained his commitment to suicide because he understood it differently than the Macedonian king. In South Asia, some ascetics like Buddhists rejected suicide, but others valorized it. Brahmanical tradition, for example, allowed it in old age for those whose health prohibited them from performing their normal duties. Jains, too, encouraged it; all the founders of the religion in fact starved themselves to death. And while most famous suicides were male, women did sometimes commit sati, burning themselves to death on the funeral pyres of their deceased husbands. For a Taxilan of Kalanos's era, choosing to end one's life was not an act of desperation. Rather, it was an appropriate response to old age after the attainment of ascetic wisdom, an empowering act. It was also an opportunity for a very public display of self-control and resolution, particularly if one chose, as Kalanos did, to die by fire.

When Alexander failed to persuade his ascetic friend to continue living, he did what he could to give him the death he wanted. The king allowed Kalanos to organize a magnificent ceremony, assigning his top general Ptolemy to help the enfeebled wise man carry it out. Together, Kalanos and Ptolemy created a huge funerary pyre. On the appointed day, Kalanos headed toward it, borne on a litter set on one of Alexander's best horses. He was adorned with garlands in Taxilan fashion and chanted hymns in his own language that no one could understand. When he reached the pyre, he distributed to his friends and followers the rich funerary gifts that Alexander had intended to be burned with him: a reminder of the disjunction between the ascetic death rituals of Kalanos's Taxila and the more materialistic and display-oriented ones of Macedonia. He also gave the horse to one of Alexander's bodyguards, because the man was one of his students (just like a good Greek philosopher, Kalanos apparently ran a school).

At the pyre, Kalanos prayed, poured a libation, and cut off a lock of hair. As the flames were lit, the soldiers raised their battle cry and the elephants trumpeted in tribute to the wise man. What Kalanos did next is disputed. One account says he lay down on the pyre and allowed the flames slowly to consume him: a slow, deliberate, and astonishingly painful form of death. Another claims instead that he let the fire build, then summoned all his strength for a terrifying brief moment, and leaped in.

The death of Kalanos made a profound impression on the Macedonian army. For some, it showed the ascetic's fortitude, his willingness to stare death in the face and to endure excruciating pain. Others had a more jaundiced opinion, calling the wise man foolhardy and vainglorious in choosing such an extreme way to die. According to his biographers, Alexander himself was uncomfortable with the whole affair: "The spectacle his friend had brought about did not seem right."

Alexander's discomfort perhaps stemmed from the fact that he bore some responsibility for the death of Kalanos. By inviting the wise man along on campaign, the king had meant to show favor to Kalanos (as well as preempting opposition from powerful ascetics like him). But removing him from his native environment was like taking a fish out of water. Kalanos had struggled, fallen ill, and finally chosen death over continuing to live like a Macedonian.

When the funeral was completed, the Macedonian king held a great feast. Kalanos had asked for it, and it offered Alexander a way to release the tension and emotion that the suicide had created. He organized athletic games and musical performances, just as he did after a military victory. In tribute to Kalanos's love of unmixed wine, the king also held a drinking contest. He gave the winner a golden crown for drinking an astonishing twelve quarts. But as Alexander's biographers noted disapprovingly, the man died four days later of alcohol poisoning. According to ancient writers, forty-one others also died. Men in the prime of life, they had not willingly chosen death like Kalanos. Still, they were gone—a sad and pitiful conclusion to the Macedonian king's banquet.

Later on, Kalanos's words about the feast were also remembered as eerie. He had told the Macedonians to make the day of his suicide one of gaiety and to drink with the king, whom he would soon see in Babylon.

For the moment, however, Alexander paid little attention to Kalanos's prophetic words. He left behind the site of his friend's suicide and journeyed west to the royal city of Susa. There he would see again, after six years, the individuals most important to his new plans: the Persian royal women.

SIXTEEN

Ninety-Two Brides

Iran
Winter–Spring 324 BCE

IN THE WINTER OF 324 BCE, the Persian Queen Mother and princesses prepared to welcome Alexander to their great palace at Susa. When he arrived, they saw a mature man, very different from the impetuous prince they had first met. They could also observe his half-Persian, half-Macedonian dress—not quite the full regalia of a proper Great King, but closer—and his more commanding, authoritative manner. And perceptive eyes like those of the Queen Mother might note his greater physical frailty after the chest wound in Pakistan and the hunger and thirst of the desert march.

The Persian royal women had been waiting a long time for Alexander's arrival. They had been his captives for the past nine years. In their captivity, they retained their fine clothes and jewelry, their servants and protocols. They may have kept more. As cuneiform tablets found at Persepolis show, Persian royal women often possessed enormous wealth, with their own estates, administrators, and networks of distribution that suggest considerable freedom of movement and power through patronage.

The Queen Mother, Sisygambis, had something more important to their survival than wealth: influence with Alexander. She knew the king favored her, even called her "Mother"—a significant gesture, but perhaps not surprising for one who had bid farewell to his own mother at twenty-two. Sisygambis used her influence sparingly, however, intervening to beg pardon only for Persians to whom she was closely tied, and watchful not to overstep.

Sisygambis was well aware of the limits to her power in her elegant glazed-brick prison. She had buried her own son (Darius III), her daughter-in-law, and likely her young grandson as well (he is mentioned at the royal family's capture in 333 BCE, and then, ominously, never again). Without them, and with her land ruled by Macedonians, Sisygambis could do little to protect her remaining family members. She may have saved her granddaughters Stateira and Drypetis from being taught to weave, that domestic task so demeaning in Persian eyes. But she had to allow their instruction in Greek, with whatever that betokened for their future. And she could not arrange marriages for her granddaughters, now likely in their early twenties and soon past the age at which Persian women expected to wed. Instead, Sisygambis and the princesses waited, year after year, for Alexander to come back.

When the Macedonian king arrived, Stateira and Drypetis, and perhaps Sisygambis, too, were able to converse with him in Greek. They may have heard his plans, in which they at last featured prominently after so many years of waiting. They were the reason for his coming to Susa, together with his high-ranking officers and whatever was left of his army. With them in mind, he had summoned the best actors, musicians, and singers in the Hellenic world from the western coast of Turkey, from Athens and Thebes on the Greek mainland, even from as far away as South Italy and Sicily. The royal women could watch Alexander setting up an enormous golden tent, likely the one he had taken from Darius many years earlier. They were the center and focus of the Macedonian king's preparations, though they had no choice in the role they would play.

On the appointed day, the Persian princesses awaited their entrance into the grandiose golden tent. It had pillars plated with gold and silver, and rods of the same precious metals hung with costly embroidered tapestries. Within it were ninety of Alexander's top officers, sitting on silver-footed couches covered with gifts worth a reported twenty minae each (about one-third of a talent, at a time when one talent was a substantial fortune for a rich man). Around them were guests, some nine to ten thousand according to the ancient sources. At the center, seated on a couch with feet of gold, was Alexander.

Before Stateira and Drypetis entered, the men stood. Holding golden cups the Macedonian king had given to each guest, they poured libations to the gods and drank a series of toasts. As they waited, the princesses had time to note that they were not the sole women invitees to the occasion. With them were ninety other aristocratic Iranian women. Some were familiar, and acknowledged as near equals, like Parysatis, daughter of the previous Great King. Others were less exalted but respectable, the children of important Persian governors like Phrataphernes as well as two sisters and one daughter of Barsine, Alexander's high-ranking mistress. One woman the princesses might have sniffed at: Apama, daughter of Alexander's Sogdian enemy Spitamenes. In the end, she proved the most fortunate of them all.

With the toasts finished, the princesses and the other women invitees were at last permitted to enter the tent. Each aristocratic Iranian woman was instructed to sit down on a couch next to the Macedonian or Greek man who would now become her husband. Stateira, the elder of Darius's daughters, seated herself next to Alexander, the man to whom her father had offered her nine years earlier. With them, and perhaps of greater importance, was Parysatis, whose father, Artaxerxes, was in the direct line of the Great Kings, while Stateira's was merely from a cadet branch.

Likely absent from the tent—but still very much in the picture— was Alexander's first wife, Roxane. Married to Alexander for three years at the time of the Susa wedding, she had probably lost one child after the Beas mutiny. She would soon become pregnant with another.

Stateira and Parysatis were probably well aware that while Alexander's marriage to Roxane perhaps had some romantic aspects, his union with them was forthrightly political. The king was securing his own place on the throne in a characteristically Persian manner; Cyrus the Great and Darius I had married into preexisting royal families in just the same way.

While the young Alexander had repeatedly rejected political marriages and preferred instead to establish his legitimacy through battle, the mature king appreciated their utility. By wedding Roxane, he had managed to stabilize Central Asia, leaving it in the hands of men like her father, Oxyarthes, during the invasion of India. Given the resistance Alexander was now facing in the imperial heartland, he likely hoped that marrying the Persian princesses would have a similar effect. Alexander had not given up his dreams of conquest. As his speech at the Beas suggested, he still hoped to extend his empire to the west. But for his plans to succeed, he needed to leave the center of his realm pacified. Political marriages were among the most effective ways he had found to do so.

At the same time, Alexander's wedding at Susa indicates that he had new dreams, new plans. Joining himself to the Persian princesses meant that any sons he had with them would have the best possible claim to rule his empire one day. As he grew older, Alexander was thinking beyond what he himself would accomplish, and considering as well his legacy for the future.

Critical to Alexander's legacy was Stateira's younger sister Drypetis. She sat on a couch with Hephaistion, the tall, good-looking man whom her grandmother had once mistaken for the king. Through Drypetis, the king and his second-in-command gained a close and official family connection. They were brothers-in-law; their children would be cousins. If anything happened to Alexander, marriage to Drypetis consolidated Hephaistion's position as the king's natural successor.

For Drypetis, marriage to Alexander's second-in-command was a good match, under the circumstances. Indeed, both Persian princesses had secured the most powerful husbands they could rationally have hoped for. Only they could know if it was enough to compensate for being forced to marry two foreigners, grooms more interested in each other than either of them.

Alexander and Hephaistion were not alone. Ninety of the king's top commanders received brides at this mass marriage, though few of their wives' names have been recorded. Alexander also made sure to invite to the wedding nine to ten thousand Macedonian common soldiers who had taken Persian partners, greatly expanding the guest list and the number of wedding favors (all those golden cups). Even by royal standards, the wedding must have been enormously expensive, but Alexander could well afford it. If it implicated his most powerful commanders and a substantial portion of his army in intercultural marriages like his, it was worth every penny.

Once Stateira, Drypetis, and all the other brides were seated by their husbands, the ceremony was ready to begin. In accordance with Iranian marriage ritual, each husband took his wife by the hand and kissed her. Then the king led a wedding song, celebrating "the partnership of the two greatest and most powerful peoples"—that is, the Macedonians and Persians.

As the Persian princesses could doubtless recognize, Alexander may have expressed his hopes for integration through the wedding song, but the reality he faced was more complicated. High-handedly, he was attempting to join in wedlock very disparate couples. For the brides, Alexander's arranged marriages were coercive though not unprecedented. Elite Iranian women likely anticipated having their marriages arranged for them, as it was the norm in their society. The princesses and their associates stood to benefit from institutionalized relationships with the Hellenic ruling elite. Still, they would probably have preferred husbands from their own cultural background, rather than the men most responsible for their land's conquest.

From the grooms' perspective, the situation looked even less promising. To be sure, powerful Greek and Macedonian men did not expect to marry for love; such matches might be a staple of the romantic comedies then popular in Athens, but they were unlikely to be common in real life. The grooms did, however, expect that they would arrange their own marriages—normally for political benefit—at a place and time of their choosing. To have their brides picked out for them, even by the king, was an abrogation of their autonomy. The grooms may also have resented being forced to marry Iranian women, with whom they shared neither religion, habits, nor even language (only one companion of Alexander's, his recently named governor Peukestas, is known to have learned Persian).

Other resentments were likely present at the Susa weddings beneath the harmonious, glittering surface. For the Persian guests, one particular source of anger was the one-sidedness of Alexander's vaunted cultural mixing. Macedonian men married Iranian women, but no brides had been summoned from the west to reward the king's loyal Persian supporters. Without Greek and Macedonian brides or Iranian husbands, the weddings appear not so much a wholehearted embrace of fusion as imperialism, with conquered women as prizes for the conquerors.

In organizing the mass marriage, Alexander may have been seeking to bind the disparate peoples of his empire together by something other than brute force. But through his interference in the most personal, intimate aspects of his subjects' lives, he had alienated them further. He would soon face the consequences of his authoritarian attempts at integration and the resentments they engendered. Dangerously for Alexander, resistance would come not from his Persian subjects, but from the Macedonians.

Soon after the Susa wedding, Alexander summoned his soldiers together for an assembly. Flush from the monumental bout of gift-giving his marriage had triggered, the king sought to spread his munificence even further. As the soldiers listened incredulously, he offered to pay off all the army's debts.

Alexander's offer was much needed. It seems incredible that the soldiers—having conquered one of the richest empires of antiquity—could be regularly in debt. Yet they were. In Alexander's army, rank-and-file infantrymen earned about one drachma a day, barely as much as a skilled craftsman. Although cavalrymen and officers earned more, their expenses were higher, too, as soldiers were generally expected to supply or at least maintain their armor, weapons, and horses. They even had to pay for their own food.

Because wages depended on the wealth of the territory through which they moved and their success, or lack thereof, in battle, soldiers' pay was intermittent. Often they went without wages for several months, then received back pay and bonuses following a victory. Their real wealth, if they were lucky, came from plunder. Soldiers were allowed to keep the coins and precious objects they took during the sack of a city, and to sell individuals they captured into slavery: a horrific, but highly lucrative, ancient practice.

Because their sources of income were both infrequent and unpredictable, Alexander's soldiers often faced liquidity crises. When they had not been paid, but still had to eat, they borrowed. They did not always pay back their loans when flush with cash.

From Alexander's perspective, repaying his soldiers' debts made good sense. No longer perfectly attuned to his men, he nonetheless recognized their financial precarity. In offering to pay, the king aimed to pave the way for demobilization by allowing the soldiers to go home debt-free. The king moved one step at a time, with the logistical finesse he had honed on his military campaigns. He didn't see fit to explain his long-term plans to the rank-and-file soldiers.

At the Susa assembly, the soldiers murmured anxiously to one another. The offer seemed to them suspicious. Perhaps, they thought, Alexander had his own ulterior motives, wanting to find out who was profligate and who was not. Perhaps he would use this knowledge against them. Generally the soldiers relished their king's attention, a key aspect of his effective leadership. But now they feared it. Their trust in him, so pronounced and powerful at the beginning of the campaign, was fraying.

Only a tiny trickle of soldiers came up. The vast majority, indebted though they were, did not move. It was an awkward, uncomfortable moment, one that made clear the gulf that now separated the soldiers from their king.

When so few volunteered, Alexander recognized his mistake. To make amends, the king set out tables piled high with coins. He invited all his soldiers to line up, show their bonds, and receive money immediately. He promised that no record would be kept of the debts of individuals. Gingerly, the soldiers came forward and took the money. Given the size of the army, the disbursement of funds must have gone on for days. By the end, the king had given out somewhere between ten and twenty thousand talents, about 280 tons of silver. The expense, for Alexander, was well worth it. With their debts paid off, his soldiers could be demobilized without fear of their creditors. One of the barriers to their homecoming was gone.

SEVENTEEN

Demobilization and Its Discontents

Iran, Iraq, and Greece
Spring–Summer 324 BCE

A SOLDIER'S HOMECOMING, as Odysseus might have warned, is always fraught. As temperate spring gave way to the blistering continental Asian summer of 324 BCE, Alexander and his troops faced epic challenges. They had been fighting for ten straight years, as long as Homer's soldiers in the Trojan War. Some had fought even longer, since they had served with Alexander's father, Philip II. Like Achilles, they had been exposed to the extraordinary brutality of constant warfare. Like Odysseus, on their winding, circuitous journeys they had suffered much. They had also formed new attachments, with romantic partners and in some cases children from the lands they had conquered. The soldiers were unsure how to reconcile these new Asian unions—nine or ten thousand of them recently formalized during the mass marriage at Susa—with the Penelopes they had left at home.

Alexander knew he owed his soldiers a homecoming. With the Great King definitively defeated and the army back in the empire's heartland, he had no excuses any longer for putting it off. But he must also have been aware how challenging it would be to get tens of thousands of men from Iran to the Greek mainland and to release them back into civilian life. At Susa, he took the tentative first step toward mass demobilization. As the response to his efforts suggested, it would prove even harder than he imagined.

Alexander began by welcoming a new group of soldiers to his camp at Susa. Selected for grace and strength, they were young Persian troops, some thirty thousand of them. As they drilled before Alexander, they wore Macedonian armor and showed off their mastery of Macedonian battle tactics. They likely used the preeminent Macedonian weapon, the eighteen-foot-long sarissa, and marched in the infantry formation with spears pointing outward that was key to the king's military success.

The Persians' demonstration of their skills also showcased their linguistic training, as these young Iranians had learned Greek. Given that few Greeks or Macedonians knew Persian, this training was clearly necessary if the young soldiers were to be incorporated into the army. At the same time, their knowledge gave them obvious advantages in Alexander's multicultural empire—advantages that the Macedonian veterans lacked.

Alexander had long been planning for this moment. He had assembled the young Persians at least four years earlier, prior to his departure for South Asia. Like the Greek allied troops whom the king had conscripted for the invasion of Persia, or the elite Macedonian Royal Pages, the young Iranians had an ambiguous status. They were honored, as they were integrated into one of the ancient world's most formidable and successful armies. They were also hostages meant to guarantee that their relatives—who must have numbered in the hundreds of thousands—did not revolt.

For Alexander's demobilization effort, the Persian soldiers were critical. As the king watched them, he could see that they were effective replacements for the men he was soon intending to send home. Alexander's veterans were aging, disapproving, and insubordinate. Particularly after their protest on the Beas, he knew he could not entirely trust them. And he couldn't depend on an endless supply of new recruits from Greece and Macedonia either. He had pulled at least thirty thousand men from there over the course of his campaigns, leaving the manpower reserves perilously close to tapped out. Persia, by contrast, had an enormous population and could easily provide more troops. The young Iranians he was observing at Susa were just the beginning.

Alexander was not immediately planning another campaign, though he had his eye on Arabia, contiguous to his empire and, with its spice trade, highly profitable. But even without another war in the offing, the king needed an army. And he wanted that army—and himself—to remain in the center of his empire, so that he could rule from Mesopotamia, not Macedonia at the far western periphery. More Aeneas than Odysseus, Alexander aimed to establish a new empire far from his homeland. Like Aeneas, he would die before his ambition was fulfilled.

Alexander was at least dimly aware of how unpopular his vision of the future would be with his Greek and Macedonian troops. The young Persians, by contrast, were accustomed to an empire centered on their homeland. They would happily accept a Middle Eastern tour of duty with the king. From Alexander's perspective, replacing Greek and Macedonian soldiers with Persians was a convenient solution. It bound his subjects more closely to him while lessening his dependence on those problematic veterans.

At the conclusion of the drilling performance, Alexander could see that his hopes for the young Persians had been abundantly fulfilled. He commended their discipline and skill, as generous with his praise to them as he had been to his Hellenic soldiers in the past. The king also gave the Iranian troops a name, striking in its suggestiveness. He called them the Epigonoi—that is, "the Successors." His Greek and Macedonian troops were less complimentary, dismissing them as "dancer-soldiers."

While the Greek and Macedonian troops clearly saw them as threatening, what the Epigonoi themselves thought of their situation is more difficult to parse. As young, strong men, the pick of the Persian Empire, they might have become potent rebels. Instead, they had been conscripted into the service of their conquerors. Still, the Epigonoi had been young when they were selected; their training was extensive and generously funded by Alexander himself; and they were, at its end, incorporated into the Macedonian army. With the Great King dead and his empire subsumed into that of Alexander, the Epigonoi had been given privileges that might well be appreciated by ambitious and resilient young men. Alexander was, it should be stressed, unusual. How few occupiers throughout history have armed and trained their subjects on a scale commensurate with their own forces?

As the summer wore on, the Epigonoi and their Greek and Macedonian counterparts moved west. The ever-more-prominent second-in-command, Hephaistion, led the heavy infantry and baggage train overland. Alexander, by contrast, sailed downriver from Susa with the elite light-armed troops to the Persian Gulf, then coasted along the shore. After the ships headed up the marshy, low-lying Tigris River, Alexander and Hephaistion met up near Opis, a strategic site near the Euphrates and thus a nexus of connectivity and communication.

For the soldiers, the heat at Opis was brutal—its current average highs hover around 100 degrees Fahrenheit in July and August—and the city was far enough inland to eliminate refreshing sea breezes. When the soldiers were summoned to another assembly, carrying their weapons and wearing their heavy bronze and iron body armor, they must have sweltered.

Only the Greek and Macedonian soldiers were invited to this assembly. The Epigonoi were in their own camp, separate from the veterans. The women and children following the army must have been nearby, but they were not invited either. They had no role in a military assembly, even when the matter under discussion intimately concerned them. They would have to wait to learn what fate the king had decreed for the men who were their lovers, partners, fathers. They must have been anxious, since the little they had, with the soldiers' departure they stood to lose. Whatever happened to the men, the women and children were unlikely to experience a homecoming.

At the Opis assembly, Alexander stood before his troops on a dais as he often did for an important speech. From there, he explained to the army his demobilization plans. The king told his soldiers he would send home those unfit for service due to age or disability, roughly half of those listening. He would not lead them himself, but instead put in charge his invalided general Krateros. The rest would stay with Alexander.

As the king spoke, blandly enumerating the honors his soldiers would receive in lieu of a homecoming, he heard angry murmurs from the crowd. The demobilized said that they were being dishonored at the end of their long service—chewed up and spit out—despite the bonuses the king was offering and the privileges he promised when they returned home. Those who were selected to stay in Persia whispered resentfully as well. They wanted to leave, and they wanted Alexander to lead them back.

Alexander kept talking, hoping to cajole his soldiers into acquiescence as he had so many times in the past. But on this occasion, his best, most charismatic efforts failed. Instead, over his speech the troops' murmurs rose to a roar. Let everyone go home, they screamed at their astonished king. If he wanted further campaigns, he could go it alone—or, they added sarcastically, with the help of his divine father, Zeus-Amun.

Abruptly and without anticipating it, Alexander found himself in an extremely dangerous situation. He was alone on the dais and highly conspicuous. Below him were at least eighteen thousand belligerent and overheated armed men. He had always enjoyed their unquestioning obedience. Now he heard for the first time their open defiance to his carefully constructed plans.

For Alexander, who cultivated a close relationship with his soldiers, what was happening was the most devastating form of betrayal. As a ruler, his very right and ability to rule was threatened. As a man who aspired to Achilles-like greatness, his heroic status was denied—mocked, even—by those who had helped make his aspirations possible

in the first place. And as an integrator seeking a stable modus vivendi
between Macedonians and Persians, the king found his efforts rejected
not by those he had conquered, but most insidiously, by his own men.
While he stood there on the dais, he was hearing what looked increasingly like a mutiny.

Back in Greece, Alexander was also dangerously close to triggering
rebellion.

In Athens particularly, men muttered to each other in the gymnasium and the marketplace, the council and the court. Alexander,
they said, was trying to demobilize. But while his soldiers wanted to
go home, many of their cities—above all Athens—did not want them
back.

The Greeks did not welcome demobilization, because many of
their veterans were exiles, explicitly forbidden to return. As the Athenians well knew, exiles had proliferated in Classical Greece. Most
were not criminals or economic migrants. Rather they were victims
of the ruthless factional politics of the fourth century BCE.

Almost from their inception, Greek cities were ridden by factions.
The few but powerful rich fought the numerous, resentful poor, urban merchants feuded with rural landowners, established old-money
families sought to keep power out of the hands of the nouveaux riches.
They argued in the assembly and sued each other in law courts, and
if a satisfactory resolution could not be reached, violence spilled out
into the streets.

This civil strife, what the Greeks called *stasis*, was a constant. But it
was exacerbated in the century before Alexander, as feuding internal
factions increasingly called on outside forces for aid. Bolstered by a
few hundred armed men, or in extreme cases a long-term military
garrison, one group could seize power and exile its opponents—at
least until the vengeful exiles called in other allies and turned the
tables on their enemies.

Once exiled from their native cities, Greek men had few professions open to them. Some talented immigrants established themselves in other cities, taking jobs for which citizenship was not required, such as teacher or speechwriter. But these were the lucky few. For those without specialized training, the best and often only career available was as a mercenary.

Many of these exile mercenaries had joined Alexander's army, hoping to improve their situations. Others had signed up with his governors, who had increased their forces during the king's long absence from the empire's heartland. Alexander had recently disbanded the governors' armies, and rumors had spread of his own mass demobilization. If the exile mercenaries sought to return and the king supported them, it would destabilize Greece.

Despite the rumors, the Athenians were not sure what to think. The king was far away, they reassured themselves. He generally respected the agreement known as the League of Corinth, which gave individual cities autonomy in internal affairs, while allowing him to control foreign policy. Forcing the cities to take back their exiles would violate the spirit if not the letter of this agreement. But Alexander, like his father, Philip, before him, did not always abide by treaties. And his regent in Macedonia, Antipater, was close enough to force the Greeks to do his bidding. The Athenians were fearful. Accustomed for centuries to fighting other Greek cities, they now had to contend with a king who was far more powerful. They nervously considered how to cope.

The natural response, in democratic Athens, was to summon an assembly. All citizens were invited to attend (because the Athenian democracy excluded women, immigrants, and enslaved persons, the citizen body was perhaps one-fifth of the city's total population). Unlike Alexander's meeting at Opis, there was no dais for a king to stand on. Nor did the men wear military garb. Instead, they put on *himatia*, long, light wool cloths they draped and twisted about their bodies. They had to stand carefully and not gesticulate too much so the cloths would stay in place.

As the Athenians gathered at the Pnyx, their vast open-air meeting place south of the Acropolis, they noted that taking back exiles would cause them special problems. Not only were their internal factional politics acute, but they had also occupied Samos two generations earlier. About a third of their citizens had departed to colonize the rich, fertile island off the coast of western Turkey. The Athenians, with their limited supply of arable land, would struggle to support the colonists if they were forced to come back.

In the dry heat of the Athenian summer, the orators who dominated the assembly argued. While no one wanted the colonists to return, they disagreed on the appropriate response to Alexander. Some hot-tempered young democrats wanted to prepare immediately for war, seeking allies and readying their navy, the best in Greece. Others sought to appease the Macedonian king as best they could. They suggested offering him crowns and statues, even worshipping him as a god.

Like Alexander's soldiers, the Athenians knew of the king's visit to the oracle of Zeus-Amun and his claim of divine sonship. Whether or not Alexander explicitly asked, the Athenians sensed his desire for godlike honors. And why not? With his money, his allies, and his army, the king had extraordinary power over the city. From a Greek religious perspective, the way to name (and possibly tame) that power was to call it divine.

As the orators debated back and forth in the assembly, Demosthenes rose from his accustomed place on the rocky hillside. Sixty years old—twice the average lifespan in his era—his curly hair was thinning, his beard gray. He wore a plain, unadorned himation, though he was a powerful man and among the wealthiest in the city.

Demosthenes was no longer the radical he had been a generation earlier, when he had rallied the Hellenes against Philip II. He had given the funeral oration after the Battle of Khaironeia, when a thousand Athenian soldiers had come back dead. Demosthenes had seen the terrible human cost of war, and he was not eager to pay that price again. But as a bitter opponent of the prerogatives of kings, neither did Demosthenes want to divinize Alexander. At the assembly, he offered a motion penalizing anyone who proposed a thirteenth addition to the Athenians' traditional twelve gods, placating, at least somewhat, the young radicals.

Demosthenes then asked the Athenians to hold off their military preparations for the present. It was rumored that Nikanor, the adopted son of the philosopher Aristotle, would announce Alexander's plan for the exiles at the Olympic Games later that summer. The orator offered himself as the leader of the official Athenian delegation to the games. There he could take the opportunity to have a word with Nikanor, an intellectual like himself. Perhaps he could persuade Nikanor of the need for an exemption for Athens. It would be better, said Demosthenes in his role as wise elder statesman, to wait.

When Demosthenes arrived at Olympia for the games, he entered a place radically different from his native Athens. Where the orator's city was spare and dry, dominated by gray-green olive trees and pinned between mountains and the sea, Olympia was lush, inland, low-lying. Located in a remote corner of the western Peloponnese, it had hosted for four centuries the Hellenic world's most prestigious athletic games.

As he moved through Olympia, Demosthenes could easily spot the courtier Nikanor and his entourage: powerful men, accustomed to respect. Also present, and adding to the enormous crowds typically on hand for the games, were masses of exiles. The rumors the orator had heard in Athens had circulated all over Greece, and many exiles had come to listen to Alexander's solution to their predicament. The scale of the problem is suggested by the fact that, according to one ancient historian, there were twenty thousand of them in attendance.

Likely exile mercenaries from the disbanded armies of Alexander's governors, these men had somehow made it back to Greece. Banned from their native cities, the exiles gathered eagerly in Olympia. After all, they had nowhere else to go.

At last came the moment that Demosthenes, the exiles, and all other visitors to the games had been anticipating. It was time for Nikanor's announcement. The courtier himself did not speak. Rather, he deputized the winner of the herald's competition (along with boxing, wrestling, running, and chariot racing, Olympia boasted events in trumpeting and voice projection). According to the herald, all exiles had the right of return, except for those guilty of murder or impiety. If a city refused to take its exiles back, Alexander's regent, Antipater, could compel them, using all necessary force. The exiles were thrilled, sending up a cheer that practically shook the sanctuary's buildings. Demosthenes was not.

With self-control born of age and bitter experience, Demosthenes nonetheless managed afterward to speak to Nikanor politely. The other members of the Athenian delegation saw the two together, although in the noisy sanctuary, they could not be certain what was said. True to his cautious nature, Demosthenes did not immediately reveal his hand.

Back in Athens, the citizens gathered in assembly once more. They considered again the question of the king's divinization, and were surprised to hear that Demosthenes had dropped his opposition to declaring Alexander a god. Drily and with his characteristic sarcasm, the orator suggested, "Let him be a son of Zeus, and of Poseidon, too, if he should wish it."

While they debated divinization, the Athenians also began preparing for war. In the midst of their preparations, they discovered off their city's coast an immense flotilla containing six thousand mercenaries led by Harpalos, Alexander's chief finance officer. Harpalos had taken fright half a year earlier when the king returned from South Asia and began summoning—and occasionally executing—his long-serving governors. The treasurer had been pardoned for financial mismanagement once already, and he knew he could not rely on his friendship with Alexander to save him a second time. So he headed with money and men for the king's foremost enemies, the Athenians, in hopes of inciting them to war.

Harpalos was premature. If he believed he could rely on Demosthenes, then he was sorely disappointed. The orator convinced the Athenians not to let Harpalos into the city accompanied by the soldiers—it was an obvious provocation—and when he returned on his own, to take him into custody. Demosthenes also advised putting the treasurer's funds on the Acropolis for safekeeping. He did not want to give the Macedonians an excuse for attacking Athens.

More politician than soldier, Demosthenes was trying to avoid a military confrontation. His conversation with Nikanor at Olympia had likely encouraged him to consider alternatives. Perhaps if the Athenians sent an embassy to Alexander, offering congratulations for his victories and addressing him as the son of Zeus, the king would relent. Perhaps he would make an exception for the colonists on Samos, just as his father, Philip II, had. Despite the temptation of Harpalos, his mercenaries, and his money, Demosthenes wanted to wait.

But Demosthenes did not want to give Harpalos up to Alexander either. It is possible that he feared, as a pious Greek, to give up someone who had come as a suppliant. Quite likely, he also accepted a bribe.

Throughout his career, Demosthenes was trailed by allegations of corruption. Despite his wealth, he seems to have taken money from those who in his mind best supported the interests of Athens. Earlier that had meant the Persian king, a surprising ally for a xenophobic Athenian but an appropriately anti-Macedonian one. Now it meant Harpalos.

In accepting money from the treasurer, Demosthenes was playing a double game. In the short term, he was pushing for an embassy and a peaceful solution. But if that failed, Harpalos and his funds would be very useful for the Athenian military. So he likely connived at the treasurer's escape from custody in the summer of 324 BCE, though he claimed to be as shocked as anyone.

Harpalos fled Athens, but made it only as far as Crete. There he was stabbed by a friend perhaps anticipating a reward from Alexander. Harpalos was betrayed and killed like a rat in a hole, though he had once been one of the most powerful men in the empire.

Demosthenes, too, suffered from the double game he had been playing. Following Harpalos's disappearance, he was prosecuted in court by Athens's foremost orators. He was accused by former friends of taking bribes and vitiating the Athenian war effort. For all his eloquence, Demosthenes lost his case. The most famous and effective anti-Macedonian politician in Greece was forced into exile: a casualty, from three thousand miles away, of Alexander's return. During the king's lifetime, Demosthenes would have no homecoming. And in his absence, the Athenians, and many other Greeks as well, grew ever more enthusiastic for war.

Back at Opis, Alexander knew he needed to act quickly. Before his soldiers' defiant shouts could lead to violence, he jumped down from the dais with his close companions and collared the thirteen most vociferous of the men. Terming them ringleaders, the king marched them off to immediate execution. Then he returned to the platform and addressed the rest of his soldiers, who listened in stunned silence.

Alexander excoriated his men for their presumption and ingratitude. Exactly what he said is unclear, but it must have been effective. At the end of the speech, the king leaped down from the platform again and left the meeting. One man against eighteen thousand, he had nonetheless managed—with his physical fearlessness, his charisma, and his split-second-reaction reflexes—to stop the potential mutiny in its tracks. Then he shut himself up within the royal quarters, admitting no one.

Alexander stayed alone in his quarters, considering his options. With the executions and his speech, he had saved himself from the immediate threat of violence. But if he anticipated that his soldiers would back down and apologize, he was wrong. As at the Beas, they remained in their camp, awaiting the king's next move. Alexander knew his troops were still mutinous, and they still vastly outnumbered him. He would have to risk more to resolve the situation. Finally, at the end of three days, he left the royal quarters and headed for the Persian camp.

Alexander could not be sure how the Persian soldiers would receive him. As he was well aware, they were his former enemies, inhabitants of a proud empire he had defeated and destroyed. Nonetheless, in his moment of need, he put his trust in the Persians rather than his own compatriots. It was an unthinkable move from the perspective of most Greeks and Macedonians. For the king, it was a leap of faith toward the new, integrated world he was trying to create.

In a voice loud enough to carry to his Greek and Macedonian troops, Alexander mustered the Persians. Doubtless to his relief, they came to him, though he was in a weak position and they could easily have rebelled. The king organized his Iranian troops into battalions with traditional Macedonian names: Persian Silver Shields, for example, and a new Persian royal guard. He appointed Iranian commanders for each battalion, and chose as well a new royal escort and personal attendants. He even called his commanders Kinsmen—a traditional Persian title signaling high status and closeness to the Great King— and allowed them to kiss him on the cheek.

Alexander had plenty of men to choose from for these honors and responsibilities. Apart from the Epigonoi, he had recruited large numbers of Bactrian and Sogdian cavalrymen. He had also created a cavalry squadron that mixed Persians with Macedonians. But his actions at Opis were far more thoroughgoing. Alexander now behaved as though he had an army without any Greeks or Macedonians at all.

With the Epigonoi as well as the other Iranian troops he had previously
summoned, Alexander had made his rebellious soldiers superfluous.

By the time Alexander had finished his muster, the Greek and
Macedonian troops were beside themselves. They had been angry
with the king at the assembly, certainly. When their hopes for return
were crushed, they had felt mutinous, and shouted their disapproval
at the king. Still, they had not taken the final steps toward rebellion,
and perhaps they had not intended to do so. At this point, they were
terrified. What would Alexander do with those Persian troops he had
just mustered? As the veterans were uncomfortably aware, the king was
ruthless in eliminating resistance. With their help, he had massacred
entire towns that had opposed him. The Greeks and Macedonians
may well have wondered what he would do to them.

The soldiers knew strong measures were called for. They ran to
the royal quarters and threw down their arms, weeping, begging
mercy, and shouting for Alexander. They asked him to kill whomever
he felt deserved the punishment. They made themselves completely
vulnerable.

At last Alexander emerged from the royal quarters. As his penitent soldiers were relieved to see, he was disposed to be merciful.
An emotional man, he wept to behold his veterans so desolate and
pitiable. Given the danger he'd been in, perhaps he also cried some
tears of relief.

As the king wept with them, the soldiers poured out their grievances. A distinguished older man spoke for them all when he told
Alexander what hurt most: to see the king calling the Persians Kinsmen and letting them kiss him, when no Macedonian was allowed to
do so. Alexander responded munificently that he regarded them all as
his kinsmen, and would in the future give them that name.

The king then permitted the man to approach and kiss him, and as
many others of the soldiers as wished. As with the repayment of debts,
this receiving of ceremonial kisses must have taken quite some time.
And it must have been a prickly process, given that men in Greece and

Macedonia rarely shaved. For the soldiers, however, it was critical: a public, physical token of their reconciliation with the king. When it was over, they went back to their camp, singing their victory song.

The veterans may have felt victorious, but it was really Alexander who had won. He had quelled a possible mutiny—how narrowly, only the troops could know. The king had used the opportunity to bring his Persian soldiers to positions of prominence, and to show the Greeks and Macedonians that they were not irreplaceable. He had achieved much, and given up little in return. Even the title of Kinsmen and the permission to kiss were distinctions permitted not to the Macedonians alone, but shared with the Persians.

The rebellion at Opis is often compared with the protest on the Beas, reasonably enough, since in both cases the king and his soldiers were at loggerheads. But the more significant comparison may be with Alexander's attempt at proskynesis, the Persian bowing-and-kissing ritual the king had sought to promulgate among Greeks and Macedonians. In the four years since that failed attempt, the king had grown far closer to his Iranian subjects and much less accessible to his veterans. While the Greeks and Macedonians had earlier disdained all customs that resembled those of Persians, now they were desperate to be allowed the same limited privileges. It was a sign of how far they had fallen in Alexander's estimation, and how far he had raised up their Iranian rivals. As the Greeks and Macedonians could see, the balance of power had shifted inexorably. During Alexander's lifetime, it would not shift back.

In the aftermath of the rebellion, Alexander invited his soldiers to a feast. Although he was reconciling with his veterans, he did not organize his dinner like a traditional Greek symposium. Instead the king appeared in the center of a series of concentric circles (a layout reminiscent, though the Greeks and Macedonians may not have known it, of the dining habits of Persian rulers). Immediately surrounding Alexander were his top-ranking Macedonian Companions: Hephaistion, Krateros, Ptolemy, and so on. Beyond them were Persians—separate and unequal, according to the seating chart, though as everyone was by now well aware, the reality was more complicated. Farther out were distinguished individuals from all the other regions incorporated into Alexander's army (Greeks, Bactrians, Sogdians, Scythians, Cypriots, Phoenicians, Egyptians, Thracians, etc.). All told, they numbered about nine thousand. They must have spoken a tremendous variety of languages, and exhibited a similar range of dress and customs. But as an ensemble they constituted the ruling military elite of the empire, gathered together under one enormous roof.

At the beginning of the banquet, Alexander had Greek soothsayers and Persian magi offer prayers. He watched as the Hellenic priests invoked the Olympian deities, the Iranians likely Ahuramazda, chief god of the Persian royal pantheon. The king drank from the same bowl as his Macedonian Companions—like the kiss, a physical token of their renewed closeness—and those surrounding him poured out the same libations. He prayed that the Macedonians and Persians would have *homonoia* and *koinonia tes arches:* powerful words in Greek, evoking harmony in thought and partnership in rule. Then all the guests poured out the same libations and gave the same victory cry. However great their differences, their actions were identical (which was what counted, at least in Greek religion).

Following the banquet, Alexander bid farewell to most of his veterans. He was sending around ten thousand soldiers west from Opis, led by Krateros. Their goal was Macedonia, where Krateros had instructions to replace Antipater as regent. Then the troops' favorite general was expected to send his predecessor back east with fresh recruits to Alexander. It was a curious mission for the long-serving regent Antipater, now at least seventy-five years old and with capable adult sons. But the soldiers likely paid scant attention to the political machinations of their leaders. What mattered was that they were going home.

Alexander sent his soldiers back with all the pay due to them till the end of their journey plus one talent of silver each—an immense sum, enough to make them the fourth-century equivalent of million-aires. He also promised them preferential treatment for the rest of their lives. By his decree, the soldiers were to receive garlands and the best seats at every athletic event and theatrical performance, a very Hellenic reward. The king provided funds as well so that the or-phaned children of those soldiers who had died would be supported, continuing to receive their father's pay.

The soldiers' other children were less fortunate. Alexander did not allow those raised in camp, and their mothers from conquered territo-ries, to accompany the departing soldiers home. Alexander promised to provide for the abandoned children, teaching them Macedonian customs and giving the sons military training. He claimed that when they were grown up, he would lead them himself to Macedonia and reunite them with their fathers. But as he and the soldiers both knew, by separating families he was leaving the wives and children highly vulnerable to the dangers of camp life. And he could guarantee what-ever protection he offered only as long as he himself was around to provide it.

In sending the soldiers home alone, Alexander claimed to be pre-venting trouble—particularly fights between his troops' new Asian families and the Macedonian ones they had left behind. He may gen-uinely have believed that as self-sustaining, well-trained adults, the children would be more acceptable in Macedonian society. He may also have hoped that with another decade of his rule, Macedonian society itself would change and become more tolerant of outsiders. What is clear is that even Alexander, for all his rhetoric at the banquet, recognized that that day had not yet come. As he separated fathers from children and wives from husbands, he implicitly acknowledged how far Macedonia was from the bicultural society he aspired to in his empire. The soldiers' personal lives were casualties of the gap between his vision for the future and the current Macedonian reality.

Perhaps that conservative, traditional Macedonian reality was one more reason Alexander intended to remain in the Middle East. He could live out his vision in his army camp, filled with soldiers from throughout the empire; in the new cities he had founded; or even in the age-old palaces of the Persian kings. In all these places, he could surround himself with his Iranian wives. He could also rely on Persian administrators and soldiers, along with select Macedonian officers like Hephaistion who gave him unquestioning support. By remaining in the empire's heartland rather than returning to Macedonia, Alexander would not have to face the separation he had just forced on his soldiers. But as he would discover, even keeping away from Macedonia would not be enough to prevent heartrending sorrow. Soon Alexander would experience the same suffering he had inflicted on his soldiers: the loss of the person he loved most.

EIGHTEEN

The Death of Patroklos

Iraq and Iran
Fall 324–Spring 323 BCE

ALEXANDER'S LOSS CAME THAT AUTUMN, in the midst of what should have been a triumphant celebration. He had left the marshy heat of Opis behind, traveling north to the cool mountain air of Ekbatana. He was planning to hold there a huge athletic and dramatic festival. After the events at Opis, he needed to reconcile with his soldiers and re-establish his fractured connection with them. Putting on a Hellenic-style celebration would help foster community among the Greek and Macedonian troops who remained with Alexander. It would also make a public demonstration of the king's generosity and his ties to traditional Greek culture, despite his increasing reliance on Persians.

While the festival was intended to court his troops, Alexander would also enjoy it. The king was fond of sports—like his hero Achilles, he was a runner—and he adored the theater. His taste in drama was conservative, and he preferred the great tragedians of the fifth century BCE—Aeschylus, Sophocles, and Euripides—to contemporary writers such as Python of Katana. Alexander and his courtiers quoted the canonical three, particularly Euripides, the way English speakers quote Shakespeare (and perhaps with a similar pretentious flair). The king even had his friend Harpalos send him their complete works when he was campaigning in Central Asia and had nothing to read.

It was during the performances at Ekbatana that Hephaistion fell sick. He and the king's other close companions were attending a busy round of events, coupled with riotous after-hours drinking parties. Hephaistion was hardly a newcomer to such parties. At Ekbatana, however, the late nights and communal libations proved dangerous to Hephaistion. He came down with a fever and was soon gravely ill.

Illness was a constant in Alexander's army. The king's forces comprised thirty thousand or more men living in close proximity, who spent their time journeying over immense territories on tough, physically demanding campaigns. Although they were generally well clothed and fed, their hygiene was rudimentary at best—unlike Roman soldiers, they were rarely provided with baths—and their doctors, though skilled surgeons, had a very limited understanding of disease. More men in Alexander's army likely died from sickness than battle.

Even high-ranking officers fell victim. Among the king's closest friends, Koinos and Erigyios both died from illness, while Krateros had just been sent home as an invalid. Hephaistion's illness was not surprising given that he had shared Alexander's many physical and mental stresses over the past year. Close as they were, Hephaistion likely suffered as much as or more than the king.

At first Alexander thought little of Hephaistion's illness. His soldiers regularly had fevers in the Middle East, and he had himself fallen victim to—and recovered from—at least two bouts of the same complaint during his campaigns. Hephaistion was young and vigorous, and after a week, he seemed to be on the mend. Alexander, whose restless temperament made him an unsuitable sickbed companion, went off to the stadium to watch the athletic competitions. Hephaistion's doctor headed to the festival likewise.

Hephaistion was left alone. The king's lover had rivals like Krateros, but he does not seem to have had a mistress or any other close friend. And if he was tended to in his sickness by his wife, Drypetis, her presence went unremarked. As far as we know, Hephaistion had no one, really, but Alexander. He was high in the king's favor, but also dangerously isolated.

On his sickbed in Ekbatana, Hephaistion decided to make the most of his solitary and unsupervised state. He had been chafing at his restricted diet, probably gruel and soup, with no wine allowed (Hippocratic medicine considered it "warming," and thus to be avoided for those with fevers).

For a young, vigorous man, accustomed to the hard-living, hard-drinking lifestyle of Alexander's court, such a diet was exasperating, as was his confinement. So Hephaistion commandeered an entire boiled chicken along with a full *psykter*—about half a gallon—of unmixed wine. He consumed them both, with gusto. Then his fever quickly worsened. Sensing his danger, he summoned Alexander from the stadium.

With his fever mounting even in the cool air of Ekbatana, Hephaistion grew weaker. For all his power, illness was beyond his control. While he struggled, Alexander was hurrying back to the palace. But the king did not come fast enough. Before he arrived, Hephaistion was dead.

In the ancient biographies of Alexander, Hephaistion is a shadowy figure. Infrequently referred to, he appears by the king's side, but does and says little. We don't know what, exactly, Hephaistion's relationship with Alexander was—friend, companion, lover?—or how it changed over time. Ancient writers are equivocal, and much influenced by the young men's tragic fate. They regularly compare the king and his companion to Achilles and Patroklos, two heroic figures whose close relationship brought about their untimely deaths. But the comparison may tell us little about what Alexander and Hephaistion were to each other in life.

What is certain about the relationship is that Hephaistion was Alexander's closest childhood friend. He was also—as second-in-command and brother-in-law—the king's designated successor. In both roles, he offered Alexander unconditional support, and received in return the king's absolute trust.

With Hephaistion's death, Alexander lost this beloved, trusted figure, along with a connection to the past and hope for the future. The death was also an unwelcome reminder of Alexander's own limitations. Powerful as he was, he could not protect the person he cared for most from dying tragically and much too young. In a life filled with astonishing successes and demoralizing reversals, this was his most personally devastating loss.

Alexander came from a culture in which intense mourning was not just socially sanctioned but expected. His was certainly passionate. When he arrived from the stadium, he threw himself on Hephaistion's body, weeping. He would not be parted from his dead friend, and had finally to be carried off to rest by his companions. He refused food and drink. In all these actions, Alexander was conforming to the cultural norms of his own day, as well as those of the Homeric heroes he emulated. Achilles had done the same for Patroklos.

Still, Alexander mourned extravagantly even by the standards of his day. As king, whatever he wished to do, in the fresh grief of his bereavement, he was able to carry out—however irrational or wrongheaded. His ancient biographers claim that Alexander hung or crucified Hephaistion's doctor, ordered the sacred fires throughout the Persian Empire extinguished, forbade the playing of music, cut his hair. Greek orators murmured mockingly that he wanted them to worship Hephaistion as a demigod, a shocking idea for pious Hellenes. Nothing could fully assuage his grief.

Characteristically for this battle-loving king, Alexander sought relief for his feelings in a military campaign. Shortly after Hephaistion's death, following a year with no recorded military activity, the king launched an attack on the Kossaians, a semiautonomous people living in the Zagros Mountains nearby. From Alexander's perspective, the Kossaians were nomads and brigands who demanded tribute from the Persian king. As a proud conqueror, Alexander could not tolerate such royal behavior, which he construed as an admission of military weakness.

In fact, the Kossaians were not true nomads, and they contributed substantially to the Persian Empire. As archaeological remains show, they had sophisticated canals and water management systems. They also served in the Great King's armies—for instance, at Gaugamela— and provided him with horses, sheep, and cattle. What Alexander saw as Danegeld was likely a more nuanced gift exchange. By offering the Kossaians coined money, the Persian king put them under an obligation to him. In return, they acknowledged his sovereignty and paid in kind with wine, military service, and their flocks.

Alexander disrupted this relationship with a violent attack. Because it was winter, the Kossaians could not respond as effectively as usual with their typical military strategies: retreating to the mountains and, from the heights, raining arrows down on their enemies. Still, they put up considerable resistance to the king. They fought, hid from, and ambushed the Macedonian army for forty days before Alexander finally declared them defeated.

Ancient biographers describe the king as annihilating the Kossaians' entire male population. But even their own records invite skepticism. As they note, a few short years after the campaign, the Kossaians were again making trouble for their Macedonian overlords. Like the Malli and Sudrakai or the inhabitants of Las Bela, the Kossaians likely combined initial resistance with eventual negotiation. Since diplomacy was rated less highly than martial valor by ancient historians, texts tend to exaggerate the toll of battles while minimizing the negotiations. But whatever Alexander's biographers claimed, the Kossaians were clearly not wiped out.

Along with his campaign against the Kossaians, Alexander also responded to Hephaistion's death by seeking comfort from Roxane. About nine months after Hephaistion's death, their child was born, a boy named Alexander. He must have been conceived in the period of intense mourning following the death of Hephaistion.

In the springtime, Alexander took the pregnant Roxane as well as the dead body of Hephaistion and set off for Babylon, the site the king had chosen for his companion's tomb. Alexander put his friend Perdikkas formally in charge of the funerary chariot, though some accounts have him taking the reins himself. The king, his wife, the army, and the corpse traveled along a lengthy, intermittently circuitous road, carrying them through the Zagros Mountains and down toward the Mesopotamian plain. They must have taken a similar route, in reverse, from Opis the previous autumn. The return was a more somber occasion.

En route to Babylon, Alexander was greeted by a flood of ambassadors. Some came from Greek cities, angling for exemptions from Alexander's mandate about exiles. But jostling among the crowd of Greeks were ambassadors from farther afield. Diplomats came from the kingdoms of the Balkan peninsula: Macedonia, Illyria, Thrace. To the south, representatives had traveled from the North African coast as far as the Straits of Gibraltar. From the west, they came from Sicily and Sardinia; from central Europe; and from Italy.

Rarely if ever in the ancient world had individuals from so many regions and cultures encountered one another. And all the visitors were well aware of the novelty of the situation. Several authors remark on the mission from the Celts, a loosely organized and migratory confederation of central Europeans who eventually spread everywhere from Hungary to Ireland. With their straight, short-cropped hair, pale skin, and torques of precious metal around their necks, the Celts were an exotic sight in Mesopotamia. Alexander's court was the first time anyone from Greece or Macedonia had ever encountered them.

As the flood of ambassadors ebbed and Alexander finally neared Babylon, he was confronted by another set of visitors with more difficult demands. These were Babylonian astronomer priests. They came to warn Alexander that according to their calculations, eclipses were coming that predicted danger. He must not, they said, enter the city of Babylon.

Alexander at first attempted to abide by the priests' warning. He may have been dubious—one story has him quoting Euripides on the untrustworthiness of prophets—and suspicious of the priests' motives. From the king's perspective, Babylonian astrologers had an ambiguous status. They were purveyors of ancient wisdom but also, potentially, charlatans. Still, they had a powerful role in the city and Alexander did not wish to antagonize them. He passed by Babylon and set up his army camp outside the city walls.

The priests likely wanted Alexander to wait outside Babylon through mid-May. They were predicting both a solar and a lunar eclipse around that time, as cuneiform tablets from their temple show. To their thinking, the king could enter when the eclipses they feared were passed, and with them, the danger.

For the impatient Alexander and his skeptical Greek and Macedonian entourage, however, the time seemed long. He had an elaborate funeral for Hephaistion planned, and he wanted to begin the preparations for it. The priests sought to be accommodating. If he had to enter the city, they said, the king should do so from the west (cardinal directions, like eclipses, were a preoccupation of Babylonian mathematicians and astrologers). Alexander tried to abide by this dictum, too. But the approach was marshy and full of pools, impossible for a man traveling with a large army.

Finally Alexander gave up. He wheeled around his soldiers and entered the city from the east in defiance of the priests' warnings. He would have to take his chances with the eclipses—even though according to the astronomers, the danger they foretold was a king's death.

NINETEEN

Babylon

Iraq
Spring–Summer 323 BCE

WHEN ALEXANDER ENTERED BABYLON in the spring of 323 BCE, he brought with him his army, his wives, and the dead body of Hephaistion. He had likely had his friend's corpse embalmed in Ekbatana, perhaps with the aid of expert Egyptian or Middle Eastern priests specializing in the preservation of bodies. He'd conveyed it over four hundred miles so that he could bury his friend in Babylon.

As he mourned, Alexander was seeking permanence in his own life. His choice of Babylon for Hephaistion's burial reflected a larger decision. After years of constant movement, Alexander had decided to make the Mesopotamian city his capital. Far from Macedonia, in the heart of the great empire he had conquered, he had found his new home. He wanted to bury Hephaistion there so that they could be together even in death. He did not foresee how soon his own death, Achilles-like, would follow his friend's.

In choosing Babylon for his home, Alexander was planning to settle in what was then one of the world's largest cities. Babylon had been a center of power since at least the time of Hammurabi, whose law code of the early 1700s BCE was created there. The city was excellently positioned for trade and diplomacy, key considerations for the king's imperial center. In addition, its rich agricultural hinterland could easily support a large population: some fifty thousand or more, at a time when the vast majority of Greek towns housed under ten thousand souls. Better than any other city, Babylon could absorb the large army and court that traveled with Alexander. It had millennia of experience in being a royal capital.

Besides its logistical and political advantages, Babylon had other attractions for Alexander. It was a cosmopolitan place, where Persian administrators mingled with Mesopotamian businessmen, Jewish priests, and Egyptian workers. The city had also been a center of learning for centuries. Its temple of Marduk, the chief Babylonian god, housed an archive of age-old cuneiform texts as well as the astronomer priests. The priests' achievements were astonishing, and included the deployment of the Pythagorean theorem—a thousand years prior to Pythagoras—along with extraordinarily accurate observations of the movements of stars and planets. Through such accomplishments, they had truly earned their prominence within Babylonian society (and, from their point of view, their right to give orders to the king).

Alexander was intrigued by the knowledge of the Babylonian astronomers, whose observations his former court historian Kallisthenes had supposedly transmitted to Aristotle. But the king's soldiers, and likely Alexander himself, found the sensual pleasures of Babylon even more entrancing. As biblical and Classical texts testify—with much pious disapprobation—the city was legendary for the luxuries and debaucheries on offer. To judge from its literary reputation, Babylon had everything a grieving heart like Alexander's could desire.

As he took full advantage of the city's pleasures, Alexander did not forget Hephaistion. He met in Babylon with his most prominent architect, Deinokrates, who was in charge of building an enormous, elaborately decorated cremation pyre for his companion. Descriptions of it in ancient texts seem incredible—its base was reported to be the length of two football fields—but archaeologists have found remains of its foundations. These suggest that the accounts, however extravagant, are likely true.

Hephaistion's pyre was not the only construction Alexander envisioned for his capital. The king was also rebuilding in a traditional
Babylonian way. He was living in a city that had last been substantially
refurbished some three hundred years earlier, during Babylon's most
recent period of independence. Constructed of baked bricks, the paradigmatic building material of Mesopotamia, Babylon's architecture
was constantly in need of upkeep.

On his first visit to Babylon in 331 BCE, Alexander had ordered repairs to the city's ziggurat as well as the astronomer priests' venerable
temple to Marduk. When he returned in 323, he reportedly put ten
thousand men to work on the repairs, an enormous expenditure of
time and effort. In accordance with traditional Mesopotamian practice, the king "cleared the dust" from the temple, a key foundation
ritual regularly recorded in Babylonian religious texts. He also issued
food rations to the workers, as a cuneiform tablet attests. In doing all
this, he was fulfilling his role as a good Mesopotamian ruler: pious,
beneficent, and respectful of the city's gods.

Alexander's rebuilding activities owed much to the powerful
Babylonian priests. Still, the contrast with his earlier behavior at
Persepolis is striking. By the time he reached Babylon, the king was
seeking to transform the enormous territory he'd conquered into a
stable empire. Alexander was learning to rebuild rather than simply
tear down.

Alexander was also planning for an expansive and culturally heterogeneous future. In Babylon, the king greeted tens of thousands
of new Persian soldiers. He decided that—rather than keeping them
separate, as most regional contingents in his army were—he would
integrate them with his Macedonian troops. He organized them into
new mixed units that mingled a handful of sarissa-bearing Macedonians along with a larger number of Persian archers or javelin throwers. By combining them, he broke up the Macedonian forces he had
come to distrust. At the same time, he stretched these expert soldiers
further, bolstered as they were by the Persian recruits.

The new mixed infantry units had a clear hierarchy, with Macedonians holding the key positions and getting paid more. Alexander's plans for the cavalry were even farther reaching. He had already incorporated into the Macedonian cavalry—the preeminent troops—those Iranians who stood out for their aristocratic birth and physical beauty (a very Hellenic set of criteria). Now he integrated the highest echelons of the army elite. To be included in their ranks was a highly sought privilege, and many went on to become Alexander's top officers. Alexander enrolled a number of Iranians into this group; for instance, the sons of his governor Phrataphernes as well as the brothers of his mistress Barsine and wife Roxane. These young men, offspring of some of the most powerful Iranians in the empire, were clearly being groomed by the king for top army positions. Even as the supply of Persian governors dwindled, the Iranian army officers show Alexander continuing to cultivate Persians as well as Macedonians for the empire's ruling elite. They were the next generation of generals for his increasingly Persianized army.

Alexander could also reflect hopefully on the beginnings of a new, even more integrated generation. By now he must have been aware that Roxane was pregnant, perhaps, if he was lucky, with his long-awaited heir. Since she had likely lost a baby during the retreat from the Beas, Alexander could not be sure that her child would survive (or indeed that Roxane herself would, given the perils of ancient childbirth). It was a time of uncertainty, perhaps nervous tension, but also anticipation: their child would be a living emblem of a bicultural future.

Still grieving for Hephaistion, but with his new home and hopes for a family to sustain him, Alexander formulated an ambitious new plan. Shortly after he arrived, he left Babylon again and sailed downriver through the marshy plains of southern Iraq. He was preparing for an invasion of Arabia.

The king headed south on a preliminary expedition. As he went, he cleaned canals, stopping up some and opening the mouths of others. His actions were those of a Mesopotamian king, carrying out the sophisticated water-management practices that had maintained the fertility of the land for thousands of years. The plains of Babylonia were the breadbasket of the Persian Empire, producing a full third of the food for the Great King and his army. With his own large army centered in the region, Alexander could not afford to neglect them.

Even as he cleared canals and dredged mud, Alexander did not forget his military goals. He had learned his lesson from the Makran, and had decided to attack the enormous, arid Arabian Peninsula by sea. To do so, he had to ensure that the Euphrates was navigable for his fleet. By securing the waterways, he made the river passable for his heavy warships. He would not leave his men stranded without vessels and supplies again.

Along his route, Alexander was no doubt rehearsing his plans and justifications for the conquest of Arabia, both to himself and to his decidedly skeptical generals. With this expedition, at least, he could reassure them that he had planned well in advance. He had sent out three scouts on ships over the past year, each venturing a little farther: the first starting from Kuwait and reaching to the island of Bahrain; the second to the Straits of Hormuz at the entrance of the Persian Gulf; the third intending to sail all the way around to Egypt, but despairing and turning back, declaring the land too vast, the desert too inhospitable.

For Alexander, however, no desert was too bleak. After all, even his scouts had to admit there were good harbors. The king also knew that Arabia was rich. The waters off Bahrain held the best supply of pearls in antiquity, at a time when pearls were the world's most valuable marine product. Alexander coveted even more strongly Arabia's other well-known products, myrrh and frankincense. As a boy, he had been chastised by his tutor for throwing handfuls of them on the gods' altars. When in 332 BCE he captured Gaza, the western terminus of the incense trade, he triumphantly sent his tutor fifteen tons of frankincense "so you may stop being stingy with the gods."

In setting his sights on Arabia, as in his care for Mesopotamian waterways, Alexander was thinking like a Babylonian king. He was focused on the Gulf Coast, contiguous to Iraq and directly opposite his empire's Iranian heartland. While from a Macedonian perspective, the region was peripheral—as his frustrated generals likely told him—from a Middle Eastern one, it was key. Arabia was a critical node in trading networks that stretched from India to the Mediterranean. At Arabian harbors, ships from the Gulf and Indian Ocean exchanged goods with caravans headed overland: spices and precious gems for pearls and incense. Given the king's long-standing interest in connectivity, it is not surprising that his ambitions turned to the Arabian Peninsula, the only major unconquered territory in the center of his empire.

Still, as Alexander wrangled with his generals up and down the Euphrates, his stated reasons may not have been the full story. Beyond them was something that looked increasingly like a compulsion for conquest. Ever since he burned down Persepolis, the king had been pushing forward from what seemed to his followers like perfectly acceptable stopping points. He always had a rationale, more or less logical. His reasons now were more Middle Eastern, less Macedonian—in that way, he had evolved—but the result was the same. Alexander was preparing yet another army for yet another war. With Babylon as his capital, he sought to settle down, to rebuild. But he could not entirely free himself from his ambitious restlessness.

On the return journey, as Alexander guided his ship through the reed-filled narrow channels close to the city, he could look forward to a triumphant return to Babylon. But while the boat slipped through the water, an overhanging reed snared his hat. The king felt his cap plucked off and with it his diadem, the sign of his rule.

At once an eager Phoenician sailor jumped off the boat and swam to retrieve both cap and diadem. While the heavy woolen cap had fallen into the water and been soaked, the ribbons of the diadem were still hanging on the reed. To keep them dry, the sailor hurriedly put on the diadem and swam with his head above the water. He returned to the boat successful, having kept the precious symbol of Alexander's kingship out of the muddy channel.

The sailor may have been pleased, but the seers Alexander kept with him were distraught. They told the king it was a bad omen to lose his crown. Some, likely Babylonians, added that the place where the reed grew was the tomb of a Mesopotamian king (who else would have known?), which intensified the dangers of the omen and required immediate action. They insisted that the man who had worn the diadem—the poor helpful Phoenician sailor—could not live.

From the Babylonian priests' perspective, signs were everywhere. Astronomers scrutinized the heavens, hieroscopists the livers of sacrificed animals. Others examined the king's body, the weather, and the planets. For hundreds of years, scholar priests had kept painstaking cuneiform records of prodigies and events, hoping to trace the connections among them. They sought a way of understanding, and with luck, predicting, the outcomes of what must have seemed a dangerously uncertain world. Scrupulous and in their own way scientific, they tested their hypotheses—a lunar eclipse signals a king's death—against what happened. Their harsh recommendation of execution for the sailor has to be seen in the context of this long-standing scholarly tradition. It also suggests the overwhelming importance, in their minds, of the king.

Alexander may not have shared the prophets' certainty that they could see the future. But he was jittery enough—and, like most Macedonians of his time, profoundly superstitious—to give an ear to their recommendation. He was also eager to keep the support of the Mesopotamian elite, which in a temple-dominated society like Babylon's meant respecting local religious customs and the dictates of scholar priests. He gave the Phoenician sailor a fortune for rescuing the diadem. Then he cut his head off.

After the grim ending to his trip downriver, Alexander returned to Babylon to carry out the long-delayed funeral of Hephaistion. On the day of the cremation, Alexander, his Companions, and no doubt many curious onlookers proceeded toward the pyre. When they arrived at its base, Alexander's friends gathered around him carrying images of Hephaistion in gold-and-ivory: the costly, technically sophisticated medium used for cult statues of the gods. They also brought their weapons and placed them on the pyre.

Alexander gave the signal, and the pyre was set alight. Given the dryness of the late Mesopotamian spring and the abundant fuel at the pyre's base, the construction likely burned quickly. The king then carried out an enormous animal sacrifice, ten thousand victims according to one source. With the gods' portion set aside, he and his companions feasted on what was left, as they had on so many happier occasions. They watched musical and athletic contests. When the performances were finished, Alexander's lengthy, drawn-out mourning period was at last officially over.

Alexander's mourning period was over, but the repercussions of Hephaistion's death lingered. They were felt by the king both politically and personally. From a political standpoint, Alexander had lost his most plausible near-term successor, the individual he trusted most to lead his armies, continue his integrative reforms, and protect his legacy. On a personal level, he was bereft of the man he loved, his closest companion and oldest friend. Without Hephaistion, and the support and stability of his second-in-command, the king appeared unmoored—increasingly sensitive to incidents he might previously have ignored. He missed Hephaistion all the more as he tried to placate the anxious astronomer priests.

For their part, the priests were watching Alexander closely and noting down his actions. In the clay tablets they deposited in the temple of Marduk, they recorded a Babylon-focused history of the king—a refreshing counterpart to the Hellenocentric perspective of the Greco-Roman literary texts. The priests documented Alexander's defeat of Darius III at Gaugamela (just eleven days after a lunar eclipse that they meticulously observed); his threatening of the unpopular treasurer of Babylon, Harpalos; his preparations for the invasion of Arabia; and perhaps most enthusiastically, his return of sacred objects to Mesopotamian temples. They also detailed a prophecy that eight years after the defeat of Darius, the crown would again change hands. From the Babylonian priests' perspective, the king's time was almost up.

The priests' concerns were infectious and clearly rattled Alexander. His nervousness was exacerbated when, shortly after his trip down the Euphrates, he experienced another uncanny episode. Alexander had left his throne and his heavy royal robes. He went off with his companions, leaving only his retinue of eunuchs to guard the throne.

In the king's absence, a man approached the throne, put on the royal robes, and sat down. He was not stopped by the eunuchs, who simply tore their garments and beat their breasts. The man remained there until Alexander returned to the eerie vision of his regal double.

When questioned, the man on the throne gave no coherent explanation for his action. By two Greek authors he is described as a prisoner, miraculously freed and divinely inspired. By a third, he claimed no motivation, even under torture; the idea just came to him, he said.

The Greek and Roman sources (and indeed, many modern scholars) present the man on the throne as a mysterious, dangerous portent. From their perspective, his actions were incomprehensible and clearly bad. But as some historians have recognized, the incident closely parallels a key Mesopotamian ritual, that of the substitute king.

Likely dating as far back as the third millennium BCE, the substitute-king ritual was performed when danger threatened the ruler. If an eclipse was predicted, or a sacrificial liver looked wrong, the ritual mandated that the real king temporarily disappear. A substitute was chosen, dressed up in the king's robes, seated on his throne, sometimes even provided with a consort, the substitute queen. His role was to attract, like a magnet, the misfortune anticipated for the ruler.

In the spring of 323 BCE, the Babylonian priests had likely decided that the substitute king ritual was necessary in order to protect Alexander. They may have informed the king, although to judge from the ancient literary sources, they did not explain their actions to his Greek-speaking followers. But even if Alexander knew ahead of time what to expect, it was still no doubt unsettling to see another man seated on his throne. And though the king consented to it, the priests' resolution of the ritual could hardly have felt reassuring. They decreed that the substitute, like the Phoenician sailor, had to die. He was quickly executed—one more casualty of the tense, fearful atmosphere surrounding Alexander.

Despite the Babylonian priests' best efforts, Alexander fell ill on the evening of the first of June, 323 BCE. He had spent the day conducting sacrifices, trying to avert danger following the execution of the man on the throne. He was heading home when invited to a drinking party by one of his friends. At the party, the king drank right through the night—or, according to Plutarch, well into the next day. Then, after sleeping it off, he met his friends for another riotous evening symposium. By that time, Alexander was already feverish.

The king summoned his physicians, but as with Hephaistion, they had little to offer. He was hot and uncomfortable as he hurried from one palace to another in search of the right breezy garden or cooling bath. But he couldn't shake the fever.

Restless and impatient, Alexander tried to act as if his illness would soon be over. He continued officiating at the sacrifices he made every day to the gods, though as he grew weaker, he had to be carried to them. He summoned his officers and discussed the planned invasion of Arabia. Even as his fever raged, the king insisted that the army and navy be readied for departure in a few days.

Throughout the first week of June, Alexander struggled against the fever, believing—or at least hoping—that he would overcome it as he had so many enemies in the past. He may have been suffering from malaria, caught during his journey down the swampy, mosquito-ridden Euphrates. Or it may have been bacteria-borne typhoid fever, a regular hazard in the ancient world. Either is possible, or some other, less recognizable disease; the descriptions in the sources vary, and the symptoms are not specific enough to make a certain diagnosis (although that has not prevented ancient-history-loving medical doctors from trying). What is clear is that Alexander's condition was weakened: by his many wounds, his earlier illnesses, his drinking, his extreme, hard-charging life.

A king like Alexander lived with the constant threat of assassination, so perhaps the thought of poison crossed his mind. He had come down with the fever at a drinking party. Had someone tampered with his wine? It's possible he considered Antipater, the Macedonian regent recently and ominously summoned to his court. Antipater had a son, cupbearer to the king, who could easily have poisoned his drink. Years later, Alexander's mother, Olympias, was rumored to have taken vengeance on this son, and scattered his ashes to the winds.

Still, if Alexander considered poison, he likely rejected the thought. Previously, whenever he had felt himself threatened, he had responded immediately and decisively—torturing and killing potential conspirators, lashing out at those who defied him. However, during those fever-ridden days in early June, Alexander carried on as though nothing untoward was happening. Given his history, it is difficult to imagine that he suspected poison and did nothing for eleven days.

As Alexander fought the fever, he knew that his soldiers were growing frantic. Despite their frustrations with him and their ever more rebellious attitude toward his authority, he was still their king. Alexander learned that the soldiers believed he had already died. They were convinced that his death was being concealed from them by his generals, whom they didn't fully trust.

Alexander determined to bid farewell to his soldiers. He arranged for all those who wished to line up outside his chamber. Then slowly, carefully, for hours on end, he had them file by his bedside. By the time they arrived, he could no longer speak or gesture, acknowledging them only with a faint motion of his eyes. It must have been an exhausting, and highly public, way to spend the moments as his strength ebbed. But as a king, Alexander had spent his life in an intense relationship with his soldiers. He had not meant to leave them so young, but he owed them at the least a chance to say goodbye. So he made time for it, as the Classical sources testify. His last words to his wives went unrecorded.

The farewell to his soldiers was Alexander's final act as ruler. He died on the eleventh of June, 323 BCE, a date recorded by the Babylonian astronomer priests. They added that the sky was cloudy that night; they could not read the future from the stars.

Epilogue

Alexander's New World

Alexandria, Egypt
c. 270 BCE

IN THE EARLY THIRD CENTURY BCE, an unusual entourage arrived in the city of Alexandria. Instead of an Athenian philosopher eager to join the staff of the library, or a Phoenician merchant bringing goods to the new center of Mediterranean trade, this group of people conveyed a corpse—the dead body of Alexander the Great.

As they moved slowly through Alexandria's busy streets, those charged with safeguarding the body saw a pioneer town. They passed new buildings still going up and immigrants speaking a cacophony of languages. They traveled along wide, grid-planned avenues, and appreciated avant-garde Greek-style architecture juxtaposed with traditional Egyptian monuments. In the distance, they glimpsed the tall tower of the famous lighthouse of Alexandria, a brilliant feat of engineering with a fire visible from more than thirty miles away. The body's guardians saw much to wonder at in Alexandria, but they could hardly meander through the city as tourists. Instead they headed for the palace quarter, the glamorous center of the new city. They took the body to a grandiose mausoleum specially constructed by the Ptolemies, and buried Alexander's well-traveled corpse.

The king had not meant to be buried in Alexandria. He himself may have wished for a funeral monument in the Siwa Oasis, near the temple of his "father," Amun. His chosen successor, Perdikkas, sought to bring the corpse instead to Vergina, the ancestral burial ground of the Macedonian royal family. But en route from Babylon, the procession bearing Alexander's dead body was waylaid by the king's close friend and newly minted governor of Egypt, Ptolemy. For the ambitious and farsighted Ptolemy, the center of power was not necessarily Macedonia. Rather, it was shifting—and he could help it shift by putting his thumb on the scale. Aware of the prestige that Alexander's tomb would have for his successors, Ptolemy snatched the body and diverted the procession to Egypt.

Alexander's corpse was pursued by Perdikkas, who had paid for its grandiose hearse and felt he had a claim on it. It was fought over on the banks of the Nile—Ptolemy, with the aid of the river's crocodiles, won—and buried first in Memphis, the traditional Egyptian royal city. But Alexander's journey was still not done. Ptolemy or his son, Ptolemy II Philadelphos, brought the body to Alexandria: the glittering cosmopolitan metropolis founded by Alexander, capital of the Hellenistic world. There the king who had sought to reach the ends of the earth and Ocean was finally laid to rest.

In Alexandria, Alexander's burial was surrounded by the tombs of Ptolemy and his descendants until the time of Kleopatra, the last, most famous Macedonian queen of Egypt. Even after her death, some three centuries after Alexander's, the king's tomb remained a site of pilgrimage. It was visited by devotees of the king, by tourists, and by other aspiring rulers; for instance, the Roman emperor Augustus, who reportedly brushed off part of the embalmed body's nose.

Though he had never meant to be buried there, Alexandria was exactly the right resting place for the Macedonian king. Far more than Vergina, or even Babylon, it was his true home: one he did not inherit but created himself. He had left the city when it was barely even a construction site, but as it grew, it fulfilled all his hopes for it and more. Like a magnet, Alexandria attracted aspiring and forward-looking individuals from all over the Mediterranean and Middle East. Not only philosophers but also poets, historians, and scientists flocked to its famous library, where their achievements included Euclidean geometry, the first accurate calculation of the earth's circumference, and—fittingly for a city founded by the *Iliad*-loving Alexander—the first editions of Homer.

These intellectuals had wide horizons. They competed for royal patronage with the Jewish theologians who produced the Septuagint, the earliest Greek translation of the Hebrew Bible. At Ptolemy's court, they could also encounter Manetho, an Egyptian priest well versed in hieroglyphics, who compiled a list of pharaonic kings and dynasties fundamental to the study of ancient Egypt. In his outreach to Egyptians like Manetho—and indeed, to a wide range of non-Macedonians— Ptolemy learned from Alexander. His city of Alexandria was an international center, where Thracian mercenaries crossed paths with North African poets, Jewish traders, and Egyptian administrators. Alexander would have loved it.

Alexandria held the king's body, but his legacy spread far beyond the city. His cults and statues proliferated throughout the Mediterranean and lasted far longer than his dynasty. His story, too, resonated for centuries. It began to be told even within his lifetime, by men like his court historian Kallisthenes. Then it was debated and embroidered by a host of Roman-era writers, most famously Plutarch. And it attained legendary status in the medieval Middle East, as Alexander became Iskandar, hero of his own romance and bit player in the Qu'ran. For all these writers—and later ones, from Marco Polo to Mary Renault—the king was always Alexander *Megas* (Alexander "the Great"). Although he has certainly had his detractors, his long-lasting popularity invites the question: What made him great?

For the Greeks and Romans, Alexander embodied greatness due to the perfect fit between his most celebrated accomplishments and the values of the time. He came from an era when what was rated most highly was political power secured through military conquest. By those standards, he succeeded brilliantly.

For more recent, more skeptical generations, Alexander the Great has also been Alexander the Terrible. An inspiration for empire builders from the Age of Exploration to the British Raj, the Macedonian king has been evaluated very differently by those with a more jaundiced view of imperialism (for instance, the colonized). From their perspective, his achievements appear no longer as the dashing exploits of a charismatic leader but violent, brutal, and gratuitous.

Yet neither those celebrating Alexander as a protoimperialist nor those condemning him as such do justice to his history. Both tend to understand him by reading history backward, extrapolating from later, better-documented empires to that of the Macedonian king. But in fact, Alexander operated very differently from later empire builders. And the key to understanding why he did so—and what made him "Great"—lies in his last years. His failures then, and the choices he made in response, were the ones that defined his legacy.

In his final years, Alexander was transformed by the crucible of his empire. When he invaded Persia, he had the best army in the world and won every major battle. But despite his speed, daring, and charisma, he learned that military success was not enough. Brilliant enemies like Spitamenes and Poros, experienced and capable allies like Artabazos and Omphis, and followers like Kleitos and Koinos—willing to speak truth to power—taught Alexander lessons he often resented, but nonetheless learned.

Alexander learned more from failure than he did from success. From the burning of Persepolis onward, years of struggle—conspiracy, guerrilla warfare, a brush with death—encouraged the king to rely less on force than on a hard-won understanding of his enemies and a willingness to compromise. Experiences like the proskynesis banquet and the protest at the Beas helped him to accept defeat, however grudgingly. From his army's march through the Makran Desert, he gained resilience and practice in making the best of a bad situation, as well as a determination never to risk and suffer so much again.

Most significant, his final years taught Alexander to embrace as-similation and integration. As he came to recognize, he was dealing with sophisticated and powerful individuals, and he needed to adopt enough of their culture to be accepted by them. With his weddings in Afghanistan and Susa, his new clothes and Persian courtiers, his restoration of the tomb of Cyrus and the ziggurat of Babylon, he put these lessons to good use. In such moments, he was reaching out to his subjects—Persians, Mesopotamians, Central and South Asians—and giving them reasons to follow him.

Alexander also learned to share power with those he conquered. Of his twenty regional governors, he named a string of eleven Irani-ans in his last years. He also cultivated South Asian client kings like Poros and Omphis, trained and incorporated at least fifty thousand Iranians into the army, and integrated Persian aristocrats into the officer corps. He did so for practical reasons, and had none of the modern interest in diversity for its own sake. He was simply trying to conquer and administer his empire in the most efficient way pos-sible. Still, the opposition from his Greek and Macedonian followers shows how strongly most Greek-speaking individuals resisted shar-ing power with non-Hellenes, even when it would have better served their interests. His final years taught Alexander a different, more flex-ible and open-minded, approach.

Alexander's evolution in his last years resonates with that of Achil-les, his mythological ancestor and the protagonist of his favorite book, the *Iliad*. Like Alexander, Achilles as portrayed by Homer was radically imperfect: brutal, callous, quick to fury. He was ambitious and competitive, relentlessly striving to be the best. And he was de-voted to a life of glory, choosing an early death and long-lasting fame over obscurity and old age.

When we think of Alexander resembling Achilles, it is often this choice that comes to mind, particularly because the king died young. But it is possible that Alexander learned other lessons as well from Achilles and the *Iliad*. As he knew, the *Iliad* does not end with the choice of Achilles, or even with his moment of greatest military glory, the killing of Hector. Instead, it ends on a somber and quiet note, with Achilles giving the body of Hector back to his grieving father. It ends, that is, with the great war hero recognizing the humanity of his enemy. In the *Iliad*, this scene is what demonstrates the evolution of Achilles's character, and brings the epic to a satisfying conclusion. Alexander, lover of the *Iliad*, surely knew it well.

As he matured, Alexander learned to appreciate the humanity of his enemies in an Achilles-like way. He did so imperfectly, and he did not cease from fighting (neither did Achilles). Still, in his final years, Alexander changed. And his world-historical importance is tied to his transformation, the repercussions of which were felt throughout and beyond his empire.

During his meteoric thirteen-year reign, Alexander not only conquered an empire, but also reached what he believed was Ocean, the literal ends of the earth. And then he turned back. He had seen, in his mind, the end of the world. Another individual might have stopped, his enormous, implausible dream satisfied. Alexander did not. Instead, having seen the end of the world, he sought to create a new one.

The Classical world is often conceived of solely in terms of Greece and Italy, with Periklean Athens and Augustan Rome as touchstones. In fact, it was far wider and more diverse, and it was the final years of Alexander above all that made it so. Because of him, Alexandria, the preeminent city of the Hellenistic world, was founded on the continent of Africa. Alexander's signature hairstyle was adopted not only for the portraits of his Macedonian successors, but also for early South Asian representations of Buddhas and Bodhisattvas. The half-Iranian, half-Macedonian grandson of his Sogdian enemy Spitamenes—the child of Spitamenes's daughter Apama and Seleukos, captain of the Silver Shields—became the dazzling Hellenistic ruler Antiokhos I, whose empire stretched from Syria to Central Asia, and whose dynasty lasted for centuries.

We tend to think of our current era as the most globally inter-connected time in history. But the world Alexander had begun to create had more incentives and fewer barriers to connectivity than our own. It was also more integrated. Of course, Greek speakers and especially Macedonians retained the upper hand, and in their own texts—the basis of most modern histories—they had little to do with non-Hellenes. But as historians come to rely less on Classical liter-ature, and more on archaeological remains and non-Greek written sources, we can begin to see how large a role the conquered played in the empire of their conquerors. Compared with the narrowly cir-cumscribed realm in which he was born, Alexander's new world was far more diverse and cosmopolitan. In this way it is an unexpected antecedent of our own global age. It also offers a new perspective on imperialism, calling into question three powerful myths about the inevitable course of European empire: first, the success of European empire builders through overwhelming military force; second, their "civilizing mission" in the Middle East; and third, their imposition of apartheid-like separation of conquerors from the conquered.

European empire builders are often thought to have prevailed due to their superior soldiers and military technology, defeating their enemies on the battlefield. Alexander's last years demonstrate how rarely, in fact, overwhelming military force guarantees lasting victory. Throughout his campaigns, Alexander always possessed better-trained, better-equipped soldiers than his enemies, along with what counted as superior military technology in his day: cornel-wood spears, siege towers, iron armor. His campaigns in Central Asia and the Indian sub-continent made abundantly clear that they were not enough. Instead, Alexander succeeded by combining his military advantages with different and less celebrated tactics such as speed, persistence, deceit, and above all, negotiation. His story suggests the dangers inherent in relying solely on overwhelming force in military operations.

Alexander's story also calls into question the myth of the "civilizing mission." European imperialists, historians contend, generally saw themselves as more advanced than those they conquered. They consequently had the right—in their self-justifying minds, the obligation—to "civilize" their imperial subjects through the imposition of, for example, new systems of government, religion, education, and so forth. The Greeks certainly believed themselves superior, and some ancient writers celebrate Alexander for founding cities, fostering trade, and bringing Greek learning to Persia. But Alexander himself did not act as though he believed his culture was necessarily superior. Instead, in his last years he used the Persian administrative system to collect taxes and feed his troops, named high-ranking Iranians to the command structure of his army, courted Babylonian priests and Iranian magi, and even followed Persian customs in dress, feasting, and wedding ceremonies. Actions like these suggest that Alexander recognized the effectiveness and sophistication of the Persian modus operandi and responded accordingly. His broad-minded and wide-ranging adoption of Persian ways offers a contrast to the behavior of later European imperialists.

Finally, Alexander's last years demonstrate that Europeans did not inevitably create empires that segregated themselves from those they ruled. While this has often been argued—or simply assumed—for Alexander himself and the Hellenistic kingdoms ruled by his Successors, recent archaeological discoveries and analysis of non-Greek texts has shown that in fact the Successors' realms saw Greeks and Macedonians educated alongside, working with, and marrying non-Hellenes. And Alexander himself was a thoroughgoing integrator, who relied on Persian administrators, fostered an astonishingly diverse court and army, and encouraged intercultural marriages among his officers and soldiers on a massive scale. His methods were often autocratic and sometimes counterproductive. But his flexibility and embrace of integration are striking, for both his own age and later on. In this way, Alexander's story does not just give us a different perspective on the past; it also helps us to imagine the future.

Acknowledgments

It gives me enormous pleasure to thank the many individuals and institutions who made this project possible. Thanks are due, to begin with, to my agent Brettne Bloom, of The Book Group, who guided me with grace, good humor, and fierce support every step of the way. I am also grateful to my editors at HarperCollins: Geoff Shandler, Peter Hubbard, and Jessica Vestuto. They understood what I was trying to do and helped me do it better; I have never received such constructive feedback, or enjoyed rewriting so much. Thanks also to my copy editor, Douglas Johnson, for his swift, good-humored, and meticulous work.

Institutional support has been critical to my research and writing, so I am very pleased to thank the National Endowment of the Humanities Public Scholars grant program, the New York Public Library Center for Research in the Humanities, and my home institutions, Brooklyn College and the Graduate Center, City University of New York. These institutions made it possible for me to give this book the time, research, and attention it needed, and encouraged my interest in bringing Classical scholarship to a wider audience; I am grateful for their support of the public humanities.

Since much of my research was conducted during the pandemic, when libraries were closed or difficult to access, I owe much to the librarians of the New York Public Library, Columbia University, and the Graduate Center. They went above and beyond to help me secure esoteric interlibrary loan items, often extremely quickly. The book would not have been possible without their help.

Over the years, I have spoken to many individuals about this project, and am particularly grateful for the advice I received from Peter Frankopan, Frantz Grenet, Frank Holt, Pierre Leriche, Laurianne Martinez-Sève, Claude Rapin, and Andrew Stewart. I was also lucky enough to have a range of very insightful readers. Paul Bachler, Kajori Chaudhuri, Sally Kousser, Sarah Leberstein, and Joon Park read early drafts of this book, and helped me clarify my thoughts and understand my audience. For a book that ranges widely over many fields, I am grateful that Zainab Bahrani, Osmund Bopearachchi, and Elizabeth Carney generously shared their expertise with me. I learned as well from audiences to whom I presented aspects of this work, including those at Columbia University, the New York Classical Club, Princeton University, the Society for Classical Studies, and the University of Indiana. And huge thanks are due to my colleagues and students in the art history and classics programs at the Graduate Center, who have been hearing about Alexander for many years. All these individuals taught me a good deal, and saved me from many mistakes; any errors remain my own.

Finally, I would like to thank my good friends and patient listeners Yvonne Elet, Mia Mochizuki, and Aileen Tsui; my parents, Morgan and Sally Kousser; and my husband and son, Erik and Andrés Fischer (Andrés once told his first-grade class that what *his* mother was an expert in was Alexander the Great, and I appreciate his enthusiasm for my topic despite all the distractions it has caused). Last but certainly not least, I would like to thank my writing partner, Ilyon Woo. Ilyon inspired me to write this book, convinced me that I could, gave tough criticism when I deserved it, cheered me on when I needed it, and essentially did everything one could ever wish for in a writing partner, and more. I dedicate to Ilyon the book that would not have existed without her.

Sources

Researching this book pushed me to read widely in order to understand, and re-create for the reader, the world Alexander inhabited. Over the course of my research, I learned about everything from Babylonian astronomy to ancient irrigation systems in Afghanistan, the behavior of elephants, and South Asian fortifications. To appreciate Alexander's challenges in Central Asia, I examined contemporary treatises on counterterrorism; to empathize with his veterans, I read about post-traumatic stress syndrome and combat fatigue. My sources for the book are in consequence broad ranging and unusual for a work on classics; this seemed to me the best way to do justice to the fullness and complexity of Alexander's world.

While archaeological material was central to my project, the Greco-Roman literary sources, despite their limitations, remain fundamental to any historical account of Alexander the Great. Foremost among them are Arrian's *Anabasis Alexandrou*, Plutarch's *Alexander*, book 17 of Diodorus Siculus's *Library of History*, Quintus Curtius Rufus's *History of Alexander the Great*, Justin's *Epitome of the Philippic History of Pompeius Trogus*, Strabo's *Geography*, and the *Epitoma Rerum Gestarum Alexandria* (also known as the Metz Epitome). Because these recur so frequently, they are cited in the notes simply by the author's name, while other works by the same author (e.g., Plutarch's *On the Fortune or Virtue of Alexander*) are given their full title. Since many differently paginated translations exist, Classical texts are often divided by book, chapter, and section; "Arrian 4.12.3" thus means Arrian's *Anabasis* book 4, chapter 12, section 3. All translations from Classical sources quoted in this book are my own.

Notes

Prologue: Alexander's Choice

1   *passes of northeastern Iran:* Throughout the book, geographical references use present-day names for clarity.

1   *bodies of exhausted men:* Plutarch 42.3.

1   *an army a fraction the size:* P. A. Brunt, *Arrian: Anabasis of Alexander* (Cambridge, MA: Harvard University Press, 1976), lxix–lxxii.

1   *leader of the hegemonic power:* Helmut Berve, *Das Alexanderreich auf prosopographischer Grundlage* (New York: Arno Press, 1973), 244; Waldemar Heckel, *Who's Who in the Age of Alexander the Great: Prosopography of Alexander's Empire* (Malden, MA: Blackwell, 2006), 103–5; Pierre Briant, *Darius in the Shadow of Alexander* (Cambridge, MA: Harvard University Press, 2015).

1   *an abandoned cart:* Curtius 5.12.20.

1   *stabbed to death by assassins:* Arrian 3.21.10; Diodorus Siculus 17.73.3.

1   *arranged for its burial:* Arrian 3.21.22; Curtius 5.13.25; Plutarch 43.3.

2   *cried at the news:* Diodorus Siculus 17.74.3; Justin 12.3.2; Curtius 6.2–3.

2   *see the Ocean:* Arrian 5.26.1–2.

2   *save that of Genghis Khan:* John Keegan, *The Mask of Command* (New York: Penguin Books, 1988), 14.

2   *has perplexed—and vexed:* A. B. Bosworth, *Alexander and the East: The Tragedy of Triumph* (Oxford, UK: Clarendon Press, 1996).

3   *Historians pass over these years:* Peter Green, *Alexander of Macedon, 356–323 B.C.: A Historical Biography* (Berkeley: University of California Press, 2012), 314–488.

3   *a few lurid incidents:* Bosworth, *Alexander and the East.*

3   *at times vulnerable empire:* Pierre Briant, *From Cyrus to Alexander: A History of the Persian Empire* (Winona Lake, IN: Eisenbrauns, 2002), 693–813; Josef Wiesehöfer, "The Achaemenid Empire in the Fourth Century B.C.E: A Period of Decline?" in *Judah and the Judeans in the Fourth Century B.C.E,* ed. Gary N. Knoppers, Oded Lipschits, and Rainer Albertz (Winona Lake, IN: Eisenbrauns, 2007), 11–30.

4   *a hundred thousand men:* Cornelius Nepos, *Datames* 8.1–2; Briant, *From Cyrus to Alexander,* 796.

4   *the empire's heartland:* Herodotus 5.52–54; Henry P. Colburn, "Connectivity and Communication in the Achaemenid Empire," *Journal of the Economic and Social History of the Orient* 56, no. 1 (2013): 29–52.

4   *internecine power struggles:* John I. W. Lee, "Xenophon and His Times," in *The Cambridge Companion to Xenophon*, ed. Michael A. Flower (Cambridge, UK: Cambridge University Press, 2016), 15–36.

4   *their cultural identity:* Edith Hall, *Inventing the Barbarian: Greek Self-Definition through Tragedy* (Oxford, UK: Clarendon Press, 1989).

4   *remote western borderlands:* T. C. Young, "480/479 B.C.—A Persian Perspective," *Iranica Antiqua* 15 (1980): 213–39.

4   *Persian power struggles:* Jeffrey Rop, "All the King's Greeks: Mercenaries, Poleis, and Empires in the Fourth Century BCE" (Ph.D. diss., Pennsylvania State University, 2013).

4   *their abundant gold:* John O. Hyland, *Persian Interventions: The Achaemenid Empire, Athens, and Sparta, 450–386 BCE* (Baltimore: Johns Hopkins University Press, 2018).

5   *the size of his kingdom:* Carol G. Thomas, *Alexander the Great in His World* (Malden, MA: Blackwell, 2007), 87.

5   *"not even a barbarian":* Demosthenes 9.31.

5   *most formidable army:* Nicholas Sekunda, "The Macedonian Army," in *A Companion to Ancient Macedonia*, ed. Joseph Roisman and Ian Worthington (Chichester, UK: Wiley-Blackwell, 2010), 449–52.

5   *ten thousand soldiers:* Polyaenus 5.44.4.

5   *large brown eyes:* Ada Cohen, *The Alexander Mosaic: Stories of Victory and Defeat* (Cambridge, UK: Cambridge University Press, 1997), 7.

5   *ambitious royal wives:* Elizabeth Carney, *Women and Monarchy in Macedonia* (Norman: University of Oklahoma Press, 2000), ch. 3.

5   *philosophy from Aristotle:* Plutarch 7.2.

5   *he dealt swiftly and effectively:* Elisabetta Poddighe, "Alexander and the Greeks: The Corinthian League," in *Alexander the Great: A New History*, ed. Waldemar Heckel and Lawrence A. Tritle (Chichester, UK: Wiley-Blackwell, 2009), 99–120.

5   *brilliantly fought campaigns:* A. R. Burn, "The Generalship of Alexander," *Greece & Rome* 12, no. 2 (1965): 148–51.

6   *nor the bureaucracy:* Pierre Briant, "The Empire of Darius III in Perspective," in *Alexander the Great: A New History*, ed. Waldemar Heckel and Lawrence A. Tritle (Chichester, UK: Wiley-Blackwell, 2009), 141–70; Pierre Briant, "Alexander and the Persian Empire, Between 'Decline' and 'Renovation,'" in *Alexander the Great: A New History*, ed. Waldemar Heckel and Lawrence A. Tritle (Chichester, UK: Wiley-Blackwell, 2009), 171–88.

7   *Greco-Roman aristocrats:* Lionel Pearson, *The Lost Histories of Alexander the Great* (New York: American Philological Association, 1960).

7   *fulminations of orators:* Elias Koulakiotis, "Attic Orators on Alexander the Great," in *Brill's Companion to the Reception of Alexander the Great*, ed. Kenneth Royce Moore (Leiden: Brill, 2018); Michael Gagarin, "Greek Oratory," in *Dinarchus, Hyperides, and Lycurgus*, ed. Ian Worthington et al. (Austin: University of Texas Press, 2001); Harvey Yunis, *Demosthenes, Speeches 18 and 19* (Austin: Univer-

sity of Texas Press, 2005); sedate inscriptions: Sviatoslav Dmitriev, "Alexander's Exiles Decree," *Klio* 86, no. 2 (2004): 348–81.

7   *cottage industry of historians:* Pearson, *Lost Histories*.

7   *Alexander's close friend:* Heckel, *Who's Who*, 235–38; Berve, *Das Alexanderreich*, 668.

7   *his official historian:* Heckel, *Who's Who*, 76–77; Berve, *Das Alexanderreich*, 408.

7   *Alexander's admiral:* Heckel, *Who's Who*, 171–73; Berve, *Das Alexanderreich*, 544; Ernst Badian, "Nearchus the Cretan," *Yale Classical Studies* 24 (1975): 147–70.

7   *his master of ceremonies:* Heckel, *Who's Who*, 83.

7   *one of his architects:* Pearson, *Lost Histories*, 150–87; Berve, *Das Alexanderreich*, 121; Heckel, *Who's Who*, 46.

7   *his helmsman:* Berve, *Das Alexanderreich*, 583; Heckel, *Who's Who*, 183–84.

7   *even his seer:* Heckel, *Who's Who*, 45–46; Alex Nice, "The Reputation of the 'Mantis' Aristander," *Acta Classica* 48 (2005): 275–302; Berve, *Das Alexanderreich*, 117.

8   *inherent biases:* Bosworth, *Alexander and the East*, 31–65; Elizabeth Baynham, *Alexander the Great: The Unique History of Quintus Curtius* (Ann Arbor: University of Michigan Press, 1998).

8   *never a Persian one:* Briant, *Darius in the Shadow of Alexander*.

8   *against the grain:* Daniel K. Richter, *Facing East from Indian Country: A Native History of Early America* (Cambridge, MA: Harvard University Press, 2001) (for methodology).

8   *contemporary Babylonian astronomers:* Robartus J. Van der Spek, "Darius III, Alexander the Great and Babylonian Scholarship," in *A Persian Perspective, Essays in Memory of Heleen Sancisi-Weerdenburg*, ed. Wouter F. M. Henkelman and Amélie Kuhrt (Leiden: Brill, 2003), 298–346; Amélie Kuhrt, *The Persian Empire* (London: Routledge, 2007), I: 447–48.

8   *inscriptions in Aramaic:* Shaul Shaked, *Le Satrape de Bactriane et son gouverneur: Documents Araméens du IVe s. avant notre ère provenant de Bactriane* (Paris: Editions De Boccard, 2004).

8   *Advances in Persian studies:* Briant, *From Cyrus to Alexander*; Briant, *Alexander the Great and His Empire: A Short Introduction* (Princeton, NJ: Princeton University Press, 2010); Wouter F. M. Henkelman, "Imperial Signature and Imperial Paradigm: Achaemenid Administrative Structure and System Across and Beyond the Iranian Plateau," *Classica et Orientalia* 17 (2017): 45–256.

8   *renaissance in Macedonian studies:* Manolēs Andronikos, *Vergina: The Royal Tombs and the Ancient City* (Athens: Ekdotike Athenon, 1984); Joseph Roisman and Ian Worthington, *A Companion to Ancient Macedonia* (Somerset, UK: Wiley, 2011); Robin J. Lane Fox, *Brill's Companion to Ancient Macedon: Studies in the Archaeology and History of Macedon, 650 BC–300 AD* (Leiden: Brill, 2011).

8   *destroyed at Persepolis:* Erich Friedrich Schmidt, *Persepolis* (Chicago: University of Chicago Press, 1953).

8   *founded in Central Asia:* Rachel Mairs, *The Hellenistic Far East: Archaeology, Language, and Identity in Greek Central Asia* (Berkeley: University of California Press, 2014).

8   *battlegrounds in Pakistan:* Mortimer Wheeler, *Flames over Persepolis: Turning Point in History* (London: Weidenfeld & Nicolson, 1968), 95–102; Luca M. Olivieri, "Notes on the Problematical Sequence of Alexander's Itinerary in Swat: A Geo-Historical Approach," *East and West* 46, no. 1/2 (1996): 45–78.

9   *power was exercised:* Robert A. Caro, *Working: Researching, Interviewing, Writing* (New York: Alfred A. Knopf, 2019), 60–61 (for methodology).

Chapter One: A City on Fire

11   *chill February air:* Donald Engels, *Alexander the Great and the Logistics of the Macedonian Army* (Berkeley: University of California Press, 1978), 73n14.

11   *fighting his way:* Diodorus Siculus 17.68.

11   *bridging rivers swollen:* Arrian 3.18.6.

11   *several orders of magnitude:* Plutarch 37.2 (fortune); Arrian 7.9.6 (inheritance), with caveats of Frank Lee Holt, *The Treasures of Alexander the Great: How One Man's Wealth Shaped the World* (New York: Oxford University Press, 2016), 23–43.

11   *above the plateau:* Ali Mousavi, "Parsa, a Stronghold for Darius: A Preliminary Study of the Defence System of Persepolis," *East and West* 42, no. 2/4 (1992): 215.

11   *thirty-three acres:* Donald Newton Wilber, *Persepolis: The Archaeology of Parsa, Seat of the Persian Kings,* 2nd rev. ed. (Princeton, NJ: Darwin Press, 1989), 3.

12   *called it his fortress:* Schmidt, *Persepolis,* 1:63.

12   *heart of the Persian Empire:* Ali Mousavi, *Persepolis: Discovery and Afterlife of a World Wonder* (Boston: De Gruyter, 2012), 51–55.

12   *he could scarcely afford:* Plutarch 15.1–2.

12   *a Panhellenic crusade:* Isokrates, *Panegyric;* Diodorus Siculus 17.4.9; Michael A. Flower, "Alexander the Great and Panhellenism," in *Alexander the Great in Fact and Fiction,* ed. E. J. Baynham and A. B. Bosworth (Oxford, UK: Oxford University Press, 2000), 96–135.

12   *Greeks had envisioned:* Michael Austin, "Alexander and the Macedonian Invasion of Asia: Aspects of the Historiography of War and Empire in Antiquity," in *War and Society in the Greek World,* ed. John Rich and Graham Shipley (Leicester: Routledge, 1993), 198–206.

12   *slightly more sanguine:* P. A. Brunt, "The Aims of Alexander," *Greece & Rome* 12, no. 2 (1965): 207.

12   *had followed success:* Burn, "Generalship of Alexander," 146–54.

13   *around his hometown:* Aeschines, *Against Ctesiphon,* 3.160.

13   *estimation of Alexander:* Poddighe, "Alexander and the Greeks," 116.

13   *advice Greek rhetoricians:* Isokrates, *To Philip.*

13   *nursed long grudges:* Isokrates, *Panegyric,* 1.125; Flower, "Alexander the Great and Panhellenism."

13 *Xerxes's sack of Athens:* Herodotus 8.54.

13 *frequently ignored advice:* Arrian 1.13.2–7, 2.25.2, 3.10.1–2, 3.18.11 (with the caveats of Elizabeth Carney, "Artifice and Alexander History," in *Alexander the Great in Fact and Fiction,* ed. E. J. Baynham and A. B. Bosworth [Oxford, UK: Oxford University Press, 2000], 263–85).

13 *Macedonian army officers:* Sabine Müller, "Philip II," in *A Companion to Ancient Macedonia,* ed. Joseph Roisman and Ian Worthington (Chichester, UK: Wiley-Blackwell, 2010), esp. 168–69 (on Philip II).

14 *some 2,300 miles:* Google Maps.

14 *decidedly less imposing:* Maria Lilimpakē-Akamatē, ed., *The Archaeological Museum of Pella* ([Athens]: J. S. Latsis Public Benefit Foundation, 2011), 57.

14 *his father had anticipated:* Brunt, "Aims of Alexander," 206–7.

14 *serious rebellion in Greece:* Ernst Badian, "Agis III," *Hermes* 95 (1967): 171–92; E. F. Bloedow, "'That Great Puzzle in the History of Alexander': Back into 'The Primal Pit of Historical Murk,'" in *Rom und der griechische Osten: Festschrift für Hatto H. Schmitt zum 65 Geburtstag,* ed. Ch. Schubert and K. Brodersen (Stuttgart: F. Steiner Verlag, 1995), 23–29.

14 *Macedonian regent, Antipater:* Heckel, *Who's Who,* 35–38; Berve, *Das Alexanderreich,* 94.

14 *overture from Darius:* Arrian 2.25.1–3; Pierre Briant, *Rois, tributs et paysans: Études sur les formations tributaires du Moyen-Orient ancien* (Paris: Les Belles Lettres, 1982), 371–72.

14 *Alexander's second-in-command:* Heckel, *Who's Who,* 190–92; Berve, *Das Alexanderreich,* 606.

14 *brevity and contempt:* Plutarch, *Alexander* 29.4.

14 *grumpily but pragmatically:* Arrian 3.18.11.

14 *his immense wealth:* Müller, "Philip II," 179.

14 *produce an heir:* Diodorus Siculus 17.16.2.

15 *was still at large:* Arrian 3.19.1.

15 *Persian Empire's borderlands:* Arrian 3.21.1.

15 *Indian subcontinent beckoned:* Arrian, *The Landmark Arrian: The Campaigns of Alexander,* ed. Pamela Mensch and James S. Romm (New York: Pantheon Books, 2010), 375–79.

15 *immense body of water:* Marie-Claire Beaulieu, *The Sea in the Greek Imagination* (Philadelphia: University of Pennsylvania Press, 2016).

15 *Ocean fascinated Alexander:* James S. Romm, *The Edges of the Earth in Ancient Thought: Geography, Exploration, and Fiction* (Princeton, NJ: Princeton University Press, 1992), 9–44; Homer, *Iliad* 14.301–10.

15 *"like ants or frogs":* Plato, *Phaedo* 109b.

15 *vast gray depths:* Beaulieu, *Sea in the Greek Imagination,* 1–20.

15 *had been encouraging:* Curtius 5.5.2.

16 *wrote two essays:* Plutarch, *Moralia* 333e–345b ("On the Fortune or Virtue of Alexander").

16 *Alexander nine months:* Arrian 2.15.6, 24.6.

16   *compared favorably in scale:* Schmidt, *Persepolis,* 1:65–68; Lilimpakē-Akamatē, *Archaeological Museum of Pella,* 58–65.

16   *roads carpeted with flowers:* Curtius 5.1.20–21.

16   *size of a soccer field:* Schmidt, *Persepolis,* 1:fig. 21.

16   *elaborate outdoor ceremonies:* Margaret Cool Root, "Achaemenid Imperial Architecture: Performative Porticoes of Persepolis," in *Persian Architecture and Kingship: Displays of Power and Politics in Iran from the Achaemenids to the Pahlavis,* ed. S. Babaie and T. Grigor (London: I. B. Tauris, 2015), 17–20.

16   *enormous audience hall:* Schmidt, *Persepolis,* 1:70–81.

16   *triple-gated building:* Schmidt, 1:107–22.

16   *after four palaces:* Schmidt, 1:222–29 (Palace of Darius I), 1:238–44 (Xerxes I), 1:269 (Palace D), 1:274–75 (Palace G).

17   *plain mudbrick walls:* Schmidt, 1:160, 73.

17   *not statistically minded:* W. W. Tarn, *Alexander the Great* (Boston: Beacon Press, 1956), 25–26; W. Heckel, "Alexander the Great and the Fate of the Enemy: Quantifying, Qualifying, and Categorizing Atrocities," in *The Many Faces of War in the Ancient World,* ed. Waldemar Heckel, Sabine Müller, and Graham Wrightson (Cambridge, UK: Cambridge University Press, 2015), 233–67.

17   *forty thousand talents:* Plutarch 37.2; cf. Curtius 5.6.9, Diodorus Siculus 17.71.1 (120,000 talents).

17   *tribute of the Athenian:* Plutarch, *Moralia* 842f.

17   *exotic, beautiful objects:* Schmidt, *Persepolis,* 2:66–67 (Penelope statue), 2:76 (jewelry), 2:83 (Egyptian bowls).

17   *let his soldiers loose:* Curtius 5.6.4–8, Diodorus Siculus 17.70.1–6.

18   *first substantial encounter:* Marek Jan Olbrycht, "Macedonia and Persia," in *A Companion to Macedonia,* ed. Joseph Roisman and Ian Worthington (Chichester, UK: Wiley-Blackwell, 2010), 343–45.

18   *broad, well-watered plains:* Slawomir Sprawski, "The Early Temenid Kings to Alexander I," in *A Companion to Ancient Macedonia,* ed. Joseph Roisman and Ian Worthington (Chichester, UK: Wiley-Blackwell, 2010), 133–34.

18   *the king's ambassadors:* Herodotus 5.17, 7.133.

18   *the Persians' demand:* Sprawski, "Early Temenid Kings," 134–38.

18   *poorly equipped army:* Sekunda, "Macedonian Army," 447–48.

18   *no Greeks, however bellicose:* Johannes Engels, "Macedonians and Greeks," in *A Companion to Ancient Macedonia,* ed. Joseph Roisman and Ian Worthington (Chichester, UK: Wiley-Blackwell, 2010), 92, 96.

18   *he went further:* Sprawski, "Early Temenid Kings," 134–38.

18   *marrying his daughter:* Herodotus 5.21.

18   *from the collaboration:* Sprawski, "Early Temenid Kings," 138–41.

19   *an impressive operator:* Herodotus 5.18–21, 8.136.

19   *few Macedonian kings:* Joseph Roisman, "Classical Macedonia to Perdiccas III," in *A Companion to Macedonia,* ed. Joseph Roisman and Ian Worthington (Chichester, UK: Wiley-Blackwell, 2010).

19   *high-ranking eunuch officials:* Briant, *From Cyrus to Alexander,* 268–70.

19 *alliances and bribery:* Brunt, "Aims of Alexander," 206.

19 *assassinated with the collusion:* Briant, *From Cyrus to Alexander,* 268–70, 563–68.

19 *traditionally autonomous province:* Briant, 619, 85–88.

19 *weak and ineffective rulers:* Roisman, "Classical Macedonia to Perdiccas III."

19 *four kings in six years:* Roisman, 159.

20 *on the losing side:* Roisman, 161–64.

20 *abundant natural resources:* Paul Millett, "The Political Economy of Macedonia," in *A Companion to Macedonia,* ed. Joseph Roisman and Ian Worthington (Chichester, UK: Wiley-Blackwell, 2010), 476.

20 *less well endowed neighbors:* William S. Greenwalt, "Macedonia, Illyria and Epirus," in *A Companion to Macedonia,* ed. Joseph Roisman and Ian Worthington (Chichester, UK: Wiley-Blackwell, 2010), 280.

20 *down from the mountains:* Greenwalt, 281–82, 85.

20 *What they wanted most:* Millett, "Political Economy of Macedonia," 484–87.

20 *spoke and wrote Greek:* Engels, "Macedonians and Greeks," 93–95.

20 *encouraged Athenian painters:* Plutarch 7.2–8.5 (Aristotle); Millett, "Political Economy of Macedonia," 479.

21 *trained their army:* Müller, "Philip II," 169.

21 *refused royal invitations:* Frances Pownall and Sarina Pal, "The Role of Greek Literature at the Argead Court," in *The History of the Argeads,* ed. Sabine Müller et al., (Wiesbaden: Harrassowitz Verlag, 2017), 219.

21 *then mocked the king:* Pownall and Pal, "Role of Greek Literature," 223.

21 *an elaborate genealogy:* Herodotus 5.22, 8.137.

21 *a fragmentary poem:* Pindar, *Siegesgesänge und Fragmente,* ed. Oskar Werner (Munich: Heimeran, 1967), 436–37 (ff. 92, 93).

21 *Macedonians' emulation of Greece:* Eugene N. Borza, *Makedonika,* ed. Carol G. Thomas (Claremont, CA: Regina Books, 1995), 125–33.

21 *far more appealing:* Janett Morgan, "Entering the Hall of Mirrors: Macedonia and the Achaemenid Empire," in *Greek Perspectives on the Achaemenid Empire: Persia Through the Looking Glass* (Edinburgh: Edinburgh University Press, 2016), 255–92; Josef Wiesehöfer and Sarina Pal, "The Persian Impact on Macedonia: Three Case Studies," in *The History of the Argeads,* ed. Sabine Müller et al. (Wiesbaden: Harrassowitz Verlag, 2017), 57–64; Agnieszka Fulińska, "The Great, Son of the Great: Alexander—Son of Darius?" in *Alexander the Great and the East,* ed. Krzysztof Nawotka and Agnieszka Wojciechowska (Wiesbaden: Harrassowitz Verlag, 2016), 223–44.

21 *analogous to the Kinsmen:* Olbrycht, "Macedonia and Persia," 345; Sekunda, "Macedonian Army," 447–48.

22 *but also instrumental:* Rolf Strootman, "Court Society," in *Courts and Elites in the Hellenistic Empires: The Near East After the Achaemenids, c. 330 to 30 BCE* (Edinburgh: Edinburgh University Press, 2014), 136–44; Olbrycht, "Macedonia and Persia," 345.

22 *counterparts, were polygamous:* Maria Brosius, *Women in Ancient Persia, 559–331 BC* (Oxford, UK: Clarendon Press, 1996); Carney, *Women and Monarchy.*

22 *the calyx cup:* Stavros Paspalas, "The Achaemenid Empire and the North-Western Aegean," *Ancient West and East* 5, no. 1 (2006): 102.

22 *burst out laughing:* Plutarch 74.1–2.

22 *lower city of Persepolis:* Athenaeus, *Deipnosophists* 13.576d-e; Curtius 5.6.4–8; Diodorus Siculus 17.70.1–4; Justin 11.14.10; Strabo 15.3.6; Arrian 3.18.11–12.

23 *attacks on civilian populations:* Adriaan Lanni, "The Laws of War in Ancient Greece," *Law and History Review* 26, no. 3 (2008): 1–17.

23 *soldiers to acquire plunder:* Sekunda, "Macedonian Army," 465–66.

23 *city of Thebes:* Arrian 1.8.5–8.

23 *the Carian Halikarnassos:* Arrian 1.23.6.

23 *the Phoenician Tyre:* Arrian 2.24.3–4.

23 *Every other military leader:* Xenophon, *Education of Cyrus* 7.5.73; Briant, *Alexander the Great and His Empire*, 108–9.

23 *so long in one place:* Plutarch 37.3–4.

23 *exactly where Darius was:* Arrian 3.19.1.

23 *as Alexander had hoped:* Plutarch 29.4.

24 *elegant columned homes:* Ali Mousavi, "La ville de Parsa: Quelques remarques sur la topographie et le système défensif de Persépolis," *Iranica Antiqua* 34 (1999): 148–51.

24 *their unfamiliar gods:* Arrian 3.16.9.

24 *in athletic competitions:* Diodorus Siculus 17.72.1.

24 *bizarre by Persians:* Donald G. Kyle, *Sport and Spectacle in the Ancient World* (Malden, MA: Blackwell Pub., 2007), 237.

24 *a brief sortie:* Curtius 5.6.11–20.

24 *the total population:* W. M. Sumner, "Achaemenid Settlement in the Persepolis Plain," *American Journal of Archaeology* 90, no. 1 (1986): 12; Curtius 5.3.3–6.

24 *Alexander was assiduous:* E.g., Plutarch 15.4, 23.2, 29.1.

24 *began by summoning:* Plutarch 37.4.

25 *388 miles away:* Engels, *Logistics of the Macedonian Army*, 73n14.

25 *behind the leaders:* Holt, *Treasures of Alexander the Great*, 87.

25 *spring day in 330 BCE:* Plutarch 38.1.

25 *Persian Empire on fire:* Arrian 3.18.11–12; Curtius 5.7.3–11; Diodorus Siculus 17.72.1–6; Plutarch 38. 1–4; N. G. L. Hammond, "The Archaeological and Literary Evidence for the Burning of the Persepolis Palace," *Classical Quarterly* 42 (1992), 358–64; E. F. Bloedow and H. M. Loube, "Alexander the Great Under Fire at Persepolis," *Klio* 79 (1997): 341–53; A. B. Bosworth, *A Historical Commentary on Arrian's History of Alexander* (Oxford, UK: Clarendon Press, 1980–1995), 1:329–33; Badian, "Agis III"; Briant, *Alexander the Great and His Empire*, 107–11.

25 *sack of the city:* Schmidt, *Persepolis*, 1:75, 76, 131, 72, 79, 85.

25 *Practiced looters, the soldiers:* Schmidt, 1:199 (metal tableware gone), 2:81–84 (stone tableware), 94 (metal remaining).

25 *shabby bronze weapons:* Schmidt, 2:97–100.

26 *a faster thoroughfare:* Schmidt, 1:186–87.

26 *soldiers dropped valuables:* Schmidt, 1:186–87.

26 *ornamented wooden couches:* Schmidt, 1:75.

26 *masses of flammable material:* Schmidt, 1:78–80 (audience hall), 131 (throne hall), 78–79 (treasury).

26 *were less meticulous:* Schmidt, 1:122 (triple-gated building, called the Council Hall by Schmidt), 72 (treasury rooms 10, 22), 75 (treasury rooms 15, 16, 35, 36).

26 *Their heat shattered:* Schmidt, 1:172 (column bases shattered), 2:4 (melted iron), 99 fig. 20B (fused arrow shafts).

26 *The fire devoured:* Schmidt, 1:75 (gold couches), 79 (mudbricks baked red, roof beams incinerated), 78 (cloth of gold).

26 *great cedar beams:* Schmidt, 1:132.

26 *heavy gray ash:* Schmidt, 1:132.

27 *Alexander's Macedonian advisers:* Arrian 3.18.11.

27 *a nexus of control:* Wouter F. M. Henkelman, "Administrative Realities: The Persepolis Archives and the Archaeology of the Achaemenid Heartland," in *The Oxford Handbook of Ancient Iran*, ed. Daniel Potts (Oxford, UK: Oxford University Press, 2013), 528–29.

27 *an Athenian courtesan:* Plutarch 38.1–4; Diodorus Siculus 17.72; Curtius 5.7.1–7.

27 *only thirty-nine coins:* Schmidt, *Persepolis*, 2:111–14.

27 *please the Greeks:* Flower, "Alexander the Great and Panhellenism," 114–15; Badian, "Agis III."

27 *the* Iliad *nearby:* Plutarch 8.2.

27 *primarily at the Persians:* Eugene Borza, "Fire from Heaven: Alexander at Persepolis," *Classical Philology* 67, no. 4 (1972): 233–45; Briant, *Rois, tributs et paysans*, 393–403.

Chapter Two: The Hunt for the Great King

29 *apple, mulberry, pear:* Henkelman, "Administrative Realities," 528–29.

29 *fertile and well watered:* Henkelman, 528–29; Rémy Boucharlat, "Southwestern Iran in the Achaemenid Period," in *The Oxford Handbook of Ancient Iran*, ed. Daniel Potts (Oxford, UK: Oxford University Press, 2013), 512–15.

29 *a rich variety:* Arrian, *Indica* 40.

29 *seventeen thousand armed men:* Curtius 5.3.3–6; Engels, *Logistics of the Macedonian Army*, 78.

29 *Darius III was there:* Arrian 3.19.1–3; Curtius 5.8.1–2; Diodorus Siculus 17.73.2.

29 *the nomads who lived:* St. John Simpson and E. V. Stepanova, eds., *Scythians: Warriors of Ancient Siberia* (London: British Museum, 2017).

29 *treasure to fund:* Arrian 3.19.5.

30 *two previous encounters:* Burn, "Generalship of Alexander," 149–51.

30 *Like Achilles:* Justin Grant Vorhis, "The Best of the Macedonians: Alexander as Achilles in Arrian, Curtius, and Plutarch" (Ph.D. diss., University of California, Los Angeles, 2017).

30 *some 514 miles:* Engels, *Logistics of the Macedonian Army*, 75.

30 *within thirty miles:* Plutarch 20.4–5; Curtius 3.8.13–14; James R. Ashley, *The Macedonian Empire: The Era of Warfare Under Philip II and Alexander the Great, 359–323 B.C.* (Jefferson, NC: McFarland, 1998), 222.

30 *governor of Armenia:* Justin 10.3.3.

31 *eighteen-foot spears:* Minor M. Markle, "The Macedonian Sarissa, Spear, and Related Armor," *American Journal of Archaeology* 81, no. 3 (1977): 323–26.

31 *unstoppable in warfare:* Polybius, *Histories* 18.29.

31 *on uneven ground:* Markle, "Macedonian Sarissa," 331–33.

31 *Their name derived:* J. F. Lazenby and David Whitehead, "The Myth of the Hoplite's Hoplon," *Classical Quarterly* 46, no. 1 (1996): 27–33.

31 *comparatively short and light:* Markle, "Macedonian Sarissa," 325.

31 *shields and jabbing spears:* Ruth Sheppard, *Alexander the Great at War: His Army, His Battles, His Enemies* (Oxford, UK: Osprey, 2008), 23–25.

31 *for the sarissa-bearers:* Markle, "Macedonian Sarissa," 329–31.

31 *carry all their gear:* Donald Engels, "Logistics: Sinews of War," in *The Oxford Handbook of Warfare in the Classical World,* ed. Brian Campbell and Lawrence A. Tritle (Oxford, UK: Oxford University Press, 2013), 354–58.

32 *speeds Alexander demanded:* R. D. Milns, "Alexander's Pursuit of Darius Through Iran," *Historia: Zeitschrift für Alte Geschichte* 15, no. 2 (1966): 256.

32 *thirteen miles per day:* Engels, *Logistics of the Macedonian Army,* 154–56.

32 *Cavalrymen, too, could wield:* Markle, "Macedonian Sarissa," 333–39.

32 *rode without stirrups:* Daniel R. Headrick, *Technology: A World History* (Oxford, UK: Oxford University Press, 2009), 59–60.

32 *helmets and breastplates:* Ann Hyland, "Horses for War: Breeding and Keeping a War-horse," in *The Oxford Handbook of Warfare in the Classical World,* ed. Brian Campbell and Lawrence A. Tritle (Oxford, UK: Oxford University Press, 2013), 505–10.

32 *expanded and transformed it:* Carolyn Willekes, "Equine Aspects of Alexander the Great's Macedonian Cavalry," in *Greece, Macedon and Persia,* ed. Timothy Howe (Oxford, UK: Oxbow Books, 2015), 56–57.

32 *ancient world's best horses:* Herodotus 3.106; Carolyn Willekes, *The Horse in the Ancient World: From Bucephalus to the Hippodrome* (London: I. B. Tauris, 2016), 119–20.

32 *cavalry in new tactics:* Willekes, "Equine Aspects," 55–57.

32 *they could not go far:* Hyland, "Horses for War," 501–3.

32 *range of other troops:* Burn, "Generalship of Alexander," 143–46; Arrian 2.26.2, 6.1.6.

33 *thirty thousand Persian:* Plutarch 47.6.

33 *those with official status:* Engels, *Logistics of the Macedonian Army,* 12–13.

33 *proved distinguished soldiers:* Plutarch 35.5, 40.1, 54.1.

33 *intellectuals and entertainers:* Plutarch 52.3–53.6; Borza, "Makedonika," 173–88, 91–205; Agnieszka Kotlińska-Toma, "On His Majesty's Secret Service—Actors at the Court of Alexander the Great," in *Alexander the Great and the East,* ed. Krzysztof Nawotka and Agnieszka Wojciechowska (Wiesbaden: Harrassowitz Verlag, 2016), 273–86.

33   *rather be Homer's Thersites: Fragmente Griecischer Historiker,* f.153 10a.

34   *unofficial camp followers:* Engels, *Logistics of the Macedonian Army,* 12–13; Diodorus Siculus 17.94.4; Justin 12.4.2–3.

34   *remote and inaccessible places:* Arrian 6.25.5.

34   *ten thousand of them:* Arrian 7.4.8 (ten thousand); Plutarch 70.2 (nine thousand).

34   *eight miles per day:* Milns, "Alexander's Pursuit of Darius."

35   *surprising his enemies:* Engels, *Logistics of the Macedonian Army,* 23.

35   *Great King Artaxerxes III:* Arrian 3.19.5; Berve, *Das Alexanderreich,* 212; Heckel, *Who's Who,* 72; M. Rahim Shayegan, "Prosopographical Notes: The Iranian Nobility During and After the Macedonian Conquest," *Bulletin of the Asia Institute* 21 (2007): no. 42.

35   *dead within two years:* Diodorus Siculus 17.5.4.

35   *three thousand cavalry:* Arrian 3.19.5; Diodorus Siculus 17.73.2; Curtius 5.8.3 (claiming thirty thousand infantry).

35   *elaborate Persian palace:* Polybius 10.27.3–13.

35   *produce of the region:* Stuart Brown, s.v. "Ecbatana," in *Encyclopedia Iranica* (1997), http://www.iranicaonline.org/articles/ecbatana.

35   *comparatively temperate climate:* Britannica Academic, s.v. "Hamadan," (2018).

36   *stripped the palace:* Polybius, *Histories* 10.27.11.

36   *he did not encourage:* Strabo 15.3.9; Arrian 3.19.5–6.

36   *regret the burning:* Curtius 5.7.10.

36   *discharging of soldiers:* Arrian 3.19.5–6; Diodorus Siculus 17.74.3–5; Curtius 6.2.17; Plutarch 3.24 (claiming it followed the death of Darius).

36   *they could settle down:* Dmitriev, "Alexander's Exiles Decree."

36   *about eight thousand men:* Diodorus Siculus 17.17.3.

36   *rich discharge payments:* Arrian 3.19.5–6; Curtius 6.2.17; Holt, *Treasures of Alexander the Great,* 120–21.

36   *to lead them west:* Arrian 3.19.6.

37   *were allowed to stay:* Arrian 3.19.6.

37   *the burning of Persepolis:* Badian, "Agis III."

37   *handing over the money:* Arrian 3.19.7.

37   *but also luxury-loving:* Heckel, *Who's Who,* 129–31; Berve, *Das Alexanderreich,* 143.

37   *to lead them east:* Arrian 3.19.7–8.

38   *a sizable portion:* Arrian 3.12.5 (total figure for the army at Gaugamela); Diodorus Siculus 17.17.3–4 (Greek mercenaries).

38   *cautious, pragmatic counsel:* Arrian 1.13.2–7, 2.25.2, 3.10.1–2, 3.18.11 (note the caveats of Carney, "Artifice and Alexander History," 264–75).

38   *an arrogant man:* Plutarch 48–49; Curtius 6.8.3.

38   *all-important Macedonian cavalry:* Arrian 3.27.4. Berve, *Das Alexanderreich,* 802; Heckel, *Who's Who,* 216–19.

38   *the rest of the army:* Arrian 3.19.1–21.10 (most detailed account, primarily followed here); Plutarch 42.5–43.7; Diodorus Siculus 17.73.2–4; Curtius 5.8.1–

5.13.25; A. F. v. Stahl, "Notes on the March of Alexander the Great from Ecbatana to Hyrcania," *Geographical Journal* 64, no. 4 (1924): 312–29; Milns, "Alexander's Pursuit of Darius"; Bosworth, *Historical Commentary,* 1:338–46.

38 *soon turned barren:* Stahl, "Notes on the March," 318; Engels, *Logistics of the Macedonian Army,* 80–83.

38 *men were left behind:* Plutarch 42.3.

38 *the Caspian Gates:* Stahl, "Notes on the March," 318–20.

39 *the nearest sizable city:* Arrian 3.20.3.

39 *from crumbling cliffs:* Stahl, "Notes on the March," 318–20.

39 *and the snakes:* Pliny the Elder, *Natural History* 6.17.

39 *rocks overhung them:* Pliny the Elder, 6.14.

39 *Artabazos, former governor:* Diodorus Siculus 16.34.1, 16.52; Curtius 3.13.13, 5.12.18; Arrian 3.21.4; Shayegan, "Prosopographical Notes," no. 23; Berve, *Das Alexanderreich,* 152; Heckel, *Who's Who,* 55.

40 *Bessos, governor of:* Curtius 4.12.6–7, 4.15.2; Michael Weiskopf, s.v. "Bessos," in *Encyclopedia Iranica* (1989), http://www.iranicaonline.org/articles/bessos -satrap-of-bactria; Shayegan, "Prosopographical Notes," no. 41; Berve, *Das Alex-anderreich,* 212; Heckel, *Who's Who,* 71–72.

40 *Satibarzanes, a governor:* Shayegan, "Prosopographical Notes," no. 99; Berve, *Das Alexanderreich,* 697; Heckel, *Who's Who,* 245.

40 *forced his abdication:* Arrian 3.21.1–2; Curtius 5.9.2–5.12.17; Justin 11.15.1–2.

40 *prevent the conspiracy:* Arrian 3.21.4; Curtius 5.12.18.

40 *two high-ranking deserters:* Arrian 3.21.1–2.

40 *a foraging expedition:* Arrian 3.20.4

40 *the trail of Darius:* Arrian 3.21.1–4.

41 *Darius had been deposed:* Arrian 3.21.4.

41 *golden chains, appropriately:* Curtius 5.12.20; Justin 11.15.1.

41 *Bessos had been named:* Arrian 3.21.5.

41 *took the shortcut:* Arrian 3.21.7–8.

42 *three thousand soldiers:* Curtius 5.13.21; Arrian 3.21.8 (suggesting, inaccurately, that he took only five hundred); R. D. Milns, "Arrian's Accuracy in Troop Details: A Note," *Historia: Zeitschrift für Alte Geschichte* 27, no. 2 (1978): 374–78.

42 *traveled forty-five miles:* Arrian 3.21.9; Stahl, "Notes on the March," 320–23.

42 *a token resistance:* Curtius 5.13.13–22; Arrian 3.21.9.

42 *They stabbed Darius:* Arrian 3.21.10; Diodorus Siculus 17.73.3; Plutarch 43.2; Curtius 5.13.23–25; Justin 11.15.5–13 (describing Darius as still alive when the Macedonians arrived; unlikely, as argued by Briant, *Darius in the Shadow of Alexander,* 314–19).

42 *the Persian Queen Mother:* Arrian 3.21.22; Curtius 5.13.25; Plutarch 43.3; Berve, *Das Alexanderreich,* 712; Heckel, *Who's Who,* 251; Shayegan, "Prosopographical Notes," no. 107.

42 *were finally going home:* Diodorus Siculus 17.74.3; Justin 12.3.2; Curtius 6.2–3.

43 *six hundred cavalrymen:* Arrian 3.21.10.

43 *provinces of Central Asia:* Briant, *From Cyrus to Alexander,* 743–54.

44 pothos, *a Greek word:* Christopher Michael Kegerreis, "Alexander the Explorer" (Ph.D. diss., University of California, Santa Barbara, 2016), 74–84; Victor Ehrenberg and Ruth Fraenkel von Velsen, *Alexander and the Greeks* (Oxford, UK: Basil Blackwell, 1938), 52–61.

Chapter Three: Old Friends and New Clothes

45 *his mistress, Barsine:* Heckel, *Who's Who*, 70; Elizabeth Carney, "Alexander and Persian Women," *American Journal of Philology* 117, no. 4 (1996): 572–75; Berve, *Das Alexanderreich*, 206; Shayegan, "Prosopographical Notes," no. 37.

45 *Mentor and Memnon:* Heckel, *Who's Who*, 162; Berve, *Das Alexanderreich*, 497.

45 *able to protect them:* Müller, "Philip II," 171–74.

45 *her uncle Memnon:* Diodorus Siculus 16.52.3.

45 *an intercultural marriage:* Fritz Schachermeyr, *Alexander der Grosse: Das Problem seiner Persönlichkeit und seines Wirkens* (Vienna: Verl. d. Österr. Akad. d. Wiss., 1973), 133.

46 *had distinguished himself:* Diodorus Siculus 16.52.3.

46 *one of the Great King's highest-ranking:* Curtius 3.13.13.

46 *ever-more-prominent:* Diodorus Siculus 16.52.1–8, 17.7.2–7.

46 *married her uncle Mentor:* Arrian 7.4.6; Carney, "Alexander and Persian Women," 572–73.

46 *both Greece and Persia:* Allison Glazebrook and Kelly Olson, *Greek and Roman Marriage* (Chichester, UK: John Wiley & Sons, 2013), 74, 78; Brosius, *Women in Ancient Persia*, 68.

46 *her other uncle, Memnon:* Plutarch 21.4.

46 *excellent Greek education:* Plutarch 21.9.

46 *any educational instruction:* Marguerite Deslauriers, "Women, Education, and Philosophy," in *Companion to Women in the Ancient World*, ed. Sharon L. James and Sheila Dillon (Oxford, UK: Wiley-Blackwell, 2012), 352; Brosius, *Women in Ancient Persia*, 83–122.

47 *loved, trusted, and promoted:* Ernst Badian, "The Death of Parmenio," *Transactions and Proceedings of the American Philological Association* 91 (1960): 337–38.

47 *brought her along:* Diodorus Siculus 20.20.21; Justin 15.2.3.

47 *were left behind:* Plutarch 43.3.

47 *surrounding the Caspian Sea:* Diodorus Siculus 17.75.3; Curtius 6.4.18–19; Strabo 11.7.4; J. R. Hamilton, *Plutarch Alexander: A Commentary* (Oxford, UK: Clarendon Press, 1969), 116–20; J. E. Atkinson, *A Commentary on Q. Curtius Rufus' Historiae Alexandri Magni, Books 5 to 7.2* (Amsterdam: A. M. Hakkert, 1994), 185–90.

47 *father and brothers arrived:* Arrian 3.23.7; Curtius 6.5.1–5.

47 *his youthful appearance:* R. R. R. Smith, *Hellenistic Royal Portraits* (Oxford, UK: Clarendon Press, 1988), 58–64; Cohen, *Alexander Mosaic*, 7.

47 *probably dressed lightly:* Vinzenz Brinkmann, "The Blue Eyes of the Persians: The Colored Sculpture of the Time of Alexander and the Hellenistic Period," in *Gods*

in Color: Painted Sculpture of Classical Antiquity, ed. Vinzenz Brinkmann and Raimund Wünsche (Munich: Stiftung Archäologie, 2007), 151.

47 *high-ranking Persian courtier:* Shapur Shahbazi, s.v. "Clothing ii. In the Median and Achaemenid Periods," in *Encyclopaedia Iranica,* 2012, http://www .iranicaonline.org/articles/clothing-ii.

47 *grandson of the Great King:* Briant, *From Cyrus to Alexander,* 782.

47 *long, luxuriant hair:* Mary G. Houston, *Ancient Egyptian, Mesopotamian & Persian Costume* (Mineola, NY: Dover Publications, 2002), 164–66.

48 *Artabazos his right hand:* Curtius 6.5.2.

48 *apprehensive Greek mercenaries:* Curtius 6.5.9–10; Arrian 3.24.4–5; Diodorus Siculus 17.76.1–2.

48 *put on kingly robes:* Arrian 3.25.3; Curtius 6.6.13; Diodorus Siculus 17.74.1–2.

48 *the upright tiara:* Shahbazi, s.v. "Clothing ii."

49 *governor, war hero:* Curtius 4.12.6–7, 4.15.2; Arrian 3.30.4.

49 *brave, calculating, ruthless:* Curtius 5.9.2–12.20.

49 *"remarkable both for generalship":* Diodorus Siculus 17.83.4.

49 *fought against Alexander:* Arrian 3.8.4.

49 *responsible for stabbing Darius:* Arrian 3.21.10.

50 *His region was a crossroads:* Claude Rapin, "Alexandre le Grand en Asie Centrale: Geographie et strategie de la conquete des Portes Caspiennes à l'Inde," in *With Alexander in India and Central Asia: Moving East and Back to West,* ed. Claudia Antonetti and Paolo Biagi (Oxford, UK: Oxbow Books, 2017), 85.

50 *offer his submission:* Curtius 6.6.13; Arrian 3.25.1–2.

50 *third regional governor:* Arrian 3.24.7, 25.4, Curtius 6.4.23–24.

50 *eleven of them were Iranian:* Briant, *Alexander the Great and His Empire,* 113.

50 *preserve his territory:* Briant, *From Cyrus to Alexander,* 65–67, 821.

51 *troop of Macedonian soldiers:* Arrian 3.25.1–2; Curtius 6.6.13.

51 *pardoned Persian governors:* Briant, *Alexander the Great and His Empire,* 111–16.

51 *difficult and uncertain route:* Rapin, "Alexandre le Grand," 80; Engels, *Logistics of the Macedonian Army,* 86.

52 *set them all alight:* Curtius 6.6.14–17; Rapin, "Alexandre le Grand," 79–81; Engels, *Logistics of the Macedonian Army,* 86–7.

53 *around five hundred:* Diodorus Siculus 17.77.4–4; Athenaeus, *Deipnosophists* 12.539d–f; Marek Jan Olbrycht, "'An Admirer of Persian Ways': Alexander the Great's Reforms in Parthia-Hyrcania and the Iranian Heritage," in *Excavating an Empire: Achaemenid Persia in Longue Durée,* ed. Touraj Daryaee, Ali Mousavi, and Khodadad Rezakhani (Costa Mesa, CA: Mazda Publishers, 2014), 49–52; A. B. Bosworth, "Alexander and the Iranians," *Journal of Hellenic Studies* 100 (1980): 5.

53 *added Darius's brother:* Plutarch 43.7; Shayegan, "Prosopographical Notes," no. 82.

53 *retinue of concubines:* Curtius 6.6.8; Diodorus Siculus 17.77.6–7; Justin 12.3.10; Briant, *From Cyrus to Alexander,* 280–82.

53 *one named Bagoas:* Curtius 6.5.23, 10.1.2–38; Plutarch 67.4; E. Badian, "The Eunuch Bagoas," *Classical Quarterly* 8, no. 3/4 (1958): 144–57; Elizabeth Baynham

and Terry Ryan, "'The Unmanly Ruler': Bagoas, Alexander's Eunuch Lover, Mary Renault's *The Persian Boy*, and Alexander Reception," in *Brill's Companion to the Reception of Alexander the Great*, ed. Kenneth Royce Moore (Leiden: Brill, 2018), 615–39; Shayegan, "Prosopographical Notes," no. 33; Heckel, *Who's Who*, 68; Berve, *Das Alexanderreich*, 195.

53 *most ancient Persian eunuchs:* Briant, *From Cyrus to Alexander*, 268–77.

54 *despised by Persian aristocrats:* Curtius 10.1.25–26.

54 *modified form of Iranian dress:* Athenaeus, *Deipnosophists* 12.537e–38b; Arrian 4.7.4; Diodorus Siculus 17.77.5; Plutarch 45.2, *Moralia* 329E, 330a; Strabo 11.13.9; Bosworth, *Historical Commentary*, 2:49–51; Shahbazi, s.v. "Clothing ii"; Hamilton, *Plutarch Alexander*, 120–23; Atkinson, *Commentary*, 167–70.

54 *purple-and-white band:* Andrew W. Collins, "The Royal Costume and Insignia of Alexander the Great," *American Journal of Philology* 133, no. 3 (2012): 377–85.

54 *his habitual costume:* Plutarch 45.2.

54 *"So this, it seems":* Plutarch 20.7–8.

55 *"to deal with the Greeks":* Plutarch, *Moralia* 329b.

55 *disgusted and bewildered:* Diodorus Siculus 17.77.4, 78.1; Justin 12.3.9.

55 *Satibarzanes had revolted:* Arrian 3.25.5; Curtius 6.6.20; Diodorus Siculus 17.78.1.

56 *capital of Artakoana:* Arrian (3.25.5–6); Rapin, "Alexandre le Grand," 85–86.

56 *the provincial capital:* Curtius 6.6.23–25; Rapin, "Alexandre le Grand," 86–88.

56 *smoked them out:* Curtius 6.6.22, 26–32; Arrian 3.25.7; Diodorus Siculus 17.78.1–3.

56 *key to his military success:* Curtius 6.6.34; Paul Bentley Kern, *Ancient Siege Warfare* (Bloomington: Indiana University Press, 1999), 201–26.

56 *Alexander pardoned them:* Curtius 6.6.34.

56 *nearby, Alexandria-in-Aria:* Strabo 15.2.8, Pliny the Elder, *Natural History* 6.25; Rapin, "Alexandre le Grand," 85.

56 *rebels of western Afghanistan:* Diodorus Siculus 17.78.3–4; Arrian 3.25.7.

56 *new Iranian governor:* Shayegan, "Prosopographical Notes," no. 18.

57 *An incident at Susa:* Curtius 5.2.18–22.

57 *high-ranking women wove:* Marie-Louise Nosch, "Voicing the Loom: Women, Weaving, and Plotting," in *Ke-Ra-Me-Ja*, ed. Dimitri Nakassis, Joann Gulizio, and Sarah A. James (Philadelphia: INSTAP Academic Press, 2014), 97–98.

57 *weaving was degrading:* Brosius, *Women in Ancient Persia*, 21–22n11.

57 *"My own customs":* Curtius 5.2.20

Chapter Four: Lovers and Conspirators

58 *too late in the year:* Rapin, "Alexandre le Grand," 88.

58 *present-day Farāh:* Rapin, 90.

58 *the next rebellion:* Plutarch 48.1–49.12, Arrian 3.26.1–27.3; Diodorus Siculus 17.79.1–80.4; Curtius 6.7.18–7.7.2.38; Justin 12.5.3; Strabo 15.2.10; Badian, "The Death of Parmenio"; Jeanne Reames, "Crisis and Opportunity: The Philotas

Affair . . . Again," in *Macedonian Legacies: Studies in Ancient Macedonian History and Culture in Honor of Eugene N. Borza*, ed. Timothy Howe and Jeanne Reames (Claremont, CA: Regina Books, 2008); Hamilton, *Plutarch Alexander*, 132–37; Bosworth, *Historical Commentary*, 1:359–67.

58 *one of Alexander's Companions:* Plutarch 49.2 ("Limnos"); Curtius 6.7.2; Diodorus Siculus 17.79.1; Heckel, *Who's Who*, 112; Berve, *Das Alexanderreich*, 269.

58 *his same-sex lover:* Diodorus Siculus 17.79.2; Curtius 6.7.2; Plutarch 49.2–3.

59 *In Macedonian society:* Elizabeth Carney, *King and Court in Ancient Macedonia: Rivalry, Treason and Conspiracy* (Swansea: Classical Press of Wales, 2015), 225–81 (men); Carney, *Women and Monarchy*, 27–29 (women).

59 *more men likely slept:* Daniel Ogden, "Homosexuality and Warfare in Ancient Greece," in *Battle in Antiquity*, ed. Alan B. Lloyd (London: Duckworth, 1996), 118–23.

59 *straight for the king:* Diodorus Siculus 17.79.2; Curtius 6.7.3–16; Plutarch 49.2–3; Heckel, *Who's Who*, 82; Berve, *Das Alexanderreich*, 418.

59 *arrived at Alexander's tent:* Athenaeus, *Deipnosophists* 12.539d–f; Andrew W. Collins, "The Persian Royal Tent and Ceremonial of Alexander the Great," *Classical Quarterly* 67, no. 1 (2017).

59 *All he could do:* Curtius 6.7.17.

60 *arrogance, boastfulness, ostentation:* Plutarch 48.1–49.2.

60 *he swaggered off:* Diodorus Siculus 17.79.3; Curtius 6.7.18–19.

60 *hadn't had the occasion:* Diodorus Siculus 17.79.3; Curtius 6.7.20–21.

60 *feared for himself:* Curtius 6.7.21, 25; Diodorus Siculus 17.79.4

60 *a young nobleman:* Curtius 6.7.22.

61 *who clearly did not:* Curtius 6.7.23–27; Plutarch 49.4; Diodorus Siculus 17.79.4–5.

61 *ancient biographers differ:* Plutarch 49.4 (killed); Diodorus Siculus 17.79.6 and Curtius 6.7.29 (suicide).

61 *Alexander shook hands:* Curtius 6.7.33–35; Diodorus Siculus 17.79.6.

61 *and often deadly:* Roisman, "Classical Macedonia to Perdiccas III," 158, 61–64.

61 *stabbed to death:* Aristotle, *Politics* 5.1311b1; Diodorus 16.93.1–94.4; Justin 9.6.4–7.14; Plutarch 10.6–8; Ernst Badian, "The Death of Philip II," *Phoenix* 17, no. 4 (1963): 244–50; Elizabeth Carney, "The Politics of Polygamy: Olympias, Alexander and the Murder of Philip," *Historia: Zeitschrift für Alte Geschichte* 41, no. 2 (1992): 169–89; Waldemar Heckel, Timothy Howe, and Sabine Müller, "'The Giver of the Bride, the Bridegroom, and the Bride': A Study of the Murder of Philip II and its Aftermath," in *Ancient Historiography on War and Empire*, ed. Timothy Howe, Sabine Müller, and Richard Stoneman (Oxford, UK: Oxbow Books, 2017), 92–124; J. R. Ellis, "The Assassination of Philip II," in *Ancient Macedonian Studies in Honour of C. F. Edson*, ed. H. J. Dell (Thessaloniki: Institute for Balkan Studies, 1981), 99–137.

61 *aristocrat named Attalos:* Heckel, *Who's Who*, 62; Berve, *Das Alexanderreich*, 182.

62 *beautiful young woman:* Plutarch 9.4.

62   *antagonized other individuals:* Plutarch 9.3–4.

62   *the most prominent:* Elizabeth Carney, *Olympias: Mother of Alexander the Great* (New York: Routledge, 2006); Heckel, *Who's Who,* 181–83; Berve, *Das Alexanderreich,* 581.

62   *a slur on Olympias:* Plutarch 9.4; Daniel Ogden, *Polygamy, Prostitutes and Death: The Hellenistic Dynasties* (London: Duckworth, with the Classical Press of Wales, 1999), 20–24.

62   *persuaded to patch up:* Plutarch 9.6; Justin 9.7.2–6.

62   *number of well-born Greeks:* Diodorus Siculus 16.91.4–6.

62   *marriage of Alexander's sister:* Diodorus Siculus 16.91.4.

63   *a religious procession:* Diodorus Siculus 16.92.5.

63   *the two Alexanders:* Justin 9.6.3.

63   *relied for his safety:* Diodorus Siculus 16.93.1.

63   *former Royal Page:* Heckel, *Who's Who,* 193–94; Berve, *Das Alexanderreich,* 614.

63   *and publicly humiliated:* Diodorus Siculus 16.92.3–93.9; Plutarch 10.4; Justin 9.6.5–7.

63   *dagger he had concealed:* Diodorus Siculus 16.94.4.

63   *he fell and was killed:* Justin 9.6.4; Diodorus Siculus 16.94.3–4.

64   *executed a cousin:* Justin 11.2.1–3; Diodorus Siculus 17.2.1–2.

64   *accused Darius III:* Arrian 2.14.5–6.

64   *rumors persisted that:* Plutarch 10.4; Justin 9.7.1–14.

64   *his childhood companion:* Waldemar Heckel, "The Conspiracy Against Philotas," *Phoenix* 31, no. 1 (1977): 9–21.

64   *called on the entire army:* Curtius 6.8.1–26; Arrian 3.26.2; Edward M. Anson, "Macedonian Judicial Assemblies," *Classical Philology* 103, no. 2 (2008): 135–49.

64   *All presented the case:* Curtius 6.9.1–31; Arrian 3.26.2.

65   *the soldiers wavered:* Curtius 6.9.25–28.

65   *seemed potentially sympathetic:* Curtius 6.10.36–11.7.

65   *delayed their decision:* Curtius 6.11.9.

65   *subjected to torture:* Curtius 6.11.13–33; Justin 12.5.3; Plutarch 49.6.

65   *a familiar punishment:* Bruce Lincoln, *Religion, Empire, and Torture: The Case of Achaemenian Persia, with a Postscript on Abu Ghraib* (Chicago: University of Chicago Press, 2007).

65   *"I offer my slaves":* Lykourgos, *Against Leocrates* 32; Antiphon, *First Tetralogy* 4.8; Demosthenes 37.40–42; David C. Mirhady, "Torture and Rhetoric in Athens," *Journal of Hellenic Studies* 116 (1996): 122.

65   *carried out on free men:* Demosthenes 15.133.

65   *torture was executed:* Curtius 6.11.10–12.

65   *leader of the torturers:* Curtius 6.11.13–19.

65   *faithful and capable general:* Heckel, *Who's Who,* 95–99; Berve, *Das Alexanderreich,* 446.

65   *brave and much-injured:* Berve, *Das Alexanderreich,* 439; Heckel, *Who's Who,* 91–93.

65   *most vociferous accusers:* Curtius 6.9.30–31.

66 *his most trusted friend:* Jeanne Reames-Zimmerman, "Hephaistion Amyn-
    toros: Eminence Grise at the Court of Alexander the Great" (Ph.D. diss.,
    Pennsylvania State University, 1998); Sabine Müller and Beatrice Poletti,
    "Hephaistion—A Re-assessment of His Career," in *Ancient Macedonians in
    Greek and Roman Sources,* ed. Timothy Howe and Frances Pownall (Swansea:
    Classical Press of Wales, 2018), 77–102; Jeanne Reames-Zimmerman, "An Atyp-
    ical Affair? Alexander the Great, Hephaestion, and the Nature of Their Rela-
    tionship," *Ancient History Bulletin* 13, no. 3 (1999): 81–96; Waldemar Heckel,
    *Alexander's Marshals: A Study of the Makedonian Aristocracy and the Politics
    of Military Leadership,* 2nd ed. (New York: Routledge, 2016), 75–100; Heckel,
    Who's Who, 133–37; Berve, *Das Alexanderreich,* 347.

66 *the real king approved:* Arrian 2.12.6–7.

66 *promoted to bodyguard:* Waldemar Heckel, "The 'Somatophylakes' of Alexan-
    der the Great: Some Thoughts," *Historia: Zeitschrift für Alte Geschichte* 27, no. 1
    (1978): 226–27.

66 *rivalry with the latter:* Curtius 6.8.17, 6.11.10; Plutarch 49.12.

66 *ability to endure hardship:* Plutarch 48.1.

66 *made a very full confession:* Curtius 6.11.17–33; Plutarch 49.6–7.

66 *left him unable to walk:* Curtius 6.11.34.

66 *carried out by the entire army:* Curtius 6.11.38 (stoning); Arrian 3.26.3 (spears).

66 *than acquiescent silence:* Ian Worthington, *Alexander the Great: Man and God*
    (Harlow, UK: Pearson/Longman, 2004), 120–21; A. B. Bosworth, *Conquest and
    Empire: The Reign of Alexander the Great* (Cambridge, UK: Cambridge Univer-
    sity Press, 1988), 101–4.

66 *a well-respected officer:* Heckel, *Who's Who,* 86–88. Berve, *Das Alexanderreich,*
    428.

67 *replaced the bodyguard:* Arrian 3.27.5.

67 *racing camels to Ekbatana:* Curtius 7.2.11–16; Arrian 3.26.3–4.

67 *a mere eleven days:* Strabo 15.2.10; Curtius 7.2.18 (ten days).

67 *He was still reading:* Curtius 7.2.15–16, 19–27.

68 *Parmenion's severed head:* Curtius 7.2.28–32.

Chapter Five: Epic Combat

69 *a second insurgency:* Arrian 3.28.2; Diodorus Siculus 17.81.3; Curtius 7.3.2. Bos-
    worth, *Historical Commentary,* 2:369; Atkinson, *Commentary,* 206–11.

69 *officer named Erigyios:* Arrian 3.28.2; Berve, *Das Alexanderreich,* 302; Heckel,
    Who's Who, 223.

69 *Persian named Phrataphernes:* Berve, *Das Alexanderreich,* 814; Heckel, *Who's
    Who,* 119; Shayegan, "Prosopographical Notes," no. 92.

71 *able to overcome:* Diodorus Siculus 17.81.3, 17.83.4–5; Curtius 7.3.2.

71 *in single combat:* Diodorus Siculus 17.83.5; Curtius 7.4.33.

71 *Erigyios, a close friend:* Arrian 3.6.5–6; Diodorus Siculus 17.57.3.

71 *calls him "white-haired":* Curtius 7.4.34.

71 *increasingly prestigious commands:* Arrian 3.6.5, 11.11; Curtius 6.4.3, 8.17.

71 *Homeric warriors fought:* Homer, *Iliad* 3.340–380, 5.627–662, 6.123–231.

72 *to wear a belt:* Aristotle, *Politics* 1324b17–19.

72 *these Homeric ideals:* Vorhis, "Best of the Macedonians."

72 *where close coordination:* Burn, "Generalship of Alexander," 148–54.

72 *cultural hero Gilgamesh:* Tzvi Abusch, "The Development and Meaning of the Epic of Gilgamesh: An Interpretive Essay," *Journal of the American Oriental Society* 121, no. 4 (2001): 615–16.

72 *king in single combat:* Justin 10.3.4–6.

72 *Alexander's battle strategy:* Minor M. Markle, "Use of the Sarissa by Philip and Alexander of Macedon," *American Journal of Archaeology* 82, no. 4 (1978): 491–93.

72 *expertise with the bow:* Chr Zutterman, "The Bow in the Ancient Near East: A Re-evaluation of Archery from the Late 2nd Millennium to the End of the Achaemenid Period," *Iranica Antiqua* xxxviii (2003): 138–44; James White, "Bows and Spears in Achaemenid Persia" (Ph.D. diss., University of California, Santa Barbara, 2020).

72 *often in a chariot:* A. Sh. Shahbazi, s.v. "Army i. Pre-Islamic Iran," in *Encyclopedia Iranica* (1986). http://www.iranicaonline.org/articles/army-i .

73 *Satibarzanes threw his spear:* Curtius 7.4.36.

73 *he sliced off:* Curtius 7.4.36–40.

73 *Satibarzanes's army melted:* Diodorus Siculus 17.83.6; Arrian 3.28.3; Curtius 7.4.38.

73 *Satibarzanes's severed head:* Curtius 7.4.40.

73 *had taken him north:* Rapin, "Alexandre le Grand," 88.

73 *spectacular natural setting:* Nancy Hatch Dupree, *An Historical Guide to Afghanistan* (Kabul: Afghan Tourist Organization, 1971), 68.

74 *desolate, treeless landscape:* Curtius 7.3.6–17; Diodorus Siculus 17.82.2–8; Arrian 3.28.1–2; Rapin, "Alexandre le Grand," 88–95; Bosworth, *Historical Commentary,* 1:367–69.

74 *"uncivilized tribe, extremely coarse":* Curtius 7.3.6.

74 *traveled extraordinary distances:* Rapin, "Alexandre le Grand," 88.

74 *struggled with frostbite:* Curtius 7.3.13.

74 *were exhausted, hungry:* Curtius 7.3.12; Arrian 3.28.1.

74 *headquarters for the winter:* Curtius 7.3.18–23; Diodorus Siculus 17.83.1–2; Arrian 3.28.4; Strabo 15.2.10.

74 *king's administrative landscape:* Henkelman, "Imperial Signature and Imperial Paradigm," 45–49, 79–80.

75 *make his conquest possible:* Briant, "Empire of Darius III in Perspective"; Briant, "Alexander and the Persian Empire."

75 *now known as Begram:* Claude Rapin, "Du Caucase au Tanaïs: Les sources de Quinte-Curce à propos de la route d'Alexandre le Grand en 330–329 av. J.-C.," in *L'histoire d'Alexandre selon Quinte-Curce,* ed. M. Mahé-Simon and J. Trinquier (Paris: Armand-Colin, 2014), 166–70; Rapin, "Alexandre le Grand," 88.

75 *some seventy all told:* Plutarch, *Moralia* 328e; P. M. Fraser, *Cities of Alexander the Great* (Oxford, UK: Clarendon Press, 1996).

75 *the difficult years:* Laurianne Martinez-Sève, "Les Grecs d'Extrême Orient: Communautés Grecques d'Asie Centrale et d'Iran," *Pallas* 89 (2012): 370–71.

76 *were easily defensible:* Leonid M. Sverchkov, "The Kurganzol Fortress (on the History of Central Asia in the Hellenistic Era)," *Ancient Civilizations from Scythia to Siberia* 14, no. 1/2 (2008): 123–25.

76 *settled them with veterans:* Martinez-Sève, "Les Grecs d'Extrême Orient," 325.

76 *they were equipped:* Laurianne Martinez-Sève, "Ai Khanoum and Greek Domination in Central Asia," *Electrum* 22 (January 2015): 17–46; Mairs, *Hellenistic Far East,* 57–101.

76 *focal points for attack:* E.g., Arrian 4.1.4.

76 *the locals' worst fears:* Frank Lee Holt, *Alexander the Great and Bactria: The Formation of a Greek Frontier in Central Asia* (Leiden: E. J. Brill, 1988).

76 *chained by Zeus:* Strabo 15.1.17; Diodorus Siculus 17.83.1

76 *a critical way station:* Joseph Hackin, *Nouvelles recherches archéologiques à Begram, Ancienne Kâpicî, 1939–1940, Rencontre de trois civilisations, Inde, Grèce, Chine* (Paris: Impr. nationale, 1954); Sanjyot Mehendale, "Begram: Along Ancient Central Asian and Indian Trade Routes," *Cahiers d'Asie Centrale* (1996), 47–64.

Chapter Six: Across the Hindu Kush

79 *Formed by the clash:* Lewis Owen, Fosco Maraini, and Nigel John Roger Allan, s.v. "Hindu Kush," in *Britannica Academic* (2009).

79 *more than 23,000 feet:* Owen, Maraini, and Allan.

79 *Mount Olympus, so tall:* Encyclopaedia Britannica, s.v. "Mount Olympus" (2018).

79 *chilly day in March:* Strabo 15.2.10; Rapin, "Alexandre le Grand."

79 *taken the Khawak Pass:* Felix Howland, "Crossing the Hindu Kush," *Geographical Review* 30, no. 2 (1940): 276–77.

80 *the armchair historians:* Rapin, "Du Caucase au Tanaïs."

80 *"one glistening sheet":* C. R. Markham, "The Upper Basin of the Kabul River," *Proceedings of the Royal Geographical Society and Monthly Record of Geography* 1, no. 2 (1879): 111–12, 15.

80 *terebinth, a shrubby tree:* Arrian 3.28.6; Strabo 15.2.10.

80 *a medicinal plant:* Strabo 15.2.10; Silvia Balatti, *Mountain Peoples in the Ancient Near East: The Case of the Zagros in the First Millennium BCE* (Wiesbaden: Harrassowitz Verlag, 2017), 226.

80 *in seventeen days:* Curtius 7.3.19–23; Diodorus Siculus 17.83.1 (sixteen days).

80 *province of Bactria-Sogdiana:* Briant, *From Cyrus to Alexander,* 746.

80 *the city of Bactra:* Arash Khazeni, "The City of Balkh and the Central Eurasian Caravan Trade in the Early Nineteenth Century," *Comparative Studies of South Asia, Africa, and the Middle East* 30, no. 3 (2010): 463–72.

81 *produced large harvests:* Curtius 7.4.26; Robert A. Lewis, "Early Irrigation in West Turkestan," *Annals of the Association of American Geographers* 56, no. 3 (1966), 567–91.

81 *land of a thousand cities:* Strabo 15.1.3; Justin 41.4.5; Edvard Rtveladze, "Monetary Circulation in Ancient Tokharistan," in *After Alexander: Central Asia Before Islam*, ed. Joe Cribb and Georgina Herrmann (Oxford, UK: British Academy, 2007), fig. 20.

81 *desert, mountains, steppe:* Lewis, "Early Irrigation in West Turkestan," 467–70.

81 *units in the Persian army:* Briant, *From Cyrus to Alexander*, 749–50.

81 *At Gaugamela, for example:* Curtius 4.12.6, 5.8.3, 10.5; Arrian 3.13.4,19.5, 21.4.

81 *He had led Sogdians:* Arrian 3.8.3; Curtius 4.12.7.

81 *summoned the Scythians:* Arrian 3.19.3–4.

82 *Darius's Greek commander:* Diodorus Siculus 17.18.2–3.

82 *taking or destroying everything:* Arrian 3.28.8.

82 *his well-organized province:* Wouter F. M. Henkelman and Margaretha L. Folmer, "*Your Tally Is Full!* On Wooden Credit Records in and After the Achaemenid Empire," in *Silver, Money and Credit: A Tribute to Robartus J. Van Der Spek on the Occasion of his 65th Birthday*, ed. Kristin Kleber and Reinhard Pirngruber (Leiden: Nederlands Instituut voor het Nabije Oosten, 2016), 200; Henkelman, "Imperial Signature and Imperial Paradigm."

82 *twenty-five thousand strong:* Brunt, *Arrian*, 530.

82 *lived off freshwater fish:* Curtius 7.4.24–25.

82 *were used to eating fish:* Peter Garnsey, *Food and Society in Classical Antiquity* (Cambridge, UK: Cambridge University Press, 1999), 113, 116–18.

82 *snow still on the ground:* Arrian 3.28.9.

82 *Bessos's capital, Bactra:* Arrian 3.29.1.

82 *foot of the Hindu Kush:* Curtius 7.4.31.

83 *withdrew from Bactra:* Arrian 3.28.8–9.

83 *heavy brick citadel:* Roland Besenval, Nicolas Engel, and Philippe Marquis, "Les travaux de la Délégation Archéologique Française en Afghanistan," *Revue Archéologique*, no. 1 (2011): 180–81.

83 *on his first attempt:* Arrian 3.29.1.

83 *met up with Erigyios:* Arrian 3.29.1; Curtius 7.4.32–5.1.

83 *most of his pack animals:* Curtius 7.5.1.

84 *suffered terribly from thirst:* Curtius 7.4.27–29, 7.5.1–5; Bosworth, *Historical Commentary*, 1:372–73.

84 *Bessos had slipped away:* Arrian 3.28.9–10; Curtius 7.4.21.

84 *boats he had burned:* Curtius 7.4.21; Arrian 3.28.9.

84 *floated across the river:* Arrian 3.29.4; Curtius 7.5.17.

84 *claimed to be Greek:* Strabo 11.11.4; Curtius 7.5.28–35; Plutarch, *Moralia* 557B; N. G. L. Hammond, "The Branchidae at Didyma and in Sogdiana," *Classical Quarterly* 48, no. 2 (1998): 339–44; Olga Kubica, "The Massacre of the Branchidae: A Reassessment; The Post-mortem Case in Defence of the Branchidae," in *Alexander the Great and the East*, ed. Krzysztof Nawotka and Agnieszka Wojciechowska (Wiesbaden: Harrassowitz Verlag, 2016), 143–50.

84 *no archaeological traces:* Claude Rapin, "On the Way to Roxanne 2: Satraps and Hyparchs between Bactra and Zariaspa/Maracanda," in *A Millennium*

of History: The Iron Age in Central Asia (2nd and 1st Millennia BC), ed. Johanna Lhuillier and Nikolaus Boroffka (Berlin: Dietrich Reimer Verlag, 2018), 280–82.

85   *a familiar practice:* Briant, *From Cyrus to Alexander*, 751.

85   *not like what they saw:* Rachel Mairs, "The Hellenistic Far East: From the Oikoumene to the Community," in *Shifting Social Imaginaries in the Hellenistic Period*, ed. Eftychia Stavrianopoulou (Leiden: Brill, 2013), 368.

85   *massacred the townspeople:* Curtius 7.5.33.

86   *Bactrian cavalry deserted:* Arrian 3.28.10; Curtius 7.4.20

86   *a man named Spitamenes:* Arrian 4.1.5; Curtius 7.6.14–15; Heckel, *Who's Who*, 254; Berve, *Das Alexanderreich*, 717; Shayegan, "Prosopographical Notes," no. 108.

86   *daughter named Apama:* Berve, *Das Alexanderreich*, 98; Heckel, *Who's Who*, 39; Shayegan, "Prosopographical Notes," no. 10.

86   *the fall of 330 BCE:* Arrian 3.28.10.

86   *sent a small force:* Arrian 3.29.6–7; Curtius 7.5.19–26.

86   *most trusted friends, Ptolemy:* Heckel, *Who's Who*, 235–38; Berve, *Das Alexanderreich*, 668.

86   *had suffered banishment:* Arrian 3.6.5.

87   *serving as his bodyguard:* Arrian 3.27.5.

87   *self-aggrandizing memoir:* Joseph Roisman, "Ptolemy and His Rivals in His History of Alexander," *Classical Quarterly* 34, no. 2 (1984): 383; Pearson, *Lost Histories*, 187–211.

87   *a ten-day march:* Arrian 3.29.7.

87   *known as Sangir-Tepe:* Arrian 3.30.1–3; Rapin, "Alexandre le Grand," 97; Claude Rapin and Muhammadjon Isamiddinov, "Entre sédentaires et nomades: Les recherches de la Mission Archéologique Franco-ouzbèke (MAFOuz) de Sogdiane sur le site de Koktepe," *Cahiers d'Asie Centrale* 21/11 (2013): 128; Johanna Lhuillier and Mutalib Hasanov, "Nouvelles recherches à Padayatak Tépé au Kashka-daria (Ouzbékistan)," *Cahiers d'Asie Centrale* 21–22 (2013): 389–98.

87   *seized Bessos and departed:* Arrian 3.30.1–2

87   *a wooden dog collar:* Arrian 3.30.3.

87   *Other ancient writers:* Arrian 3.30.5 (quoting Aristoboulos); Curtius 7.5.36; Diodorus Siculus 17.83.8–9.

87   *stripped of his upright tiara:* Curtius 7.5.24.

88   *to be whipped in public:* Arrian 3.30.4–5

88   *to his own fiefdom:* Arrian 3.30.2, 4.1.5.

Chapter Seven: Fighting the Hydra

89   *rumblings of dissent:* Curtius 7.6.1–4.

89   *ambassador named Derdas:* Arrian 4.1.1–2; Curtius 7.6.11–12; Heckel, *Who's Who*, 111; Berve, *Das Alexanderreich*, 250.

89   *plains of waist-high grass:* Claude Rapin, "Aux origines de la cartographie: L'em-

pire Achéménide sous Darius I et Xerxès," *Ancient Civilizations from Scythia to Siberia* 24 (2018): 36.

89   *these roaming pastoralists:* Simpson and Stepanova, *Scythians,* 10–15.

90   *they possessed weapons:* Simpson and Stepanova, 262.

90   *spoke an Iranian dialect:* A. Yu. Alexeyev, "The Scythians in Eurasia," in *Scythians: Warriors of Ancient Siberia,* ed. St. John Simpson and E. V. Stepanova (London: British Museum, 2017), 8.

90   *Scythians loved to drink:* St. John Simpson and E. V. Stepanova, "Eating, Drinking and Everyday Life," in *Scythians: Warriors of Ancient Siberia,* ed. St. John Simpson and E. V. Stepanova (London: British Museum, 2017), 159.

90   *Greek-style golden quiver:* Alexeyev, "Scythians in Eurasia," 26 fig. 21.

90   *fermented mare's milk:* Simpson and Stepanova, "Eating, Drinking and Everyday Life," 159–60.

90   *low tables and stools:* Simpson and Stepanova, "Eating, Drinking and Everyday Life," 156–57.

90   *their living as farmers:* Léopold Migeotte, *The Economy of the Greek Cities from the Archaic Period to the Early Roman Empire,* trans. Janet Lloyd (Berkeley: University of California Press, 2009), 67.

90   *was strongly discouraged:* Paul McKechnie, *Outsiders in the Greek Cities in the Fourth Century B.C.* (London: Routledge, 1989), 16–33.

91   *six hundred miles per year:* Jeannine Davis-Kimball, "Asia Central Steppes," in *Encyclopedia of Archaeology,* ed. Deborah M. Pearsall (Oxford, UK: Academic Press, 2008), 538; Lorenzo Crescioli, "The Scythians and the Eastern Limits of the Greek Influence: The Pazyryk Culture and Its Foreign Artistic Influences," in *With Alexander in India and Central Asia: Moving East and Back to West,* ed. Paolo Biagi and Claudia Antonetti (Oxford, UK: Oxbow Books, 2017), 139–41.

91   *not identical tribes:* Davis-Kimball, "Asia Central Steppes."

91   *Even their jewelry:* Crescioli, "Scythians and the Eastern Limits," 127–37.

91   *mutually beneficial relationship:* Crescioli, 139–41; Alexeyev, "Scythians in Eurasia," 23–24.

91   *another potential function:* Arrian 4.1.3–4; Curtius 7.6.13; Justin 12.5.12–13.

91   *erupted into a revolt:* Bosworth, *Historical Commentary,* 2:15–19; Holt, *Alexander the Great and Bactria,* 52–69.

92   *exercised greater autonomy:* Briant, *From Cyrus to Alexander,* 750.

92   *threatened their way of life:* Holt, *Alexander the Great and Bactria,* 54–55.

92   *a pharaoh in Egypt:* Agnieszka Wojciechowska, *From Amyrtaeus to Ptolemy: Egypt in the Fourth Century B.C.* (Wiesbaden: Harrassowitz Verlag, 2016), 84–91.

92   *"freedom and autonomy":* Ernst Badian, "The Administration of the Empire," *Greece & Rome* 12, no. 2 (1965): 166–69.

92   *Alexander had imposed:* Arrian 4.1.4.

92   *a military review:* Arrian 4.1.5; Curtius 7.6.15.

92   *failed to recognize:* Michael Iliakis, "Flipping the Coin: Alexander the Great's Bactrian-Sogdian Expedition from a Local Perspective," *Studia Hercynia* 25, no. 1 (2021): 38.

93   *then kill them all:* Arrian 4.1.5; Curtius 7.6.15.

93   *an optimistic messenger:* Curtius 7.6.14.

93   *Sogdian capital, Marakanda:* Arrian 4.3.6.

93   *nearly four miles long:* Frantz Grenet, "Maracanda/Samarkand, une métropole Pré-Mongole: Sources écrites et archéologie," *Annales: Histoire, Sciences Sociales* 59, no. 5/6 (2004): 1054.

93   *stores of grain and treasure:* Sebastian Stride, Bernardo Rondelli, and Simone Mantellini, "Canals versus Horses: Political Power in the Oasis of Samarkand," *World Archaeology* 41, no. 1 (2009): 75–80; Charlotte Baratin, "Le grenier Grec de Samarkand," 2009, https://hal.science/hal-00483708.

93   *critical choke hold:* Frantz Grenet, personal communication, April 25, 2019.

93   *brought fresh water:* Stride, Rondelli, and Mantellini, "Canals versus Horses," 75–80.

94   *led by the cavalarymen:* Arrian 4.1.4–5; Curtius 7.6.13–15.

95   *Iranian named Pharnoukhes:* Arrian 4.3.6–7; Curtius 7.6.24; Heckel, *Who's Who,* 207; Berve, *Das Alexanderreich,* 768.

95   *the oasis of Marakanda:* Arrian 4.5.3–6.2; Curtius 7.7.31–39; Bosworth, *Historical Commentary,* 2:22–25, 32–37.

96   *Macedonians unwisely followed:* Arrian 4.5.3; Curtius 7.7.31–33; Rapin, "On the Way to Roxanne 2," 285.

96   *Persian hunting preserve:* Arrian 4.6.1; Curtius 7.7.32.

96   *that Spitamenes struck:* Arrian 4.6.1–2.

96   *on open, level ground:* Robin Waterfield, *Taken at the Flood: The Roman Conquest of Greece* (New York: Oxford University Press, 2014), 128–34.

97   *a barrage of arrows:* Arrian 4.5.4–6; Curtius 7.7.32–33; K. V. Chugunov, T. V. Rjabkova, and St. John Simpson, "Mounted Warriors," in *Scythians: Warriors of Ancient Siberia,* ed. St. John Simpson and E. V. Stepanova (London: British Museum, 2017); Mike Loades, "Scythian Archery," in *Masters of the Steppe: The Impact of the Scythians and Later Nomad Societies of Eurasia,* ed. Svetlana V. Pankova and John Simpson (Oxford, UK: Archaeopress, 2020), 258–67.

97   *all of them were slaughtered:* Arrian 4.5.7–9.

97   *the survivors to silence:* Curtius 7.7.39.

97   *a place called Cyropolis:* Arrian 4.2.1–3.5; Curtius 7.6.7–23; Bosworth, *Historical Commentary,* 2:19–22.

97   *his close friend Krateros:* Arrian 4.2.1–2; Curtius 7.6.16.

98   *all the adult males:* Arrian 4.2.3–6; Curtius 7.6.16–21.

98   *hammered the walls:* Arrian 4.3.1–4; Curtius 7.6.17–23 (calling it the city of the Memaceni); Hamilton, *Plutarch Alexander,* 122; Bosworth, *Historical Commentary,* 2:21.

98   *the mudbrick walls:* E.g., Koktepe (near Samarkand), Rapin and Isamiddinov, "Entre sédentaires et nomades," 128.

98   *crept beneath the walls:* Arrian 4.3.2–3; Curtius 7.6.23 (tunneled beneath the walls).

98   *they faced fierce resistance:* Arrian 4.3.3.

99   *lost an eye:* N. Hammond, G. T. Griffith, and F. W. Walbank, *A History of Macedonia* (Oxford, UK: Clarendon Press, 1972–1988), 2:257.

99   *Pyrrhus of Epirus:* Plutarch, *Pyrrhus* 34.2–3.

99   *everything went dark:* Arrian 4.3.3; Curtius 7.6.22.

99   *laying out his city:* Arrian 4.4.1; Curtius 7.6.25–27; Justin 12.5.12–13; Bosworth, *Historical Commentary,* 2:26.

99   *ceremonies and athletic games:* Arrian 4.4.1.

99   *encounter the Scythians:* Arrian 4.4.2–5.1; Curtius 7.7.1–29, 8.1–9.16; Bosworth, *Historical Commentary,* 2:27–32.

99   *in no fit condition to lead:* Curtius 7.7.5–6.

100   *his soothsayer Aristander:* Arrian 4.4.2–3; Curtius 7.7.8; Heckel, *Who's Who,* 45–46; Nice, "The Reputation of the 'Mantis' Aristander"; Berve, *Das Alexanderreich,* 117.

100   *already in Homer's Iliad:* Homer, *Iliad* 1.68–100.

100   *attacking the Scythians:* Curtius 7.7.8–9.

100   *"the signs from the gods":* Arrian 4.4.3; Curtius 7.7.22–29 (where the second set of entrails fortuitously improves).

100   *a long, sleepless night:* Curtius 7.8.2.

100   *an impatient Parmenion:* Curtius 4.13.16–25.

101   *Scythians' myriad campfires:* Curtius 7.8.2.

101   *went out to speak:* Curtius 7.8.3.

101   *the soldiers greeted him:* Curtius 7.8.3–5.

101   *several thousand rafts:* Metz Epitome 10 (2,000 rafts); Curtius 7.8.6–7 (12,000 rafts).

101   *planned battle strategy:* Curtius 7.9.2–4; Bosworth, *Historical Commentary,* 2:28–29.

102   *reached the farther shore:* Curtius 7.9.5–9.

102   *across the river:* Arrian 4.4.1–2.

102   *by wheeling around:* Arrian 4.4.6.

102   *mixed light-armed troops:* Arrian 4.4.6–7.

103   *a thousand enemy deaths:* Arrian 4.4.8

103   *collapsed and lost consciousness:* Arrian 4.4.9; Curtius 7.9.13.

103   *consent to the offers:* Arrian 4.5.1; Curtius 7.9.17–19.

103   *driven insatiably to conquest:* Arrian 5.24.8; Brunt, "Aims of Alexander"; Worthington, *Alexander the Great,* 215–16; Ehrenberg and Velsen, *Alexander and the Greeks,* 52–61.

103   *he had led Pharnoukhes:* Arrian 4.6.3–4; Curtius 7.9.20.

104   *a full military funeral:* Arrian 4.6.5; Curtius 7.9.21.

104   *long and difficult process:* Stella G. Miller, *The Tomb of Lyson and Kallikles: A Painted Macedonian Tomb* (Mainz: P. von Zabern, 1993), 64–65.

104   *as far as the desert:* Arrian 4.6.5–7.

104   *south toward Bactria:* Arrian 4.7.1.

104   *Now called Cheshme Shafa:* Polybius, *Histories* 10.49.15; Strabo 11.11.2 (suggesting it was the same as Bactra); Pliny, *Natural History* 6.45; Besenval, Engel, and

Marquis, "Les travaux de la Délégation Archéologique Française en Afghanistan," 181–84; Andrew Lawler, "Edge of an Empire," *Archaeology* 64, no. 5 (2011): 42–47.

105 *Persian governor Phrataphernes:* Arrian 4.7.1

105 *a Cretan naval officer:* Arrian 4.7.2; Curtius 7.10.11–12; Heckel, *Who's Who*, 171–73; Berve, *Das Alexanderreich*, 544; Badian, "Nearchus the Cretan."

105 *triumphant military review:* Arrian 4.1.5; Curtius 7.6.15; Briant, *From Cyrus to Alexander*, 748–50.

105 *fought the Bactrian cavalry:* Arrian 3.11.3; Curtius 4.12.6.

106 *they go unmentioned:* Arrian 4.17.3.

106 *nose and ears cut off:* Arrian 4.7.3.

106 *before an assembly:* Arrian 4.7.3; Curtius 7.10.10; Plutarch 43.6 (killed by Alexander in person); Bosworth, *Historical Commentary*, 2:43–45; Briant, *From Cyrus to Alexander*, 741.

106 *intelligence-gathering strategy:* Mirhady, "Torture and Rhetoric in Athens," 119.

106 *Persian-style barbarism:* E.g., Arrian 4.7.4.

106 *punished in just this way:* Briant, *From Cyrus to Alexander*, 123; inscriptions of Darius I proudly describe him giving the same treatment to attempted usurpers in his reign (*DB* paragraph 33; *DB Bab.* paragraph 25).

Chapter Eight: Murder at the Feast

107 *the Hissar Mountains:* Rapin, "On the Way to Roxanne 2," 286–92.

107 *the Iron Gates:* Claude Rapin, "On the Way to Roxane," in *Zwischen Ost und West: Neue Forschung zum antiken Zentralasien*, ed. Gunvor Lindström et al. (Darmstadt: Verlag Philipp von Zabern, 2013), 64.

107 *ruler named Sisimithres:* Arrian 4.21.1, 6, 8–10 (called Khorienes); Curtius 8.2.19–33, 8.4.19; Plutarch 58.2–3; Strabo 11.5.17; Heckel, *Who's Who*, 250; Shayegan, "Prosopographical Notes," no. 104; Berve, *Das Alexanderreich*, 708.

107 *present-day Mount Kyzkurgan:* Rapin, "On the Way to Roxane," 74–78; Rapin, "On the Way to Roxanne 2," 288–89.

107 *cut down junipers:* Frantz Grenet (personal communication, April 25, 2019).

108 *They worked constantly:* Arrian 4.21.3–5.

108 *his engineers, who built:* Eric William Marsden, "Macedonian Military Machinery and its Designers under Philip and Alexander," in *Archaia Makedonia 2* (Thessaloniki: Institute for Balkan Studies, 1977).

108 *rocks, nets, and cedars:* Arrian 2.18.3–6.

108 *aristocrat from Bactria:* Heckel, *Who's Who*, 187–88; Shayegan, "Prosopographical Notes," no. 81; Berve, *Das Alexanderreich*, 587; Rapin, "On the Way to Roxane," 73–78.

109 *his own free will:* Arrian 4.21.6–10.

109 *He divided his forces:* Arrian 4.16.2; Curtius 8.1.1 (into thirds); A. B. Bosworth, "A Missing Year in the History of Alexander the Great," *The Journal of Hellenic Studies* 101 (1981): 17–39; Rapin, "On the Way to Roxane."

110 *Perdikkas, a young bodyguard:* Arrian 4.16.2; Heckel, *Who's Who*, 197–202; Berve, *Das Alexanderreich*, 627.

110 *tutored for three years:* Diogenes Laertius 5.27; Plutarch 7.4.

110 *lectures on geography:* Romm, *Edges of the Earth*, 41–44.

110 *lifelong love of Homer:* Hamilton, *Plutarch Alexander*, 18, 20.

110 *treat his Persian subjects:* Plutarch, *Moralia* 328c–329d.

110 *never explicitly say so:* Reames-Zimmerman, "Hephaistion Amyntoros," 164.

110 *placed his seal ring:* Plutarch 39.5–6.

110 *Greek pederastic ideal:* Kenneth Dover, *Greek Homosexuality* (London: Duckworth, 1978), 56–58.

111 *writers and Macedonian realities:* Carney, *King and Court*, 155–65.

111 *bear them legitimate heirs:* Carney, *Women and Monarchy*, 18–23.

111 *monogamy was not expected:* Carney, "Politics of Polygamy."

111 *his relationship with Hephaistion:* Reames-Zimmerman, "An Atypical Affair?"

111 *to found cities and establish:* Arrian 4.16.2–3.

111 *heavy-walled fortress:* Grenet, "Maracanda/Samarkand, une Métropole Pré-Mongole: Sources Écrites et Archéologie," 1051–55.

111 *news from elsewhere:* Arrian 4.16.3; Curtius 8.1.7–10.

112 *soldiers south to Bactria:* Arrian 4.16.4.

112 *He first attacked:* Arrian 4.16.4–5.

112 *moved on to Zariaspa:* Arrian 4.16.5–17.2.

112 *now he was resigning:* Arrian 4.17.3; Curtius 8.1.19 (slightly later).

113 *promise of an alliance:* Arrian 4.15.1–6; Curtius 7.1.7–9.

113 *a royal hunting preserve:* Curtius 8.1.10–13

113 *the English* paradise: Wouter F. M. Henkelman, *The Other Gods Who Are: Studies in Elamite-Iranian Acculturation Based on the Persepolis Fortification Texts* (Leiden: Nederlands Instituut voor het Nabije Oosten, 2008), 426n983.

114 *hunts in Macedonia:* Carney, *King and Court*, 265–81; Hallie Franks, *Hunters, Heroes, Kings: The Frieze of Tomb II at Vergina* (Princeton, NJ: American School of Classical Studies at Athens, 2012), 36–48.

114 *a boar without a net:* Athenaeus, *Deipnosophists* 1.18a.

114 *Assyrian and then Persian:* Maureeen Alden, "Lions in Paradise: Lion Similes in the Iliad and the Lion Cubs of IL. 18.318–22," *Classical Quarterly* 55, no. 2 (2005): 340–42.

114 *far from native species:* Henri-Paul Francfort, "Scythians, Persians, Greeks and Horses: Reflections on Art, Culture, Power and Empires in the Light of Frozen Burials and Other Excavations," in *Masters of the Steppe: The Impact of the Scythians and Later Nomad Societies of Eurasia*, ed. Svetlana V. Pankova and John Simpson (Oxford, UK: Archaeopress, 2020), 143.

114 *famous for his deed:* Curtius 8.1.15.

114 *facing the beast alone:* Curtius 8.1.14.

114 *was no longer allowed:* Curtius 8.1.15–18.

115 *the king gave a feast:* Arrian 4.8.1–9.8; Curtius 8.1.20–2.12; Justin 12.6.1–16; Plutarch 50.1–52.2; Bosworth, *Historical Commentary*, 2:51–68; Elizabeth Carney,

"The Death of Clitus," *Greek, Roman and Byzantine Studies* 22, no. 2 (1981): 149–60; Hamilton, *Plutarch Alexander*, 139–48.

115 *bringing Hellenic fruit:* Plutarch 50. 2.

115 *saved his life in battle:* Arrian 1.14.8.

115 *it featured meat:* Carney, *King and Court*, 241.

115 *nomadic pastoralists nearby:* Johanna Lhuillier and Marjan Mashkour, "Animal Exploitation in the Oases: An Archaeozoological Review of Iron Age Sites in Southern Central Asia," *Antiquity* 91, no. 357 (2017): 665–68.

115 *There was bread:* Carney, *King and Court*, 241.

115 *popular, long-lasting grain:* Baratin, "Le Grenier Grec de Samarkand."

115 *likely mixed it:* Carney, *King and Court*, 238–40.

116 *passed a cup:* Plutarch 54.3–4; Hallie Franks, *The World Underfoot: Mosaics and Metaphor in the Greek Symposium* (New York: Oxford University Press, 2018), 17–29.

116 *silver drinking vessels:* Angeliki Kottaridi, *Macedonian Treasures: A Tour Through the Museum of the Royal Tombs of Aigai*, trans. Alexandra Doumas (Athens: Kapon Editions, 2011), 98–105.

116 *the king and his guests:* Carney, *King and Court*, 225–64.

116 *governor of Bactria-Sogdiana:* Curtius 8.1.19.

116 *offended by a poet:* Plutarch 50.4–5.

116 *angered by the king himself:* Curtius 8.1.22–23.

117 *antiauthoritarian content:* Gherardo Ugolini, "Φόβος φυτεύει τύραννον: The Tyrant's Fears on the Attic Tragic Stage," *Comparative Drama* 51, no. 4 (2017): 462.

117 *"Alas, how terribly":* Curtius 8.1.28; Plutarch 51.5; Euripides, *Andromache* 693.

117 *They all likely recognized:* Pownall and Pal, "Role of Greek Literature," 223–25.

117 *inscribed their trophies:* Euripides, *Andromache* 694–99.

117 *only by prudent silence:* Curtius 8.1.29–30.

117 *began praising Philip:* Arrian 4.8.4–6; Curtius 8.1.30–37.

117 *saved Alexander's life:* Arrian 4.8.6–7; Curtius 8.1.34–37.

117 *barbarians and slaves:* Plutarch 51.1–3.

118 *He ridiculed the oracle:* Curtius 8.1.42.

118 *Zeus-Amun in the Siwa Oasis:* Arrian 3.3.1–4.5; Diodorus Siculus 17.49.2–51.4; Strabo 17.1.43; Andrew Collins, "Alexander's Visit to Siwah: A New Analysis," *Phoenix* 68, no. 1/2 (2014): 62–77; Daniel Ogden, "Alexander and Africa (332–331 BC and Beyond): The Facts, the Traditions and the Problems," *Acta Classica* 2014, no. sup-5 (2014): 9–14; Wojciechowska, *From Amyrtaeus to Ptolemy*, 84–85.

118 *His dagger was gone:* Arrian 4.8.7; Curtius 8.1.43; Plutarch 51.4.

118 *No one obeyed:* Arrian 4.8.7–8; Curtius 8.1.44–47; Plutarch 51.4–5.

119 *grabbed a sarissa:* Arrian 4.8.8–9; Curtius 8.1.49–52; Plutarch 51.5–6.

119 *Alexander contemplated suicide:* Arrian 4.9.1–2; Curtius 8.2.1–4; Plutarch 51.6.

119 *the king's feeling of guilt:* Arrian 4.9.3–4; Curtius 8.2.5–12; Plutarch 52.1.

119 *Aristotle's nephew, Kallisthenes:* Arrian 4.9.5–6; Plutarch 52.2; Heckel, *Who's Who*, 76–77; Berve, *Das Alexanderreich*, 408.

119 *An odd, ambivalent man:* Gordon Shrimpton, "The Callisthenes Engima," in *Greece, Macedon, and Persia,* ed. Timothy Howe, Erin Garvin, and Graham Wrightson (Oxford, UK: Oxbow Books, 2015), 114–17.

119 *speaking softly of ordinary things:* Plutarch 52.2.

120 *the philosopher Anaxarkhos:* Heckel, *Who's Who,* 27; Eugene Borza, "Anaxarchus and Callisthenes: Academic Intrigue at Alexander's Court," in *Ancient Macedonian Studies in Honor of Charles F. Edson,* ed. H. J. Dell (Thessaloniki: Institute for Balkan Studies 1981), 73–80; Berve, *Das Alexanderreich,* 70.

120 *"whatever is ratified":* Arrian 4.9.7; Plutarch 52.3–4.

120 *formal funeral ceremony:* Curtius 8.2.12.

120 *Dionysos, god of wine:* Arrian 4.9.5.

120 *ten days at Marakanda:* Curtius 8.2.13.

Chapter Nine: Three Banquets and a Conspiracy

122 *he fell in love:* Arrian 4.19.4–6; Curtius 8.4.22–30; Plutarch 47.7–8; Plutarch, *Moralia* 332E, 338D; Metz Epitome 28–31; Athenaeus, *Deipnosophists* 5.197c; Carney, "Alexander and Persian Women," 575–77; Sabine Müller, "Stories of the Persian Bride: Alexander and Roxane," in *The Alexander Romance in Persia and the East,* ed. Ian Richard Netton, Kyle Erickson, and Richard Stoneman (Groningen: Barkhuis, 2012), 295–309; Marcel Renard and Jean Servais, "À propos du mariage d'Alexandre et de Roxane," *L'Antiquité Classique* 24, no. 1 (1955): 29–50.

122 *hosted by Sisimithres:* Strabo 11.11.4.

122 *his most beautiful clothes:* Athenaeus, *Deipnosophists* 4.145b.

122 *the center of the feast:* Wouter F. M. Henkelman, "Parnakka's Feast: Sip in Parsa and Elam," in *Elam and Persia,* ed. J. Alvarez-Mon and M. B. Garrison (Winona Lake, IN: Eisenbrauns, 2011), 116–18.

123 *He ate the meat:* Elspeth R. M. Dusinberre, "Satrapal Sardis: Achaemenid Bowls in an Achaemenid Capital," *American Journal of Archaeology* 103, no. 1 (1999): 94–95.

123 *nuts, seeds, and fruit:* Wouter F. M. Henkelman, "'Consumed Before the King': The Table of Darius, that of Irdabama and Irtaštuna, and that of his Satrap, Karkiš," in *Der Achämenidenhof. Akten des 2 internationalen Kolloquiums zum Thema "Vorderasien im Spannungsfeld klassischer und altorientalischer Überlieferungen," Landgut Castelen bei Basel, 23–25 Mai 2007,* ed. B. Jacobs and R. Rollinger (Wiesbaden: Harrassowitz Verlag, 2010), 679–82; Athenaeus, *Deipnosophists* 4.145e-f; Polyaenus, *Stratagems* 4.3.32.

123 *small handleless bowls:* Dusinberre, "Satrapal Sardis," 76.

123 *like a bull's horn:* Susanne Ebbinghaus, "Feasting Like the Persian King," in *Animal-Shaped Vessels in the Ancient World: Drinking with Gods, Heroes, and Kings,* ed. Susanne Ebbinghaus (Cambridge, MA: Harvard University Press, 2018), 136–84.

123 *enjoyed a departure:* Athenaeus, *Deipnosophists* 4.145c; Franks, *World Underfoot,* 15–29.

123 *Central Asian aristocrats:* Curtius 8.4.23.

123 *the hands of Alexander:* Arrian 4.18.4–4.19.4 (though he calls the fortress the "Rock of Sogdiana"); Strabo 11.11.4.

123 *wide-sleeved Persian robes:* Shahbazi, s.v. "Clothing ii"; Jalilian Shahram and Fatemi Seyed Ali, "Women's Clothing in Ancient Iran (Case Study: Achaemenid Period)," *Taḥqīqāt-i Farhangī-i Īrān* 4, no. 3 (2012): 1–22.

123 *Their dances, too:* A. Shapur Shahbazi and Robyn C. Friend, s.v. "Dance," in *Encyclopaedia Iranica* (2011); Lillian Brady Lawler, "The Dance in Ancient Greece," *Classical Journal* 42, no. 6 (1947): 343–49.

123 *Her name was Roxane:* Rüdiger Schmitt, s.v. "Rhoxane," in *Encyclopaedia Iranica,* http://www.iranicaonline.org/articles/rhoxane-name; Shayegan, "Prosopographical Notes," no. 97; Heckel, *Who's Who,* 241–42; Berve, *Das Alexanderreich,* 688.

123 *beautiful than any woman:* Arrian 4.19.5.

124 *he proposed marriage:* Plutarch 47.7–8; Plutarch, *Moralia* 332e, 338d; Curtius 8.2.26–9; Strabo 11.11.4; Arrian 4.19.5.

124 *nothing like the ideal:* Briant, *From Cyrus to Alexander,* 225–27.

124 *in splendid isolation:* Maria Brosius, "New Out of Old? Court and Court Ceremonies in Achaemenid Persia," in *The Court and Court Society in Ancient Monarchies,* ed. Antony Spawforth (Cambridge, UK: Cambridge University Press, 2007), 49.

124 *not been brought up:* Brosius, *Women in Ancient Persia,* 79.

124 *sense of its practical value:* Carney, "Alexander and Persian Women," 575–77.

125 *a homely tradition:* Curtius 8.4.27; Renard and Servais, "A Propos du Mariage."

125 *Oxyarthes was ecstatic:* Metz Epitome 31.

125 *royal Macedonian males:* William S. Greenwalt, "The Marriageability Age at the Argead Court: 360–317 B.C," *Classical World* 82, no. 2 (1988): 93–94.

125 *reject the eligible daughters:* Elizabeth Baynham, "Why Didn't Alexander Marry Before Leaving Macedonia? Observations on Factional Politics at Alexander's Court in 336–334 B.C," *Rheinisches Museum für Philologie* 141, no. 2 (1998): 148.

125 *were settled at Susa:* Diodorus Siculus 17.67.1; Carney, *Women and Monarchy,* 108–11; Brosius, *Women in Ancient Persia,* 77.

125 *high-profile assignments:* Reames-Zimmerman, "Hephaistion Amyntoros"; Heckel, *Alexander's Marshals,* 75–100.

126 *birth to a son, Herakles:* Diodorus Siculus 20.20.1; Justin 11.10.3; Plutarch, *Eumenes* 1.7; Justin 15.2.3 (son's birth in 325 BCE).

126 *So did her siblings:* Carney, "Alexander and Persian Women," 572–75.

126 *left Alexander's service:* Arrian 4.17.3; Curtius 8.1.19.

126 *marry his captive, Briseis:* Curtius 8.4.26; Homer, *Iliad* 1.184–88.

126 *provoke the king:* Curtius 8.4.30.

127 *lightning-cum-hailstorm:* Curtius 8.4.2–17; Metz Epitome 24–27.

127 *severed head of Spitamenes:* Arrian 4.17.7 (Spitamenes's followers responsible for his death); Metz Epitome 20–23; Curtius 8.3.1–12 (Spitamenes's wife).

128 *convince the Persians:* Plutarch 47.8; Curtius 8.4.25.

128 *Greek island of Samothrace:* William Greenwalt, "Philip II and Olympias on Samothrace: A Clue to Macedonian Politics during the 360s," in *Macedonian Legacies: Studies in Ancient Macedonian History and Culture in Honor of Eugene N. Borza,* ed. Timothy Howe and Jeanne Reames (Claremont, CA: Regina Books, 2008), 86–88.

128 *mysteries of Samothrace:* Yves Lehmann, "La théologie des mystères de Samothrace: Mythe, rites et philosophie," in *Les mystères: Nouvelles perspectives,* ed. Marc Philonenko, Yves Lehmann, and Laurent Pernot (Turnhout, Belgium: Brepols, 2017), 125–47.

128 *intense religious experience:* Plutarch 2.1.

128 *they married soon after:* Greenwalt, "Philip II and Olympias on Samothrace," 86–88.

129 *reaffirmed their ties:* Greenwalt, "Macedonia, Illyria and Epirus," 289–95.

129 *fusion and power sharing:* Briant, *Alexander the Great and His Empire,* 101–2; Badian, "Administration of the Empire."

129 *Greeks called* proskynesis: Arrian 4.10.5–12.5; Curtius 8.5.9–24; Plutarch 54.3–55.1; Justin 12.7; Takuji Abe, "Proskynēsis: From a Persian Court Protocol to a Greek Religious Practice," *Tekmeria* 14 (2017–18): 1–45; J. P. V. D. Balsdon, "The 'Divinity' of Alexander," *Historia: Zeitschrift für Alte Geschichte* 1, no. 3 (1950): 371–82; Federicomaria Muccioli, "Classical Sources and *Proskynesis:* History of a Misunderstanding," in *Alexander's Legacy: Atti del Convegno Università Cattolica del Sacro Cuore Milano 2015,* ed. Cinzia Bearzot and Franca Landucci (Rome: "L'Erma" di Bretschneider, 2016), 41–59; Bosworth, *Historical Commentary,* 2:68–90.

129 *a simple greeting:* Herodotus 1.134.

130 *"sending a kiss forward":* Abe, "Proskynēsis," 15.

130 *near-infinite calibration:* Abe, 5–11.

130 *Persian minds, a king at all:* Abe, 11–15.

130 *himself increasingly surrounded:* Collins, "Persian Royal Tent," 74n16.

131 *everyone on equal footing:* Balsdon, "'Divinity' of Alexander," 376; Antony Spawforth, "The Court of Alexander the Great between Europe and Asia," in *The Court and Court Society in Ancient Monarchies,* ed. Antony Spawforth (Cambridge, UK: Cambridge University Press, 2007), 103–6.

131 *kind of "loving-cup":* Arrian 4.12.3–5; Plutarch 54.3–4; Theophrastus, *Characters* 23.3 (jewel-encrusted cup popular in Alexander's court).

131 *most likely with Hephaistion:* Collins, "Persian Royal Tent," 74.

131 *each one performed proskynesis:* Arrian 4.12.3; Plutarch 54.3–4.

131 *departure from Persian custom:* Xenophon, *Cyropaidia* 8.3.14; Plutarch, *Themistokles* 27.4.

131 *older men in particular:* Plutarch 54.2.

131 *to evade the ritual:* Plutarch, *Artaxerxes* 22; Herodotus 7.136.

132 *no way implied the divinity:* Muccioli, "Classical Sources and *Proskynesis*"; Ernst Badian, "The Deification of Alexander the Great," in *Ancient Macedonian Studies in Honor of Charles F. Edson,* ed. H. J. Dell (Thessaloniki: Institute for Balkan Studies, 1981), 52–53.

132 *the appearance of subordination:* Abe, "Proskynēsis," 22–28.

132 *forced to comply:* Herodotus 7.136.

132 *pliant philosopher Anaxarkhos:* Borza, "Anaxarchus and Callisthenes."

132 *and likely embellished:* Strabo 17.1.43.

132 *ebbing of the tide: Fragmente Griechischer Historiker* 124 F 31 (Kallisthenes); Waldemar Heckel, "Creating Alexander: The Official History of Kallisthenes of Olynthos," in *Celebrity, Fame, and Infamy in the Hellenistic World,* ed. Riemer A. Faber (Toronto: University of Toronto Press, 2020), 199–216.

133 *omitted the gesture:* Arrian 4.12.4; Plutarch 54.5–6.

133 *Kallisthenes made a speech:* Arrian 4.11.1–9; Curtius 8.5.14–20; Plutarch 54.3.

133 *made Kallisthenes a model:* Richard Stoneman, "The Legacy of Alexander in Ancient Philosophy," in *Brill's Companion to Alexander the Great,* ed. Joseph Roisman (Leiden: Brill, 2003), 336–38.

133 *also likely apocryphal:* Balsdon, "'Divinity' of Alexander," 371–82; Truesdell S. Brown, "Callisthenes and Alexander," *American Journal of Philology* 70, no. 3 (1949): 240–45; Hamilton, *Plutarch Alexander,* 151.

133 *is another story told:* Arrian 4.12.5; Plutarch 54.6.

133 *"I will depart":* Plutarch 54.6.

133 *to have scotched:* Badian, "Deification of Alexander the Great," 48–54.

133 *friend of the king's:* Heckel, *Who's Who,* 147–51; Berve, *Das Alexanderreich,* 466.

134 *bursting out in laughter:* Arrian 4.12.2; Waldemar Heckel, "Leonnatos, Polyperchon and the Introduction of Proskynesis," *American Journal of Philology* 99, no. 4 (1978): 459–61.

134 *abandoned his effort:* Arrian 4.12.2; Curtius 8.5.22–24 (identified as Polyperchon).

134 *"as though he were":* Plutarch 55.2.

134 *reputation among philosophers:* Stephen White, "Theophrastus and Callisthenes," in *Influences on Peripatetic Rhetoric: Essays in Honor of William W. Fortenbaugh,* ed. David C. Mirhady (Leiden: Brill, 2007), 211–30.

135 *conspiracy of the Royal Pages:* Arrian 4.13.1–14.4; Curtius 8.6.1–8.23; Plutarch 55.3–9; Elizabeth Carney, "The Conspiracy of Hermolaus," *Classical Journal* 76, no. 3 (1981): 223–31; Carney, *King and Court,* 207–23; Hamilton, *Plutarch Alexander,* 153–57; Bosworth, *Historical Commentary,* 2:90–101.

135 *not entirely voluntary post:* N. G. L. Hammond, "Royal Pages, Personal Pages, and Boys Trained in the Macedonian Manner during the Period of the Temenid Monarchy," *Historia: Zeitschrift für Alte Geschichte* 39, no. 3 (1990): 261–90; Strootman, "Court Society," 136–44; Miltiadēs V. Hatzopoulos, *Cultes et rites de passage en Macédoine* (Athènes: Kentron Hellēnikēs kai Rōmaïkēs Archaiotētos, Ethnikon Hidryma Ereunōn, 1994), 87–102.

135 *combined extraordinary intimacy:* Arrian 4.13.1; Curtius 8.6.2–6.

135 *painful and servile punishment:* Virginia J. Hunter, *Policing Athens: Social Control in the Attic Lawsuits, 420–320 B.C.* (Princeton, NJ: Princeton University Press, 1994), 182–83.

135 *the acme of attractiveness:* Ogden, "Homosexuality and Warfare in Ancient Greece," 108–9.

135 *the king's erotic needs:* Carney, *King and Court,* 162, 210.

135 *as lovers of Philip II:* Diodorus Siculus 16.93.3–4.

135 *a youth named Hermolaos:* Heckel, *Who's Who,* 138–39; Berve, *Das Alexanderreich,* 305.

135 *fifty new pages:* Curtius 5.1.42; Carney, *King and Court,* 211.

135 *unnerving, and physically demanding:* Carney, *King and Court,* 211.

136 *tutored by Kallisthenes:* Arrian 4.13.2; Curtius 8.6.24–25; Plutarch 55.4.

136 *felt like punishment:* Carney, *King and Court,* 211–15.

136 *Hermolaos threw a spear:* Arrian 4.13.2; Curtius 8.6.7.

136 *now recline like a man:* Athenaeus, *Deipnosophists* 1.18a.

136 *not bear to be preempted:* Curtius 8.1.14.

136 *began plotting to assassinate:* Arrian 4.13.3–4; Curtius 8.6.7–8.

137 *confiding in his lover:* Arrian 4.13.3; Curtius 8.6.8.

137 *recruited other pages:* Arrian 4.13.4 (four pages); Curtius 8.6.9 (seven pages).

137 *moderately prominent men:* Carney, "Conspiracy of Hermolaus," 228–29.

137 *in a month's time:* Arrian 4.13.4; Curtius 8.6.10–11.

138 *a Syrian prophetess:* Curtius 8.6.16; Arrian 4.13.5–6.

138 *a superstitious man:* Lowell Edmonds, "The Religiosity of Alexander," *Greek, Roman and Byzantine Studies* 12, no. 3 (1971): 363–91.

138 *had time to reflect:* Curtius 8.6.14–15.

138 *a considerable tip:* Curtius 8.6.18–19.

138 *the conspirators, Epimenes:* Arrian 4.13.7; Curtius 8.6.20; Heckel, *Who's Who,* 118; Berve, *Das Alexanderreich,* 300.

139 *likely witnessed the trial:* Curtius 8.6.21.

139 *close friend Ptolemy:* Arrian 4.13.7; Curtius 8.6.22.

139 *Ptolemy sprang into action:* Arrian 4.13.7; Curtius 8.6.27; Plutarch 55.5–6.

139 *the plot involved no one:* Arrian 4.14.1; Curtius 8.6.24; Plutarch 55.5–6.

139 *as instigator of the plot:* Arrian 4.14.1.

139 *he made his opinion:* Arrian 4.13.2; Curtius 8.6.24–25; Plutarch 55.2–4.

140 *had no more planned:* Arrian 4.14.1; Curtius 8.8.21; Carney, "Conspiracy of Hermolaus," 229; Brown, "Callisthenes and Alexander," 245–48; Hamilton, *Plutarch Alexander,* 153–57.

140 *just enough plausibility:* Plutarch 55.2.

140 *were put on trial:* Arrian 4.13.7–14.3; Curtius 8.6.29–8.20 (trial before torture).

140 *reportedly defended himself:* Arrian 4.14.2; Curtius 8.7.1–15.

140 *His grievances, however:* Carney, "Conspiracy of Hermolaus," 229–30; Carney, *King and Court,* 216.

140 *they were stoned to death:* Arrian 4.14.3; Plutarch 55.7; Curtius 8.28.0 (tortured to death).

140 *was hanged on the spot:* Arrian 4.14.3; Plutarch 55.9.

140 *delayed a decision:* Plutarch 55.9; Arrian 4.14.3.

140 *dominated by pro-Macedonians:* Poddighe, "Alexander and the Greeks."

140 *ill health, obesity, and lice:* Plutarch 55.9; Arrian 4.14.3.

Chapter Ten: Following in the Footsteps of the Gods

143 *all the way to Ocean:* Aristotle, *Meteorologica* 350a19–23; A. B. Bosworth, "Aristotle, India and the Alexander Historians," *Topoi Orient Occident* 3, no. 2 (1993): 421–22.

143 *high as 120,000 men:* Curtius 8.5.1–4, 8.9.1.

143 *enormous, implausible number:* Engels, *Logistics of the Macedonian Army,* 149.

143 *Argryaspides (Silver Shields):* Curtius 8.5.4; Elizabeth Baynham, "Alexander's Argyraspids: Tough Old Fighters or Antigonid Myth?" in *After Alexander,* ed. Víctor Alonso Troncoso and Edward M. Anson (Oxford, UK: Oxbow Books, 2013), 110–20.

144 *"India" was not limited:* Herodotus 3.91.4, 3.94.2; Klaus Karttunen, "Gandhāra and the Greeks," *Bulletin of the Asia Institute* 23 (2009): 131–34.

144 *conquered by Darius I:* Briant, *From Cyrus to Alexander,* 140.

144 *Greco-Persian Wars:* Herodotus 7.65, 70, 86.

144 *fought for Darius III:* Arrian 3.8.36.

144 *neither as strong:* David Fleming, "Where Was Achaemenid India?" *Bulletin of the Asia Institute* 7 (1993): 67–72; Peter Magee et al., "The Achaemenid Empire in South Asia and Recent Excavations in Akra in Northwest Pakistan," *American Journal of Archaeology* 109, no. 4 (2005): 711–41; Pierfrancesco Callieri, s.v. "India iii: Relations: Achaemenid Period," in *Encyclopaedia Iranica* (2012), https://www.iranicaonline.org/articles/india-iii-relations-achaemenid-period; R. S. Sharma, *India's Ancient Past* (Delhi: Oxford University Press, 2007).

144 *was politically fragmented:* Callieri, "India iii"; Romila Thapar, *Early India: From the Origins to AD 1300* (Berkeley: University of California Press, 2003), 146–50.

144 *only theoretically subordinate:* Henkelman, "Imperial Signature and Imperial Paradigm," 175–85.

144 *bountiful, and wondrous:* Romm, *Edges of the Earth,* 82–120.

144 *two harvests a year:* Strabo 15.1.13.

144 *less given to thieving:* Strabo 15.1.53.

144 *were also healthier:* Strabo 15.1.45.

144 *them were vegetarians:* Herodotus 3.100; Richard Stoneman, "Who Are the Brahmans? Indian Lore and Cynic Doctrine in Palladius' De Bragmanibus and Its Models," *Classical Quarterly* 44, no. 2 (1994): 506–10.

145 *"wool that grows":* Herodotus 3.106.

145 *colored and ornamented:* Curtius 8.9.21; Arrian, *Indica* 16.1–3.

145 *purple, and grass green:* Arrian, *Indica* 16.4.

145 *rivers ran with gold:* Curtius 8.9.18–19.

145 *spices, rare as Arabia's:* Strabo 15.1.22.

145 *Its oxen so impressed:* Arrian 4.25.4.

145 *writers maintained inaccurately:* Curtius 8.9.17; Richard Glover, "The Elephant in Ancient War," *Classical Journal* 39, no. 5 (1944): 267–68.

145 *Afghanistan and Pakistan:* Claude Rapin and Frantz Grenet, "How Alexander Entered India," *Afghanistan* 1, no. 1 (2018): 156–72; Olivieri, "Notes on the Problematical Sequence"; Aurel Stein, "Alexander's Campaign on the Indian North-West Frontier: Notes from Explorations Between Upper Swāt and the Induṣ," *Geographical Journal* 70, no. 5 (1927): 417–40; Aurel Stein, "Alexander's Campaign on the Indian North-West Frontier: Notes from Explorations Between Upper Swāt and the Induṣ (Continued)," *Geographical Journal* 70, no. 6 (1927): 515–40; P. H. L. Eggermont, "Alexander's Campaign in Gandhāra and Ptolemy's List of Indo-Scythian Towns," *Orientalia Lovaniensia Periodica* 1 (1970): 63–125.

145 *Macedonians called Nysa:* Arrian 5.1.1–2.7; Curtius; 8.10.7–18; Justin 12.7.6–8; Metz Epitome 36–38; Strabo 15.9; Ory Amitay, *From Alexander to Jesus* (Berkeley: University of California Press, 2010), ch. 3; Rapin and Grenet, "How Alexander Entered India"; Giuseppe Tucci, "On Swāt. The Dards and Connected Problems," *East and West* 27, no. 1/4 (1977): 33, 40–41; Bosworth, *Historical Commentary*, 2:197–213.

146 *metal-tipped arrows:* Arrian, *Indica* 16.6–9; Uma Prasad Thapliyal, *Military Costume and Accoutrements in Ancient India* (New Delhi: Manohar Publishers & Distributors, 2012), 90–113.

146 *wily, clever civic elder:* Berve, *Das Alexanderreich*, 36; Heckel, *Who's Who*, 3.

146 *likely oligarchic town:* Arrian 5.2.2–3; Bosworth, *Historical Commentary*, 2:203; Thapar, *Early India*, 146–50.

147 *the Greek god Dionysos:* Arrian 5.1.5–6.

147 *Krishna, and Indra:* R. D. Karmarkar, "The First Greek Conqueror of India," *Annals of the Bhandarkar Oriental Research Institute* 31, no. 1/4 (1950): 243–45; Ildikó Puskás, "Magasthenes and the 'Indian Gods' Herakles and Dionysos," *Mediterranean Studies* 2 (1990): 46–47.

147 *belief in sacred mountains:* Tucci, "On Swāt," 26–28.

147 *knowledge of Greek mythology:* Amitay, *From Alexander to Jesus*, ch. 3.

147 *had long-standing ties:* E. A. Fredricksmeyer, "The Ancestral Rites of Alexander the Great," *Classical Philology* 61, no. 3 (1966): 179–82; Albert Henrichs, "Greek Maenadism from Olympias to Messalina," *Harvard Studies in Classical Philology* 82 (1978): 121–60.

147 *have been performed:* Dēmētrios Pantermalēs, *Gods and Mortals at Olympus: Ancient Dion, City of Zeus* (New York: Alexander S. Onassis Foundation, 2016), 21.

147 *"I have left":* Euripides, *Bacchai* 13–15.

148 *sovereignty, as opposed:* Bosworth, *Historical Commentary*, 2:209.

148 *the envoy compromised:* Arrian 5.2.2–4.

148 *but rare in Persia:* Theophrastus, *Enquiry into Plants* 4.4.1.

148 *hymns to the god:* Arrian 5.2.6–7.

148 *libations of wine:* Susan Guettel Cole, "Finding Dionysus," in *A Companion to Greek Religion*, ed. Daniel Ogden (Oxford, UK: Blackwell, 2007), 336–37.

148 *bulls or goats:* Cole, "Finding Dionysus," 327.

149 *dazzling alpine landscape:* Stein, "Alexander's Campaign," 417.

149 *he responded brutally:* Arrian 4.23.1–25.7; Curtius 8.10.4–6; Heckel, "Alexander the Great and the Fate of the Enemy."

149 *there was Massaga:* Arrian 4.26.1–27.4, *Indica* 1.8; Curtius 8.10.22–36; Diodorus Siculus 17.84.1–6; Justin 12.7; Metz Epitome 39–45; Plutarch 59.6; Polyaenus, *Stratagems* 4.3.20; Strabo 15.1.27; Elizabeth Baynham, "'The Abominable Quibble': Alexander's Massacre of Indian Mercenaries at Massaga," in *Theatres of Violence,* ed. Philip G. Dwyer and Lyndall Ryan (New York: Berghahn Books, 2012); Bosworth, *Historical Commentary,* 2:169–76.

149 *the present-day site:* Olivieri, "Notes on the Problematical Sequence," 61–62; Tucci, "On Swāt," 49.

149 *Queen Kleophis had been:* Heckel, *Who's Who,* 90–91; Berve, *Das Alexanderreich,* 435.

149 *managed to avoid* sati: Aelian, *Varia Historia* 7.18; Diodorus 19.33.1–34.7; Strabo 15.1.62; Stefano Beggiora, "Indian Ethnography in Alexandrian Sources: A Missed Opportunity?" in *With Alexander in India and Central Asia: Moving East and Back to West,* ed. Claudia Antonetti and P. Biagi (Oxford, UK: Oxbow Books, 2017), 245–46.

150 *propelled by the gods:* Curtius 8.10.31–32.

150 *and unburied skeletons:* Olivieri, "Notes on the Problematical Sequence," 61–62.

150 *she sued for peace:* Curtius 8.10.33–35.

151 *Kleophis bore a son:* Curtius 8.10.36; Justin 12.7.9–11.

151 *faced a higher price:* Arrian 4.27.3–4; Plutarch 59.6; Polyaenus, *Stratagems* 4.3.20.

151 *it was a terrible blot:* Plutarch 59.6.

151 *the ceaseless apologist:* Arrian 4.27.3–4.

151 *from faulty translation:* Tarn, *Alexander the Great,* 125.

151 *machinations of the queen:* Baynham, "'Abominable Quibble,'" 34–35.

151 *campaign of terror:* Bosworth, *Historical Commentary,* 2:174–75.

151 *useful martial stratagems:* Polyaenus, *Stratagems* 4.3.20; cf. 4.2.4 (Philip II).

151 *as gratuitously violent:* Richard Stoneman, *The Greek Experience of India: From Alexander to the Indo-Greeks* (Princeton, NJ: Princeton University Press, 2019), 74; Bosworth, *Historical Commentary,* 158.

152 *barely been touched:* Olivieri, "Notes on the Problematical Sequence," 63; Thapar, *Early India,* 146–50.

152 *town by resistant town:* Olivieri, "Notes on the Problematical Sequence," 72–73.

152 *the Rock of Aornos:* Arrian 4.28.1–30.4; Curtius 8.11.2–25; Diodorus Siculus 17.85.1–86.1; Justin 12.7.12–13; Metz Epitome 45–47; Stein, "Alexander's Campaign (Continued)"; Tucci, "On Swāt"; Olivieri, "Notes on the Problematical Sequence"; Stein, "Alexander's Campaign"; Bosworth, *Historical Commentary,* 2:178–91.

152 *present-day Mount Ilam:* Tucci, "On Swāt," 52–55; Olivieri, "Notes on the Problematical Sequence," 62–70.

152 *far-off paternal ancestor:* Amitay, *From Alexander to Jesus,* ch. 3.

152 *appointed a governor:* Arrian 4.22.5, 28.6.

153 *the surrounding countryside:* Arrian 4.29.1.

153 *sent up a fire signal:* Arrian 4.29.2.

153 *maintain his position: Arrian:* 4.29.2–3.

153 *boulders, and other missiles:* Curtius 8.11.13.

154 *elaborate man-made mountain:* Arrian 4.29.7–30.1.

154 *form of negotiated surrender:* Arrian 4.30.2.

154 *killing some as they fled:* Arrian 4.29.3–4; Curtius 8.11.22–23.

154 *an altar to Athena:* Curtius 8.11.24.

154 *stories about Herakles:* Ory Amitay, "Vagantibus Graeciae Fabulis: The North African Wanderings of Antaios and Herakies," *Mediterranean Historical Review* 29, no. 1 (2014): 1–28.

154 *great traveler Theseus:* Karl Schefold, *Die Urkönige, Perseus, Bellerophon, Herakles und Theseus in der klassischen und hellenistischen Kunst,* ed. Franz Jung (Munich: Hirmer, 1988), 97–114.

154 *hubris, a combination:* L. Cairns Douglas, "Hybris, Dishonour, and Thinking Big," *Journal of Hellenic Studies* 116 (1996): 1–32.

155 *they called* nemesis: David Konstan, "Nemesis and Phthonos," in *Gestures: Essays in Ancient History, Literature, and Philosophy Presented to Alan L. Boegehold,* ed. Geoffrey W. Bakewell and James P. Sickinger (Oxford, UK: Oxbow Books, 2003), 74–87.

155 *the Macedonian king:* Strabo 15.1.16; Arrian 6.1.2–4; Stoneman, *Greek Experience of India,* 39.

155 *to cross the Indus:* Arrian 5.3.5–6, 7.1–2; Curtius 8.12.4; Diodorus Siculus 17.86.3–4; Aurel Stein, "From Swat to the Gorges of the Indus," *Geographical Journal* 100, no. 2 (1942): 49–56; Bosworth, *Historical Commentary,* 2:219–27.

156 *Greeks called Omphis:* Berve, *Das Alexanderreich,* 739; Heckel, *Who's Who,* 260–61 ("Taxiles").

156 *all these encounters:* Curtius 8.12.5–6; Diodorus Siculus 17.86.4; Rapin and Grenet, "How Alexander Entered India," 161–63.

156 *had a rival: Poros:* Buddha Prakash, "Poros," *Annals of the Bhandarkar Oriental Research Institute* 32, no. 1/4 (1951): 198–233; Heckel, *Who's Who,* 231–32; Berve, *Das Alexanderreich,* 683.

156 *celebrated in the Mahabharata:* Mahabharata 5.167.19–20; Stoneman, *Greek Experience of India,* 150.

156 *of wealth and power:* Curtius 8.9.23–25, 29; Diodorus Siculus 17.86.5–7; Metz Epitome 48–53; Strabo 15.1.28.

156 *five thousand soldiers:* Arrian 5.8.5.

157 *he feared that Omphis:* Diodorus Siculus 17.86.5.

157 *had inadvertently alarmed:* Diodorus Siculus 17.86.6.

157 *the exchange of gifts:* Arrian 5.8.2–3; Plutarch 59.2–3.

157 *conventions of gift-giving:* Josef Wiesehöfer, s.v. "GIFT GIVING ii. In Pre-Islamic Persia," in *Encyclopaedia Iranica* (2016), http://www.iranicaonline.org/articles /gift-giving-ii; Marc Domingo Gygax, "Gift-Giving and Power Relationships in

Greek Social Praxis and Public Discourse," in *The Gift in Antiquity*, ed. M. L. Satlow (Hoboken, NJ: Wiley-Blackwell, 2013), 45–60.

157 *Taxila, the capital:* Beggiora, "Indian Ethnography in Alexandrian Sources," 240–48; Alia Jawad, "Taxila: A Type Site of the Rich Cultural and Educational Heritage of Pakistan," *Journal of Asian Civilizations* 35, no. 2 (2012); Anna Maria Quagliotti, "Taxila," *Oxford Art Online* (Oxford, UK: Oxford University Press, 2019); John Hubert Marshall, *A Guide to Taxila*, 4th ed. (Cambridge, UK: Dept. of Archeology in Pakistan at the University Press, 1960); Gérard Fussman, "Taxila: The Central Asian Connection," *Studies in the History of Art* 31 (1993): 83–100; F. Raymond Allchin, "The Urban Position of Taxila and Its Place in Northwest India-Pakistan," *Studies in the History of Art* 31 (1993): 69–81.

157 *three major trade routes:* Jason Neelis, "Trade Networks in Ancient South Asia," in *Early Buddhist Transmission and Trade Networks, Mobility and Exchange Within and Beyond the Northwestern Borderlands of South Asia* (Leiden: Brill, 2011), 201–4.

158 *Buddhist monk Hsüan-tsang:* Sally Hovey Wriggins, *Xuanzang: A Buddhist Pilgrim on the Silk Road* (Boulder, CO: Westview Press, 1996), 65–69.

158 *young, grid-planned city:* Photios M. Petsas, *Pella, Alexander the Great's Capital* (Thessaloniki: Institute for Balkan Studies, 1978).

158 *passed by large houses:* Marshall, *Guide to Taxila*, 51–52.

158 *the city's official center:* Marshall, *Guide to Taxila*, 56.

158 *famous grammarian Panini:* Tauqeer Ahmad, "Cultural Impact of the Achaemenian on Ancient Pakistan," *South Asian Studies* 27, no. 1 (2012): 228–29.

159 *the Mauryan dynasty:* Thapar, *Early India*, 174–78.

159 *hunting, military strategy:* Jawad, "Taxila."

159 *have conquered it all:* Plutarch 62.4.

159 *"naked wise men":* Arrian, *Indica* 11.1–8; Plutarch 59.4, 64.1–65.4; Strabo 15.1.39, 59–68; Patrick Olivelle, *Ascetics and Brahmins: Studies in Ideologies and Institutions* (London: Anthem Press, 2011), 249–62; Stoneman, *Greek Experience of India*, 290–331; Andrea Zambrini, "Megasthenes Thirty Years Later," in *With Alexander in India and Central Asia: Moving East and Back to West*, ed. Claudia Antonetti and P. Biagi (Oxford, UK: Oxbow Books, 2017), 231–37.

159 *Alexander's own ship:* Berve, *Das Alexanderreich*, 583; Heckel, *Who's Who*, 183–84.

159 *in his memoir, which:* Pearson, *Lost Histories*, 83–111; Udai Prakash Arora, "The Fragments of Onesikritos on India—An Appraisal," *Indian Historical Review* 32, no. 1 (2005): 35–102; Reinhold Bichler, "On the Traces of Onesicritus: Some Historiographical Aspects of Alexander's Indian Campaign," in *The Historiography of Alexander the Great*, ed. Krzysztof Nawotka et al. (Wiesbaden: Harrassowitz Verlag, 2018), 51–70; Truesdell S. Brown, *Onesicritus: A Study in Hellenistic Historiography* (Berkeley: University of California Press, 1949).

159 *early form of yoga:* Strabo 15.1.63.

159 *one of the leaders:* Berve, *Das Alexanderreich*, 396; Heckel, *Who's Who*, 73–74.

160 *teacher named Mandanis:* Heckel, *Who's Who,* 102 ("Dandamis"); Berve, *Das Alexanderreich,* 243.

160 *his own teachings:* Strabo 15.1.64–65.

161 *Kalanos would remain:* Plutarch 65.3; Stoneman, "Who Are the Brahmans?" 505–6; A. B. Bosworth, "Strabo, India, and Barbequed Brahmans," in *After Alexander: The Time of the Diadochi (323–281 BC),* ed. Víctor Alonso Troncoso and Edward M. Anson (Oxford, UK: Oxbow Books, 2013), 75–81.

161 *terms them* Brachmanes: Strabo 15.1.59, 61–64; Stoneman, "Who Are the Brahmans?"; Richard Stoneman, "Naked Philosophers: The Brahmans in the Alexander Historians and the Alexander Romance," *Journal of Hellenic Studies* 115 (1995): 99–114; Stoneman, *Greek Experience of India,* 290–331.

161 *a caste system:* Arrian, *Indica* 11.1–12.9; Strabo 15.1.39–49; Stoneman, *Greek Experience of India,* 212–17.

161 *resemble Cynic philosophers:* Stoneman, "Naked Philosophers," 103–4.

161 *a period of flux:* Thapar, *Early India,* 164–73.

162 *a high-ranking ambassador:* Arrian 5.8.4; Curtius 8.13.1–2; Diodorus Siculus 17.87.1–2; Justin 12.8.1–2; Metz Epitome 54–57; Plutarch 60.

162 *Put one hostile foot":* Metz Epitome 57.

Chapter Eleven: How to Fight an Elephant

163 *in late April:* Arrian 5.19.3; Bosworth, *Historical Commentary,* 2:270–72.

163 *the river's eastern banks:* Arrian 5.8.4–9.1; Curtius 8.13.5–7; Diodorus Siculus 17.87.1–2.

163 *a distinctive presence:* Marie L. Thompson, s.v. "Elephant," in *The Gale Encyclopedia of Science,* ed. K. Lee Lerner and Brenda Wilmoth Lerner (Detroit: Gale, 2014), 1558–59.

164 *before Alexander's journeys:* J. M. Bigwood, "Aristotle and the Elephant Again," *American Journal of Philology* 114, no. 4 (1993): 549–52.

164 *"it has a nose":* Aristotle, *History of Animals* 2.1.

164 *Aristotle also commented:* Aristotle, *History of Animals* 2.1 (penis), 2.5 (tusks), 5.14 and 6.27 (gestation), and 9.1 (war).

164 *on the Persian side:* Arrian 3.8.6, 11.6, 15.4, 15.6.

164 *His ally Omphis:* Arrian 4.22.6 (Omphis's initial gift); Arrian 5.3.5; Curtius 8.12.7, Diodorus Siculus 17.86.4–5 (procession).

165 *Indian elephant-catchers:* Arrian 4.30.5–8; Diodorus Siculus 17.86.2–3.

165 *three hundred pounds:* Thompson, s.v. "Elephant," 1560–61.

165 *fascinated by peacocks:* Aelian, *On the Nature of Animals* 5.21.

165 *strength with delicacy:* Thompson, s.v. "Elephant," 1558–59.

165 *intelligent, sensitive animals:* Thompson, 1559–60.

166 *of spoken commands:* Jeheskel Shoshani, *Elephants: Majestic Creatures of the Wild* (Emmaus, PA: Rodale Press, 1992), 150.

166 *strength, and powerful tusks:* Thompson, s.v. "Elephant."

166 *between the two armies:* Arrian 5.9.4; Curtius 8.13.8–9.

166 *some 160 miles:* Bosworth, *Historical Commentary on Arrian's History of Alexander,* II: 264.

167 *terrified by the elephants:* Arrian 5.10.2.

167 *fondness for rivers:* Philip Sabin and Philip de Souza, "Battle," in *The Cambridge History of Greek and Roman Warfare,* ed. Hans van Wees, Michael Whitby, and Philip Sabin, vol. 1, *Greece, The Hellenistic World and the Rise of Rome* (Cambridge, UK: Cambridge University Press, 2007), 403–4.

167 *four most famous battles:* Burn, "Generalship of Alexander," 148–54.

167 *roused his soldiers:* Arrian 5.10.3.

168 *a massive store of grain:* Arrian 5.9.3.

168 *Jhelum would be low:* Arrian 5.9.3.

168 *sending out scouts:* Arrian 5.9.2.

168 *Seventeen miles from camp:* Arrian 5.11.2.

168 *pathless, and covered in trees:* Arrian 5.11.1–2.

168 *gave the order to cross:* Arrian 5.11.1–12.4; Curtius 8.13.17–27; Metz Epitome 59; Plutarch 60.2–3.

169 *heavy-armed infantry:* Arrian 5.12.2.

169 *man named Seleukos:* Berve, *Das Alexanderreich,* 700; Heckel, *Who's Who,* 246–48.

169 *the Macedonian cavalry:* Arrian 5.12.2.

169 *had been with Alexander:* Arrian 5.11.3–13.1.

169 *not even the majority:* Brunt, *Arrian,* 530–31.

169 *brought in his train:* Arrian 5.12.2.

169 *more exotic soldiers:* Arrian 5.11.3–12.2; Curtius 8.14.5.

170 *scouts spotted them:* Arrian 5.12.2–13.1.

170 *around 5,300 cavalry:* A. M. Devine, "The Battle of Hydaspes: A Tactical and Source-Critical Study," *Ancient World* 16, no. 3 (1987): 98.

170 *at least 20,000 men:* Plutarch 62.1.

170 *had his elephants:* Arrian 5.14.4–5 (200 elephants); Curtius 8.13.6 and Metz Epitome 54 (85); Diodorus Siculus 17.87.1–2 (130 elephants).

170 *found places to ford:* Arrian 5.13.2–4; Bosworth, *Historical Commentary,* 2:282.

170 *how small horses were:* Markle, "Macedonian Sarissa," 334.

171 *with an advance force:* Arrian 5.13.3–14.6; Curtius 8.14.2–3; Plutarch 60.5.

171 *well-made, beautiful armor:* Arrian 5.18.5.

171 *with light-armed forces:* Arrian 5.15.1–2; Curtius 8.14.2–5.

171 *after the pouring rain:* Arrian 5.15.1–2; Curtius 8.14.2–5.

171 *He picked a sandy site:* Arrian 5.15.5.

171 *massed elephant charge:* Glover, "Elephant in Ancient War," 259–61.

171 *towers from a distance:* Arrian 5.15.5–7; Curtius 8.14.9–13; Diodorus Siculus 17.87.3–5.

172 *to circle defensively:* Arrian 5.16.1–2.

172 *twice what they covered:* Milns, "Alexander's Pursuit of Darius," 256.

172 *to move into position:* Arrian 5.16.2–3; Curtius 8.14.14–16; Polyaenus, *Stratagems* 4.3.22.

172 *Alexander started the battle:* Burn, "Generalship of Alexander," 151–4; J. R. Hamilton, "The Cavalry Battle at the Hydaspes," *Journal of Hellenic Studies* 76 (1956): 26–31; Bosworth, *Historical Commentary,* 2:262–87; Glover, "Elephant in Ancient War," 264–65; Devine, "Battle of Hydaspes"; J. F. C. Fuller, *The Generalship of Alexander the Great* (New Brunswick, NJ: Rutgers University Press, 1960), 180–99.

172 *king pulled his cavalry:* Arrian 5.16.4–17.1; Polyaenus, *Stratagems* 4.33.22.

172 *three to four thousand:* Arrian 5.15.4, Diodorus Siculus 17.87.1.

172 *his close friend Koinos:* Arrian 5.16.3, 17.1; Polyaenus, *Stratagems* 4.33.22; Bosworth, *Historical Commentary,* 2:294–95.

173 *rearrange themselves to fight:* Bosworth, *Historical Commentary,* 2:296–300; Hamilton, "Cavalry Battle at the Hydaspes," 29–30.

173 *"as if to a friendly":* Arrian 5.17.2.

173 *the elephants charged:* Curtius 8.14.26–27; Diodorus Siculus 17.88.1.

173 *sickle-shaped Persian swords:* Arrian 5.17.3; Curtius 8.14.28–29.

173 *devastated the Punjab one:* Arrian 5.17.3–4.

174 *to draw a noose:* Bosworth, *Historical Commentary,* 2:302.

174 *ships backing water:* Arrian 5.17.7.

174 *they suddenly stampeded:* Arrian 5.17.5–7; Curtius 8.14.30; Diodorus Siculus 17.88.3.

174 *bold and careless:* Shoshani, *Elephants,* 146.

174 *Carthaginian general Hasdrubel:* Glover, "Elephant in Ancient War," 263.

174 *Alexander's work for him:* Arrian 5.17.6–7; Curtius 8.14.30; Diodorus Siculus 17.88.3.

175 *nine thousand men:* Diodorus Siculus 17.89.1–2.

175 *on the Punjab side:* Arrian 5.18.1–2 (likely exaggerated).

175 *His infantry had suffered:* Arrian 5.18.3; Diodorus Siculus 17.89.3 Bosworth, *Historical Commentary,* 2:304.

175 *Boukephalos, the horse:* Plutarch 6.1–8.

175 *perished after the Battle:* Arrian 5.19.4–6; Metz Epitome 62; Plutarch 61; Strabo 15.1.29.

175 *Poros himself escaped:* Arrian 5.18.4–19.3; Curtius 8.14.31–46; Diodorus Siculus 17.88.4–89.3; Justin 12.8.5–7; Plutarch 60.8.

175 *the young Chandragupta:* Prakash, "Poros," 224.

176 *"Like a king":* Plutarch 60.8.

176 *restored Poros's kingdom:* Arrian 5.19.3; Curtius 8.14.45–46; Diodorus Siculus 17.89.6; Plutarch 60.8.

176 *with client kings:* Briant, *From Cyrus to Alexander,* 766–67; David Braund, *Rome and the Friendly King: The Character of the Client Kingship* (London: Croom Helm, 1984).

176 *extravagant gift-giving:* Arrian 5.20.1–2; Curtius 9.1.1–6; Diodorus Siculus 17.89.3–6.

Chapter Twelve: Monsoon and Mutiny

178 *for seventy days:* Diodorus Siculus 17.94.3.

178 *leaving standing water:* "Monsoon," in *UXL Encyclopedia of Weather and Natural Disasters,* ed. Amy Hackney Blackwell and Elizabeth Manar (Detroit: Gale, 2016).

178 *spreading nutrient-rich soil:* "Monsoon," 522–23.

179 *averaging 100 degrees:* Lawrence Ziring and Shahid Javed Burki, s.v. "Pakistan," in *Encyclopaedia Britannica* (2020).

179 *drenching it continuously:* James Marti, s.v. "Monsoon," in *The Gale Encyclopedia of Science,* ed. K. Lee Lerner and Brenda Wilmoth Lerner (Detroit: Gale, 2014), 2883–84; "Monsoon," 521–22.

179 *contradictory, and largely erroneous:* Francesco Prontera, "The Indian Caucasus from Alexander to Eratosthenes," in *With Alexander in India and Central Asia: Moving East and Back to West,* ed. Claudia Antonetti and Paolo Biagi (Oxford, UK: Oxbow Books, 2017), 212–21.

179 *Rain in Macedonia:* Alfred Philippson, *Das Klima Griechenlands* (Bonn: F. Dümmler, 1948), 78–103.

180 *frightened the Macedonians:* Diodorus Siculus 17.90.2–3; Strabo 15.1.29.

180 *were the snakes:* Arrian, *Indica* 15.10–12; Curtius 9.1.12; Diodorus Siculus 17.90.1, 5–7; Strabo 15.1.28, 37, 45.

180 *The soldiers encountered:* Waqas Ali et al., "Diversity and Habitat Preferences of Amphibians and Reptiles in Pakistan: A Review," *Journal of Asia-Pacific Biodiversity* 11, no. 2 (2018): 173; Y. Gupta and S. Peshin, "Do Herbal Medicines Have Potential for Managing Snake Bite Envenomation?" *Toxicology International* 19, no. 2 (2012): 89.

180 *was equally painful:* H. Alistair Reid, "Snakebite in the Tropics," *British Medical Journal* 3, no. 5614 (1968): 360.

180 *sleeping in hammocks:* Diodorus Siculus 17.90.5–7; Strabo 15.1.45.

180 *plant-based antidotes:* Curtius 9.1.12; Strabo 15.1.45; Gupta and Peshin, "Do Herbal Medicines?" 96.

180 *thirty thousand strong:* Devine, "Battle of Hydaspes."

180 *and other camp followers:* Engels, *Logistics of the Macedonian Army,* 13.

181 *perhaps 3.7 million acres:* Bosworth, *Historical Commentary,* 2:263.

181 *were the Kathaians:* Arrian 5.22.1–24.6; Diodorus Siculus 17.91.3–4; Polyaenus, *Stratagems* 4.3.30; Strabo 15.1.30; Prakash, "Poros," 227–29; Vincent A. Smith, "The Position of the Autonomous Tribes of the Panjâb Conquered by Alexander the Great," *Journal of the Royal Asiatic Society of Great Britain and Ireland* (1903): 699–700; Bosworth, *Historical Commentary,* 2:327–37.

181 *the Malli and Sudrakai:* Stoneman, "Naked Philosophers," 102; Adrish Chandra Banerji, "The Malavas," *Annals of the Bhandarkar Oriental Research Institute* 13, no. 3/4 (1931): 218.

181 *a cousin of Poros:* Arrian 5.21.2–3; Diodorus Siculus 17.91.1.

181 *troops and elephants:* Arrian 5.21.1–22.2.

181 *unusual marriage customs:* Strabo 15.1.30.

181 *brick, not stone:* Arrian 5.23.4; Dieter Schlingloff, *Fortified Cities of Ancient India: A Comparative Study* (London: Anthem Press, 2013), 17–26.

182 *refused to come out:* Arrian 5.22.3–23.1.

182 *hand-to-hand melee:* Arrian 5.23.1–5.

182 *They built a stockade:* Arrian 5.23.6–24.3.

182 *and take the city:* Arrian 5.23.6–24.5; Curtius 9.1.14–18; Diodorus Siculus 17.91.4.

182 *were unusually brutal:* Arrian 5.24.5–8; Diodorus Siculus 17.91.4; N. G. L. Hammond, "Some Passages in Polyaenus 'Stratagems' Concerning Alexander," *Greek, Roman and Byzantine Studies* 37, no. 1 (1996): 42–44.

182 *No archaeological evidence:* Smith, "Position of the Autonomous Tribes," 701–2.

183 *"bloody, barbarian manner":* Polyaenus, *Stratagems* 4.3.30.

183 *five hundred invalid Kathaians:* Arrian 5.24.7.

183 *the inhabitants capitulated:* Curtius 9.1.32–33; Polyaenus, *Stratagems* 4.3.30.

183 *"for it seemed":* Arrian 5.24.8.

183 *frustrated modern historians:* E.g., Worthington, *Alexander the Great,* 215–17.

183 *to the Indus River:* Briant, *From Cyrus to Alexander,* 754–57.

184 *biographers blame pothos:* Kegerreis, "Alexander the Explorer," 74–84; Ehrenberg and Velsen, *Alexander and the Greeks,* 52–61.

184 *love of warfare:* Keegan, *Mask of Command.*

184 *megalomania:* Bosworth, *Alexander and the East.*

184 *a civilizing mission:* Tarn, *Alexander the Great;* Johann Gustav Droysen, *History of Alexander the Great,* ed. Flora Kimmich (Philadelphia: American Philosophical Society, 2012), 207.

184 *next powerful king:* Berve, *Das Alexanderreich,* 770; Heckel, *Who's Who,* 207.

184 *for military intelligence:* Curtius 9.1.35–2.2; Diodorus Siculus 17.93.1–2.

184 *The Ganges king:* Curtius 9.2.2–4; Diodorus Siculus 17.93.2; Metz Epitome 68; Plutarch 62.2.

185 *demanding to know:* Curtius 9.2.5.

185 *killed the previous king:* Curtius 9.2.5–7; Diodorus Siculus 17.93.3; Metz Epitome 69.

185 *may well have been accurate:* Plutarch 62.2.

185 *a powerful kingdom:* Jim G. Shaffer, "Reurbanization: The Eastern Punjab and Beyond," *Studies in the History of Art* 31 (1993): 53–67; Romila Thapar, *The Past Before Us: Historical Traditions of Early North India* (Cambridge, MA: Harvard University Press, 2013); Federica Barba, "The Fortified Cities of the Ganges Plain in the First Millennium B.C.," *East and West* 54, no. 1/4 (2004): 223–50.

185 *a Greek ambassador:* Truesdell S. Brown, "The Merits and Weaknesses of Megasthenes," *Phoenix* 11, no. 1 (1957), 12–24; Puskás, "Magasthenes and the 'Indian Gods'"; Zambrini, "Megasthenes Thirty Years Later."

185 *wooden-walled capital:* Strabo 15.1.36; Arrian, *Indike* 10.5–7; Schlingloff, *Fortified Cities of Ancient India,* 32–45.

186 *clothes long gone:* Curtius 9.3.10.

186 *more than two months:* Diodorus Siculus 17.94.1–3.

186 *their women and children:* Diodorus Siculus 17.94.3–4.

186 *mentioned by ancient writers:* Justin 12.4.2–11; Engels, *Logistics of the Macedonian Army,* 12–13.

187 *sought to make amends:* Diodorus Siculus 17.94.4–5.

187 *war widows and war orphans:* Angelos Chaniotis, *War in the Hellenistic World: A Social and Cultural History* (Malden, MA: Blackwell Publishing, 2005), 86.

187 *on the future army:* Justin 12.4.5–11.

187 *he called an assembly:* Arrian 5.25.2; Curtius 9.2.12; Diodorus Siculus 17.94.5; Justin 12.8.10–11; Bosworth, *Historical Commentary,* 2:337–60; R. M. Errington, "The Nature of the Macedonian State Under the Monarchy," *Chiron* 8 (1978): 110–11.

188 *used to learning:* Edward M. Anson, "Macedonia's Alleged Constitutionalism," *Classical Journal* 80, no. 4 (1985): 246–48.

188 *the Pillars of Herakles:* Arrian 5.25.3–26.8; Curtius 9.2.12–30; Diodorus Siculus 17.94.5.

188 *a long silence followed:* Arrian 5.27.1; Curtius 9.2.31–3.2.

189 *dissolved into tears:* Curtius 9.3.3.

189 *relatively egalitarian atmosphere:* Carney, *King and Court,* 242–43.

189 *front lines at Khaironeia:* Plutarch 9.2.

189 *his early days as king:* Diodorus Siculus 17.2.2; Justin 11.1.7–10.

189 *Physically daring, he still:* Elizabeth Carney, "Macedonians and Mutiny: Discipline and Indiscipline in the Army of Philip and Alexander," *Classical Philology* 91, no. 1 (1996): 29–30.

189 *he maintained his grasp:* Burn, "Generalship of Alexander."

189 *honored the dead:* Arrian 1.16.5; 2.12.1; Carney, "Macedonians and Mutiny," 28.

189 *military science of logistics:* Engels, *Logistics of the Macedonian Army.*

189 *chose his subordinates well:* Burn, "Generalship of Alexander," 142–43.

191 *haltingly began to speak:* Arrian 5.27.1–2; Curtius 9.3.3–4.

191 *His men were exhausted:* Arrian 5.27.2–28.1; Curtius 9.3.5–17; Justin 12.8.10–15.

191 *tears and acclamations:* Curtius 9.3.16–17.

191 *remained there angrily:* Curtius 39.3.18–19; Arrian 5.28.3.

192 *arguments over back pay:* Polyaenus, *Stratagems* 4.2.6.

192 *Classical Athenian generals:* Carney, "Macedonians and Mutiny," 20–24.

192 *famous Julius Caesar:* Stefan G. Chrissanthos, "Caesar and the Mutiny of 47 B.C.," *Journal of Roman Studies* 91 (2001): 68.

192 *peaceful political protest:* Lee Brice, "Military Unrest in the Age of Philip and Alexander of Macedon: Defining the Terms of Debate," in *Greece, Macedon and Persia,* ed. Timothy Howe (Oxford, UK: Oxbow Books, 2015), 72–73.

193 *soothsayers conduct sacrifices:* Arrian 5.28.4.

193 *turn back at the Beas:* Arrian 5.28.4–5; Curtius 9.3.19.

193 *unquestionable, stinging defeat:* Ernst Badian, "Harpalus," *Journal of Hellenic Studies* 81 (1961): 19–20; Carney, "Macedonians and Mutiny," 37.

193 *with tears of joy:* Arrian 5.29.1; Justin 12.8.17.

193 *no constitutional right:* Anson, "Macedonian Judicial Assemblies"; Errington, "Nature of the Macedonian State."

193 *altars by the river:* Arrian 5.29.1–2; Curtius 9.3.19; Diodorus Siculus 17.95; Plutarch 62.4.

193 *twins of the altars:* Arrian 1.11.7.

194 *permanent abandoned monument:* Curtius 9.3.19; Diodorus Siculus 17.95.1–2; Plutarch 62.3–4.

194 *no traces of the site:* Smith, "Position of the Autonomous Tribes," 701–2.

194 *as well as ancient historians:* E.g., Curtius 10.5.33; Plutarch 50.3–6; Bosworth, *Alexander and the East,* 133–65.

Chapter Thirteen: The End of the World

196 *a farther 2,300 or so:* Calculated on Google Maps, May 20, 2023.

196 *as well as thrill-seeking:* Arrian, *Indica* 20.1; Kegerreis, "Alexander the Explorer," contra James S. Romm, "Aristotle's Elephant and the Myth of Alexander's Scientific Patronage," *American Journal of Philology* 110, no. 4 (1989): 566–75.

197 *as had the Persians:* Henkelman, "Imperial Signature and Imperial Paradigm."

197 *supplied the timber:* Millett, "Political Economy of Macedonia," 484–87.

197 *easier than by land:* Peregrine Horden and Nicholas Purcell, *The Corrupting Sea: A Study of Mediterranean History* (Oxford, UK: Blackwell Publishers, 2000), 133.

197 *buried by Alexander:* Arrian 6.2.1; Curtius 9.3.20.

197 *timing of Koinos's death:* Badian, "Harpalus," 19; Bosworth, *Historical Commentary,* 2:354–55.

198 *sickened and died:* Donato Gómez-Díaz, "Cholera: First Through Third Pandemics, 1816–1861," in *Encyclopedia of Pestilence, Pandemics, and Plagues,* ed. Joseph P. Byrne (Westport, CT: Greenwood Press, 2008), 98–99.

198 *newborn, unnamed son:* Metz Epitome 70.

198 *abbreviated, and gossipy:* E. J. Baynham, "An Introduction to the Metz Epitome: Its Traditions and Value," *Antichthon* 29 (1995): 60–77.

199 *to his ancestral gods:* Arrian 6.3.1–2.

199 *even the horses:* Arrian 6.3.2.

199 *commander of the fleet:* Arrian 6.2.3.

199 *helmsman of the king's ship:* Arrian 6.2.3.

199 *Hephaistion was* philalexandros: Plutarch 47.5–6.

200 *broke up the fight:* Plutarch 47.6–7.

200 *leading important troops:* Arrian 6.2.1–3.2; Curtius 9.3.24; Diodorus Siculus 17.95.3–5; Justin 12.9.1.

200 *astonishing and colorful:* Arrian 6.3.2–5.

200 *grandiose cruise downriver:* Pierre Herman Leonard Eggermont, *Alexander's Campaigns in Southern Punjab* (Leuven: Uitgeverij Peeters en Departement Oriëntalistiek, 1993).

200 *Rumors of insurrection:* Arrian 6.4.3.

200 *promise to head home:* Curtius 9.4.16–23.

200 *back to war:* Eggermont, *Alexander's Campaigns in Southern Punjab,* 26–48, 64–80.

200 *to call an assembly:* Curtius 9.4.19–23.

201 *Malavas and Sudrakas:* Stoneman, "Naked Philosophers," 102; Banerji, "The Malavas," 218.

201 *"trained in arms":* Mahabharata 2.48; 6.47; 8.4.

201 *bamboo, cane, and wood:* Kaushik Roy, *Hinduism and the Ethics of Warfare in South Asia: From Antiquity to the Present* (New York: Cambridge University Press, 2012), 22.

201 *looked down on archery:* Todd Davis, "Archery in Archaic Greece" (Ph.D. diss., Columbia University, 2013), 261–70.

201 *venerable and heroic mode:* Roy, *Hinduism and the Ethics of Warfare in South Asia,* 20–22.

201 *They were both farmers:* Arrian 6.5.3.

201 *hunters, catching and taming:* Curtius 9.7.12, 9.8.1–2.

201 *called "white iron":* Banerji, "The Malavas," 223.

201 *rings of fortifications:* Schlingloff, *Fortified Cities of Ancient India,* 17–26.

201 *high mudbrick walls:* Arrian 6.10.3–4.

201 *caught his victims unawares:* Arrian 6.6.1–3.

202 *a negotiated surrender:* Fuller, *Generalship of Alexander the Great,* 264–72.

202 *soldiers had chafed:* Arrian 7.6.5.

202 *he massacred the Malli:* Arrian 6.6.5.

202 *crossing the Ravi River:* Arrian 6.7.1.

202 *captured and enslaved:* Arrian 6.7.3.

202 *set fire to their houses:* Arrian 6.7.4–6; Curtius 9.4.6–7 (slightly earlier).

202 *appropriately heroic response:* Stoneman, *Greek Experience of India,* 305–12; Enrica Garzilli, "First Greek and Latin Documents on Sahagamana and Some Connected Problems (Part 1)," *Indo-Iranian Journal* 40, no. 3 (1997): 205–43; Olivelle, *Ascetics and Brahmins,* 207–29.

203 *fleeing to the desert:* Arrian 6.8.1–2.

203 *well-defended town:* Arrian 6.9.1–11.8; Curtius 9.4.30–5.20; Diodorus Siculus 17.98.2–6; Justin 12.9.5–13; Metz Epitome 75–77; Plutarch 63.1–6; Vorhis, "Best of the Macedonians," 115–28, 67–76; J. M. Mossman, "Tragedy and Epic in Plutarch's Alexander," *Journal of Hellenic Studies* 108 (1988): 83–93.

203 *a strong outer wall:* Arrian 6.7.4.

203 *called for siege ladders:* Arrian 6.9.3.

203 *Macedonians were moving slowly:* Curtius 9.4.30.

203 *the first siege ladder:* Arrian 6.9.3–5; Curtius 9.5.1–18; Diodorus Siculus 17.98.5–99.4; Justin 12.9.5–10; Plutarch 63.4.

203 *a high-ranking infantryman:* Heckel, *Who's Who,* 203–5; Berve, *Das Alexander-reich,* 634.

203 *siege ladders broke:* Arrian 6.9.4.

203 *down within the walls:* Arrian 6.9.5; Plutarch 63.2–3; Curtius 9.5.2.

204 *his iron helmet:* E. N. Borza, "The Royal Macedonian Tombs and the Parapher-nalia of Alexander the Great," *Phoenix* 41, no. 2 (1987): 110–16.

204 *hoplite-style shield:* Minor M. Markle, "Macedonian Arms and Tactics Under Alexander the Great," *Studies in the History of Art* 10 (1982): 99.

204 *shot in the chest:* Curtius 9.5.9; Plutarch 63.3; Arrian 6.10.1–2.

204 *he killed the man:* Curtius 9.5.11.

204 *to climb the walls:* Arrian 6.10.3.

204 *pierced three times:* Curtius 9.5.17.

204 *sacred shield of Troy:* Arrian 6.8.3, 6.9.2.

204 *taken this shield:* Pierre Briant, "Alexandre à Troie: Images, mythe et realia," in *The Historiography of Alexander the Great,* ed. Krzysztof Nawotka et al. (Wiesbaden: Harrassowitz Verlag, 2018); Charles Brian Rose, "Troy and the Historical Imagina-tion," *The Classical World* 91, no. 5 (1998): 407.

205 *They slaughtered everyone:* Arrian 6.11.1; Curtius 9.5.19–22; Diodorus Siculus 17.99.4.

205 *experienced army doctor:* Waldemar Heckel, "Two Doctors from Kos?" *Mnemosyne* 34, no. 3/4 (1981): 396–98; Berve, *Das Alexanderreich,* 452–3; Heckel, *Who's Who,* 100.

205 *famed healing center:* Molly Jones-Lewis, "Physicians and 'Schools,'" in *A Com-panion to Science, Technology, and Medicine in Ancient Greece and Rome,* ed. Georgia Irby (Hoboken, NJ: John Wiley & Sons, 2016).

205 *treated Alexander's father:* Pliny, *Natural History* 7.37.

205 *and precise instruments:* Lawrence J. Bliquez, *The Tools of Asclepius: Surgical Instruments in Greek and Roman Times* (Leiden: Brill, 2015), 23–50.

205 *they were cautious:* Frédéric Le Blay, "Surgery," in *A Companion to Science, Tech-nology, and Medicine in Ancient Greece and Rome,* ed. Georgia Irby (Hoboken, NJ: John Wiley & Sons, Inc, 2016).

205 *encouraged his doctor:* Arrian 6.11.1–2; Curtius 9.5.22–29.

205 *leather pillows for support:* Blay, "Surgery."

205 *three finger lengths:* Plutarch 63.5–6.

206 *Alexander's attendants wailed:* Curtius 9.5.29.

206 *the king's purported death:* Arrian 6.12.1–3; Curtius 9.5.30–6.1.

206 *the restive province:* Mairs, *Hellenistic Far East;* Martinez-Sève, "Les Grecs d'Ex-trême Orient," 370–74.

206 *the long journey back:* Curtius 7.1–11; Diodorus Siculus 17.99.5–6; Michael Il-iakis, "Greek Mercenary Revolts in Bactria: A Re-appraisal," *Historia: Zeitschrift für Alte Geschichte* 62, no. 2 (2013): 182–95; Holt, *Alexander the Great and Bac-tria,* 79–85; Badian, "Harpalus," 25–31.

206 *finally willing to leave:* Curtius 9.5.30.

207 *suspected a forgery:* Arrian 6.12.2–3.

207 *a waterborne procession:* Arrian 6.13.1; Curtius 9.6.1–2.

207 *carefully choreographed display:* Arrian 6.13.2–3.

208 *they reproached him:* Arrian 13.4–5; Curtius 9.6.4–16.

208 *a life of glory:* Curtius 9.6.16–26.

208 *gorgeously dressed in linen:* Curtius 9.7.12.

208 *It was little enough:* Arrian 6.14.1–3; Curtius 9.7.12–15; Metz Epitome 78; Banerji, "The Malavas," 222; Eggermont, *Alexander's Campaigns in Southern Punjab,* 42.

208 *one hundred golden couches:* Curtius 9.7.15.

208 *the chief quarrel:* Curtius 9.7.16–18; Diodorus Siculus 17.100.1–4; Elizabeth Baynham, "Quintus Curtius Rufus on the 'Good King': The Dioxippus Episode in Book 9.7.16–26," in *A Companion to Greek and Roman Historiography,* ed. John Marincola (Oxford, UK: Blackwell, 2007).

209 *radically unequal contest:* Curtius 9.7.19–22; Diodorus Siculus 17.100.5–8.

209 *then committed suicide:* Curtius 9.7.23–26; Diodorus Siculus 17.101.3–6.

209 *pardoning those who:* Arrian 6.15.6–7, 16.3–4, 17.2–3.

209 *attacking those who:* Arrian 6.16.1–2, 16.5, 17.1; Curtius 9.8.4–30; Diodorus Siculus 17.102.1–103.8.

209 *coaxing back to:* Arrian 6.17.5–6; Stoneman, *Greek Experience of India,* 74; Stephen Peter Rosen, *Societies and Military Power: India and Its Armies* (Cornell University Press, 1996), 76–84.

210 *governor and garrison soldiers:* Arrian 6.14.3–15.3.

210 *were the Brachmanes:* Arrian 6.7.4, 16.5; Diodorus Siculus 17.102.7; Plutarch 64.1–5; Thapar, *Early India,* 132–33, 64–73.

210 *condemned them to death:* Arrian 6.16.5.

210 *smeared with the venom:* Curtius 9.8.17–20; Diodorus Siculus 17.103.1–6; Justin 12.10.1–2; Pierre Herman Leonard Eggermont, *Alexander's Campaigns in Sind and Baluchistan and the Siege of the Brahmin Town of Harmatelia* (Leuven: Leuven University Press, 1975), 109–12.

211 *Ptolemy recovered, as did:* Curtius 9.8.21–28; Diodorus Siculus 17.103.6–8; Justin 12.10.3; Strabo 15.2.7 (during the march through the Makran).

211 *new medical research:* Muhammad Hassham Hassan Bin Asad et al., "Compensatory Effects of Medicinal Plants of Pakistan upon Prolongation of Coagulation Assays Induced by Naja Naja Karachiensis Bite," *Current Science* 106, no. 6 (2014): 870–73; Gupta and Peshin, "Do Herbal Medicines Have Potential?"; W. Mors et al., "Plant Natural Products Active Against Snake Bite—The Molecular Approach," *Phytochemistry* 55, no. 6 (2000): 627–42.

211 *"the bitter water":* Curtius 9.9.6.

211 *Marsh-filled and swampy:* Paolo Biagi, "Changing the Prehistory of Sindh and Las Bela Coast: Twenty-Five Years of Italian Contribution," *World Archaeology: Debates in World Archaeology* 43, no. 4 (2011): 527–30.

211 *Greek-style boats:* Paolo Biagi, "Uneasy Riders: With Alexander and Nearchus from Pattala to Rhambakia," in *With Alexander in India and Central Asia: Moving East and Back to West,* ed. Claudia Antonetti and P. Biagi (Oxford, UK: Oxbow Books, 2017), 271.

211 *island named Cilluta:* Arrian 6.18.2–19.3; Curtius 9.9.7–26; Plutarch 66.1.

211 *seacoast in early summer:* Plutarch 66.1.

211 *beginnings of monsoon season:* Arrian, 6.21.1–3.

212 *Ahead was the gray sky:* Gemma Sharpe (personal communication).

212 *twelve species of dolphins:* Quddusi Kazmi, "Marine Biodiversity of Pakistan," Zoological Congress of Pakistan, 2013.

212 *made to hug the shore:* Horden and Purcell, *Corrupting Sea*, 126.

212 *recitations of Homer:* Homer, *Iliad* 18.605–8 (Ocean as place), 18.398 (Thetis, mother of Achilles, as the daughter of Ocean), 14.302–4 (acrimonious marital relations with Tethys).

212 *"the outer sea":* Aristotle, *Metrology* 1.13.

213 *he consented to stop:* Curtius 9.9.27.

213 *an offering to Poseidon:* Arrian 6.19.5; Plutarch 66.2.

Chapter Fourteen: The Land of the Fish Eaters

215 *In the Makran desert:* Arrian 6.23.1–25.6; Curtius 9.10.11–16; Diodorus Siculus 17.105.3–8; Plutarch 66.2–3; Strabo 15.2.5–7.

215 *eating dates and the pith:* Strabo 15.2.5.

215 *slaughtered pack animals:* Arrian 6.25.1.

215 *Men, too, left behind:* Arrian 6.25.2.

216 *responsible for thousands:* Plutarch 66.2–3.

216 *bid his old friend farewell:* Arrian 6.17.3.

216 *With them came the elephants:* Arrian 6.17.3.

216 *to the Bolan Pass:* Mahnaz Z. Ispahani, "Baluchistan and Its Environs: The Motives for Access," in *Roads and Rivals, The Political Uses of Access in the Borderlands of Asia* (Ithaca, NY: Cornell University Press, 1989), 36–45.

216 *four hundred pack animals:* Engels, *Logistics of the Macedonian Army*, 18.

216 *as long as the pass itself:* Engels, 19n28.

217 *Even the elephants:* H. H. Scullard, *The Elephant in the Greek and Roman World* (Ithaca, NY: Cornell University Press, 1974), 74.

217 *journey across the Alps:* Scullard, 158–59.

217 *Ozines and Zariaspes:* Curtius 9.10.19; Arrian 6.27.3 ("Ordanes"); Heckel, *Who's Who*, 185 ("Ordanes"), 273 ("Zariaspes"); Berve, *Das Alexanderreich*, 590, 335; Shayegan, "Prosopographical Notes," nos. 74, 84, 118.

217 *Alexander's Persian appointees:* Badian, "Harpalus," 19–20.

218 *ten miles per day:* Engels, *Logistics of the Macedonian Army*, 155–56.

218 *the Baluchistan region:* Brian Spooner, s.v. "Baluchistan: Geography, History, and Ethnography," in *Encyclopaedia Iranica*, vol. 3 (1988), https://www.iranicaonline.org/articles/baluchistan-i.

218 *The king ordered them:* Diodorus Siculus 17.104.3.

218 *Nearkhos and Onesikritos:* Engels, *Logistics of the Macedonian Army*, 112.

219 *a different account:* Arrian 6.24.3.

219 *four months' worth:* Arrian 6.20.5.

219 *elided his responsibility:* Engels, *Logistics of the Macedonian Army,* 112–13.

219 *the Sinai Peninsula:* Engels, 59–60.

219 *He didn't bring camels:* Henkelman, "Imperial Signature and Imperial Paradigm," 55–63.

219 *The missing pilot:* Engels, *Logistics of the Macedonian Army,* 115–16n83.

219 *the last fertile area:* Arrian 6.21.3–5; Curtius 9.10.4–7; Diodorus Siculus 17.104.3–8; Aurel Stein, "On Alexander's Route into Gedrosia: An Archaeological Tour in Las Bela," *Geographical Journal* 102, no. 5/6 (1943): 212–17; Engels, *Logistics of the Macedonian Army,* 138.

220 *preemptively surrendered:* Engels, "Logistics," 354–58.

220 *and relatively numerous:* Diodorus Siculus 17.104.6–7; Curtius 9.10.7.

220 *since caravan routes:* Robert H. McDowell, "The Indo-Parthian Frontier," *American Historical Review* 44, no. 4 (1939): 787–88; Henkelman, "Imperial Signature and Imperial Paradigm," 45–63.

220 *empire's second-in-command:* Andrew W. Collins, "Alexander and the Persian Court Chiliarchy," *Historia: Zeitschrift für Alte Geschichte* 61, no. 2 (2012): 159–67.

220 *faced fierce resistance:* Ispahani, "Baluchistan and Its Environs," 62.

220 *north to the hills:* Arrian 6.22.1.

220 *was a choke point:* Engels, *Logistics of the Macedonian Army,* 137–39.

221 *utterly barren mountains:* Aurel Stein, *An Archaeological Tour to Gedrosia: Memoirs of the Archaeological Survey of India* (Calcutta: Government of India Central Publication Branch, 1931), 5–12.

221 *Macedonian-appointed governor:* Arrian 6.22.2.

221 *founded by Hephaistion:* 6.21.5, 6.22.3.

221 *parting from the king:* Strabo 15.1.17.

222 *to a good harbor:* Arrian, *Indica* 21.10–12.

222 *So they built a wall:* Arrian, *Indica* 21.13.

222 *their leader, Agamemnon:* Aeschylus, *Agamemnon* 225–50.

222 *mussels and oysters:* Arrian, *Indica* 21.13.

223 *most of the surplus food:* Curtius 9.10.13.

223 *third, least bad option:* Engels, *Logistics of the Macedonian Army,* 114–15.

223 *for agricultural territory:* Stein, *Archaeological Tour,* 7–12.

223 *best-watered tracts:* Stein, "On Alexander's Route into Gedrosia," 212–26; Engels, 138–43; Roland Besenval, "Le peuplement de l'ancienne Gédrosie, de la protohistoire à la période islamique: Travaux archéologiques récents dans le Makran pakistanais," *Comptes Rendus des Séances de l'Année—Académie des Inscriptions et Belles-lettres* 138, no. 2 (1994): 525–28; Biagi, "Uneasy Riders."

223 *organic substances: myrrh:* Arrian 6.22.4; Strabo 14.2.3; Eggermont, *Alexander's Campaigns in Sind and Baluchistan,* 116–25.

223 *incense, and medicine:* Shimshon Ben-Yehoshua, Carole Borowitz, and Lumír Ondřej Hanuš, *Frankincense, Myrrh, and Balm of Gilead: Ancient Spices of Southern Arabia and Judea* (Hoboken, NJ: John Wiley & Sons, 2011), 39–46.

223 *The Phoenician traders:* Arrian 6.22.5–6.

224 *"washed by the sea":* Arrian 6.22.6–7; Eggermont, *Alexander's Campaigns in Sind and Baluchistan,* 120–225.

224 *eroded sandstone cliffs:* Stein, *Archaeological Tour;* Stein, "On Alexander's Route into Gedrosia."

224 *the deep, hot sand:* Arrian 6.24.4; Strabo 15.2.6.

224 *they felt lost:* Arrian 6.26.4.

224 *"perished in the sand":* Arrian 6.25.3.

224 *their fallen comrades:* Curtius 9.10.16.

225 *most distressing loss:* Arrian 6.25.4–6; cf. Stein, *Archaeological Tour,* 57–58.

225 *with disastrous repercussions:* Diodorus Siculus 17.105.6; Curtius 9.10.11–16; Bosworth, *Alexander and the East,* 166–85; Hamilton, *Plutarch Alexander,* 181–85.

225 *chose the harsh route:* Badian, "Harpalus," 21.

225 *further military campaigns:* Arrian 7.1.1–4.

226 *He barely passed:* Engels, *Logistics of the Macedonian Army,* 116–17; Stein, "On Alexander's Route into Gedrosia," 224–26.

226 *food was more plentiful:* Arrian 6.23.4–6; Strabo 15.2.5.

226 *the Turbat Oasis:* Stein, "On Alexander's Route into Gedrosia," 220–21; Besenval, "Le peuplement de l'ancienne Gédrosie," 525–28.

226 *grinding the grain:* Arrian 6.23.6; Henkelman, "Imperial Signature and Imperial Paradigm," 48.

226 *Persian imperial system:* Henkelman, "Imperial Signature and Imperial Paradigm."

226 *best Persian manner:* Arrian 6.23.4; Henkelman, "Imperial Signature and Imperial Paradigm," 49.

226 *to his nearby governors:* Arrian 6.27.6; Curtius 9.10.17–18; Diodorus Siculus 17.105.6–7; Plutarch 66.3.

226 *final stage of his route:* Arrian 6.26.4–5; Stein, "On Alexander's Route into Gedrosia," 221–23.

226 *sixty days after:* Plutarch 66.3.

226 *loyal governor Phrataphernes:* Arrian 6.27.6; Diodorus Siculus 17.105.7–8; Henkelman, "Imperial Signature and Imperial Paradigm," 55–63.

227 *thousands of his followers:* Plutarch 66.2.

227 *a larger population:* Mogens Herman Hansen, *Polis: An Introduction to the Ancient Greek City-State* (Oxford, UK: Oxford University Press, 2006), 29.

227 *wine-fueled march:* Arrian 6.28.1–2 (skeptical); Curtius 9.10.24–29; Diodorus Siculus 17.106.1; Plutarch 67.1–3.

227 *able to set sail:* Arrian, *Indica* 21.1; Strabo 15.2.5 Engels, *Logistics of the Macedonian Army,* 135–36.

227 *albeit often inaccurately:* Brunt, *Arrian,* 2:523–25.

227 *present-day Karachi:* Arrian *Indica* 22.4; Biagi, "Uneasy Riders," 263.

227 *and observant memoirist:* Pearson, *Lost Histories,* 128–29.

227 *rendezvous with Leonnatos:* Arrian, *Indica* 22.5–8.

228 *offered him baked fish:* Arrian, *Indica* 28.1–9.

228 *Iranian named Hydrakes:* Arrian, *Indica* 27.1; Arora, "Fragments of Onesikritos," 47–48; Berve, *Das Alexanderreich*, 760; Heckel, *Who's Who*, 141.
228 *myrtle, and flower gardens:* Arrian, *Indica* 27.2.
228 *their rate of travel:* cf. Arrian, *Indica* 21.3–4, 27.2.
228 *dangerous, forbidden island:* Arrian, *Indica* 31.1–9; Strabo 15.2.13.
229 *a sign of good luck:* Eunice Burr Stebbins, *The Dolphin in the Literature and Art of Greece and Rome* (Menasha, WI: George Banta, 1929), 1–8.
229 *a pod of blue whales:* Arrian, *Indica* 30.1–7; Curtius 10.1.11–12; Diodorus Siculus 17.106.6–7; Strabo 15.2.13; L. Harrison Matthews, *The Whale* (New York: Crescent Books, 1975), 66–92.
229 *sailors called* Ichthyophagoi: Arrian 6.23.1–3, *Indica* 29.9–16; Curtius 9.10.8–10; Diodorus Siculus 17.105.3–5; Strabo 15.2.2; Oddone Longo, "I Mangiatori di Pesci: Regime alimentare e quadro culturale," *Materiali e discussioni per l'analisi dei testi classici*, no. 18 (1987): 9–55.
229 *at least the 1970s:* Biagi, "Uneasy Riders," 272.
229 *well-watered coastline:* Arrian, *Indica* 32.2.
230 *full of incense and spices:* Ben-Yehoshua, Borowitz, and Hanuš, *Frankincense, Myrrh, and Balm of Gilead*, 7–9.
230 *best-recorded feuds:* Arrian, *Indica* 32.6–13.
230 *except olives, Nearkhos:* Arrian, *Indica* 32.5.
230 *and speaking Greek:* Arrian, *Indica* 33.5–6.
230 *great show of hastening:* Arrian 6.27.3–6, *Indica* 33.7–8; Curtius 10.1.1–9; Diodorus Siculus 17.106.2–3; Justin 12.10.8.
230 *built a double stockade:* Arrian, *Indica* 33.10.
230 *long haired, unwashed:* Arrian, *Indica* 34.7.
231 *the ships were safe:* Arrian, *Indica* 35.1–6; Curtius 10.1.10; Plutarch 68.1.
231 *a substantial proportion:* Engels, *Logistics of the Macedonian Army*, 117.
231 *Sacrificing to the gods:* Arrian, *Indica* 35.7–36.3.

Chapter Fifteen: A Ransacked Tomb and a Fiery Death

232 *been there once before:* Strabo 15.3.7; Arrian 6.29.9.
232 *regretted the destruction:* Arrian 6.30.1.
232 *carefully planted trees:* Boucharlat, "Southwestern Iran in the Achaemenid Period," 507–9; David Stronach and Hilary Gopnik, s.v. "Pasargadae," in *Encyclopaedia Iranica* (2009), http://www.iranicaonline.org/articles/pasargadae.
232 *an important role model:* Strabo 11.11.4.
233 *the best Greek craftsmen:* Stronach and Gopnik, "Pasargadae."
233 *tomb's rich accoutrements:* Arrian 6.29.5–7; Strabo 15.3.7.
233 *tomb had been ransacked:* Arrian 6.29.4–11; Curtius 10.1.30–32; Plutarch 69.2–3; Strabo 15.3.7; Josef Wiesehöfer, "Cyrus the Great and the Sacrifices for a Dead King," in *Ancient Historiography on War and Empire*, ed. Timothy Howe, Sabine Müller, and Richard Stoneman (Oxford, UK: Oxbow Books, 2017), 55–61; Briant, *Rois, tributs et paysans*, 386–92.

233 *by seizing the Magi:* Arrian 6.29.7, 11.

233 *Persian ritual experts:* Briant, *From Cyrus to Alexander,* 245–46.

233 *guard the tomb of Cyrus:* Henkelman, *Other Gods Who Are,* 424–26.

233 *self-appointed to his role:* Arrian 3.8.5; 6.29.2, 30.1–2; Curtius 4.12.8, 10.1.22–38; Shayegan, "Prosopographical Notes," no. 79; Heckel, *Who's Who,* 186; Berve, *Das Alexanderreich,* 592.

234 *his eunuch lover, Bagoas:* John Yardley and J. E. Atkinson, *Quintus Curtius Rufus: Histories of Alexander the Great,* vol. 10 (Oxford, UK: Oxford University Press, 2009), 93–97.

234 *"not his whores":* Curtius 10.1.26.

234 *had him hanged:* Arrian 6.30.2; Curtius 10.1.37.

234 *a Macedonian officer:* Plutarch 69.2; Hamilton, *Plutarch Alexander,* 192 (calling Plutarch's account into question).

234 *deluged by complaints:* Arrian 6.30.1–2; Curtius 10.1.1–9, 39–42.

235 *caves of Wadi el-Daliyeh:* Peter Machinist, "The First Coins of Judah and Samaria: Numismatics and History in the Achaemenid and Early Hellenistic Periods," in *Continuity and Change: Proceedings of the Last Achaemenid History Workshop,* ed. H. Sancisi-Weerdenburg, Amélie Kuhrt, and Margaret Cool Root, (Leiden: Nederlands Institut voor het Nabije Oosten, 1994), 377.

235 *Far away, at Kyzyltepa:* Xin Wu, "Exploiting the Virgin Land: Kyzyltepa and the Effects of the Achaemenid Persian Empire on its Central Asian Frontier," in *A Millennium of History: The Iron Age in Southern Central Asia (2nd and 1st Millennia BC),* ed. Johanna Lhuillier and Nikolaus Boroffka (Berlin: Dietrich Reimer Verlag, 2018), 189–214; Xin Wu, "10 Land of the Unrule-ables: Bactria in the Achaemenid Period," in *Fitful Histories and Unruly Publics: Rethinking Temporality and Community in Eurasian Archaeology,* ed. Kathryn O. Weber et al. (Leiden: Brill, 2017), 258–88.

235 *destroyed by conflagration:* Igor Kreimerman and Débora Sandhaus, "Political Trends as Reflected in the Material Culture: A New Look at the Transition Between the Persian and Early Hellenistic Periods," in *Times of Transition: Judea in the Early Hellenistic Period,* ed. Sylvia Honigman, Christophe Nihan, and Oded Lipschits (Pittsburgh: Penn State University Press, 2021), 119–31.

235 *fully 90 percent:* Jakub Havlík, *"Terra Mulitplex et Varia Natura.* On the Settlement Patterns of Bactria in the Hellenistic Period," *Studia Hercynia* 25, no. 2 (2021), 9–41.

236 *was swift and violent:* Arrian 6.27.5, 7.4.1–3; Curtius 10.1.1–9; Diodorus Siculus 17.108.6; Justin 12.10.8; Plutarch 68.2–4; Badian, "Harpalus"; Badian, "Administration of the Empire," 180.

236 *Death could be the penalty:* Briant, *From Cyrus to Alexander,* 45, 338; Lincoln, *Religion, Empire, and Torture.*

236 *still concentrated power:* Reames-Zimmerman, "Hephaistion Amyntoros," 26.

237 *the architect or engineer:* Pearson, *Lost Histories,* 150–87; Berve, *Das Alexanderreich,* 121; Heckel, *Who's Who,* 46.

237 *restoration of the tomb:* Arrian 6.29.10; Strabo 15.3.7.

237 *permission to commit suicide:* Arrian 7.2.2–3.6; Diodorus Siculus 17.107.1–6; Plutarch 69.3–4; Strabo 15.1.63–5, 68; Stoneman, *Greek Experience of India,* 302–5, 12–19; Zambrini, "Megasthenes Thirty Years Later," 231–37.

237 *the province of women:* Nicole Loraux, *Tragic Ways of Killing a Woman,* trans. Anthony Forster (Cambridge, MA: Harvard University Press, 1987), 8–11.

238 *some ascetics like Buddhists:* Olivelle, *Ascetics and Brahmins,* 207–8.

238 *sometimes commit sati:* Aelian, *Varia Historia* 7.18; Diodorus 19.33.1–34.7; Strabo 15.1.62.

238 *a magnificent ceremony:* Arrian 7.3.2–3.

238 *materialistic and display-oriented:* Andronikos, *Vergina.*

238 *was one of his students:* Arrian 7.3.4.

239 *What Kalanos did next:* Strabo 15.1.68.

239 *more jaundiced opinion:* Diodorus Siculus 17.107.5; Strabo 15.1.68.

239 *Alexander himself was uncomfortable:* Arrian 7.3.5.

239 *preempting opposition:* Zambrini, "Megasthenes Thirty Years Later," 234.

239 *held a great feast:* Athenaeus, *Deipnosophists* 436f–37b; Plutarch 70.1.

240 *remembered as eerie:* Plutarch 69.3–4

Chapter Sixteen: Ninety-Two Brides

241 *great palace at Susa:* Strabo 15.3.21, Rémy Boucharlat, "Suse, Marché Agricole ou Relais du Grand Commerce," *Paléorient* 11, no. 2 (1985); Rémy Boucharlat, s.v. "Susa: The Achaemenid Period," in *Encyclopaedia Iranica* (2009), https://www.iranicaonline.org/articles/susa-iii-the-achaemenid-period; Henkelman, "Imperial Signature and Imperial Paradigm," 113–29.

241 *had been his captives:* Arrian 2.11.9.

241 *retained their fine clothes:* Plutarch 21.1–3.

241 *possessed enormous wealth:* Henkelman, "'Consumed Before the King,'" 693–703.

241 *called her "Mother":* Diodorus Siculus 17.37.6.

242 *intervening to beg pardon:* Arrian 3.17.6.

242 *buried her own son:* Arrian 3.22.1.

242 *her young grandson:* Curtius 3.11.24, 12.26.

242 *taught to weave:* Curtius 5.2.18–22.

242 *instruction in Greek:* Diodorus Siculus 17.67.1.

242 *have heard his plans:* Bosworth, "Alexander and the Iranians," 10–14; Branko van Oppen de Rutter, "The Susa Marriages—A Historiographical Note," *Ancient Society* 44 (2014): 25–41; Carney, "Alexander and Persian Women," 577–81; Sabine Müller, "The Female Element of the Political Self-Fashioning of the Diadochi: Ptolemy, Seleucus, Lysimachus, and Their Iranian Wives," in *After Alexander: The Time of the Diadochi (323–281 BC),* ed. Víctor Alonso Troncoso and Edward M. Anson (Oxford, UK: Oxbow Books, 2013), 199–214; Corinna Hoff, "The Mass Marriage at Susa in 324 BC and Achaemenid Tradition," in *Sex and Gender in the Ancient Near East: Proceedings of the 47th Rencontre Assyriologique Internationale, Helsinki, July 2–6, 2001,* ed. S. Par-

pola and R. M. Whiting (Helsinki: Neo-Assyrian Text Corpus Project, 2002), 239–44.

242 *summoned the best:* Athenaeus, *Deipnosophists* 12.538b–539a; Kotlińska-Toma, "On His Majesty's Secret Service," 279–85.

242 *enormous golden tent:* Aelian, *Varia Historia* 8.7; Athenaeus, *Deipnosophists* 12.538b–539a; Víctor Alonso Troncoso, Mauricio Álvarez Rico, and Sarina Pal, "Alexander's Tents and Camp Life," in *The History of the Argeads,* ed. Sabine Müller et al. (Wiesbaden: Harrassowitz Verlag, 2017), 117–23.

243 *reported twenty minae:* Athenaeus, *Deipnosophists* 12.538b.

243 *some nine to ten thousand:* Plutarch 70.2; Arrian 7.4.8.

243 *a series of toasts:* Plutarch 70.2.

243 *like Parysatis, daughter:* Berve, *Das Alexanderreich,* 607; Heckel, *Who's Who,* 192; Shayegan, "Prosopographical Notes," no. 87.

243 *Others were less exalted:* Arrian 7.4.4–6.

243 *to enter the tent:* Arrian 7.4.7–8; Athenaeus, *Deipnosophists* 12.538b–539a.

243 *of greater importance:* Hoff, "Mass Marriage at Susa," 240.

244 *was forthrightly political:* Sabine Müller, "Drypetis in Fact and (Fan) Fiction," in *Orientalism and the Reception of Powerful Women from the Ancient World,* ed. Fillipo Carla-Uhink and Anja Weber (London: Bloomsbury Academic, 2020), 60.

244 *Cyrus the Great:* Briant, *From Cyrus to Alexander,* 33, 132.

244 *younger sister Drypetis:* Müller, "Drypetis in Fact and (Fan) Fiction"; Müller and Poletti, "Hephaistion"; Shayegan, "Prosopographical Notes," no. 49; Berve, *Das Alexanderreich,* 290; Heckel, *Who's Who,* 116.

245 *the king's top commanders:* Athenaeus, *Deipnosophists* 12.538b–539a.

245 *nine to ten thousand:* Arrian 7.4.6, 8; Plutarch 70.2, *Moralia* 329e; van Oppen de Rutter, "The Susa Marriages."

245 *been enormously expensive:* Plutarch 70.2–3.

245 *his most powerful commanders:* Justin 12.10.9.

245 *the ceremony was ready:* Arrian 7.4.6–8.

245 *"the partnership of the two":* Plutarch, *Moralia* 329e.

245 *the norm in their society:* Brosius, *Women in Ancient Persia,* 38.

246 *the romantic comedies:* T. B. L. Webster, *An Introduction to Menander* (Manchester, UK: Manchester University Press, 1974), 23–24.

246 *their own marriages:* Carney, *Women and Monarchy,* 98.

246 *marry Iranian women:* Arrian 7.6.2.

246 *only one companion:* Federicomaria Muccioli, "Peucesta, tra lealismo Macedone e modello Persiano," *Electrum: Studia z Historii Starożytnej* 24, no. 24 (2017): 75–91; Bosworth, "Alexander and the Iranians," 11–12.

246 *women as prizes:* Bosworth, "Alexander and the Iranians," 11–12.

246 *all the army's debts:* Arrian 7.5. 1–3; Curtius 10.2.9–11; Diodorus Siculus 17.109.1–2; Justin 12.11.1–3; Plutarch 70; Joseph Roisman, *Alexander's Veterans and the Early Wars of the Successors* (Austin: University of Texas Press, 2012), 40–44; Holt, *Treasures of Alexander the Great,* 124–27.

247 *rank-and-file infantrymen:* R. D. Milns, "Army Pay and the Military Budget of Alexander the Great," in *Zu Alexander d. Gr. Festschrift G. Wirth,* ed. W. Will and J. Heinrichs (Amsterdam: Hakkert, 1987), 233–56; Sekunda, "Macedonian Army," 465–66.

247 *as a skilled craftsman:* Harvey F. Miller, "The Practical and Economic Background to the Greek Mercenary Explosion," *Greece & Rome* 31, no. 2 (1984): 155.

247 *supply or at least maintain:* Sekunda, "Macedonian Army," 467–70; Paul McKechnie, "Greek Mercenary Troops and Their Equipment," *Historia: Zeitschrift für alte Geschichte* 43, no. 3 (1994): 297–305.

247 *for their own food:* John W. I. Lee, "Daily Life in Classical Greek Armies, c. 500–330 BCE," in *New Approaches to Greek and Roman Warfare,* ed. Lee Brice (Newark, NJ: John Wiley and Sons, 2020), 43–46.

247 *back pay and bonuses:* Sekunda, "Macedonian Army," 465–66.

247 *individuals they captured:* Borja Antela Bernárdez, "La campaña de Alejandro: Esclavismo y dependencia en el espacio de conquista," *Actes du groupe de recherches sur l'esclavage depuis l'antiquité* 35, no. 1 (2015): 281–96.

247 *did not always pay back:* Holt, *Treasures of Alexander the Great,* 126–27.

247 *use this knowledge against them:* Arrian 7.5.1; Curtius 10.2.10.

248 *tiny trickle of soldiers:* Arrian 7.5.1.

248 *recognized his mistake:* Arrian 7.5.2–3; Curtius 10.2.10–11.

248 *280 tons of silver:* Holt, *Treasures of Alexander the Great,* 126.

Chapter Seventeen: Demobilization and Its Discontents

249 *is always fraught:* Jonathan Shay, Max Cleland, and John McCain, *Odysseus in America: Combat Trauma and the Trials of Homecoming* (New York: Scribner, 2002), 120–46.

249 *served with Alexander's father:* Baynham, "Alexander's Argyraspids," 118.

250 *new group of soldiers:* Arrian 7.6.1–2; Diodorus Siculus 17.108.1–3; Plutarch 71.1–2. Hammond, "Royal Pages," 272–79; N. G. L. Hammond, "Alexander's Newly-Founded Cities," *Greek, Roman and Byzantine Studies* 39, no. 3 (1998): 243–68; Marek Jan Olbrycht, "The Epigonoi: The Iranian Phalanx of Alexander the Great," in *The Many Faces of War in the Ancient World,* ed. Waldemar Heckel, Sabine Müller, and Graham Wrightson (Cambridge, UK: Cambridge University Press, 2015), 196–212.

250 *four years earlier:* Curtius 8.5.1; Plutarch 47.3.

250 *They were also hostages:* Bosworth, "Alexander and the Iranians," 17–18.

250 *thirty thousand men:* A. B. Bosworth, "Alexander the Great and the Decline of Macedon," *Journal of Hellenic Studies* 106 (1986): 8–9.

251 *had his eye on Arabia:* Arrian 7.19.5–20.2; Strabo 16.1.

251 *rule from Mesopotamia:* Curtius 10.2.8.

251 *called them the Epigonoi:* Arrian 7.6.1; Plutarch 71.1.

251 *as "dancer-soldiers":* Plutarch 71.2.

252 *counterparts moved west:* Arrian 7.7.1–2, 6–7.

252 *nexus of connectivity:* Paolo Gentili, "Opis e le altere," *Studi Classici e Orientali* 51 (2005), 25–53.

252 *current average highs:* https://www.accuweather.com, consulted July 3, 2023.

252 *to another assembly:* Arrian 7.8.1–11.1; Curtius 10.2.12–30; Diodorus Siculus 17.108.3, 109.2–3; Justin 12.11.4–9; Plutarch 71.2–3; Carney, "Macedonians and Mutiny," 37–42; Carney, "Artifice and Alexander History," 273–85; Roisman, *Alexander's Veterans*, 44–60; Marek Jan Olbrycht, "The Military Reforms of Alexander the Great During his Campaign in Iran, Afghanistan, and Central Asia," in *Miscellanea Eurasiatica Cracoviensia*, ed. C. Galewicz, J. Pstrusińska, and L. Sudyka (Kraków: Księgarnia Akademicka, 2007), 317–19.

253 *half of those listening:* Roisman, *Alexander's Veterans*, 56.

253 *invalided general Krateros:* N. Ashton, "Craterus Revisited," in *East and West in the World Empire of Alexander: Essays in Honour of Brian Bosworth*, ed. Pat Wheatley and E. J. Baynham (Oxford, UK: Oxford University Press, 2015), 107–16.

253 *murmurs from the crowd:* Plutarch 71.2–3; Arrian 7.8.2.

253 *divine father, Zeus-Amun:* Arrian 7.8.3; Justin 12.11.6.

254 *In Athens particularly:* Hyperides 5.4.

254 *exiles had proliferated:* McKechnie, *Outsiders in the Greek Cities*, 34–78.

254 *violence spilled out:* Hans Van Wees, "'Stasis, Destroyer of Men': Mass, Elite, Political Violence and Security in Archaic Greece," *Entretiens sur l'antiquité classique* 54 (2008): 1–48.

254 *the century before Alexander:* Matthew Trundle, *Greek Mercenaries: From the Late Archaic Period to Alexander* (Abingdon, Oxon: Routledge, 2004), 62.

255 *Some talented immigrants:* McKechnie, *Outsiders in the Greek Cities*, 142–77.

255 *only career available:* McKechnie, 79–100; Trundle, *Greek Mercenaries*, 40–79.

255 *the governors' armies:* Diodorus Siculus 17.106.3.

255 *the League of Corinth:* Poddighe, "Alexander and the Greeks."

255 *did not always abide:* Pseudo-Demosthenes 17.12; *Fragmente Griechische Historiker* 153 f 5 (*P. Oxy.* 216): Sam Hitchings, "The Date of [Demosthenes] 17, 'On the Treaty with Alexander,'" *Harvard Studies in Classical Philology* 109 (2017): 171–72 (Alexander); N. G. L. Hammond, *Philip of Macedon* (Baltimore: Johns Hopkins University Press, 1994), 30–31, 90–92 (Philip II).

255 *one-fifth of the city's total:* Hansen, *Polis*, 93; Mogens Herman Hansen, *Demography and Democracy: The Number of Athenian Citizens in the Fourth Century BC* (Herning, Denmark: Systime, 1986), 66.

255 *would stay in place:* Paul Zanker, *The Mask of Socrates: The Image of the Intellectual in Antiquity*, Sather Classical Lectures, vol. 59, (Berkeley: University of California Press, 1995), 87–88.

256 *open-air meeting place:* John Camp, *The Archaeology of Athens* (New Haven, CT: Yale University Press, 2001), 153–54.

256 *two generations earlier:* Christian Habicht, "Athens, Samos, and Alexander the Great," *Proceedings of the American Philosophical Society* 140, no. 3 (1996): 397–405.

256 *prepare immediately for war:* Hyperides 5.4.

256 *worshipping him as a god:* Dinarchus 1.94; Hyperides 5.7; Polybius, *Histories* 12.12b3; Diogenes Laertius 6.63; Aelian, *Varia Historia* 5.12; Plutarch, *Moralia* 804b, 842d; Balsdon, "'Divinity' of Alexander"; Edmonds, "Religiosity of Alexander"; Badian, "Deification of Alexander the Great," 54–59; Edward M. Anson, *Alexander the Great: Themes and Issues* (London: Bloomsbury Academic, 2013), 83–120.

256 *the way to name:* S. R. F. Price, *Rituals and Power: The Roman Imperial Cult in Asia Minor* (Cambridge, UK: Cambridge University Press, 1984), 25–40.

256 *on the rocky hillside:* Hyperides 5.3.

256 *Sixty years old:* Yunis, *Demosthenes, Speeches 18 and 19*, 3–5.

256 *twice the average lifespan:* Hansen, *Demography and Democracy*, 65.

256 *plain, unadorned himation:* Zanker, *Mask of Socrates*, 83–85.

256 *among the wealthiest:* Heckel, *Who's Who*, 110–11; Berve, *Das Alexanderreich*, 263.

256 *the funeral oration:* Demosthenes 18.285, 60.

256 *thousand Athenian soldiers:* Diodorus Siculus 16.86.5.

257 *a thirteenth addition:* Dinarchus 1.94.

257 *Nikanor, the adopted son:* A. B. Bosworth, "A New Macedonian Prince," *Classical Quarterly* 44, no. 1 (1994): 57–58.

257 *himself as the leader:* Dinarchus 1.81–82.

257 *Olympia was lush:* Olympia Vikatou, *Olympia: The Archaeological Site and the Museums* (Athens: Ekdotike Athenon, 2006), 17–18.

257 *twenty thousand of them:* Diodorus Siculus 18.8.5.

258 *trumpeting and voice projection:* Donald G. Kyle, *Sport and Spectacle in the Ancient World*, 2nd ed., Ancient Cultures, vol. 4 (Chichester, UK: John Wiley and Sons, 2015), 115.

258 *had the right of return:* Curtius 10.2.4–7; Dinarchus 1.82; Diodorus Siculus 17.109.1; 18.8.2–5; Hyperides 5.4; Justin 13.5.2–6; Wilhelm Dittenberger, *Sylloge Inscriptionum Graecarum*, 3rd ed. (1915), 306, 312; Dmitriev, "Alexander's Exiles Decree"; Robert Garland, *Wandering Greeks: The Ancient Greek Diaspora from the Age of Homer to the Death of Alexander the Great* (Princeton, NJ: Princeton University Press, 2014), 190–94; A. J. Heisserer and R. Hodot, "The Mytilenean Decree on Concord," *Zeitschrift für Papyrologie und Epigraphik* 63 (1986): 109–28.

258 *speak to Nikanor politely:* Dinarchus 1.103

258 *"Let him be a son":* Hyperides 5.7.

258 *mercenaries led by Harpalos:* Curtius 10.2.1–3; Dinarchus 1.4–6, 68–70, 81–82, 89–94, 103; Hyperides 5.1–5, 7; Diodorus Siculus 17.108.6–7; Justin 13.5.9; Pausanias 1.37.5; Plutarch, *Demosthenes* 25.1–26.1, *Phocion* 21–22; E. Badian, "The First Flight of Harpalus," *Historia: Zeitschrift für Alte Geschichte* 9, no. 2 (1960): 245–46; Badian, "Harpalus"; Yardley and Atkinson, *Quintus Curtius Rufus*, 107–14.

259 *was sorely disappointed:* Dinarchus 1.68, 89; Hyperides 5.3; Plutarch, *Demosthenes* 25.1–5.

259 *to consider alternatives:* Badian, "Harpalus," 32–33.

259 *just as his father, Philip II:* Habicht, "Athens, Samos, and Alexander the Great," 399.

259 *also accepted a bribe:* Dinarchus 1.68; Hyperides 5.1–2; Plutarch, *Demosthenes* 25.1–26.1.

259 *meant the Persian King:* Hyperides 5.4; Dinarchus 1.10, 18–22; Aeschines, *Against Ctesiphon* 3.239–40.

260 *at the treasurer's escape:* Hyperides 5.3.

260 *betrayed and killed:* Diodorus Siculus 17.108.7–8.

260 *prosecuted in court:* Dinarchus 1.1; Hyperides 5.1–3.

260 *was forced into exile:* Plutarch, *Demosthenes* 26.1

260 *to immediate execution:* Curtius 10.2.30–3.4; Arrian 7.8.3; Justin 12.11.8.

260 *excoriated his men:* D. Brendan Nagle, "The Cultural Context of Alexander's Speech at Opis," *Transactions of the American Philological Association (1974)* 126 (1996): 151–72.

260 *admitting no one:* Arrian 7.11.1; Curtius 10.3.5.

261 *mustered the Persians:* Arrian 7.11.2–4; Curtius 10.3.6–14; Diodorus Siculus 17.108.3; Justin 12.12.1–5; Plutarch 71.3.

261 *men to choose from:* Arrian 7.6.3–5; Olbrycht, "The Epigonoi."

262 *themselves completely vulnerable:* Arrian 7.11.4; Curtius 10.4.3; Diodorus Siculus 10.108.3; Justin 12.12.6; Plutarch 71.4.

262 *to behold his veterans:* Arrian 7.11.5; Plutarch 71.5.

262 *poured out their grievances:* Arrian 7.11.6–7.

262 *approach and kiss him:* Arrian 7.11.6–7.

263 *Macedonia rarely shaved:* Daniel Ogden, *Alexander the Great: Myth, Genesis and Sexuality* (Exeter: University of Exeter Press, 2011), 181–82.

263 *their victory song:* Arrian 7.11.7–8.

263 *to positions of prominence:* Olbrycht, "The Epigonoi."

263 *the protest on the Beas:* Brice, "Military Unrest"; Carney, "Macedonians and Mutiny."

263 *habits of Persian rulers:* Arrian 7.11.8–9; Konrad Vössing, "Royal Feasting," in *A Companion to Food in the Ancient World*, ed. John Wilkins and Robin Nadeau (Chichester, UK: John Wiley and Sons, 2015), 245–48; Henkelman, "Parnakka's Feast," 116–18.

264 *about nine thousand:* Arrian 7.11.9.

264 *soothsayers and Persian magi:* Arrian 7.11.8.

264 koinonia tes arches: Arrian 7.11.9; R. J. Klonoski, "Homonoia in Aristotle's Ethics and Politics," *History of Political Thought* 17, no. 3 (1996): 313–25.

264 *at least in Greek religion:* Robert Parker, *On Greek Religion* (Ithaca, NY: Cornell University Press, 2011), 31–34.

264 *ten thousand soldiers:* Arrian 7.12.1–4; Justin 12.12.7–10 (eleven thousand); Plutarch 71.5.

264 *long-serving regent Antipater:* Arrian 7.12.5–7; E. M. Pitt and W. P. Richardson, "Hostile Inaction? Antipater, Craterus and the Macedonian Regency," *Classical Quarterly* 67, no. 1 (2017): 77–87.

265 *fourth-century equivalent:* Arrian 7.12.1; Plutarch 71.5; Holt, *Treasures of Al-exander the Great*, 120–21; Phillip Harding, *Athens Transformed, 404–262 BC: From Popular Sovereignty to the Dominion of the Elite* (London: Routledge, 2015), 90–91.

265 *The soldiers' other children:* Arrian 7.12.2–3.

265 *to be preventing trouble:* Arrian 7.12.2.

Chapter Eighteen: The Death of Patroklos

267 *came that autumn:* Hamilton, *Plutarch Alexander,* 199.

267 *cool mountain air:* Strabo 11.13.

267 *and dramatic festival:* Arrian 7.14.1; Athenaeus, *Deipnosophists* 538a; Diodorus Siculus 17.110.7–8; Plutarch 72; Kotlińska-Toma, "On His Majesty's Secret Service"; Sebastiana Nervegna, "Lycurgus, Alexander the Great, and the Texts of Greek Tragedy," *Classical Philology* 115, no. 3 (2020): 578–85; Brigitte Le Guen, "Theatre, Religion, and Politics at Alexander's Travelling Royal Court" in *Greek Theatre in the Fourth Century BC,* ed. Eric Csapo et al. (Berlin: De Gruyter, 2014), 249–74.

267 *he was a runner:* Plutarch 4.5.

267 *His taste in drama:* Nervegna, "Lycurgus, Alexander the Great, and the Texts of Greek Tragedy"; Pownall and Pal, "Role of Greek Literature."

267 *the canonical three:* Bosworth, *Alexander and the East,* 142–46.

267 *their complete works:* Plutarch 8.2–3.

267 *Hephaistion fell sick:* Arrian 7.14.1; Diodorus Siculus 17.110.7–8; Justin 12.12.11–12; Plutarch 72.1–4; Hamilton, *Plutarch Alexander,* 199–202; Jeanne Reames-Zimmerman, "The Mourning of Alexander the Great," *Syllecta Classica* 12 (2001): 98–145; *Arrian, Anabasi di Alessandro,* ed. Francesco Sisti and Andrea Zambrini ([Rome, Italy]: Fondazione Lorenzo Valla, 2001), 614–18.

268 *unlike Roman soldiers:* Philip Rance, "Health, Wounds, and Medicine in the Late Roman Army (250–600 CE)," in *New Approaches to Greek and Roman Warfare,* ed. Lee Brice (Hoboken, NJ: John Wiley & Sons, 2020).

268 *understanding of disease:* Richard A. Gabriel, *Man and Wound in the Ancient World: A History of Military Medicine from Sumer to the Fall of Constantinople* (Washington, D.C: Potomac Books, 2012), 149–54.

268 *Erigyios both died:* Curtius 8.2.40 (Erigyios); 9.3.20 (Koinos).

268 *the same complaint:* Spyros Retsas, "Alexander's (356–323 BC) Expeditionary Medical Corps, 334–323 BC," *Journal of Medical Biography* 17, no. 3 (2009): 167–68.

268 *Hephaistion was left alone:* Arrian 7.14.1; Plutarch 72.

269 *his restricted diet:* Plutarch 72.1; Jacques Jouanna and Ph J. van der Eijk, *Greek Medicine from Hippocrates to Galen: Selected Papers,* Studies in Ancient Medicine (Leiden: Brill, 2012), 146–47.

269 *entire boiled chicken:* Plutarch 72.1; Hamilton, *Plutarch Alexander,* 199.

269 *Hephaistion was dead:* Arrian 7.14.1; Plutarch 72.2.

269 *Achilles and Patroklos:* Arrian 7.16.8; Arrian, *Discourses* 2.22.17–18; Aelian, *Varia Historia* 12.7.

270 *was certainly passionate:* Arrian 7.14.2–4; Plutarch 72.2.

270 *Achilles had done the same:* Homer, *Iliad* 19.305–08.

270 *Alexander mourned extravagantly:* Arrian 7.14.2; Diodorus Siculus 17.110.8; Justin 12.12.12; Plutarch 72.2; Reames-Zimmerman, "Mourning of Alexander the Great."

270 *Greek orators murmured:* Hyperides 6.21–22.

270 *attack on the Kossaians:* Arrian 7.15.1–3; Diodorus Siculus 17.111.4–6; Plutarch 72.3; Strabo 11.13.6.

271 *to the Persian Empire:* Balatti, *Mountain Peoples,* 220–26, 304–26; Pierre Briant, "Brigandage, dissidence et conquête en Asie Achéménide et Hellénistique," *Dialogues d'histoire ancienne* 2, no. 1 (1976): 196–209.

271 *typical military strategies:* Balatti, *Mountain Peoples,* 230.

271 *for forty days before:* Diodorus Siculus 17.111.6.

271 *entire male population:* Plutarch 72.3; Diodorus Siculus 17.111.5.

271 *again making trouble:* Diodorus Siculus 19.19.3–4; Balatti, *Mountain Peoples,* 230.

271 *after Hephaistion's death:* Justin 13.2.5 (calculated relative to Alexander's death); Curtius 10.6.9 (eleven months).

272 *taking the reins himself:* Arrian 7.14.5; Diodorus Siculus 17.110.8.

272 *a flood of ambassadors:* Arrian 7.15.4–6; Diodorus Siculus 17.113.1–4; Justin 12.13.1–2. Brunt, *Arrian,* 495–99; Arrian, *Anabasi di Alessandro,* 619–24.

272 *Celts were an exotic sight:* Arrian 7.14.4; Diodorus Siculus 17.113.2; John Haywood, *The Celts: Bronze Age to New Age* (London: Taylor and Francis, 2014).

272 *Babylonian astronomer priests:* Arrian 7.16.5–6; Diodorus Siculus 17.112.2–4; Justin 12.13.3; Plutarch 73.1; Van der Spek, "Darius III, Alexander the Great and Babylonian Scholarship"; Micah T. Ross, "Belephantes to Alexander: An Astrological Report to a Macedonian King?" in *Alexander the Great and the East,* ed. Krzysztof Nawotka and Agnieszka Wojciechowska (Wiesbaden: Harrassowitz Verlag, 2016), 89–102; Willem Smelik, "The 'Omina Mortis' in the Histories of Alexander the Great," *Talanta* 10/11 (1978/79): 93–96.

273 *the priests' motives:* Arrian 7.16.6–17.5.

273 *outside the city walls:* Arrian 7.17.5; Diodorus Siculus 17.112.4; Justin 12.13.4.

273 *and a lunar eclipse:* Van der Spek, "Darius III, Alexander the Great and Babylonian Scholarship," 338.

273 *and Macedonian entourage:* Diodorus Siculus 17.112.4–5; Justin 12.13.5.

273 *do so from the west:* Arrian 7.17.5.

273 *cardinal directions, like eclipses:* Ross, "Belephantes to Alexander," 100.

273 *marshy and full of pools:* Arrian 7.17.6; Van der Spek, "Darius III, Alexander the Great and Babylonian Scholarship," 334–35.

273 *the priests' warnings:* Arrian 7.17.6.

273 *a king's death:* Van der Spek, "Darius III, Alexander the Great and Babylonian Scholarship"; Ross, "Belephantes to Alexander"; Smelik, "'Omina Mortis,'" 93–96.

Chapter Nineteen: Babylon

274 *city his capital:* Strabo 15.2.9; Wilhelm Völcker-Janssen, *Kunst und Gesellschaft an den Höfen Alexanders d. Gr. und seiner Nachfolger* (Munich: Tuduv, 1993), 100–116.

274 *the time of Hammurabi:* Michael Seymour, *Babylon: Legend, History and the Ancient City* (London: I. B. Tauris, 2014), 9.

274 *some fifty thousand:* Tom Boiy, *Late Achaemenid and Hellenistic Babylon* (Dudley, MA: Peeters, 2004), 233.

275 *ten thousand souls:* Hansen, *Polis,* 76.

275 *a cosmopolitan place:* R. J. van der Spek, "Multi-ethnicity and Ethnic Segregation in Hellenistic Babylon," in *Ethnic Constructs in Antiquity: The Role of Power and Tradition,* ed. Ton Derks and Nico Roymans (Amsterdam: Amsterdam University Press, 2009), 103–7.

275 *the astronomer priests:* Boiy, *Late Achaemenid and Hellenistic Babylon,* 272–74, 297–303.

275 *the Pythagorean theorem:* Asger Aaboe, "Babylonian Mathematics, Astrology, and Astronomy," in *The Assyrian and Babylonian Empires and Other States of the Near East, from the Eighth to the Sixth Centuries BC,* ed. John Boardman et al., Cambridge Ancient History (Cambridge, UK: Cambridge University Press, 1992).

275 *transmitted to Aristotle:* Simplicius, *On Aristotle's On the Heavens* 2.12.

275 *its literary reputation:* Andrew Scheil, *Babylon Under Western Eyes: A Study of Allusion and Myth* (Toronto: University of Toronto Press, 2016).

275 *prominent architect, Deinokrates:* Plutarch 72.3–4; Bonna D. Wescoat, "The Patronage of Greek and Roman Architecture," in *The Oxford Handbook of Greek and Roman Art and Architecture,* ed. Clemente Marconi (Oxford, UK: Oxford University Press, 2014), 176–77.

275 *decorated cremation pyre:* Arrian 7.14.8–9; Diodorus Siculus 17.115.1–6; Plutarch 72.3–4; Olga Palagia, "Hephaestion's Pyre and the Royal Hunt of Alexander," in *Alexander the Great in Fact and Fiction,* ed. Elizabeth Baynham and A. B. Bosworth (Oxford, UK: Oxford University Press, 2010), 167–206; Jeanne Reames, "The Cult of Hephaestion," in *Responses to Oliver Stone's* Alexander: *Film, History, and Cultural Studies,* ed. Paul Cartledge and Fiona Greenland (Madison: University of Wisconsin Press, 2010), 183–216; Völcker-Janssen, *Kunst und Gesellschaft,* 100–116.

276 *three hundred years earlier:* Seymour, *Babylon,* 21.

276 *Constructed of baked bricks:* Hansjörg Schmid, *Der Tempelturm Etemenanki in Babylon* (Mainz: Verlag Philipp von Zabern, 1995), 47–48.

276 *of time and effort:* Arrian 3.16.4, 7.17.1–4; Strabo 16.1.5; Jennifer Finn, "Alexander's Return of the Tyrannicide Statues to Athens," *Historia: Zeitschrift für Alte Geschichte* 63, no. 4 (2014): 387–89; Amélie T. L. Kuhrt, "The Achaemenid Empire: A Babylonian Perspective," *Proceedings of the Cambridge Philological Society* 34 (1988): 68–71.

276 *"cleared the dust":* Arrian 7.17.2; Finn, "Alexander's Return," 389.

276 *issued food rations:* Tom Boiy, "Dating Methods during the Early Hellenistic Period," *Journal of Cuneiform Studies* 52, no. 1 (2000): 118n14; Finn, "Alexander's Return," 390.

276 *new mixed units:* Arrian 7.23.1–4; Bosworth, "Alexander and the Iranians," 18–20.

277 *plans for the cavalry:* Arrian 7.6.3–4.

277 *of the army elite:* Arrian 7.6.4–5.

277 *of ancient childbirth:* Nancy H. Demand, *Birth, Death, and Motherhood in Classical Greece* (Baltimore: Johns Hopkins University Press, 1994), 71–86.

278 *he cleaned canals:* Arrian 7.21.1–7; Strabo 16.1.10–11.

278 *water-management practices:* Briant, *From Cyrus to Alexander,* 719–23.

278 *full third of the food:* Herodotus 1.192.

278 *made the river passable:* Briant, *From Cyrus to Alexander,* 719–23.

278 *sent out three scouts:* Arrian 7.20.7–10; Jan Retso, *The Arabs in Antiquity: Their History from the Assyrians to the Umayyads* (Abingdon, UK: RoutledgeCurzon, 2003), 269–71.

278 *there were good harbors:* Arrian 7.20.3–5; Jean-François Salles, "The Arab Persian Gulf Under the Seleucids," in *Hellenism in the East: The Interaction of Greek and Non-Greek Civilizations from Syria to Central Asia After Alexander,* ed. Amélie Kuhrt and Susan Sherwin-White (London: Duckworth, 1987), 105–8.

278 *best supply of pearls:* Jean-François Salles, "Arab Persian Gulf," 80–82.

278 *valuable marine product:* Pliny, *Natural History* 9.54.

279 *fifteen tons of frankincense:* Plutarch 25.5.

279 *focused on the Gulf Coast:* Jan Retso, *Arabs in Antiquity,* 273.

279 *spices and precious gems:* Salles, "Arab Persian Gulf," 82–88.

279 *compulsion for conquest:* Arrian 7.19.6; Strabo 16.1.9.

279 *the sign of his rule:* Arrian 7.22.2–5; Diodorus Siculus 17.116.5–7; Arrian, *Anabasi di Alessandro,* 640–42.

280 *a Mesopotamian king:* Samuel K. Eddy, *The King Is Dead: Studies in the Near Eastern Resistance to Hellenism, 334–31 BC* (Lincoln: University of Nebraska Press, 1961), 106–12.

280 *signs were everywhere:* Van der Spek, "Darius III, Alexander the Great and Babylonian Scholarship," 289–97.

280 *their own way scientific:* Aaboe, "Babylonian Mathematics, Astrology, and Astronomy," 279–90.

280 *temple-dominated society:* Kuhrt, "Achaemenid Empire," 70.

281 *friends gathered around him:* Arrian 7.14.9; Diodorus Siculus 17.115.1.

281 *ten thousand victims:* Diodorus Siculus 17.115.6.

281 *his companions feasted:* Arrian 7.14.10; Diodorus Siculus 17.115.6–116.1.

282 *Babylon-focused history:* Van der Spek, "Darius III, Alexander the Great and Babylonian Scholarship"; Finn, "Alexander's Return."

282 *detailed a prophecy:* Van der Spek, "Darius III, Alexander the Great and Babylonian Scholarship," 338.

282 *another uncanny episode:* Arrian 7.21.1–3; Diodorus Siculus 17.116.2–4; Plutarch 73.3–4.

282 *described as a prisoner:* Diodorus Siculus 17.116.2–4; Plutarch 73.3–4.

282 *he claimed no motivation:* Arrian 7.21.1–3.

282 *mysterious, dangerous portent:* Paul McKechnie, "Omens of the Death of Alexander the Great" in *Alexander & His Successors: Essays from the Antipodes,* ed. Pat Wheatley and Robert Hannah (Claremont, CA: Regina Books, 2009), 206–26; Robin Lane Fox, "Alexander and Babylon: A Substitute King?" in *Alexander the Great and the East,* ed. Krzysztof Nawotka and Agnieszka Wojciechowska (Wiesbaden: Harrassowitz Verlag, 2016), 103–16.

282 *the substitute king:* Smelik, "'Omina Mortis'"; Van der Spek, "Darius III, Alexander the Great and Babylonian Scholarship," 338–39; cf. Ross, "Belephantes to Alexander," 96–99.

283 *third millennium BCE:* Claus Ambos, "Rites of Passage in Ancient Mesopotamia: Changing Status by Moving through Space: Bit Rimki and the Ritual of the Substitute King," *Rivista degli studi orientali* 86 (2013): 39.

283 *ritual was necessary:* Van der Spek, "Darius III, Alexander the Great and Babylonian Scholarship," 338–39.

283 *informed the king:* Kuhrt, *Persian Empire,* 622.

283 *was quickly executed:* Diodorus Siculus 17.116.4; Plutarch 74.1.

283 *Alexander fell ill:* Yardley and Atkinson, *Quintus Curtius Rufus,* 141–49.

283 *first of June, 323 BCE:* John Atkinson, Elsie Truter, and Etienne Truter, "Alexander's Last Days: Malaria and Mind Games?" *Acta Classica* 52 (2009): 25.

283 *to a drinking party:* Arrian 7.24.4; Diodorus Siculus 17.1171.1; Justin 12.13.7; Plutarch 75.3.

283 *well into the next day:* Plutarch 75.3.

283 *was already feverish:* Arrian 7.25.1; Plutarch 75.3–4; Alan E. Samuel, "Alexander's 'Royal Journals,'" *Historia: Zeitschrift für alte Geschichte* 14, no. 1 (1965): 3–6.

283 *summoned his physicians:* Diodorus Siculus 17.117.3.

283 *one palace to another:* Arrian 7.25.1–6; Plutarch 76.1–4.

284 *had to be carried:* Arrian 7.25.2; Plutarch 76.3.

284 *invasion of Arabia:* Arrian 7.25.2–5.

284 *suffering from malaria:* Donald Engels, "A Note on Alexander's Death," *Classical Philology* 73, no. 3 (1978): 224–28; David W. Oldach et al., "A Mysterious Death," *New England Journal of Medicine* 338, no. 24 (1998): 1767.

284 *bacteria-borne typhoid fever:* Oldach et al., "Mysterious Death."

284 *medical doctors from trying:* E.g., Oldach et al.

284 *tampered with his wine?:* Arrian 7.27.1–3; Diodorus Siculus 17.117.5–118.2; Plutarch 77.1–3; Justin 12.13.10–14.9; Metz Epitome 97–98; A. B. Bosworth, "The Death of Alexander the Great: Rumour and Propaganda," *Classical Quarterly* 21, no. 1 (1971): 112–36.

284 *he considered Antipater:* Arrian 7.27.1–2; Diodorus Siculus 17.117.1–2; Justin 12.14.1–8.

284 *scattered his ashes:* Plutarch 77.1–2.

284 *difficult to imagine:* Engels, "Note on Alexander's Death," 224.

285 *were growing frantic:* Arrian 7.26.1; Curtius 10.5.1–3; Justin 12.15.2–4; Plutarch 76.4.

285 *eleventh of June, 323 BCE:* L. Depuydt, "The Time of Death of Alexander the Great: 11 June 323 B.C. (−322), ca. 4:00–5:00 PM," *Die Welt des Orients* 28 (1997): 117–35.

Epilogue: Alexander's New World

286 *the staff of the library:* Andrew Erskine, "Culture and Power in Ptolemaic Egypt: The Museum and Library of Alexandria," *Greece & Rome* 43 (1995).

286 *center of Mediterranean trade*: Brian Gottesman, "Alexandria," in *Encyclopedia of World Trade: From Ancient Times to the Present,* ed. Cynthia Clark Northrup et al. (London: Taylor and Francis, 2004), 21.

286 *body of Alexander the Great*: Andrew Erskine, "Life after Death: Alexandria and the Body of Alexander," *Greece & Rome* 49, no. 2 (2002).

286 *Greek-style architecture:* J. McKenzie, *The Architecture of Alexandria and Egypt, c. 300 B.C. to A.D. 700* (New Haven, CT: Yale University Press, 2007).

286 *lighthouse of Alexandria:* McKenzie, 41–45.

286 *more than thirty miles*: Josephus, *Jewish War* 4.10.5.

286 *constructed by the Ptolemies:* Strabo 17.1.8.

286 *a funeral monument:* Curtius 10.5.4; Justin 12.15.7.

287 *instead to Vergina:* Pausanias 1.6.3.

287 *diverted the procession:* Diodorus Siculus 18.28.2–3; Curtius 10.10.20; Erskine, "Life after Death," 167–71.

287 *the banks of the Nile:* Diodorus Siculus 18.33.1–36.7.

287 *Ptolemy II Philadelphos:* Curtius 10.10.20 (Ptolemy I); Diodorus Siculus 18.28.3–5 (Ptolemy I); Pausanias 1.7.1 (Ptolemy II).

287 *the tombs of Ptolemy:* Strabo 17.1.8; Erskine, "Life after Death," 163–67.

287 *embalmed body's nose:* Cassius Dio 51.16.5.

288 *included Euclidean geometry:* J. V. Luce, "Greek Science in Its Hellenistic Phase," *Hermathena*, no. 145 (1988): 27–28.

288 *first editions of Homer:* Erskine, "Culture and Power in Ptolemaic Egypt," 45.

288 *produced the Septuagint:* Nina L. Collins, *The Library in Alexandria and the Bible in Greek* (Leiden: Brill, 2000).

288 *Manetho, an Egyptian priest:* Ian S. Moyer, *Egypt and the Limits of Hellenism* (Cambridge, UK: Cambridge University Press, 2011), 86–103.

288 *an international center:* Susan A. Stephens, *Seeing Double: Intercultural Poetics in Ptolemaic Alexandria* (Berkeley: University of California Press, 2003), 238–57.

288 *cults and statues proliferated:* Carlos Noreña, "Rituals and Memory: Hellenistic Ruler Cults in the Roman Empire," in *Cultural Memories in the Roman Empire,* ed. Carl Galinsky and Kenneth Lapatin (Los Angeles: Getty Publications, 2015).

288 *attained legendary status:* Haila Manteghi, "Alexander the Great in the Shāhnāmeh of Ferdowsī," in *The Alexander Romance in Persia and the East,* ed. Richard Stoneman, Kyle Erickson, and Ian Netton (Netherlands: Barkhuis, 2012).

288 *Marco Polo to Mary Renault:* Barbara Blythe, "Medieval and Renaissance Italian Receptions of the Alexander Romance Tradition," in *Brill's Companion to the Reception of Alexander the Great,* ed. Kenneth Royce Moore (Leiden: Brill, 2018); Elizabeth Baynham and Terry Ryan, "'The Unmanly Ruler': Bagoas, Alexander's Eunuch Lover, Mary Renault's *The Persian Boy,* and Alexander Reception," in *Brill's Companion to the Reception of Alexander the Great,* ed. Kenneth Royce Moore (Leiden: Brill, 2018).

289 *inspiration for empire builders:* Rachel Mairs, "The Men Who Would Be Alexander: Alexander the Great and His Graeco-Bactrian Successors in the Raj," in *Brill's Companion to the Reception of Alexander the Great,* ed. Kenneth Royce Moore (Leiden: Brill, 2018).

289 *a more jaundiced view:* A. K. Narain, "Alexander and India," *Greece & Rome* 12, no. 2 (1965).

291 *Buddhas and Bodhisattvas:* Marian Wenzel, *Echoes of Alexander the Great: Silk Route Portraits from Gandhara: A Private Collection* (London: Eklisa Anstalt, 2000).

291 *Hellenistic ruler Antiokhos I:* Susan M. Sherwin-White and Amélie Kuhrt, *From Samarkhand to Sardis: A New Approach to the Seleucid Empire* (Berkeley: University of California Press, 1993), 38–39.

292 *the conquered played:* Sherwin-White and Kuhrt.

292 *and military technology:* Jared M. Diamond, *Guns, Germs, and Steel: The Fates of Human Societies* (New York: W. W. Norton, 2005).

293 *their imperial subjects:* Caroline Elkins, *Legacy of Violence: A History of the British Empire* (New York: Alfred A. Knopf, 2022).

293 *bringing Greek learning:* Plutarch, *Moralia* 328d–f; Arrian 7.7.6–7.

293 *from those they ruled:* Carl Husemoller Nightingale, *Segregation: A Global History of Divided Cities* (Chicago: University of Chicago Press, 2012).

293 *argued—or simply assumed:* A. B. Bosworth, "Alexander and the Iranians," *Journal of Hellenic Studies* 100 (1980); Peter Green, *Alexander to Actium: The Historical Evolution of the Hellenistic Age* (Berkeley: University of California Press, 1990), 312–35.

293 *working with, and marrying:* Sherwin-White and Kuhrt, *From Samarkhand to Sardis;* Claudia Horst, "Politics and Hybrid Identities—The Greek Theatre in Hellenistic Babylon," in *Evidence Combined: Western and Eastern Sources in Dialogue,* ed. Raija Mattila, Sebastian Fink, and Sanae Ito (Vienna: Austrian Academy of Sciences Press, 2022); Willy Clarysse, "Ptolémées et temples," in *Le Décret de Memphis,* ed. Dominique Valbelle and Jean Leclant (Paris: De Boccard, 1999), 4–65); W. Peremans, "Les Lagides, les élites indigènes et la monarchie bicéphale," in *Le système palatial en Oriente, en Grèce et à Rome,* ed. E. Levy (Leiden: E. J. Brill 1987), 326–43.

Bibliography

Aaboe, Asger. "Babylonian Mathematics, Astrology, and Astronomy." In *The Assyrian and Babylonian Empires and Other States of the Near East, from the Eighth to the Sixth Centuries BC,* edited by John Boardman, I. E. S. Edwards, E. Sollberger, and N. G. L. Hammond, 276–92. Cambridge, UK: Cambridge University Press, 1992.

Abe, Takuji. "Proskynēsis: From a Persian Court Protocol to a Greek Religious Practice." *Tekmeria* 14 (2017–18): 1–45.

Abusch, Tzvi. "The Development and Meaning of the Epic of Gilgamesh: An Interpretive Essay." *Journal of the American Oriental Society* 121, no. 4 (2001): 614–22.

Ahmad, Tauqeer. "Cultural Impact of the Achaemenian on Ancient Pakistan." *South Asian Studies* 27, no. 1 (2012): 228–29.

Alden, Maureeen. "Lions in Paradise: Lion Similes in the Iliad and the Lion Cubs of Il. 18.318–22." *Classical Quarterly* 55, no. 2 (2005): 335–42.

Alexeyev, A. Yu. "The Scythians in Eurasia." In *Scythians: Warriors of Ancient Siberia,* edited by St. John Simpson and E. V. Stepanova, 20–26. London: British Museum, 2017.

Ali, Waqas, Arshad Javid, Ali Hussain, and Syed Mohsin Bukhari. "Diversity and Habitat Preferences of Amphibians and Reptiles in Pakistan: A Review." *Journal of Asia-Pacific Biodiversity* 11, no. 2 (2018): 173.

Allchin, F. Raymond. "The Urban Position of Taxila and Its Place in Northwest India-Pakistan." *Studies in the History of Art* 31 (1993): 69–81.

Ambos, Claus. "Rites of Passage in Ancient Mesopotamia: Changing Status by Moving through Space: Bit Rimki and the Ritual of the Substitute King." *Rivista degli Studi Orientali* 86 (2013): 39–54.

Amitay, Ory. *From Alexander to Jesus.* Berkeley: University of California Press, 2010.

———. "Vagantibus Graeciae Fabulis: The North African Wanderings of Antaios and Herakies." *Mediterranean Historical Review* 29, no. 1 (2014): 1–28.

Andronikos, Manolēs. *Vergina: The Royal Tombs and the Ancient City.* Athens: Ekdotike Athenon, 1984.

Anson, Edward M. *Alexander the Great: Themes and Issues.* London: Bloomsbury Academic, 2013.

———. "Macedonia's Alleged Constitutionalism." *Classical Journal* 80, no. 4 (1985): 303–16.

———. "Macedonian Judicial Assemblies." *Classical Philology* 103, no. 2 (2008): 135–49.

Antela Bernárdez, Borja. "La campaña de Alejandro: Esclavismo y dependencia en el espacio de conquista." *Actes du groupe de recherches sur l'esclavage depuis l'antiquité* 35, no. 1 (2015): 281–96.

Arora, Udai Prakash. "The Fragments of Onesikritos on India: An Appraisal." *Indian Historical Review* 32, no. 1 (2005): 35–102.

Arrian. *Anabasi di Alessandro*. Edited by Francesco Sisti and Andrea Zambrini. [Rome]: Fondazione Lorenzo Valla, 2001.

———. *The Landmark Arrian: The Campaigns of Alexander*. Edited by Pamela Mensch and James S. Romm. New York: Pantheon Books, 2010.

Asad, Muhammad Hassham Hassan Bin, Sabih Durre, Bashir Ahmad Choudary, Arooj Fatima Asad, Ghulam Muratza, and Izhar Hussain. "Compensatory Effects of Medicinal Plants of Pakistan Upon Prolongation of Coagulation Assays Induced by Naja Naja Karachiensis Bite." *Current Science* 106, no. 6 (2014): 870–73.

Ashley, James R. *The Macedonian Empire: The Era of Warfare Under Philip II and Alexander the Great, 359–323 B.C.* Jefferson, NC: McFarland, 1998.

Ashton, N. "Craterus Revisited." In *East and West in the World Empire of Alexander: Essays in Honour of Brian Bosworth,* edited by Pat Wheatley and E. J. Baynham, 107–16. Oxford, UK: Oxford University Press, 2015.

Atkinson, J. E. *A Commentary on Q. Curtius Rufus' Historiae Alexandri Magni, Books 5 to 7.2.* Amsterdam: A. M. Hakkert, 1994.

Atkinson, John, Elsie Truter, and Etienne Truter. "Alexander's Last Days: Malaria and Mind Games?" *Acta Classica* 52 (2009): 23–46.

Austin, Michael. "Alexander and the Macedonian Invasion of Asia: Aspects of the Historiography of War and Empire in Antiquity." In *War and Society in the Greek World,* edited by John Rich and Graham Shipley, 197–223. Leicester: Routledge, 1993.

Badian, Ernst. "The Administration of the Empire." *Greece & Rome* 12, no. 2 (1965): 166–82.

———. "Agis III." *Hermes* 95 (1967): 171–92.

———. "The Death of Parmenio." *Transactions and Proceedings of the American Philological Association* 91 (1960): 324–38.

———. "The Death of Philip II." *Phoenix* 17, no. 4 (1963): 244–50.

———. "The Deification of Alexander the Great." In *Ancient Macedonian Studies in Honor of Charles F. Edson,* edited by H. J. Dell, 27–71. Thessaloniki: Institute for Balkan Studies, 1981.

———. "The Eunuch Bagoas." *Classical Quarterly* 8, no. 3/4 (1958): 144–57.

———. "The First Flight of Harpalus." *Historia: Zeitschrift für Alte Geschichte* 9, no. 2 (1960): 245–46.

———. "Harpalus." *Journal of Hellenic Studies* 81 (1961): 16–43.

———. "Nearchus the Cretan." *Yale Classical Studies* 24 (1975): 147–70.

Balatti, Silvia. *Mountain Peoples in the Ancient Near East: The Case of the Zagros in the First Millennium BCE*. Wiesbaden: Harrassowitz Verlag, 2017.

Balsdon, J. P. V. D. "The 'Divinity' of Alexander." *Historia: Zeitschrift für Alte Geschichte* 1, no. 3 (1950): 363–88.

Banerji, Adrish Chandra. "The Mālavas." *Annals of the Bhandarkar Oriental Research Institute* 13, no. 3/4 (1931): 218–29.

Baratin, Charlotte. "Le grenier grec de Samarkand." 2009–12. https://hal.archives -ouvertes.fr/hal-00483708.

Barba, Federica. "The Fortified Cities of the Ganges Plain in the First Millennium B.C." *East and West* 54, no. 1/4 (2004): 223–50.

Baynham, E. J. "An Introduction to the Metz Epitome: Its Traditions and Value." *Antichthon* 29 (1995): 60–77.

Baynham, Elizabeth. "'The Abominable Quibble': Alexander's Massacre of Indian Mercenaries at Massaga." In *Theatres of Violence*, edited by Philip G. Dwyer and Lyndall Ryan, 27–37. London: Berghahn Books, 2012.

———. *Alexander the Great: The Unique History of Quintus Curtius*. Ann Arbor: University of Michigan Press, 1998.

———. "Alexander's Argyraspids: Tough Old Fighters or Antigonid Myth?" In *After Alexander: The Time of the Diadochi (323–281 BC)*, edited by Víctor Alonso Troncoso and Edward M. Anson, 110–20. Oxford, UK: Oxbow Books, 2013.

———. "Quintus Curtius Rufus on the 'Good King': The Dioxippus Episode in Book 9.7.16–26." In *Companion to Greek and Roman Historiography*, edited by John Marincola, 405–11. Oxford, UK: Blackwell Publishing, 2007.

———. "Why Didn't Alexander Marry Before Leaving Macedonia? Observations on Factional Politics at Alexander's Court in 336–334 B.C." *Rheinisches Museum für Philologie* 141, no. 2 (1998): 141–52.

Baynham, Elizabeth, and Terry Ryan. "'The Unmanly Ruler': Bagoas, Alexander's Eunuch Lover, Mary Renault's the Persian Boy, and Alexander Reception." In *Brill's Companion to the Reception of Alexander the Great*, edited by Kenneth Royce Moore, 615–39. Leiden: Brill, 2018.

Beaulieu, Marie-Claire. *The Sea in the Greek Imagination*. Philadelphia: University of Pennsylvania Press, 2016.

Beggiora, Stefano. "Indian Ethnography in Alexandrian Sources: A Missed Opportunity?" In *With Alexander in India and Central Asia: Moving East and Back to West*, edited by Claudia Antonetti and P. Biagi, 238–54. Oxford, UK: Oxbow Books, 2017.

Ben-Yehoshua, Shimshon, Carole Borowitz, and Lumír Ondřej Hanuš. *Frankincense, Myrrh, and Balm of Gilead: Ancient Spices of Southern Arabia and Judea*. Hoboken, NJ: John Wiley & Sons, 2011.

Berve, Helmut. *Das Alexanderreich auf prosopographischer Grundlage*. New York: Arno Press, 1973.

Besenval, Roland. "Le peuplement de l'ancienne Gédrosie, de la protohistoire à la période islamique: Travaux archéologiques récents dans le Makran pakistanais." *Comptes rendus des séances de l'année—Académie des inscriptions et belles-lettres* 138, no. 2 (1994): 513–35.

Besenval, Roland, Nicolas Engel, and Philippe Marquis. "Les travaux de la Délégation Archéologique Française en Afghanistan." *Revue archéologique*, no. 1 (2011): 172–88.

Biagi, Paolo. "Changing the Prehistory of Sindh and Las Bela Coast: Twenty-Five Years of Italian Contribution." *World Archaeology: Debates in World Archaeology* 43, no. 4 (2011): 523–37.

———. "Uneasy Riders: With Alexander and Nearchus from Pattala to Rhambakia." In *With Alexander in India and Central Asia: Moving East and Back to West*, edited by Claudia Antonetti and P. Biagi, 255–78. Oxford, UK: Oxbow Books, 2017.

Bichler, Reinhold. "On the Traces of Onesicritus: Some Historiographical Aspects of Alexander's Indian Campaign." In *The Historiography of Alexander the Great*, edited by Krzysztof Nawotka, Robert Rollinger, Josef Wiesehöfer, and Agnieszka Wojciechowska, 51–70: Wiesbaden: Harrassowitz Verlag, 2018.

Bigwood, J. M. "Aristotle and the Elephant Again." *American Journal of Philology* 114, no. 4 (1993): 537–55.

Blay, Frédéric Le. "Surgery." In *A Companion to Science, Technology, and Medicine in Ancient Greece and Rome,* edited by Georgia Irby. Hoboken, NJ: John Wiley & Sons, 2016.

Bliquez, Lawrence J. *The Tools of Asclepius: Surgical Instruments in Greek and Roman Times.* Studies in Ancient Medicine, vol. 43. Leiden: Brill, 2015.

Bloedow, E. F. "'That Great Puzzle in the History of Alexander': Back into 'the Primal Pit of Historical Murk.'" In *Rom und der griechische Osten: Festschrift für Hatto H. Schmitt zum 65 Geburtstag,* edited by Ch. Schubert and K. Brodersen, 23–41. Stuttgart: F. Steiner Verlag, 1995.

Bloedow, E. F., and H. M. Loube. "Alexander the Great Under Fire at Persepolis." *Klio* 79 (1997): 341–53.

Blythe, Barbara. "Medieval and Renaissance Italian Receptions of the Alexander Romance Tradition." In *Brill's Companion to the Reception of Alexander the Great,* 503–24, Leiden: Brill, 2018.

Boiy, Tom. "Dating Methods During the Early Hellenistic Period." *Journal of Cuneiform Studies* 52, no. 1 (2000): 115–21.

———. *Late Achaemenid and Hellenistic Babylon.* Dudley, MA: Peeters, 2004.

Borza, Eugene. "Anaxarchus and Callisthenes: Academic Intrigue at Alexander's Court." In *Ancient Macedonian Studies in Honor of Charles F. Edson,* edited by H. J. Dell, 73–86. Thessaloniki: Institute for Balkan Studies, 1981.

———. "Fire from Heaven: Alexander at Persepolis." *Classical Philology* 67, no. 4 (1972): 233–45.

———. *Makedonika,* edited by Carol G. Thomas. Claremont, CA: Regina Books, 1995.

———. "The Royal Macedonian Tombs and the Paraphernalia of Alexander the Great." *Phoenix* 41, no. 2 (1987): 105–21.

Bosworth, A. B. *Alexander and the East: The Tragedy of Triumph.* Oxford, UK: Clarendon Press, 1996.

———. "Alexander and the Iranians." *Journal of Hellenic Studies* 100 (1980): 1–21.

———. "Alexander the Great and the Decline of Macedon." *Journal of Hellenic Studies* 106 (1986): 1–12.

———. "Aristotle, India and the Alexander Historians." *Topoi Orient Occident* 3, no. 2 (1993): 407–24.

———. *Conquest and Empire: The Reign of Alexander the Great.* Cambridge, UK: Cambridge University Press, 1988.

———. "The Death of Alexander the Great: Rumour and Propaganda." *Classical Quarterly* 21, no. 1 (1971): 112–36.

———. *A Historical Commentary on Arrian's History of Alexander.* 2 vols. Oxford, UK: New York: Clarendon Press, 1980–1995.

———. "A Missing Year in the History of Alexander the Great." *Journal of Hellenic Studies* 101 (1981): 17–39.

———. "A New Macedonian Prince." *Classical Quarterly* 44, no. 1 (1994): 57–65.

———. "Strabo, India and Barbequed Brahmans." In *After Alexander: The Time of the Diadochi (323–281 BC),* edited by Víctor Alonso Troncoso and Edward M. Anson, 71–83. Oxford, UK: Oxbow Books, 2013.

Boucharlat, Rémy. "Southwestern Iran in the Achaemenid Period." In *The Oxford Handbook of Ancient Iran,* edited by Daniel Potts, 503–29. Oxford, UK: Oxford University Press, 2013.

———. "Susa: The Achaemenid Period." In *Encyclopaedia Iranica*, 2009. https://www.iranicaonline.org/articles/susa-iii-the-achaemenid-period.

———. "Suse, marché agricole ou relais du grand commerce." *Paléorient* 11, no. 2 (1985): 71–81.

Braund, David. *Rome and the Friendly King: The Character of the Client Kingship*. London: Croom Helm, 1984.

Briant, Pierre. "Alexander and the Persian Empire, Between 'Decline' and 'Renovation.'" In *Alexander the Great: A New History*, edited by Waldemar Heckel and Lawrence A. Tritle, 171–88. Chichester, UK: Wiley-Blackwell, 2009.

———. *Alexander the Great and His Empire: A Short Introduction*. Princeton, NJ: Princeton University Press, 2010.

———. "Alexandre à Troie: Images, mythe et realia." In *The Historiography of Alexander the Great*, edited by Krzysztof Nawotka, Robert Rollinger, Josef Wiesehöfer, and Agnieszka Wojciechowska, 9–20. Wiesbaden: Harrassowitz Verlag, 2018.

———. "'Brigandage,' dissidence et conquête en asie achéménide et hellénistique." *Dialogues d'histoire ancienne* 2, no. 1 (1976): 163–259.

———. *Darius in the Shadow of Alexander*. Cambridge, MA: Harvard University Press, 2015.

———. "The Empire of Darius III in Perspective." In *Alexander the Great: A New History*, edited by Waldemar Heckel and Lawrence A. Tritle, 141–70. Chichester, UK: Wiley-Blackwell, 2009.

———. *From Cyrus to Alexander: A History of the Persian Empire*. Winona Lake, IN: Eisenbrauns, 2002.

———. *Rois, tributs et paysans: Études sur les formations tributaires du Moyen-Orient ancien*. Paris: Les Belles Lettres, 1982.

Brice, Lee. "Military Unrest in the Age of Philip and Alexander of Macedon: Defining the Terms of Debate." In *Greece, Macedon and Persia*, edited by Timothy Howe, 69–76. Oxford, UK: Oxbow Books, 2015.

Brinkmann, Vinzenz. "The Blue Eyes of the Persians: The Colored Sculpture of the Time of Alexander and the Hellenistic Period." In *Gods in Color: Painted Sculpture of Classical Antiquity*, edited by Vinzenz Brinkmann and Raimund Wünsche, 151–67. Munich: Stiftung Archäologie, 2007.

Britannica Academic. s.v. "Hamadan." 2018.

Brosius, Maria. "New Out of Old? Court and Court Ceremonies in Achaemenid Persia." In *The Court and Court Society in Ancient Monarchies*, edited by Antony Spawforth, 17–57. Cambridge, UK: Cambridge University Press, 2007.

———. *Women in Ancient Persia, 559–331 BC*. Oxford, UK: Clarendon Press, 1996.

Brown, Stuart. s.v. "Ecbatana." In *Encyclopedia Iranica*, 80–84, 1996. http://www.iranicaonline.org/articles/ecbatana.

Brown, Truesdell S. "Callisthenes and Alexander." *American Journal of Philology* 70, no. 3 (1949): 225–48.

———. "The Merits and Weaknesses of Megasthenes." *Phoenix* 11, no. 1 (1957): 12–24.

———. *Onesicritus: A Study in Hellenistic Historiography*. Berkeley: University of California Press, 1949.

Brunt, P. A. "The Aims of Alexander." *Greece & Rome* 12, no. 2 (1965): 205–15.

———. *Arrian: Anabasis of Alexander*. Cambridge, MA: Harvard University Press, 1976.

Burn, A. R. "The Generalship of Alexander." *Greece & Rome* 12, no. 2 (1965): 140–54.

Callieri, Pierfrancesco. s.v. "India iii: Relations: Achaemenid Period." In *Encyclopaedia Iranica*, 10–13, 2006. https://www.iranicaonline.org/articles/india-iii-relations -achaemenid-period.

Camp, John. *The Archaeology of Athens.* New Haven, CT: Yale University Press, 2001.

Carney, Elizabeth. "Alexander and Persian Women." *American Journal of Philology* 117, no. 4 (1996): 563–83.

———. "Artifice and Alexander History." In *Alexander the Great in Fact and Fiction*, edited by E. J. Baynham and A. B. Bosworth, 263–85. Oxford, UK: Oxford University Press, 2000.

———. "The Conspiracy of Hermolaus." *Classical Journal* 76, no. 3 (1981): 223–31.

———. "The Death of Clitus." *Greek, Roman and Byzantine Studies* 22, no. 2 (1981): 149.

———. *King and Court in Ancient Macedonia: Rivalry, Treason and Conspiracy.* Swansea: Classical Press of Wales, 2015.

———. "Macedonians and Mutiny: Discipline and Indiscipline in the Army of Philip and Alexander." *Classical Philology* 91, no. 1 (1996): 19–44.

———. *Olympias: Mother of Alexander the Great.* New York: Routledge, 2006.

———. "The Politics of Polygamy: Olympias, Alexander and the Murder of Philip." *Historia: Zeitschrift für Alte Geschichte* 41, no. 2 (1992): 169–89.

———. *Women and Monarchy in Macedonia.* Norman: University of Oklahoma Press, 2000.

Caro, Robert A. *Working: Researching, Interviewing, Writing.* New York: Alfred A. Knopf, 2019.

Chaniotis, Angelos. *War in the Hellenistic World: A Social and Cultural History.* Malden, MA: Blackwell Publishing, 2005.

Chrissanthos, Stefan G. "Caesar and the Mutiny of 47 B.C." *Journal of Roman Studies* 91 (2001): 63–75.

Chugunov, K. V., T. V. Rjabkova, and St. John Simpson. "Mounted Warriors." In *Scythians: Warriors of Ancient Siberia*, edited by St. John Simpson and E. V. Stepanova, 192–201. London: British Museum, 2017.

Clarysse, Willy. "Ptolémées et temples." In *Le Décret de Memphis*, edited by Dominique Valbelle and Jean Leclant, 41–65. Paris: De Boccard, 1999.

Cohen, Ada. *The Alexander Mosaic: Stories of Victory and Defeat.* Cambridge, UK: Cambridge University Press, 1997.

Colburn, Henry P. "Connectivity and Communication in the Achaemenid Empire." *Journal of the Economic and Social History of the Orient* 56, no. 1 (2013): 29–52.

Cole, Susan Guettel. "Finding Dionysus." In *A Companion to Greek Religion*, edited by Daniel Ogden. Oxford, UK: Blackwell Publishing, 2007, 325–41.

Collins, Andrew. "Alexander and the Persian Court Chiliarchy." *Historia: Zeitschrift für Alte Geschichte* 61, no. 2 (2012): 159–67.

———. "Alexander's Visit to Siwah: A New Analysis." *Phoenix (Toronto)* 68, no. 1/2 (2014): 62–77.

———. "The Persian Royal Tent and Ceremonial of Alexander the Great." *Classical Quarterly* 67, no. 1 (2017): 71–76.

———. "The Royal Costume and Insignia of Alexander the Great." *American Journal of Philology* 133, no. 3 (2012): 371–402.

Collins, Nina L. *The Library in Alexandria and the Bible in Greek.* Leiden: Brill, 2000.

Crescioli, Lorenzo. "The Scythians and the Eastern Limits of the Greek Influence: The Pazyryk Culture and Its Foreign Artistic Influences." In *With Alexander in India and Central Asia: Moving East and Back to West,* edited by Paolo Biagi and Claudia Antonetti, 122–51. Oxford, UK: Oxbow Books, 2017.

Davis, Todd. "Archery in Archaic Greece." Ph.D. diss., Columbia University, 2013.

Davis-Kimball, Jeannine. "Asia Central Steppes." In *Encyclopedia of Archaeology,* edited by Deborah M. Pearsall, 532–53. Oxford, UK: Academic Press, 2008.

Demand, Nancy H. *Birth, Death, and Motherhood in Classical Greece.* Ancient Society and History. Baltimore: Johns Hopkins University Press, 1994.

Depuydt, L. "The Time of Death of Alexander the Great: 11 June 323 B.C. (–322), Ca. 4:00–5:00 pm." *Die Welt des Orients* 28 (1997): 117–35.

Deslauriers, Marguerite. "Women, Education, and Philosophy." In *Companion to Women in the Ancient World,* edited by Sharon L. James and Sheila Dillon, 343–53. Oxford, UK: Wiley-Blackwell, 2012.

Devine, A. M. "The Battle of Hydaspes: A Tactical and Source-Critical Study." *Ancient World* 16, no. 3 (1987): 91–112.

Diamond, Jared M. *Guns, Germs, and Steel: The Fates of Human Societies.* New York: W. W. Norton, 2005.

Dmitriev, Sviatoslav. "Alexander's Exiles Decree." *Klio* 86, no. 2 (2004): 348–81.

Douglas, L. Cairns. "Hybris, Dishonour, and Thinking Big." *Journal of Hellenic Studies* 116 (1996): 1–32.

Dover, Kenneth. *Greek Homosexuality.* London: Duckworth, 1978.

Droysen, Johann Gustav. *History of Alexander the Great.* Edited by Flora Kimmich. Philadelphia: American Philosophical Society, 2012.

Dupree, Nancy Hatch. *An Historical Guide to Afghanistan.* Kabul: Afghan Tourist Organization, 1971.

Dusinberre, Elspeth R. M. "Satrapal Sardis: Achaemenid Bowls in an Achaemenid Capital." *American Journal of Archaeology* 103, no. 1 (1999): 73–102.

Ebbinghaus, Susanne. "Feasting Like the Persian King." In *Animal-Shaped Vessels in the Ancient World: Drinking with Gods, Heroes, and Kings,* edited by Susanne Ebbinghaus, 136–84. Cambridge, MA: Harvard University Press, 2018.

Eddy, Samuel K. *The King Is Dead: Studies in the Near Eastern Resistance to Hellenism, 334–31 BC.* Lincoln: University of Nebraska Press, 1961.

Edmonds, Lowell. "The Religiosity of Alexander." *Greek, Roman and Byzantine Studies* 12, no. 3 (1971): 363–91.

Eggermont, P. H. L. "Alexander's Campaign in Gandhāra and Ptolemy's List of Indo-Scythian Towns." *Orientalia Lovaniensia Periodica* 1 (1970): 63–125.

———. *Alexander's Campaigns in Sind and Baluchistan and the Siege of the Brahmin Town of Harmatelia.* Leuven: Leuven University Press, 1975.

———. *Alexander's Campaigns in Southern Punjab.* Leuven: Uitgeverij Peeters en Departement Oriëntalistiek, 1993.

Ehrenberg, Victor, and Ruth Fraenkel von Velsen. *Alexander and the Greeks.* Oxford, UK: Basil Blackwell, 1938.

Elkins, Caroline. *Legacy of Violence: A History of the British Empire.* New York: Alfred A. Knopf, 2022.

Ellis, J. R. "The Assassination of Philip II." In *Ancient Macedonian Studies in Honour of C. F. Edson,* edited by H. J. Dell, 99–137. Thessaloniki: Institute for Balkan Studies, 1981.

Encyclopaedia Britannica. s.v. "Mount Olympus." 2018. https://www.britannica.com /place/Mount-Olympus-mountain-Greece.

Engels, Donald. *Alexander the Great and the Logistics of the Macedonian Army.* Berkeley: University of California Press, 1978.

———. "Logistics: Sinews of War." In *The Oxford Handbook of Warfare in the Classical World,* edited by Brian Campbell and Lawrence A. Tritle. Oxford: Oxford University Press, 2013.

———. "A Note on Alexander's Death." *Classical Philology* 73, no. 3 (1978): 224–28.

Engels, Johannes. "Macedonians and Greeks." In *A Companion to Ancient Macedonia,* edited by Joseph Roisman and Ian Worthington, 81–98. Chichester, UK: Wiley-Blackwell, 2010.

Errington, R. M. "The Nature of the Macedonian State Under the Monarchy." *Chiron* 8 (1978): 77–133.

Erskine, Andrew. "Culture and Power in Ptolemaic Egypt: The Museum and Library of Alexandria." *Greece & Rome* 43 (1995): 38–48.

———. "Life after Death: Alexandria and the Body of Alexander." *Greece & Rome* 49, no. 2 (2002): 163–79.

Finn, Jennifer. "Alexander's Return of the Tyrannicide Statues to Athens." *Historia: Zeitschrift für Alte Geschichte* 63, no. 4 (2014): 385–403.

Fleming, David. "Where Was Achaemenid India?" *Bulletin of the Asia Institute* 7 (1993): 67–72.

Flower, Michael A. "Alexander the Great and Panhellenism." In *Alexander the Great in Fact and Fiction,* edited by E. J. Baynham and A. B. Bosworth, 96–135. Oxford: Oxford University Press, 2000.

Fox, Robin Lane. "Alexander and Babylon: a Substitute King?" In *Alexander the Great and the East,* edited by Krzysztof Nawotka and Agnieszka Wojciechowska, 103–16. Wiesbaden: Harrassowitz Verlag, 2016.

Francfort, Henri-Paul. "Scythians, Persians, Greeks and Horses: Reflections on Art, Culture, Power and Empires in the Light of Frozen Burials and Other Excavations." In *Masters of the Steppe: The Impact of the Scythians and Later Nomad Societies of Eurasia,* edited by Svetlana V. Pankova and John Simpson, 134–55. Oxford: Archaeopress, 2020.

Franks, Hallie. *Hunters, Heroes, Kings: The Frieze of Tomb II at Vergina.* Princeton, NJ: American School of Classical Studies at Athens, 2012.

———. *The World Underfoot: Mosaics and Metaphor in the Greek Symposium.* New York: Oxford University Press, 2018.

Fraser, P. M. *Cities of Alexander the Great.* Oxford: Clarendon Press, 1996.

Fredricksmeyer, E. A. "The Ancestral Rites of Alexander the Great." *Classical Philology* 61, no. 3 (1966): 179–82.

Fulińska, Agnieszka. "The Great, Son of the Great: Alexander—Son of Darius?" In *Alexander the Great and the East,* edited by Krzysztof Nawotka and Agnieszka Wojciechowska, 223–44. Wiesbaden: Harrassowitz Verlag, 2016.

Fuller, J. F. C. *The Generalship of Alexander the Great.* New Brunswick, NJ: Rutgers University Press, 1960.

Fussman, Gérard. "Taxila: The Central Asian Connection." *Studies in the History of Art* 31 (1993): 83–100.

Gabriel, Richard A. *Man and Wound in the Ancient World: A History of Military Medicine from Sumer to the Fall of Constantinople.* Washington, DC: Potomac Books, 2012.

Gagarin, Michael. "Greek Oratory." In *Dinarchus, Hyperides, and Lycurgus,* edited by Ian Worthington, Craig Cooper, Edward M. Harris, and Michael Gagarin, ix-xxviii. Austin: University of Texas Press, 2001.

Garland, Robert. *Wandering Greeks: The Ancient Greek Diaspora from the Age of Homer to the Death of Alexander the Great.* Princeton, NJ: Princeton University Press, 2014.

Garnsey, Peter. *Food and Society in Classical Antiquity.* Cambridge, UK: Cambridge University Press, 1999.

Garzilli, Enrica. "First Greek and Latin Documents on Sahagamana and Some Connected Problems (Part 1)." *Indo-Iranian Journal* 40, no. 3 (1997): 205–43.

Gentili, Paolo. "Opis e le altre." *Studi Classici e Orientali* 51 (2005): 25–53.

Glazebrook, Allison, and Kelly Olson. *Greek and Roman Marriage.* Chichester, UK: John Wiley & Sons, 2013.

Glover, Richard. "The Elephant in Ancient War." *Classical Journal* 39, no. 5 (1944): 257–69.

Gómez-Díaz, Donato. "Cholera: First through Third Pandemics, 1816–1861." In *Encyclopedia of Pestilence, Pandemics, and Plagues,* edited by Joseph P. Byrne, 96–105. Westport, CT: Greenwood Press, 2008.

Gottesman, Brian. "Alexandria." In *Encyclopedia of World Trade: from Ancient Times to the Present,* edited by Cynthia Clark Northrup, Jerry H. Bentley Jr., Alfred E. Eckes, Patrick Manning, Kenneth Pomeranz, Steven Topik, and Spencer Tucker, 21–22. London: Taylor and Francis, 2004.

Green, Peter. *Alexander of Macedon, 356–323 B.C.: A Historical Biography.* Berkeley: University of California Press, 2012.

———. *Alexander to Actium: The Historical Evolution of the Hellenistic Age.* Berkeley: University of California Press, 1990.

Greenwalt, William. "Macedonia, Illyria and Epirus." In *A Companion to Macedonia,* edited by Joseph Roisman and Ian Worthington, 279–305. Chichester, UK: Wiley-Blackwell, 2010.

———. "The Marriageability Age at the Argead Court: 360–317 B.C." *The Classical World* 82, no. 2 (1988): 93–97.

———. "Philip II and Olympias on Samothrace: A Clue to Macedonian Politics During the 360s." In *Macedonian Legacies: Studies in Ancient Macedonian History and Culture in Honor of Eugene N. Borza,* edited by Timothy Howe and Jeanne Reames, 79–106. Claremont, CA: Regina Books, 2008.

Grenet, Frantz. "Maracanda/Samarkand, une métropole pré-mongole: Sources écrites et archéologie." *Annales: Histoire, Sciences Sociales* 59, no. 5/6 (2004): 1043–67.

Gupta, Y., and S. Peshin. "Do Herbal Medicines Have Potential for Managing Snake Bite Envenomation?" *Toxicology International* 19, no. 2 (2012): 89–99.

Gygax, Marc Domingo. "Gift-Giving and Power Relationships in Greek Social Praxis and Public Discourse." In *The Gift in Antiquity,* edited by M. L. Satlow, 45–60. Hoboken, NJ: Wiley-Blackwell, 2013.

Habicht, Christian. "Athens, Samos, and Alexander the Great." *Proceedings of the American Philosophical Society* 140, no. 3 (1996): 397–405.

Hackin, Joseph. *Nouvelles recherches archéologiques à Begram, Ancienne Kâpicî, 1939–1940: Rencontre de trois civilisations, Inde, Grèce, Chine.* Paris: Impr. nationale, 1954.

Hall, Edith. *Inventing the Barbarian: Greek Self-Definition through Tragedy.* Oxford: Clarendon Press, 1989.

Hamilton, J. R. "The Cavalry Battle at the Hydaspes." *Journal of Hellenic Studies* 76 (1956): 26–31.

——. *Plutarch Alexander: A Commentary.* Oxford: Clarendon Press, 1969.

Hammond, N. G. L. "Alexander's Newly-Founded Cities." *Greek, Roman and Byzantine Studies* 39, no. 3 (1998): 243.

——. "The Archaeological and Literary Evidence for the Burning of the Persepolis Palace." *Classical Quarterly* 42 (1992): 358–64.

——. "The Branchidae at Didyma and in Sogdiana." *Classical Quarterly* 48, no. 2 (1998): 339–44.

——. *Philip of Macedon.* Baltimore: Johns Hopkins University Press, 1994.

——. "Royal Pages, Personal Pages, and Boys Trained in the Macedonian Manner During the Period of the Temenid Monarchy." *Historia: Zeitschrift für Alte Geschichte* 39, no. 3 (1990): 261–90.

——. "Some Passages in Polyaenus 'Stratagems' Concerning Alexander." *Greek, Roman and Byzantine Studies* 37, no. 1 (1996): 23.

Hammond, N., G. T. Griffith, and F. W. Walbank. *A History of Macedonia.* Oxford: Clarendon Press, 1972–1988.

Hansen, Mogens Herman. *Demography and Democracy: The Number of Athenian Citizens in the Fourth Century B.C.* Herning, Denmark: Systime, 1986.

——. *Polis: An Introduction to the Ancient Greek City-State.* Oxford: Oxford University Press, 2006.

Harding, Phillip. *Athens Transformed, 404–262 BC: From Popular Sovereignty to the Dominion of the Elite.* London: Routledge, 2015.

Hatzopoulos, Miltiadēs V. *Cultes et rites de passage en Macédoine.* Athènes: Kentron Hellēnikēs kai Rōmaïkēs Archaiotētos, Ethnikon Hidryma Ereunōn, 1994.

Havlík, Jakub. "*Terra Mulitplex et Varia Natura:* On the Settlement Patterns of Bactria in the Hellenistic Period." *Studia Hercynia* 25, no. 2 (2021): 9–41.

Haywood, John. *The Celts: Bronze Age to New Age.* London: Taylor and Francis, 2014.

Headrick, Daniel R. *Technology: A World History.* Oxford: Oxford University Press, 2009.

Heckel, Waldemar. "Alexander the Great and the Fate of the Enemy: Quantifying, Qualifying, and Categorizing Atrocities." In *The Many Faces of War in the Ancient World*, edited by Waldemar Heckel, Sabine Müller, and Graham Wrightson, 233–67. Cambridge, UK: Cambridge University Press, 2015.

——. *Alexander's Marshals: A Study of the Macedonian Aristocracy and the Politics of Military Leadership.* 2nd ed. New York: Routledge, 2016.

——. "The Conspiracy against Philotas." *Phoenix* 31, no. 1 (1977): 9–21.

——. "Creating Alexander: The Official History of Kallisthenes of Olynthos." In *Celebrity, Fame, and Infamy in the Hellenistic World*, edited by Riemer A. Faber, 199–216. Toronto: University of Toronto Press, 2020.

——. "Leonnatos, Polyperchon and the Introduction of Proskynesis." *American Journal of Philology* 99, no. 4 (1978): 459–61.

——. "The 'Somatophylakes' of Alexander the Great: Some Thoughts." *Historia: Zeitschrift für Alte Geschichte* 27, no. 1 (1978): 224–28.

——. "Two Doctors from Kos?" *Mnemosyne* 34, no. 3/4 (1981): 396–98.

——. *Who's Who in the Age of Alexander the Great: Prosopography of Alexander's Empire.* Malden, MA: Blackwell, 2006.

Heckel, Waldemar, Timothy Howe, and Sabine Müller. "'The Giver of the Bride, the Bridegroom, and the Bride': A Study of the Murder of Philip II and Its Aftermath." In *Ancient Historiography on War and Empire,* edited by Timothy Howe, Sabine Müller, and Richard Stoneman, 92–124. Oxford: Oxbow Books, 2017.

Heisserer, A. J., and R. Hodot. "The Mytilenean Decree on Concord." *Zeitschrift für Papyrologie und Epigraphik* 63 (1986): 109–28.

Henkelman, Wouter F. M., and Margaretha L. Folmer. "*Your Tally Is Full!* On Wooden Credit Records in and After the Achaemenid Empire." In *Silver, Money and Credit: A Tribute to Robartus J. Van Der Spek on the Occasion of His 65th Birthday,* edited by Kristin Kleber and Reinhard Pirngruber, 133–239. Leiden: Nederlands Instituut voor het Nabije Oosten, 2016.

Henkelman, Wouter F. M. "Administrative Realities: The Persepolis Archives and the Archaeology of the Achaemenid Heartland." In *The Oxford Handbook of Ancient Iran,* edited by Daniel Potts, 529–53. Oxford: Oxford University Press, 2013.

——. "'Consumed Before the King': The Table of Darius, That of Irdabama and Irtaštuna, and That of His Satrap, Karkiš." In *Der Achämenidenhof: Akten Des 2 Internationalen Kolloquiums zum Thema "Vorderasien im Spannungsfeld Klassischer und Altorientalischer Überlieferungen," Landgut Castelen bei Basel, 23–25 Mai 2007,* edited by B. Jacobs and R. Rollinger, 667–775. Wiesbaden: Harrassowitz Verlag, 2010.

——. "Imperial Signature and Imperial Paradigm: Achaemenid Administrative Structure and System Across and Beyond the Iranian Plateau." *Classica et Orientalia* 17 (2017): 45–256.

——. *The Other Gods Who Are: Studies in Elamite-Iranian Acculturation Based on the Persepolis Fortification Texts.* Leiden: Nederlands Instituut voor het Nabije Oosten, 2008.

——. "Parnakka's Feast: Sip in Parsa and Elam." In *Elam and Persia,* edited by J. Alvarez-Mon and M. B. Garrison, 89–166. Winona Lake, IN: Eisenbrauns, 2011.

Henrichs, Albert. "Greek Maenadism from Olympias to Messalina." *Harvard Studies in Classical Philology* 82 (1978): 121–60.

Hitchings, Sam. "The Date of [Demosthenes] 17, 'On the Treaty with Alexander.'" *Harvard Studies in Classical Philology* 109 (2017): 167–97.

Hoff, Corinna. "The Mass Marriage at Susa in 324 Bc and Achaemenid Tradition." In *Sex and Gender in the Ancient Near East: Proceedings of the 47th Rencontre Assyriologique Internationale, Helsinki, July 2–6, 2001,* edited by S. Parpola and R. M. Whiting. Helsinki: Neo-Assyrian Text Corpus Project, 2002.

Holt, Frank Lee. *Alexander the Great and Bactria: The Formation of a Greek Frontier in Central Asia.* Leiden: E. J. Brill, 1988.

——. *The Treasures of Alexander the Great: How One Man's Wealth Shaped the World.* New York: Oxford University Press, 2016.

Horden, Peregrine, and Nicholas Purcell. *The Corrupting Sea: A Study of Mediterranean History.* Oxford: Blackwell Publishers, 2000.

Horst, Claudia. "Politics and Hybrid Identities—the Greek Theatre in Hellenistic Babylon." In *Evidence Combined: Western and Eastern Sources in Dialogue,* edited by Raija Mattila, Sebastian Fink, and Sanae Ito, 11–26. Vienna: Austrian Academy of Sciences Press, 2022.

Houston, Mary G. *Ancient Egyptian, Mesopotamian & Persian Costume.* Mineola, NY: Dover Publications, 2002.

Howland, Felix. "Crossing the Hindu Kush." *Geographical Review* 30, no. 2 (1940): 272–78.

Hunter, Virginia J. *Policing Athens: Social Control in the Attic Lawsuits, 420–320 B.C.* Princeton, NJ: Princeton University Press, 1994.

Hyland, Ann "Horses for War: Breeding and Keeping a Warhorse." In *The Oxford Handbook of Warfare in the Classical World,* edited by Brian Campbell and Lawrence A. Tritle, 493–510. Oxford: Oxford University Press, 2013.

Hyland, John O. *Persian Interventions: The Achaemenid Empire, Athens, and Sparta, 450–386 BCE.* Baltimore: Johns Hopkins University Press, 2018.

Iliakis, Michael. "Flipping the Coin: Alexander the Great's Bactrian-Sogdian Expedition from a Local Perspective." *Studia Hercynia* 25, no. 1 (2021): 34–47.

———. "Greek Mercenary Revolts in Bactria: A Re-appraisal." *Historia: Zeitschrift für Alte Geschichte* 62, no. 2 (2013): 182–95.

Ispahani, Mahnaz Z. "Baluchistan and Its Environs: The Motives for Access." In *Roads and Rivals: The Political Uses of Access in the Borderlands of Asia,* 31–82. Ithaca, NY: Cornell University Press, 1989.

Jawad, Alia. "Taxila: A Type Site of the Rich Cultural and Educational Heritage of Pakistan." *Journal of Asian Civilizations* 35, no. 2 (2012) Gale Academic OneFile (accessed September 11, 2023). https://link-gale-com.ezproxy.gc.cuny.edu/apps/doc/A335804416/AONE?u=cuny_gradctr&sid=bookmark-AONE&xid=81f75f6f.

Jones-Lewis, Molly. "Physicians and 'Schools.'" In *A Companion to Science, Technology, and Medicine,* edited by Georgia Irby. Hoboken, NJ: John Wiley & Sons, 2016.

Jouanna, Jacques, and Ph. J. van der Eijk. *Greek Medicine from Hippocrates to Galen: Selected Papers.* Leiden: Brill, 2012.

Karmarkar, R. D. "The First Greek Conqueror of India." *Annals of the Bhandarkar Oriental Research Institute* 31, no. 1/4 (1950): 239–49.

Karttunen, Klaus. "Gandhāra and the Greeks." *Bulletin of the Asia Institute* 23 (2009): 131–34.

Kazmi, Quddusi. "Marine Biodiversity of Pakistan." Zoological Congress of Pakistan, 2013.

Keegan, John. *The Mask of Command.* New York: Penguin Books, 1988.

Kegerreis, Christopher Michael. "Alexander the Explorer." Ph.D. diss., University of California, Santa Barbara, 2016.

Kern, Paul Bentley. *Ancient Siege Warfare.* Bloomington: Indiana University Press, 1999.

Khazeni, Arash. "The City of Balkh and the Central Eurasian Caravan Trade in the Early Nineteenth Century." *Comparative Studies of South Asia, Africa, and the Middle East* 30, no. 3 (2010): 463–72.

Klonoski, R. J. "Homonoia in Aristotle's Ethics and Politics." *History of Political Thought* 17, no. 3 (1996): 313–25.

Konstan, David. "Nemesis and Phthonos." In *Gestures: Essays in Ancient History, Literature, and Philosophy Presented to Alan L Boegehold,* edited by Geoffrey W. Bakewell and James P. Sickinger, 74–87. Oxford: Oxbow Books, 2003.

Kotlińska-Toma, Agnieszka. "On His Majesty's Secret Service—Actors at the Court of Alexander the Great." In *Alexander the Great and the East*, edited by Krzysztof Nawotka and Agnieszka Wojciechowska, 273–86. Wiesbaden: Harrassowitz Verlag, 2016.

Kottaridi, Angeliki. *Macedonian Treasures: A Tour Through the Museum of the Royal Tombs of Aigai*. Translated by Alexandra Doumas. Athens: Kapon Editions, 2011.

Koulakiotis, Elias. "Attic Orators on Alexander the Great." In *Brill's Companion to the Reception of Alexander the Great*, edited by Kenneth Royce Moore, 41–71. Leiden: Brill, 2018.

Kreimerman, Igor, and Débora Sandhaus. "Political Trends as Reflected in the Material Culture: A New Look at the Transition Between the Persian and Early Hellenistic Periods." In *Times of Transition: Judea in the Early Hellenistic Period*, edited by Sylvia Honigman, Christophe Nihan, and Oded Lipschits, 119–31. Unversity Park, PA: Penn State University Press, 2021.

Kubica, Olga. "The Massacre of the Branchidae: A Reassessment; The Post-Mortem Case in Defence of the Branchidae." In *Alexander the Great and the East*, edited by Krzysztof Nawotka and Agnieszka Wojciechowska, 143–50. Wiesbaden: Harrassowitz Verlag, 2016.

Kuhrt, Amélie. "The Achaemenid Empire: A Babylonian Perspective." *Proceedings of the Cambridge Philological Society* 214, no. 34 (1988): 60–76.

———. *The Persian Empire*. London: Routledge, 2007.

Kyle, Donald G. *Sport and Spectacle in the Ancient World*. Malden, MA: Blackwell, 2007.

———. *Sport and Spectacle in the Ancient World*. 2nd ed. Chichester, UK: John Wiley and Sons, 2015.

Lane Fox, Robin J. *Brill's Companion to Ancient Macedon: Studies in the Archaeology and History of Macedon, 650 BC–300 AD*. Leiden: Brill, 2011.

Lanni, Adriaan. "The Laws of War in Ancient Greece." *Law and History Review* 26, no. 3 (2008): 1–17.

Lawler, Andrew. "Edge of an Empire." *Archaeology* 64, no. 5 (2011): 42–47.

Lawler, Lillian Brady. "The Dance in Ancient Greece." *Classical Journal* 42, no. 6 (1947): 343–49.

Lazenby, J. F., and David Whitehead. "The Myth of the Hoplite's Hoplon." *Classical Quarterly* 46, no. 1 (1996): 27–33.

Le Guen, Brigitte "Theatre, Religion, and Politics at Alexander's Travelling Royal Court." In *Greek Theatre in the Fourth Century B.C.*, edited by Eric Csapo, Hans Rupprecht Goette, J. Richard Green, and Peter Wilson, 249–74. Berlin: De Gruyter, 2014.

Lee, John I. W. "Daily Life in Classical Greek Armies, c. 500–330 BCE." In *New Approaches to Greek and Roman Warfare*, edited by Lee Brice, 39–51. Newark, NJ: John Wiley and Sons, 2020.

———. "Xenophon and His Times." In *The Cambridge Companion to Xenophon*, edited by Michael A. Flower, 15–36. Cambridge, UK: Cambridge University Press, 2016.

Lehmann, Yves. "La théologie des mystères de Samothrace: Mythe, rites et philosophie." In *Les mystères: Nouvelles perspectives*, edited by Marc Philonenko, Yves Lehmann, and Laurent Pernot, 125–47. Turnhout, Belgium: Brepols, 2017.

Lewis, Robert A. "Early Irrigation in West Turkestan." *Annals of the Association of American Geographers* 56, no. 3 (1966): 467–91.

Lhuillier, Johanna, and Mutalib Hasanov. "Nouvelles recherches à Padayatak Tépé au Kashka-Daria (Ouzbékistan)." *Cahiers d'Asie Centrale* 21–22 (2013): 389–98.

Lhuillier, Johanna, and Marjan Mashkour. "Animal Exploitation in the Oases: An Archaeozoological Review of Iron Age Sites in Southern Central Asia." *Antiquity* 91, no. 357 (2017): 655–73.

Lilimpakē-Akamatē, Maria, ed. *The Archaeological Museum of Pella.* [Athens]: J. S. Latsis Public Benefit Foundation, 2011.

Lincoln, Bruce. *Religion, Empire, and Torture the Case of Achaemenian Persia, with a Postscript on Abu Ghraib.* Chicago: University of Chicago Press, 2007.

Loades, Mike. "Scythian Archery." In *Masters of the Steppe: The Impact of the Scythians and Later Nomad Societies of Eurasia,* edited by Svetlana V. Pankova and St. John Simpson, 258–67. Oxford: Archaeopress, 2020.

Longo, Oddone. "I Mangiatori di Pesci: Regime alimentare e quadro culturale." *Materiali e discussioni per l'analisi dei testi classici,* no. 18 (1987): 9–55.

Loraux, Nicole. *Tragic Ways of Killing a Woman.* Translated by Anthony Forster. Cambridge, MA: Harvard University Press, 1987.

Luce, J. V. "Greek Science in Its Hellenistic Phase." *Hermathena,* no. 145 (1988): 23–38.

Machinist, Peter. "The First Coins of Judah and Samaria: Numismatics and History in the Achaemenid and Early Hellenistic Periods." In *Continuity and Change: Proceedings of the Last Achaemenid History Workshop,* edited by H. Sancisi-Weerdenburg, Amélie Kuhrt, and Margaret Cool Root, 365–79. Leiden: Nederlands Institut voor het Nabije Oosten, 1994.

Magee, Peter, Cameron Petrie, Robert Knox, Farid Khan, and Ken Thomas. "The Achaemenid Empire in South Asia and Recent Excavations in Akra in Northwest Pakistan." *American Journal of Archaeology* 109, no. 4 (2005): 711–41.

Mairs, Rachel. *The Hellenistic Far East: Archaeology, Language, and Identity in Greek Central Asia.* 1st ed. Berkeley: University of California Press, 2014.

———. "The Hellenistic Far East: From the Oikoumene to the Community." In *Shifting Social Imaginaries in the Hellenistic Period,* edited by Eftychia Stavrianopoulou, 365–85. Leiden: Brill, 2013.

———. "The Men Who Would Be Alexander: Alexander the Great and His Graeco-Bactrian Successors in the Raj." In *Brill's Companion to the Reception of Alexander the Great,* edited by Kenneth Royce Moore, 576–95. Leiden: Brill, 2018.

Manteghi, Haila. "Alexander the Great in the Shāhnāmeh of Ferdowsī." In *The Alexander Romance in Persia and the East,* edited by Richard Stoneman, Kyle Erickson, and Ian Netton, 161–74. Groningen, Netherlands: Barkhuis, 2012.

Markham, C. R. "The Upper Basin of the Kabul River." *Proceedings of the Royal Geographical Society and Monthly Record of Geography* 1, no. 2 (1879): 110–21.

Markle, Minor M. "Macedonian Arms and Tactics Under Alexander the Great." *Studies in the History of Art* 10 (1982): 86–111.

———. "The Macedonian Sarissa, Spear, and Related Armor." *American Journal of Archaeology* 81, no. 3 (1977): 323–39.

———. "Use of the Sarissa by Philip and Alexander of Macedon." *American Journal of Archaeology* 82, no. 4 (1978): 483–97.

Marsden, Eric William. "Macedonian Military Machinery and Its Designers Under Philip and Alexander." In *Archaia Makedonia 2.* Thessaloniki: Institute for Balkan Studies, 1977.

Marshall, John Hubert. *A Guide to Taxila.* 4th ed. Cambridge, UK: For the Dept. of Archeology in Pakistan at the University Press, 1960.

Marti, James. s.v. "Monsoon." In *The Gale Encyclopedia of Science,* edited by K. Lee Lerner and Brenda Wilmoth Lerner, 2882–85. Detroit: Gale, 2014.

Martinez-Sève, Laurianne. "Ai Khanoum and Greek Domination in Central Asia." *Electrum* 22 (January 2015): 17–46.

———. "Les Grecs d'Extrême Orient: Communautés Grecques d'Asie Centrale et d'Iran." *Pallas* 89 (2012): 367–91.

Matthews, L. Harrison. *The Whale.* New York: Crescent Books, 1975.

McDowell, Robert H. "The Indo-Parthian Frontier." *American Historical Review* 44, no. 4 (1939): 781–801.

McKechnie, Paul. "Greek Mercenary Troops and Their Equipment." *Historia: Zeitschrift für alte Geschichte* 43, no. 3 (1994): 297–305.

———. "Omens of the Death of Alexander the Great." In *Alexander & His Successors: Essays from the Antipodes,* edited by Pat Wheatley and Robert Hannah, 206–26. Claremont, CA: Regina Books, 2009.

———. *Outsiders in the Greek Cities in the Fourth Century B.C.* London: Routledge, 1989.

McKenzie, J. *The Architecture of Alexandria and Egypt, c. 300 B.C. to A.D. 700.* New Haven, CT: Yale University Press, 2007.

Mehendale, Sanjyot. "Begram: Along Ancient Central Asian and Indian Trade Routes." *Cahiers d'Asie Centrale* (1996): 47–64.

Migeotte, Léopold. *The Economy of the Greek Cities from the Archaic Period to the Early Roman Empire.* Translated by Janet Lloyd. Berkeley: University of California Press, 2009.

Miller, Harvey F. "The Practical and Economic Background to the Greek Mercenary Explosion." *Greece & Rome* 31, no. 2 (1984): 153–60.

Miller, Stella G. *The Tomb of Lyson and Kallikles: A Painted Macedonian Tomb.* Mainz: P. von Zabern, 1993.

Millett, Paul. "The Political Economy of Macedonia." In *A Companion to Macedonia,* edited by Joseph Roisman and Ian Worthington, 472–504. Chichester, UK: Wiley-Blackwell, 2010.

Milns, R. D. "Alexander's Pursuit of Darius Through Iran." *Historia: Zeitschrift für Alte Geschichte* 15, no. 2 (1966): 256–56.

———. "Army Pay and the Military Budget of Alexander the Great." In *Zu Alexander d. Gr. Festschrift G. Wirth,* edited by W. Will and J. Heinrichs, 233–56. Amsterdam: Hakkert, 1987.

———. "Arrian's Accuracy in Troop Details: A Note." *Historia: Zeitschrift für Alte Geschichte* 27, no. 2 (1978): 374–78.

Mirhady, David C. "Torture and Rhetoric in Athens." *Journal of Hellenic Studies* 116 (1996): 119–31.

"Monsoon." In *UXL Encyclopedia of Weather and Natural Disasters,* edited by Amy Hackney Blackwell and Elizabeth Manar, 520–25. Detroit: Gale, 2016.

Morgan, Janett. "Entering the Hall of Mirrors: Macedonia and the Achaemenid Empire." In *Greek Perspectives on the Achaemenid Empire: Persia through the Looking Glass,* 255–92. Edinburgh: Edinburgh University Press, 2016.

Mors, W., M. C. Do Nascimento, Bmr Pereira, and Na Pereira. "Plant Natural Products Active Against Snake Bite—the Molecular Approach." *Phytochemistry* 55, no. 6 (2000): 627–42.

Mossman, J. M. "Tragedy and Epic in Plutarch's Alexander." *Journal of Hellenic Studies* 108 (1988): 83–93.

Mousavi, Ali. "La ville de Parsa: Quelques remarques sur la topographie et le système défensif de Persépolis." *Iranica Antiqua* 34 (1999): 145–55.

———. "Parsa, a Stronghold for Darius: A Preliminary Study of the Defence System of Persepolis." *East and West* 42, no. 2/4 (1992): 203–26.

———. *Persepolis: Discovery and Afterlife of a World Wonder.* Boston: De Gruyter, 2012.

Moyer, Ian S. *Egypt and the Limits of Hellenism.* Cambridge, UK: Cambridge University Press, 2011.

Muccioli, Federicomaria. "Classical Sources and *Proskynesis*: History of a Misunderstanding." In *Alexander's Legacy: Atti Del Convegno Università Cattolica Del Sacro Cuore Milano 2015,* edited by Cinzia Bearzot and Franca Landucci, 41–59. Rome: "L'Erma" di Bretschneider, 2016.

———. "Peucesta, tra lealismo Macedone e modello Persiano." *Electrum: Studia z historii starożytnej* 24, no. 24 (2017): 75–91.

Müller, Sabine. "Drypetis in Fact and (Fan) Fiction." In *Orientalism and the Reception of Powerful Women from the Ancient World,* edited by Fillipo Carla-Uhink and Anja Weber, 57–69. London: Bloomsbury Academic, 2020.

———. "The Female Element of the Political Self-Fashioning of the Diadochi: Ptolemy, Seleucus, Lysimachus, and Their Iranian Wives." In *After Alexander: The Time of the Diadochi (323–281 BC),* edited by Víctor Alonso Troncoso and Edward M. Anson. 199–214: Oxford: Oxbow Books, 2013.

———. "Philip II." In *A Companion to Ancient Macedonia,* edited by Joseph Roisman and Ian Worthington, 166–85. Chichester, UK: Wiley-Blackwell, 2010.

———. "Stories of the Persian Bride: Alexander and Roxane." In *The Alexander Romance in Persia and the East,* edited by Ian Richard Netton, Kyle Erickson, and Richard Stoneman, 295–309. Groningen: Barkhuis, 2012.

Müller, Sabine, and Beatrice Poletti. "Hephaistion—a Re-Assessment of His Career." In *Ancient Macedonians in Greek and Roman Sources,* edited by Timothy Howe and Frances Pownall, 77–102. Swansea: Classical Press of Wales, 2018.

Nagle, D. Brendan. "The Cultural Context of Alexander's Speech at Opis." *Transactions of the American Philological Association (1974)* 126 (1996): 151–72.

Narain, A. K. "Alexander and India." *Greece & Rome* 12, no. 2 (1965): 155–65.

Neelis, Jason. "Trade Networks in Ancient South Asia." In *Early Buddhist Transmission and Trade Networks: Mobility and Exchange Within and Beyond the Northwestern Borderlands of South Asia,* 183–228. Leiden: Brill, 2011.

Nervegna, Sebastiana. "Lycurgus, Alexander the Great, and the Texts of Greek Tragedy." *Classical Philology* 115, no. 3 (2020): 578–85.

Nice, Alex. "The Reputation of the 'Mantis' Aristander." *Acta Classica* 48 (2005): 87–102.

Nightingale, Carl Husemoller. *Segregation: A Global History of Divided Cities.* Chicago: University of Chicago Press, 2012.

Noreña, Carlos. "Rituals and Memory: Hellenistic Ruler Cults in the Roman Empire." In *Cultural Memories in the Roman Empire,* edited by Carl Galinsky and Kenneth Lapatin, 86–100. Los Angeles: Getty Publications, 2015.

Nosch, Marie-Louise. "Voicing the Loom: Women, Weaving, and Plotting." In *Ke-Ra-Me-Ja,* edited by Dimitri Nakassis, Joann Gulizio, and Sarah A. James, 91–102. Philadelphia: INSTAP Academic Press, 2014.

Ogden, Daniel. "Alexander and Africa (332–331 BC and Beyond): The Facts, the Traditions and the Problems." *Acta Classica* 2014, no. sup-5 (2014): 1–37.

———. *Alexander the Great: Myth, Genesis and Sexuality.* Exeter: University of Exeter Press, 2011.

———. "Homosexuality and Warfare in Ancient Greece." In *Battle in Antiquity,* edited by Alan B. Lloyd, 107–68. London: Duckworth, 1996.

———. *Polygamy, Prostitutes and Death: The Hellenistic Dynasties.* London: Duckworth, with the Classical Press of Wales, 1999.

Olbrycht, Marek Jan. "'An Admirer of Persian Ways': Alexander the Great's Reforms in Parthia-Hyrcania and the Iranian Heritage." In *Excavating an Empire: Achaemenid Persia in Longue Durée,* edited by Touraj Daryaee, Ali Mousavi, and Khodadad Rezakhani, 37–62. Costa Mesa, CA: Mazda Publishers, 2014.

———. "The Epigonoi: The Iranian Phalanx of Alexander the Great." In *The Many Faces of War in the Ancient World,* edited by Waldemar Heckel, Sabine Müller, and Graham Wrightson, 196–212. Cambridge, UK: Cambridge University Press, 2015.

———. "Macedonia and Persia." In *A Companion to Macedonia,* edited by Joseph Roisman and Ian Worthington, 342–69. Chichester, UK: Wiley-Blackwell, 2010.

———. "The Military Reforms of Alexander the Great During His Campaign in Iran, Afghanistan, and Central Asia." In *Miscellanea Eurasiatica Cracoviensia,* edited by C. Galewicz, J. Pstrusi´nska, and L. Sudyka, 309–21. Kraków: Księgarnia Akademicka, 2007.

Oldach, David W., R. Michael Benitez, Eugene N. Borza, and Robert E. Richard. "A Mysterious Death." *New England Journal of Medicine* 338, no. 24 (1998): 1764–69.

Olivelle, Patrick. *Ascetics and Brahmins: Studies in Ideologies and Institutions.* London: Anthem Press, 2011.

Olivieri, Luca M. "Notes on the Problematical Sequence of Alexander's Itinerary in Swat: A Geo-Historical Approach." *East and West* 46, no. 1/2 (1996): 45–78.

Owen, Lewis, Fosco Maraini, and Nigel John Roger Allan. s.v. "Hindu Kush." In *Britannica Academic.* 2009, https://academic-eb-com.central.ezproxy.cuny.edu/levels/collegiate/article/Hindu-Kush/110522.

Palagia, Olga. "Hephaestion's Pyre and the Royal Hunt of Alexander." In *Alexander the Great in Fact and Fiction,* edited by Elizabeth Baynham and A. B. Bosworth, 167–206. Oxford: Oxford University Press, 2010.

Pantermalēs, Dēmētrios. *Gods and Mortals at Olympus: Ancient Dion, City of Zeus.* New York: Alexander S. Onassis Foundation, 2016.

Parker, Robert. *On Greek Religion.* Ithaca, NY: Cornell University Press, 2011.

Paspalas, Stavros. "The Achaemenid Empire and the North-Western Aegean." *Ancient West and East* 5, no. 1 (2006): 90–120.

Pearson, Lionel. *The Lost Histories of Alexander the Great.* New York: American Philological Association, 1960.

Peremans, W. "Les Lagides, les élites indigènes et la monarchie bicéphale." In *Le système palatial en Oriente, en Grèce et à Rome,* edited by E. Levy, 326–43. Leiden: E. J. Brill, 1987.

Petsas, Photios M. *Pella, Alexander the Great's Capital.* Thessaloniki: Institute for Balkan Studies, 1978.

Philippson, Alfred. *Das Klima Griechenlands.* Bonn: F. Dümmler, 1948.

Pindar. *Siegesgesänge und Fragmente,* edited by Oskar Werner. Munich: Heimeran, 1967.

Pitt, E. M., and W. P. Richardson. "Hostile Inaction? Antipater, Craterus and the Macedonian Regency." *Classical Quarterly* 67, no. 1 (2017): 77–87.

Poddighe, Elisabetta. "Alexander and the Greeks: The Corinthian League." In *Alexander the Great: A New History,* edited by Waldemar Heckel and Lawrence A. Tritle, 99–120. Chichester, UK: Wiley-Blackwell, 2009.

Pownall, Frances, and Sarina Pal. "The Role of Greek Literature at the Argead Court." In *The History of the Argeads,* edited by Sabine Müller, Tim Howe, Hugh Bowden, and Robert Rollinger, 215–30. Wiesbaden: Harrassowitz Verlag, 2017.

Prakash, Buddha. "Poros." *Annals of the Bhandarkar Oriental Research Institute* 32, no. 1/4 (1951): 198–233.

Price, S. R. F. *Rituals and Power: The Roman Imperial Cult in Asia Minor.* Cambridge, UK: Cambridge University Press, 1984.

Prontera, Francesco. "The Indian Caucasus from Alexander to Eratosthenes." In *With Alexander in India and Central Asia: Moving East and Back to West,* edited by Claudia Antonetti and Paolo Biagi, 212–21. Oxford: Oxbow Books, 2017.

Puskás, Ildikó. "Magasthenes and the 'Indian Gods' Herakles and Dionysos." *Mediterranean Studies* 2 (1990): 39–47.

Quagliotti, Anna Maria. "Taxila." In *Oxford Art Online.* Oxford University Press, 2019, https://www.oxfordartonline.com/groveart/view/10.1093/gao/9781884446054.001 .0001/oao-9781884446054-e-7000083510.

Rance, Philip. "Health, Wounds, and Medicine in the Late Roman Army (250–600 CE)." In *New Approaches to Greek and Roman Warfare,* edited by Lee Brice. Hoboken, NJ: John Wiley & Sons, 2020.

Rapin, Claude. "Alexandre le Grand en Asie Centrale: Geographie et strategie de la conquete des Portes Caspiennes à l'Inde." In *With Alexander in India and Central Asia: Moving East and Back to West,* edited by Claudia Antonetti and Paolo Biagi, 37–121. Oxford: Oxbow Books, 2017.

———. "Aux origines de la cartographie: L'Empire Achéménide sous Darius I et Xerxès." *Ancient Civilizations from Scythia to Siberia* 24 (2018): 1–67.

———. "Du Caucase au Tanaïs: Les sources de Quinte-Curce à propos de la route d'Alexandre le Grand en 330–329 av. J.-C." In *L'histoire d'Alexandre selon Quinte-Curce,* edited by M. Mahé-Simon and J. Trinquier, 141–86. Paris: Armand-Colin, 2014.

———. "On the Way to Roxane." In *Zwischen Ost und West: Neue Forschung zum antiken Zentralasien,* edited by Gunvor Lindström, Svend Hansen, Alfried Wieczorek, and Michael Tellenbach, 43–82. Darmstadt: Verlag Philipp von Zabern, 2013.

———. "On the Way to Roxanne 2: Satraps and Hyparchs between Bactra and Zariaspa/ Maracanda." In *A Millennium of History: The Iron Age in Central Asia (2nd and 1st Millennia BC),* edited by Johanna Lhuillier and Nikolaus Boroffka, 257–98. Berlin: Dietrich Reimer Verlag, 2018.

Rapin, Claude, and Frantz Grenet. "How Alexander Entered India." *Afghanistan* 1, no. 1 (2018): 141–81.

Rapin, Claude, and Muhammadjon Isamiddinov. "Entre sédentaires et nomades: Les recherches de la Mission Archéologique Franco-Ouzbèke (Mafouz) de Sogdiane sur le site de Koktepe." *Cahiers d'Asie Centrale* 21/11 (2013): 113–33.

Reames, Jeanne. "An Atypical Affair? Alexander the Great, Hephaestion, and the Nature of Their Relationship." *Ancient History Bulletin* 13, no. 3 (1999): 81–96.

———. "Crisis and Opportunity: The Philotas Affair . . . Again." In *Macedonian Legacies: Studies in Ancient Macedonian History and Culture in Honor of Eugene N. Borza*, edited by Timothy Howe and Jeanne Reames, 165–81. Claremont, CA: Regina Books, 2008.

———. "The Cult of Hephaestion." In *Responses to Oliver Stone's Alexander: Film, History, and Cultural Studies*, edited by Paul Cartledge and Fiona Greenland, 183–216. Madison: University of Wisconsin Press, 2010.

———. "Hephaistion Amyntoros: Eminence Grise at the Court of Alexander the Great." Ph.D. diss., Pennsylvania State University, 1998.

———. "The Mourning of Alexander the Great." *Syllecta Classica* 12 (2001): 98–145.

Reid, H. Alistair. "Snakebite in the Tropics." *British Medical Journal* 3, no. 5614 (1968): 359–62.

Renard, Marcel, and Jean Servais. "A propos du Mariage d'Alexandre et de Roxane." *L'Antiquité Classique* 24, no. 1 (1955): 29–50.

Retsas, Spyros. "Alexander's (356–323 BC) Expeditionary Medical Corps 334–323 BC." *Journal of Medical Biography* 17, no. 3 (2009): 165–69.

Retso, Jan. *The Arabs in Antiquity: Their History from the Assyrians to the Umayyads.* Abingdon, UK: RoutledgeCurzon, 2003.

Richter, Daniel K. *Facing East from Indian Country: A Native History of Early America.* Cambridge, MA: Harvard University Press, 2001.

Roisman, Joseph. *Alexander's Veterans and the Early Wars of the Successors.* Austin: University of Texas Press, 2012.

———. "Classical Macedonia to Perdiccas III." In *A Companion to Macedonia*, edited by Joseph Roisman and Ian Worthington, 145–65. Chichester, UK: Wiley-Blackwell, 2010.

———. "Ptolemy and His Rivals in His History of Alexander." *Classical Quarterly* 34, no. 2 (1984): 373–85.

Roisman, Joseph, and Ian Worthington. *A Companion to Ancient Macedonia.* Malden, MA: Wiley-Blackwell, 2011.

Romm, James S. "Aristotle's Elephant and the Myth of Alexander's Scientific Patronage." *American Journal of Philology* 110, no. 4 (1989): 566–75.

———. *The Edges of the Earth in Ancient Thought: Geography, Exploration, and Fiction.* Princeton, NJ: Princeton University Press, 1992.

Root, Margaret Cool. "Achaemenid Imperial Architecture: Performative Porticoes of Persepolis." In *Persian Architecture and Kingship: Displays of Power and Politics in Iran from the Achaemenids to the Pahlavis*, edited by S. Babaie and T. Grigor, 1–63. London: I. B. Tauris, 2015.

Rop, Jeffrey. "All the King's Greeks: Mercenaries, Poleis, and Empires in the Fourth Century BCE." Ph.D. diss., Pennsylvania State University, 2013.

Rose, Charles Brian. "Troy and the Historical Imagination." *The Classical World* 91, no. 5 (1998): 405–13.

Rosen, Stephen Peter. *Societies and Military Power: India and Its Armies.* Ithaca, NY: Cornell University Press, 1996.

Ross, Micah T. "Belephantes to Alexander: an Astrological Report to a Macedonian King?" In *Alexander the Great and the East*, edited by Krzysztof Nawotka and Agnieszka Wojciechowska, 89–102. Wiesbaden: Harrassowitz Verlag, 2016.

Roy, Kaushik. *Hinduism and the Ethics of Warfare in South Asia: From Antiquity to the Present.* New York: Cambridge University Press, 2012.

Rtveladze, Edvard. "Monetary Circulation in Ancient Tokharistan." In *After Alexander: Central Asia Before Islam,* edited by Joe Cribb and Georgina Herrmann, 389–97. Oxford: British Academy, 2007.

Sabin, Philip, and Philip de Souza. "Battle." In *The Cambridge History of Greek and Roman Warfare.* Vol. 1, *Greece, the Hellenistic World and the Rise of Rome,* edited by Hans van Wees, Michael Whitby, and Philip Sabin, 399–460. Cambridge, UK: Cambridge University Press, 2007.

Salles, Jean-François. "The Arab Persian Gulf Under the Seleucids." In *Hellenism in the East: The Interaction of Greek and Non-Greek Civilizations from Syria to Central Asia after Alexander,* edited by Amélie Kuhrt and Susan Sherwin-White, 75–109. London: Duckworth, 1987.

Samuel, Alan E. "Alexander's 'Royal Journals.'" *Historia: Zeitschrift für alte Geschichte* 14, no. 1 (1965): 1–12.

Schachermeyr, Fritz. *Alexander der Grosse: Das Problem seiner Persönlichkeit und seines Wirkens.* Vienna: Verl. d. Österr. Akad. d. Wiss., 1973.

Schefold, Karl. *Die Urkönige, Perseus, Bellerophon, Herakles und Theseus in der klassischen und hellenistischen Kunst,* edited by Franz Jung. Munich: Hirmer, 1988.

Scheil, Andrew. *Babylon Under Western Eyes: A Study of Allusion and Myth.* Toronto: University of Toronto Press, 2016.

Schlingloff, Dieter. *Fortified Cities of Ancient India: A Comparative Study.* Cultural, Historical, and Textural Studies of South Asian Regions, edited by Frederico Squarcini. New York: Anthem Press, 2013.

Schmid, Hansjörg. *Der Tempelturm Etemenanki in Babylon.* Mainz: Verlag Philipp von Zabern, 1995.

Schmidt, Erich Friedrich. *Persepolis.* Chicago: University of Chicago Press, 1953.

Schmitt, Rüdiger. s.v. "Cadusii." In *Encyclopaedia Iranica.* 1990, https://www.iranicaonline.org/articles/cadusii-lat.

———. "Rhoxane." In *Encyclopaedia Iranica.* 2018, http://www.iranicaonline.org/articles/rhoxane-name.

Scullard, H. H. *The Elephant in the Greek and Roman World.* Ithaca, NY: Cornell University Press, 1974.

Sekunda, Nicholas. "The Macedonian Army." In *A Companion to Ancient Macedonia,* edited by Joseph Roisman and Ian Worthington, 446–71. Chichester, UK: Wiley-Blackwell, 2010.

Seymour, Michael. *Babylon: Legend, History and the Ancient City.* London: I. B. Tauris, 2014.

Shaffer, Jim G. "Reurbanization: The Eastern Punjab and Beyond." *Studies in the History of Art* 31 (1993): 53–67.

Shahbazi, A. Sh. s.v. "Army I. Pre-Islamic Iran." In *Encyclopedia Iranica,* 489–99, 1986. http://www.iranicaonline.org/articles/army-i.

Shahbazi, A. Shapur, and Robyn C. Friend. s.v. "Dance." In *Encyclopaedia Iranica,* 2011, https://www.iranicaonline.org/articles/dance-raqs#pt1.

Shahbazi, Shapur. s.v. "Clothing ii. In the Median and Achaemenid Periods." In *Encyclopaedia Iranica,* 2012. http://www.iranicaonline.org/articles/clothing-ii.

Shahram, Jalilian, and Fatemi Seyed Ali. "Women's Clothing in Ancient Iran (Case Study: Achaemenid Period)." *Tahqīqāt-i Farhangī-i Īrān* 4, no. 3 (2012): 1–22.

Shaked, Shaul. *Le satrape de Bactriane et son gouverneur: Documents Araméens du Ive s. avant notre ère provenant de Bactriane.* Paris: Editions De Boccard, 2004.

Sharma, R. S. *India's Ancient Past.* Delhi: Oxford University Press, 2007.

Shay, Jonathan, Max Cleland, and John McCain. *Odysseus in America: Combat Trauma and the Trials of Homecoming.* New York: Scribner, 2002.

Shayegan, M. Rahim. "Prosopographical Notes: The Iranian Nobility During and After the Macedonian Conquest." *Bulletin of the Asia Institute* 21 (2007): 97–126.

Sheppard, Ruth. *Alexander the Great at War: His Army, His Battles, His Enemies.* Oxford: Osprey, 2008.

Sherwin-White, Susan M., and Amélie Kuhrt. *From Samarkhand to Sardis: A New Approach to the Seleucid Empire.* Berkeley: University of California Press, 1993.

Shoshani, Jeheskel. *Elephants: Majestic Creatures of the Wild.* Emmaus, PA: Rodale Press, 1992.

Shrimpton, Gordon. "The Callisthenes Engima." In *Greece, Macedon, and Persia,* edited by Timothy Howe, Erin Garvin, and Graham Wrightson, 114–17. Oxford: Oxbow Books, 2015.

Simpson, St. John, and E. V. Stepanova. "Eating, Drinking and Everyday Life." In *Scythians: Warriors of Ancient Siberia,* edited by St. John Simpson and E. V. Stepanova, 154–63. London: British Museum, 2017.

———, eds. *Scythians: Warriors of Ancient Siberia.* London: British Museum, 2017.

Smelik, Willem. "The 'Omina Mortis' in the Histories of Alexander the Great." *Talanta* 10/11 (1978/79): 92–111.

Smith, R. R. R. *Hellenistic Royal Portraits.* Oxford: Clarendon Press, 1988.

Smith, Vincent A. "The Position of the Autonomous Tribes of the Panjāb Conquered by Alexander the Great." *Journal of the Royal Asiatic Society of Great Britain and Ireland* (1903): 685–702.

Spawforth, Antony. "The Court of Alexander the Great between Europe and Asia." In *The Court and Court Society in Ancient Monarchies,* edited by Antony Spawforth, 82–120. Cambridge, UK: Cambridge University Press, 2007.

Spooner, Brian. s.v. "Baluchistan: Geography, History, and Ethnography." In *Encyclopaedia Iranica,* 1988. https://www.iranicaonline.org/articles/baluchistan-i.

Sprawski, Slawomir. "The Early Temenid Kings to Alexander I." In *A Companion to Ancient Macedonia,* edited by Joseph Roisman and Ian Worthington, 127–44. Chichester, UK: Wiley-Blackwell, 2010.

Stahl, A. F. v. "Notes on the March of Alexander the Great from Ecbatana to Hyrcania." *Geographical Journal* 64, no. 4 (1924): 312–29.

Stebbins, Eunice Burr. *The Dolphin in the Literature and Art of Greece and Rome.* Menasha, WI: George Banta, 1929.

Stein, Aurel. "Alexander's Campaign on the Indian North-West Frontier: Notes from Explorations Between Upper Swāt and the Induṣ." *Geographical Journal* 70, no. 5 (1927): 417–40.

———. "Alexander's Campaign on the Indian North-West Frontier: Notes from Explorations Between Upper Swāt and the Induṣ (Continued)." *Geographical Journal* 70, no. 6 (1927): 515–40.

———. *An Archaeological Tour to Gedrosia: Memoirs of the Archaeological Survey of India.* Calcutta: Government of India Central Publication Branch, 1931.

———. "From Swat to the Gorges of the Indus." *Geographical Journal* 100, no. 2 (1942): 49–56.

———. "On Alexander's Route into Gedrosia: An Archaeological Tour in Las Bela." *Geographical Journal* 102, no. 5/6 (1943): 193–227.

Stephens, Susan A. *Seeing Double: Intercultural Poetics in Ptolemaic Alexandria.* Berkeley: University of California Press, 2003.

Stoneman, Richard. *The Greek Experience of India: From Alexander to the Indo-Greeks.* Princeton, NJ: Princeton University Press, 2019.

———. "The Legacy of Alexander in Ancient Philosophy." In *Brill's Companion to Alexander the Great,* edited by Joseph Roisman, 325–45. Leiden: Brill, 2003.

———. "Naked Philosophers: The Brahmans in the Alexander Historians and the Alexander Romance." *Journal of Hellenic Studies* 115 (1995): 99–114.

———. "Who Are the Brahmans? Indian Lore and Cynic Doctrine in Palladius' *De Bragmanibus* and Its Models." *Classical Quarterly* 44, no. 2 (1994): 500–510.

Stride, Sebastian, Bernardo Rondelli, and Simone Mantellini. "Canals Versus Horses: Political Power in the Oasis of Samarkand." *World Archaeology* 41, no. 1 (2009): 73–87.

Stronach, David, and Hilary Gopnik. s.v. "Pasargadae." In *Encyclopaedia Iranica.* 2009. http://www.iranicaonline.org/articles/pasargadae.

Strootman, Rolf. "Court Society." In *Courts and Elites in the Hellenistic Empires: The Near East after the Achaemenids, c. 330 to 30 BCE,* 111–35. Edinburgh University Press, 2014.

Sumner, W. M. "Achaemenid Settlement in the Persepolis Plain." *American Journal of Archaeology* 90, no. 1 (1986): 3–31.

Sverchkov, Leonid M. "The Kurganzol Fortress (on the History of Central Asia in the Hellenistic Era)." *Ancient Civilizations from Scythia to Siberia* 14, no. 1/2 (2008): 123–91.

Tarn, W. W. *Alexander the Great.* Boston: Beacon Press, 1956.

Thapar, Romila. *Early India: From the Origins to AD 1300.* Berkeley: University of California Press, 2003.

———. *The Past Before Us: Historical Traditions of Early North India.* Cambridge, MA: Harvard University Press, 2013.

Thapliyal, Uma Prasad. *Military Costume and Accoutrements in Ancient India.* New Delhi: Manohar, 2012.

Thomas, Carol G. *Alexander the Great in His World.* Malden, MA: Blackwell, 2007.

Thompson, Marie L. s.v. "Elephant." In *The Gale Encyclopedia of Science,* edited by K. Lee Lerner and Brenda Wilmoth Lerner, 1557–61. Detroit: Gale, 2014.

Troncoso, Víctor Alonso, Mauricio Álvarez Rico, and Sarina Pal. "Alexander's Tents and Camp Life." In *The History of the Argeads,* edited by Sabine Müller, Tim Howe, Hugh Bowden, and Robert Rollinger, 113–24. Wiesbaden: Harrassowitz Verlag, 2017.

Trundle, Matthew. *Greek Mercenaries: From the Late Archaic Period to Alexander.* Abingdon, UK: Routledge, 2004.

Tucci, Giuseppe. "On Swāt: The Dards and Connected Problems." *East and West* 27, no. 1/4 (1977): 9–103.

Ugolini, Gherardo. "Φόβος Φυτεύει Τύραννον: The Tyrant's Fears on the Attic Tragic Stage." *Comparative Drama* 51, no. 4 (2017): 456–74.

van der Spek, Robartus J. "Darius III, Alexander the Great and Babylonian Scholarship." In *A Persian Perspective: Essays in Memory of Heleen Sancisi-Weerdenburg,* edited by Wouter F. M. Henkelman and Amélie Kuhrt, 289–346. Leiden: Brill, 2003.

———. "Multi-Ethnicity and Ethnic Segregation in Hellenistic Babylon." In *Ethnic Constructs in Antiquity: The Role of Power and Tradition,* edited by Ton Derks and Nico Roymans, 101–16. Amsterdam: Amsterdam University Press, 2009.

van Oppen de Rutter, Branko. "The Susa Marriages—a Historiographical Note." *Ancient Society* 44 (2014): 25–41.

Van Wees, Hans. "'Stasis, Destroyer of Men': Mass, Elite, Political Violence and Security in Archaic Greece." *Entretiens sur l'antiquité classique* 54 (2008): 1–48.

Vikatou, Olympia. *Olympia: The Archaeological Site and the Museums.* Athens: Ekdotike Athenon, 2006.

Völcker-Janssen, Wilhelm. *Kunst und Gesellschaft an den Höfen Alexanders d. Gr. und seiner Nachfolger.* Munich: Tuduv, 1993.

Vorhis, Justin Grant. "The Best of the Macedonians: Alexander as Achilles in Arrian, Curtius, and Plutarch." Ph.D. diss., University of California, Los Angeles, 2017.

Vössing, Konrad. "Royal Feasting." In *A Companion to Food in the Ancient World,* edited by John Wilkins and Robin Nadeau, 243–52. Chichester, UK: John Wiley and Sons, 2015.

Waterfield, Robin. *Taken at the Flood: The Roman Conquest of Greece.* New York: Oxford University Press, 2014.

Webster, T. B. L. *An Introduction to Menander.* Manchester: Manchester University Press, 1974.

Weiskopf, Michael. s.v. "Bessos." In *Encyclopedia Iranica,* 174–75, 1989. http://www.iranicaonline.org/articles/bessos-satrap-of-bactria.

Wenzel, Marian. *Echoes of Alexander the Great: Silk Route Portraits from Gandhara: A Private Collection.* London: Eklisa Anstalt, 2000.

Wescoat, Bonna D. "The Patronage of Greek and Roman Architecture." In *The Oxford Handbook of Greek and Roman Art and Architecture,* edited by Clemente Marconi, 176–202. Oxford: Oxford University Press, 2014.

Wheeler, Mortimer. *Flames Over Persepolis: Turning Point in History.* London: Weidenfeld & Nicolson, 1968.

White, James. "Bows and Spears in Achaemenid Persia." Ph.D. diss., University of California, Santa Barbara, 2020.

White, Stephen. "Theophrastus and Callisthenes." In *Influences on Peripatetic Rhetoric: Essays in Honor of William W. Fortenbaugh,* edited by David C. Mirhady, 211–30. Leiden: Brill, 2007.

Wiesehöfer, Josef. "The Achaemenid Empire in the Fourth Century B.C.E: A Period of Decline?" In *Judah and the Judeans in the Fourth Century B.C.E,* edited by Gary N. Knoppers, Oded Lipschits, and Rainer Albertz, 11–30. Winona Lake, IN: Eisenbrauns, 2007.

———. "Cyrus the Great and the Sacrifices for a Dead King." In *Ancient Historiography on War and Empire,* edited by Timothy Howe, Sabine Müller, and Richard Stoneman, 55–61. Oxford: Oxbow Books, 2017.

———. s.v. "Gift Giving II. In Pre-Islamic Persia." In *Encyclopaedia Iranica,* 604–9, 2016. http://www.iranicaonline.org/articles/gift-giving-ii.

Wiesehöfer, Josef, and Sarina Pal. "The Persian Impact on Macedonia: Three Case Studies." In *The History of the Argeads,* edited by Sabine Müller, Tim Howe, Hugh Bowden, and Robert Rollinger. 57–64. Wiesbaden: Harrassowitz Verlag, 2017.

Wilber, Donald Newton. *Persepolis: The Archaeology of Parsa, Seat of the Persian Kings.* 2nd rev. ed. Princeton, NJ: Darwin Press, 1989.

Willekes, Carolyn. "Equine Aspects of Alexander the Great's Macedonian Cavalry." In *Greece, Macedon and Persia,* edited by Timothy Howe, 47–58. Oxford: Oxbow Books, 2015.

———. *The Horse in the Ancient World: From Bucephalus to the Hippodrome.* London: I. B. Tauris, 2016.

Wojciechowska, Agnieszka. *From Amyrtaeus to Ptolemy: Egypt in the Fourth Century B.C.* Wiesbaden: Harrassowitz Verlag, 2016.

Worthington, Ian. *Alexander the Great: Man and God.* Harlow, UK: Pearson/Longman, 2004.

Wriggins, Sally Hovey. *Xuanzang: A Buddhist Pilgrim on the Silk Road.* Boulder, CO: Westview Press, 1996.

Wu, Xin. "10 Land of the Unrule-Ables: Bactria in the Achaemenid Period." In *Fitful Histories and Unruly Publics: Rethinking Temporality and Community in Eurasian Archaeology,* edited by Kathryn O. Weber, Emma Hite, Lori Khatchadourian, and Adam T. Smith, 258–88. Leiden: Brill, 2017.

———. "Exploiting the Virgin Land: Kyzyltepa and the Effects of the Achaemenid Persian Empire on Its Central Asian Frontier." In *A Millennium of History: The Iron Age in Southern Central Asia (2nd and 1st Millennia BC),* edited by Johanna Lhuillier and Nikolaus Boroffka, 189–214. Berlin: Dietrich Reimer Verlag, 2018.

Yardley, John, and J. E. Atkinson. *Quintus Curtius Rufus: Histories of Alexander the Great.* Vol. 10. Clarendon Ancient History Series. Oxford: Oxford University Press, 2009.

Young, T. C. "480/479 B.C.—a Persian Perspective." *Iranica Antiqua* 15 (1980): 213–39.

Yunis, Harvey. *Demosthenes, Speeches 18 and 19.* Austin: University of Texas Press, 2005.

Zambrini, Andrea. "Megasthenes Thirty Years Later." In *With Alexander in India and Central Asia: Moving East and Back to West,* edited by Claudia Antonetti and P. Biagi, 222–37. Oxford: Oxbow Books, 2017.

Zanker, Paul. *The Mask of Socrates: The Image of the Intellectual in Antiquity.* Berkeley: University of California Press, 1995.

Ziring, Lawrence, and Shahid Javed Burki. s.v. "Pakistan." In *Encyclopaedia Britannica,* 2020, https://www.britannica.com/place/Pakistan.

Zutterman, Chr. "The Bow in the Ancient Near East: A Re-Evaluation of Archery from the Late 2nd Millennium to the End of the Achaemenid Period." *Iranica Antiqua* xxxviii (2003): 119–66.

Index

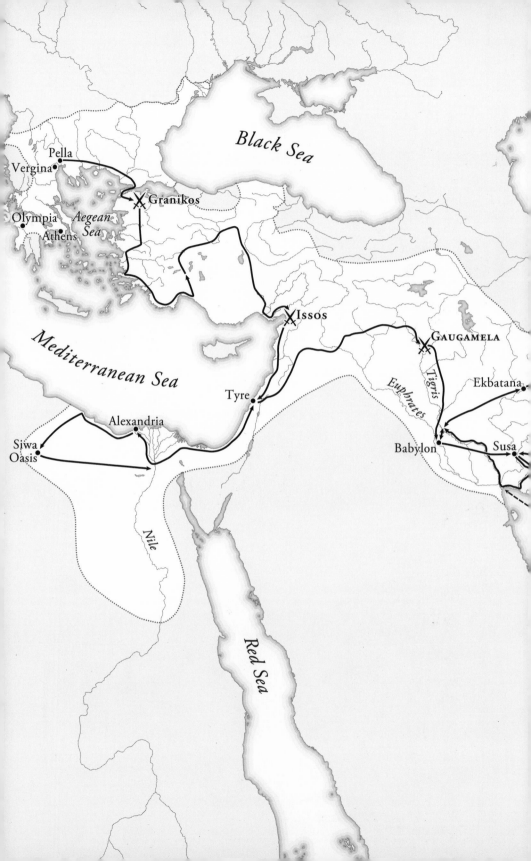

Black Sea

Pella
Vergina
Olympia
Athens
Aegean Sea
Granikos

Mediterranean Sea

Issos
Gaugamela

Tyre
Euphrates
Tigris
Ekbatana

Alexandria
Siwa Oasis
Babylon
Susa

Nile

Red Sea